Women's Oral History

Women's Oral History
The *Frontiers* Reader

EDITED BY

SUSAN H. ARMITAGE

WITH PATRICIA HART

AND KAREN WEATHERMON

University of Nebraska Press, Lincoln and London

© 2002 by the Frontiers Pub-
lishing, Inc.
Library of Congress Catalog-
ing-in-Publication Data
Women's oral history : the
Frontiers reader / edited by
Susan H. Armitage, with
Patricia Hart and Karen
Weathermon. p. cm.
Includes bibliographical refer-
ences and index.
ISBN 0-8032-5944-1
(pa. : alk. paper)
1. Women—History.
2. Oral history.
I. Armitage, Susan H.
(Susan Hodge), 1937–
II. Hart, Patricia, 1950–
III. Weathermon, Karen, 1961–
IV. Frontiers.
HQ1122 .W675 2002
305.4' 09—dc21
2002022623

To Kathi George,
  The woman who kept Frontiers *alive*

Contents

Introduction

Frontiers: A Journal of Women Studies began publication in 1975. Along with *Signs* and *Feminist Studies*, it was one of the first academic journals to emerge from the second wave of the Women's Movement. Like its sister journals *Frontiers* was dedicated to the publication of the new feminist scholarship, but it also sought to bridge the gap between the academy and the community. It published articles of interest not just to academic feminists (who were not all that plentiful in the mid-1970s), but also to feminist activists. In the 1970s a lot of women fit that description: They started women's health clinics, rape crisis lines, battered women's shelters, displaced homemakers programs, women's legal services, welfare rights organizations, lesbian organizations, and women's labor organizations. All of these women—whether they were designing and teaching their first women's studies courses or building women's community organizations—were starved for information about women. At that time little was published about women's history, and scanty knowledge existed about the deep and sustaining tradition of feminist activism that we now know has existed for centuries. We didn't even know very much about how most women conducted and thought about their own lives because few researchers before us had thought to look beyond the handful of famous women. We urgently needed to know more about all women.

The first landmark *Frontiers* issue on women's oral history (1977) was intended to fill this information gap. Oral history—interviewing people for the purpose of recording their personal and historical memories—was the perfect tool for the grassroots effort of interviewing ordinary women. Tape recorders were inexpensive, and the basic interviewing methods were easy to learn; all one had to do was to find a few elderly women who were willing to talk. In 1977, however, there was one remaining problem: There were no guides to interviewing women. Until that time, most of the nationally known and established oral history projects had focused on interviewing elite men for their "behind the scenes" recollections of notable political events. Interviewing women was at first hobbled by the all-but-universal belief that questions designed for men would be just as suitable for women (or, if you prefer a darker view, that all intelligent women agreed with the masculine view of the world, and those who didn't were just spoilers). A *Frontiers* special issue, guest-edited by women's oral history pioneers Sherna Gluck and Joan Jensen, provided "how-to" guides for interviewing women and articles illustrating a wide range of information that could be gained through oral history interviews. In 1983 *Frontiers* published a follow-up issue, just as the initial surge in interest in women's oral history was tapering off, and in 1998 the journal brought the field up to date with two issues devoted to women's oral history.

"Basic Approaches," the first section of this volume, is drawn largely from the landmark 1977 issue. It seemed to us, as we reviewed past issues for possible inclusion, that the "why" and the "how" are just as important today as they were in 1977. We begin with Sherna Gluck's "What's So Special About Women?" which provided the basic rationale for women's oral history and offered the practical instruction that was so needed in 1977 — and so hard to find. One of the interview guides included in the resource section that follows her article is drawn from Gluck's own women's oral history project at California State University, Long Beach. As her essay shows, Gluck clearly understands the multiple purposes of women's oral history, which she summarizes as recovery, validation, communication, and continuity in the historical experience of women. The next three articles offer thoughtful later essays written by practitioners reflecting on their own experiences: Margaret Strobel writes about the classic "insider/outsider" dilemma that all oral historians grapple with, Sherry Thomas offers a frank discussion about her experiences interviewing farm women, and Susan Armitage encourages the wider focus necessary when one moves beyond individual interviews to larger oral history projects.

By 1983 women's oral history was changing. Money for large oral history projects dried up, and the focus of women's history as a whole shifted decisively toward the study of difference rather than commonality. Individual in-depth interviews that explored the lives of the most overlooked women, such as Fran Leeper Buss's study *Forged under the Sun* set a new standard in the field of women's oral history.[1] Some of the changes that have occurred in the years 1983 to 1998 are the topic of the next article, a conversation between Sherna Gluck and Susan Armitage. In this valuable retrospective, Gluck points out the lack of attention to difference in her 1977 oral history advice, and Armitage states that much more interviewing needs to be done. The section closes with an exemplary article by Judy Yung that illustrates how effectively she used oral history in *Unbound Feet*, her prizewinning study of Chinese and Chinese American women in San Francisco.[2]

The second section of this volume, "Oral History Applications," illustrates some of the many ways in which women's oral history has been used. The most common and apparently straightforward use is biography, as the opening article by Sally Roesch Wagner explains as she tells us about some of her research for a biography of Matilda Joslyn Gage. Another biography, based on an interview with Icy Norman by Mary Murphy, was one of the building blocks of *Like a Family*, the collective history of North Carolina mill life that Jacquelyn Dowd Hall, James Leloudis, Robert Korstad, Murphy, Lu Ann Jones, and Charistopher B. Daly published in 1987.[3] Next, Harriet Wrye and Jacqueline Churilla explain another personal use of oral history: to encourage elderly people to undertake a life review.

Oral histories have frequently been used in public presentations and especially in the slide-tape show format that was so popular in the 1980s. "*Good Work, Sister!* The Making of An Oral History Production," by Amy Kesselman, Tina Tau, and Karen Wickre in Portland, Oregon, presents one of the first studies of women shipyard workers during World War II. Today, video is a much more common medium, and in "Filming Nana," Connie Broughton tells us about the dilemmas she encountered when she interviewed her grandmother for a television documentary about an Idaho mining town. Oral histories are also increasingly used in historical art and museum exhibits, as an exhibit by Alison Marchant in an old textile mill in Lancashire, England, shows. This section closes with an example of by far the most common use of oral history; that is, as a discovery tool in the classroom, as Anne M. Butler and Gerri W. Sorenson explain.

The third section of this volume, "Oral History Discoveries and Insights," shows a few of the ways in which oral history is being used to recover lost segments of women's history. Oral history is an unparalleled tool for reaching below the surface and uncovering hidden stories and points of view. Diane Sands shows this clearly in her discussion of her use of oral history to understand how the network of illegal abortion worked in Montana. Another common use of oral history, to help in finding the hidden participants of events, is evident in Dolores Delgado Bernal's discussion of the role of female students in the 1968 Los Angeles School Blowouts. The "media stars" of the riots were young men; only through oral history is female activity recaptured. Oral history provides another rarely documented phenomenon when it catches women in transition—in motion, as it were, rather than frozen in place. Two essays illustrate the insights that can be gained: Lucille Jake, Evelyn James, and Pamela Bunte's interviews with Southern Paiute women about the ways in which their lives were changing, and Valerie Grim's study of African American women moving from rural Mississippi to Chicago and adjusting to the city. Another frequently overlooked use of oral history is the documentation of the impact of public policy on the people affected by it. Two very different examples are included: Jean Calterone Williams's study of homeless women trying to balance the conflicting requirements of homeless and battered women's shelters, and Rosemary Sayigh's exploration of the ways in which the national struggle shapes the lives of Palestinian women. This section concludes with a study of how the oral tradition of a famous British strike in the 1920s shaped the responses of women strikers in the 1980s by Jaclyn Gier-Viskovatoff and Abigail Porter.

This collection of articles about women's oral history from the pages of *Frontiers* has been gathered together in part to illustrate the important role that women's oral history has played in our developing knowledge about the history of women. Our hope also is that the instruction and inspiration in this volume will encourage our readers to undertake oral histories of their own, thereby contributing another small piece to the still incomplete mosaic of recorded and recovered histories of the lives of women.

Sue Armitage, Patricia Hart, and Karen Weathermon for Frontiers

NOTES

1. Maria Elena Lucas, *Forged under the Sun/Forjado Bajo el Sol: The Life of Maria Elena Luca*, ed. Fran Leeper Buss (Ann Arbor: University of Michigan Press, 1993).

2. Judy Yung, *Unbound Feet: A Social History of Chinese Women in San Francisco* (Berkeley: University of California Press, 1995).

3. Jacquelyn Dowd Hall et al., *Like a Family: The Making of a Southern Cotton Mill World* (Chapel Hill: University of North Carolina Press, 1987).

Women's Oral History

Basic Approaches

1

What's So Special about Women?

Women's Oral History

SHERNA BERGER GLUCK

Refusing to be rendered historically voiceless any longer, women are creating a new history—using our own voices and experiences. We are challenging the traditional concepts of history, of what is "historically important," and we are affirming that our everyday lives *are* history. Using an oral tradition, as old as human memory, we are reconstructing our own past.

When women historians first began the task of creating and expanding the field of women's history, we relied on traditional historical concepts and methods. We busily searched for hidden clues to direct us to "lost heroines," and, whenever possible, we sought out those who were still alive in order to record their past experiences. Because so little documentation was available on the lives and activities of these women, we found ourselves in a situation similar to that of Allan Nevins, who "developed" the method of oral history in 1948.[1] With the advent of the telephone and the decline in the practice of journal writing and lengthy correspondence, historians were faced with a "drying up" of many of the sources on which they traditionally depended. Oral history, emerging then as the sound recording of the reminiscences of public figures, was hailed as a method that could create alternative sources.

Fitting women into this new scheme of things was essential and not very difficult. There were and are women who have been "important" figures in public life, both those who have functioned in the public eye and those who have worked behind the scenes. Some women achieved recognition as a result of their struggle for women's rights, while others who participated in that struggle remain unrecognized. But the majority of women did not lead public lives. Most women were not women's rights activists or union leaders or public participants in social movements. Until relatively recently, most women in the United States did not engage in wage-earning labor. By virtue of acculturation and socialization in a sexist society, women's lives were and are different from most men's. Whether women have played out public roles or adopted the traditional female role in the private realm, their lives have been governed by what Gerda Lerner has called a special rhythm.[2] In tracing this rhythm, it is important to document the lives and experiences of all of these women: to pore over newspaper accounts and organization papers, to seek out their living associates, to research fully their lives and activities, and to record their stories, for only then can we see the whole picture of women's lives, and how their rhythm has affected our lives.

Women all over the country have been using oral history to explore this rhythm of women's lives. In doing so, we are harking back to an oral tradition much older than that developed by white male historians in the United States in the 1940s. We are part of the tradition in which the life and experiences of "everywoman/man" was considered worthy of remembering and passing on to others—because it was history. It was this tradition, brought from Africa, which black historians tapped in the 1920s when they started to record the stories of former slaves.[3] It was this same tradition that both inspired Alex Haley to trace his roots and helped him to reconstruct the kidnap of his ancestors from West Africa.[4]

For women, using this model of oral history not only leads us to "anywoman," but it also raises a different set of questions to be explored. (Please see the Resource Section beginning on page 27 for examples of interviewing guides used in women's oral histories.) We ask about clothing and physical activity, menstruation, knowledge and attitudes about sex and birth control, childbirth, economic functions in the household, household work, the nature of relationships among women, the magazines and books they read, the menopausal experience, and the relationship of the private life to the public life. Thus, not only is the political base of women's oral history different from the Nevins model, but also, and just as important, the content is special. No matter what women we choose to interview, regardless of how typical or atypical their life experiences have been, there are certain common threads that link all women.

It is the recognition that women's oral history is so special and, significantly, that it has developed as a field unto itself—primarily through the work of women outside the major university oral history centers—that inspired us to devote an entire issue of a women studies journal to the subject.

Women's oral history is a feminist encounter, even if the interviewee is not herself a feminist. It is the creation of a new type of material on women; it is the validation of women's experiences; it is the communication among women of different generations; it is the discovery of our own roots and the development of a continuity that has been denied us in traditional historical accounts.

II

Oral history, the creation of a new "document" through the tape-recorded interview, traditionally has been divided into three types: topical, biographical, and autobiographical. The topical interview is, in many ways, most akin to the open-ended sociological interview; the interviewer brings in a specific focus in order to gather information about a particular event. It might center on something that applies to both women and men, like Judy Yung's interviews with Chinese immigrants about their detention on Angel Island, or it might focus on those experiences particular to women only, such as hysterectomy.[5] The biographical oral history interview is characterized by this same kind of specificity, but the focus is, instead, on a specific individual — usually a public figure such as Sally Roesch Wagner's interviews about Matilda Joslyn Gage.

In the autobiographical interview, the course of the individual *interviewee's* life is what determines both the form and content of the oral history. Even when one interviews a group of women who participated in the same kind of activity, the question will be tailormade to each individual's experience and the information will be recorded as part of a total memoir. In other words, in biographical and topical interviews, a slice of the interviewee's life is explored; in the autobiographical interview, the total life history is recorded.

In reality, there is a great deal of overlapping among the three forms. In both the topical and biographical interview, enough autobiographical material must be recorded to establish the specific relationship of the interviewee to the event or the individual being researched. On the other hand, when autobiographical interviews are collected from a group of women who shared a similar activity, for example, participation in the labor movement, some common questions would be explored with all. (See the Resource Section for an outline developed by the University of Michigan for interviews with trade union women.) Further, in our efforts to revise women's historiography, there are certain areas that should be explored with all women as part of their autobiographical accounts, such as their reactions to the onset of menses.

The distinction between the autobiographical and topical interviews is further blurred by the fact that ultimately, specific materials might be extracted from several different autobiographical interviews and clustered together around a specific topic, such as exploration of mother-daughter relationships or work on older women from different ethnic groups.

In fact, the so-called autobiographical oral history should be as complete a document as possible so that a variety of uses can be made of it. Much like the anthropological life history, it should reflect the experiences, values, attitudes, and relationships of the interviewee—the patterns and rhythms of her life and times. It can stand on its own, as an autobiography of an individual, or sections can be extracted from it for analysis or use in documentation.

As with any source, questions about the validity of the material must be raised. Despite their awareness of the obvious bias of contemporary newspaper reports, historians traditionally have relied on journalistic accounts as primary sources. The same criteria should be used to assess the validity of *any* source, written or oral: How does it "fit" with what we know about the subject? The usual questions about the reliability of memory and the problem of retrospective interpretation must also be raised, as they would be for any autobiographical account.

The autobiographical oral history, however, is a rather strange hybrid, not like conventional autobiography, which is usually characterized by a certain amount of studied reconsideration by the "author" and by her self-selection of both form and content. The so-called autobiographical oral history is a collaborative effort of the interviewer (archivist/historian) and the interviewee (source/history). This very collaboration makes the oral history memoir unique. Based on face-to-face interaction, during which the source can be both questioned and evaluated, it becomes more than the sound of one voice.

Based on the background research and the historical perspective that the interviewer brings to the process, the life of the interviewee is reconstructed within a broader social context—a context not ordinarily provided by the self-recorded memoirist. An understanding of this context guides the interviewer in deciding which spontaneous material should be elaborated on more fully. Though the best interviewer will encourage spontaneity and self-direction, it is intellectually dishonest to discount the interviewer's role in creating the oral history. The advantages derived from her knowledge and perspective can, ideally, sensitize her to personal and cultural inconsistencies in the content of the interview. Such inconsistencies might be indicative of a highly idiosyncratic woman; they might be an important source of information about the complex patterns in women's lives; or, they might raise questions about memory and candor.

Besides subtle nuances in the content of the interview and voice inflections—which are captured on tape—there are nonverbal gestures that only the sensitive interviewer (or—if the interview is being filmed or videotaped—the sensitive photographer) will observe. These nonverbal cues reveal the emotional tone of the interview and should be carefully noted afterwards; they will become part of the record used by both the interviewee and others to evaluate the validity and reliability of the material recorded.

Despite the obvious advantages of the collaborative reconstruction of the interviewee's life, there are, of course, drawbacks. The perspective of the interviewer cannot help but influence, even subtly, the content of the material—particularly what the interviewee will judge as "important." After we completed an interview, one woman commented that she could tell by the way my eyes sparkled at various times that I was particularly interested in the problems she faced as a woman in the male world of science. Although we can console ourselves with the knowledge that there is no such thing as "objective" reporting, we must recognize our own influence in the interview process and make a concerted effort to maintain a balance between what we, as feminist historians, think is important and what the women we are interviewing think was important about their own lives.

As will become obvious from the richness of language in the oral histories included in this volume, the collaboration between interviewer and interviewee results in more than new "historical" documents. It allows for the creation of a new literature, a literature that can tap the language and experiences of those who do not ordinarily have access to such public expression except, perhaps, through the more anonymous forms of folk culture.

III

Oral history is not, nor should it be, the province of experts. On the contrary, some of the best work today is being done by individuals and groups outside "the groves of academe" and often by those without any formal training in history or journalism. Anyone who can listen to the women who are speaking can do oral history. It is not enough, however, to rush off to the nearest senior citizen center with a tape recorder. It is important to be prepared.

Reading about interviewing technique is a helpful first step. Despite the proliferation of "how to" articles and manuals, the most useful discussion of technique is still to be found in two older works by Willa Baum and Norman Hoyle.[6] Discretion and common sense must be used in evaluating recommendations for interviewing technique. Patently absurd suggestions are sometimes made, for example, the edict not to laugh when the interviewee says something funny. The oral history interview is a human interaction and the same kind of warm, human responses expected in other interactions should govern our behavior. Reading the instructional articles will heighten awareness of the interview process, but nothing will contribute to this awareness more than the actual interview experience. The best training for conducting an oral history interview is actual practice—practice interviews that are carefully listened to and evaluated and analyzed. These "mock" interviews should be conducted with persons other than the intended subject.

The more practice the interviewer has, and the more experience she gains, the more partisan she becomes to her own methods. Although there is widespread agreement among oral history practitioners on some points, there is also disagreement. The oral history interview, above all, is specialized, and therefore highly variable; it is tailored to the experiences and style of the individual interviewee. Keeping in mind the proviso that there is no *one* perfect method of collecting oral histories, I offer the following ideas based on my own experiences over the past five years in personally interviewing an enormous number and wide range of women, and in training students to gather in-depth women's oral history. The methods of making contact, choosing equipment, adopting an interview style, and processing the interviews have all worked successfully for me. Although these suggestions are based on autobiographical oral history interviews with women in their seventies, eighties, nineties, and even one-hundreds, many of the points are equally valid for the topical and biographical interviews and for women of almost any age group.

Making Contact

Whom we select to interview obviously will be governed by our own specific interest. In my classes for the past three years, randomly selected women have been contacted and "everywoman" interviews were conducted. Fully exploring the life of each individual woman became the basis for a study of women's lives in the early twentieth century. To locate women who have had a particular kind of experience, such as involvement in the labor movement or defense industry work during World War II, different methods might be used. I have successfully located union women through the retiree groups of various unions, through widespread advertisement of my work among older radicals, and through public speaking. Other oral historians and interviewers have placed ads in local and national newspapers.

In selecting the women to interview, the question of cultural likeness—including gender, race, class, ethnic, and even regional identification—immediately arises. As Margaret Strobel points out in her article, there are not yet sufficient numbers of women in Africa, for instance, who are trained to record their own history. The combined forces of racism and sexism have also limited the number of "minority" women in the United States who have had access to the skills and equipment that would enable them to record their own past. Until these skills are learned—and each of us must do everything in her power to share these skills—the role of the "outsider" will remain crucial. Otherwise, the history of black, Hispanic, Asian, and Native American women will be lost.

Besides being governed by necessity, the outsider can sometimes delve into certain kinds of experiences that insiders cannot.[7] There might be specific topics that are more easily discussed with "outsiders." Also, because outsiders are less conversant with the culture or subculture, they may take less for granted and ask for more clarification than insiders. On the whole, though, my experience has been that cultural likeness can greatly promote trust and openness, whereas dissimilarity reinforces cultural and social distance.

Because of my own light complexion and hair, the Jewish immigrant women I have interviewed have assumed that I was not Jewish. As soon as I dropped a clue for them, both the content of the interview (particularly about their childhood in the shtetls of Europe or the ghettos of America) and the nature of our relationship changed. On the other hand, because of my appearance and my socialization into the larger Anglo culture I have "passed" when I have conducted interviews with Anglo-Saxon women. A very light-skinned black student of mine from Texas was politely treated and her interview with a black ninety-two-year-old woman and her seventy-year-old daughter progressed uneventfully until, during the third session, the interviewees realized that she was "one of us." The nature of the interview changed dramatically. Similarly, the few male students I have had in my women's oral history classes, despite their efforts, never overcame the barriers of gender difference.

It is not only a matter of trust; the subtle cues to which culturally similar women can respond might mean the difference between a good and bad interview. Though these nuances cannot be thoroughly learned by an outsider, the interviewer must prepare as best she can so that she can understand the attitudes, vocabulary, and body language of the group or subgroup with which the interviewee identifies.

No matter whom we choose to interview or how we have located her, the first contact with our interviewee is crucial, particularly since she might be subtly influenced by the way in which we located her. One of the activists whom I found through her union was convinced, despite all my explanations and protestations, that I was from the "union office." She was, therefore, guarded in her description of the difficulties she had faced as a woman in her union. On the other hand, when a particularly respected or loved friend was the source of my contact, the door was opened wide and the interviews were quite candid.

It is important in contacting the person to make clear how her name was obtained and to explain to her, in advance, what the interest in her is. For most women, especially those who did not participate in "important" events or in organizations outside of the home, there is tremendous initial reluctance to being interviewed; it is the reluctance that comes from being socialized female in this society. It is important to establish for her, at the very outset, why we feel her life and experiences are important. This might mean not only an explanation about our specific project, but also a discussion of how we view the daily life experiences of all women to be a part of history.

The interviewer's own credibility must also be established; this can be accomplished by reference to a relationship with someone the interviewer knows and/or by the use of letterhead stationery or a brochure that describes her work. (Though a letter from the instructor might be helpful for students, I have found that the "grandmother role," which the elderly so often adopt towards the student, makes their entrée relatively easy.)

Because it is often difficult for the elderly to hear well on the telephone, it is best to try to communicate this essential introductory material first by mail. Then, when contact is made, she will be clear about who is calling and what is wanted, and an appointment can be made. It is important to determine what time of day is best for her; her stamina and memory will vary.

All the women I have interviewed have been sufficiently in tune with their own body rhythms to tell me *exactly* what was the best time to interview; then I adjusted *my* schedule accordingly.

It is still that initial face-to-face meeting that will make or break the oral history. Rather personal and intimate details about the women's life will be openly discussed, and to do so means that there must be an attitude of trust. She will, rightfully, want to know how the material will be used. Although it is important to be open about both the purpose of the interview and the use of the material, I usually wait until after some sort of trusting relationship has developed before asking her to sign any releases or agreements; there is no subterfuge here, but even the simplest agreement forms can raise specters and create suspicions. (See the Resource Section for a sample interview agreement.) I have had only two women refuse to sign an agreement once the interviews were completed; in both cases their oral histories were made anonymous and all identifiable references were deleted.

Open communication is crucial to establishing trust with an interviewee. Since we are asking a stranger to be self-revealing, we, in turn, must be willing to divulge information about ourselves. I have had some interviewees question me at length about my own background and life, whereas others have asked nothing. It is with the former that I have developed the most intimate mutual relationships and with whom I have probably created the richest oral histories. I do not mean to imply that the interviewer should insert her own life story into the actual interview. However, before beginning the first interview or while chatting over coffee, tea, or juice after the interview, the interviewer may talk about herself—to whatever extent is natural and the interviewee seems to expect. The interviewer's sharing her own feelings about the interview (her nervousness, for example), encourages the interviewee to talk about *her* feelings, and both parties can be placed at ease.

The first interview is not "just to get acquainted." The expectations and relationship that develop during that first encounter can determine the course of the other interviews. For this reason, the practice interviews, during training, should be done with others than those to be actually interviewed for a project. That first interview might be the only one conducted with a woman or, on the other hand, it might represent the first of some twenty sessions. The decision about how many interviews will be recorded can best be made on the basis of the outline developed and the research undertaken *after* the initial interview. Though it is best not to make a definite commitment to the interviewee until you can be more precise, she should be prepared for the eventuality that more than one interview may be recorded.

How much preparation is done before the first interview will depend largely on who the woman is. For a prominent individual, a "local figure," or someone involved in a well-documented activity, it is possible to research existing sources such as newspapers, organization records, and histories ahead of time. However, many of those we will interview are women about whom a great deal is not recorded; they are the "voiceless" unknown women who worked in the home, the women who worked at office jobs pushing the huge carriages of old typewriters, the women who rose at five in the morning to chop cotton, the women who bore three, four, five, and more children, the women who panicked at their frequent pregnancies and performed abortions on themselves. The best preparation for a first interview with these women is a familiarity with the time period, especially the living conditions and tenor of life in both rural and urban settings.

Familiarity with the texture of life allows us to explore fully her family history and her early years. The same principles will guide us as in later interviews; her own experiences and style of reminiscing provide the framework, while our general topical outline sensitizes us to certain areas and provides suggestions for probing. After covering the early years, usually to adolescence (which might require more than one interview), a general biographical sketch is recorded in roughly chronological sequence. It is this sketch that will then be used as the basis for both structuring the subsequent interviews and directing us to the areas that should be researched.

Though most of the women whom we will interview probably do not have "papers," almost all do have photographs and various objects that they have kept from their past. Looking over these helps to inform the interviewer and to jog the memory of the interviewee.

I thought I had fully exhausted the recollections of a union woman about the various strikes in which she had participated until we looked over her photographs, late in the interview series. A picture of an ILGWU (International Ladies' Garment Workers Union) picnic reminded her that this was a victory celebration; she was then able to recount her activities in yet another strike. It is best to look over these records early in the project, ideally during the first interview. Furthermore, it is a good idea to let the tape recorder run as she comments on her photo album or a newspaper clipping or displays her yellowed wedding dress. Although the material should be recorded again later, in the context of the period in which it took place, the second version of the story might be quite different from that first rendition—which could become a lost gem were we not to record it when the memory spontaneously surfaced.

The Interview Process

The interview is a transaction between the interviewer and the interviewee, and their responses to each other form the basis for the creation of the oral history. Each woman has her own style of recollecting, as well as her own specific experiences. As sensitive interviewers, we respond to each individually, and the interview process will therefore vary. This variability is one of the most distinctive features of the oral history interview and is what makes it different from the standardized interviews used by social scientists.

Despite experience and careful planning by the interviewer, there are several common tendencies that can mar any interview. These are a function of our own impatience and (in our eagerness to use our background research) a dependency on our prepared outlines or guides. We fear lapses of silence. We squirm at what appear to be long, irrelevant digressions. We become impatient at the chaotic manner in which memory divulges the past. In our fear and impatience, and also in our enthusiasm for the material we are uncovering, we succumb to talking too much, asking too many questions too soon.

The best oral history is a quasi-monologue on the part of the interviewee that is encouraged by approving nods, appreciative smiles, and enraptured listening and stimulated by understanding comments and intelligent questions. Though the ideal interviewer is there primarily to provide a broad leeway in which to help the interviewee structure her recollections, sensitivity to both individual idiosyncrasies and class or culturally determined characteristics, might lead to more direct questioning in some cases and total silence in others.

For example, despite her protestations that she would not be able to talk without a lot of questions, an old Jewish immigrant woman whom I interviewed would embark on an hour-long monologue at the beginning of each session. She had self-selected that material that was important to her, or that she thought was of general interest. I quickly learned that asking questions—except for points of clarification—was an intrusion. She demanded total eye contact at all times! During her spontaneous reminiscing, I remained virtually silent. Then, toward the end of the session, or at the beginning of the next one, I would ask some additional questions relating to the material she had provided or to my own outline.

In planning for the interview, I review the types of questions I wish to ask and the order in which I want to ask them, but I also try to avoid too much "preordering" of the material. The principle that I generally use is to ask the most general question first, waiting to see where that question leads. It might lead to a detailed description, to what appears to be a digression, or to a blank. My own reaction, then, is tailored to the woman's response. If the general question, for example, about living conditions during her childhood, yields detailed information, I can sit back, keeping a sharp ear for unexpected information, new directions to explore, and confusing material. If, on the other hand, the general question leads to a vague or general response, then the questions can be re-cast or phrased more specifically. If we are clear in our own minds what it is we are looking for, this is not difficult to do. For instance, when I ask about living conditions during the woman's youth, what I am seeking is sufficient information to re-create the basic social setting as well as the financial circumstances of the family. A general response such as "we were very poor," or "we lived in a tenement" does not tell me much. Asking more specific questions (for example, how many slept in a room, a bed; was there water/plumbing in the living space, in the corridor, outside) can yield sufficiently rich descriptions so that no further questioning is necessary.

A general or vague response might indicate that the interviewee did not consider the subject very important. If we have touched upon an area that is not part of her basic self-definition, but is important to us as feminist archivists, then we must devise a way to get the information without letting our questions overdetermine the interview. It might mean that we wait until the very end of the oral history recording sessions to ask some of our questions, even though they might be out of context. Otherwise, we can easily end up with an oral history that is defined not by the values and rhythm of the individual's life, but by the perspective that *we* bring about women, about class, about race.

If our general questions lead to a lengthy digression, then we must be prepared to follow that line until it is exhausted. It is imperative that we learn to let the train of memory association run its course; that we be able to scrap totally the direction in which we were originally headed; that we know when to ignore our outlines and pick up new avenues of inquiry. If, at the end of this new track, we still do not have the information we were initially seeking, then we can return to our original line of inquiry, perhaps asking for the same content in a different way.

Sometimes, though, the interviewee truly cannot recall the information we are seeking. As little as we know about memory function, we do know that it is related to blood flow and that it will vary at different times of the day and on different occasions during the week. Thus, sensitivity to the health and stamina of the interviewee is important; it is also a basic sign of human respect. This generally means determining what time of day is best to interview her; being prepared to cancel an interview if, when you arrive, she seems tired, upset, or "under the weather"; and, knowing when to cut the session short. During the course of the interview, as she tires, there will be noticeable memory loss and increased difficulty in remembering words. That should signal that it is time to end the interview for the day. (I have found that the ninety-minute interview is about the right length for most elderly women, though for some, one hour is the maximum. I openly discuss this with the interviewee.) When a question draws a blank or a line of inquiry is not productive, we have to be willing to give up. If it is important, we might want to make a mental note of it and try again on another occasion.

How do we keep track of our own line of thought during the various passages into the byways of memory? With attentive listening we can easily forget our own questions. How do we quickly note a new line of inquiry that was triggered by a comment of the interviewee; how do we keep some chronological sense when an interviewee's style is to rush headlong from one anecdote to another? There is as much diversity of opinion on note-taking during the interview as there is on sharing the outline or guide with the interviewee. My own experiences vary from one interviewee to the next, though invariably I do not share with her my outline or specific questions. My fear is that this outline, which is really just a guide for myself, will determine the course of the interview too much. I will suggest at the end of each session the *general areas* we might want to cover at the following session.

As for note-taking during the interviews, I usually try to avoid making notations of more than a single word or phrase—just enough to keep *my* memory intact. Stopping to take notes signifies to her either that what she is saying is not very important and that you do not have to listen, or that it is *very* important and you are taking notes in order to ask her more about it. In any event, the loss of eye contact, even for a brief moment, the break in the pattern of concentrated listening, can be very disruptive. In reviewing the tape later, the interviewer can note names, places, and dates, and can then ask for clarification of confusing material at the next session.

Perhaps the most difficult and frustrating task is to keep clear in our own minds some sense of chronology and the order of events. Some women, particularly less educated working-class women, are not accustomed to reflecting about themselves, to viewing their lives as important. The stories they are used to repeating are those that recount a courageous act, a funny episode, or a tragic event in their families. Consequently, the interview might be a string of anecdotes with little connecting material or insufficient descriptions to place these anecdotes in a context adequately understandable to outsiders. This is her style and rather than interfere (which would be useless anyway) the interviewer has to develop some systematic way of keeping time references clear and to ask questions *in relation to* the anecdote that helps to provide the total context. I have found it helpful to actually develop a chronological chart, based on the first contact interview, which clearly outlines the various stages in the woman's life. In this way, it becomes easier to keep straight which anecdote fits where.

The interview with the more educated, middle-class woman usually is quite a different process. She is more accustomed to reflecting about life, and also to articulating ideas. As a result the interview is more "orderly"; thoughts are more often completed, and sentences hang together. This is not to say that one interview is better or worse than another, but rather that we have to be aware of the ways in which class, particularly, affect thought processes and speaking patterns, and to adapt ourselves to these variations.

In addition to those differences related to class origins there are certain cultural characteristics that are a function of both ethnicity and generation. Though older and/or immigrant women might talk without much hesitation about "female concerns," they often find it difficult to be very explicit. For instance, most women will freely talk about the onset of menses. However, they might find it more difficult to describe the "pads" they used, where they were collected, washed, and so on. By the same token, though women might be willing to talk about birth control, they might be embarrassed to describe specific techniques and might speak in euphemisms, such as, "My husband took precautions." She might be referring to his using condoms, or to coitus interruptus. It will be up to the interviewer to then phrase questions that elicit the information without requiring the interviewee to use words with which she has difficulty or that embarrass her. Faced with the timidity of some older women, the interviewer must have sufficient knowledge about birth control practices in the earlier part of the century to step in and provide words as well as to ask for more details. This is part of the preparation that any good interviewer will have done, and these cultural differences may have important implications for the editing process.

Processing the Interview

Once we have successfully recorded one or a series of interviews, the initial product (and, perhaps, the final one) is the raw tape recording. Since an important primary document has been created, it is important to take measures both to protect it and, at the same time, to make it accessible to others.[8] Minimally, this requires some summarizing and indexing of the contents of the tapes and either depositing them in archives or making their existence known to those who would have an interest in the materials. By using either extensive funding or a willingness to put in countless unpaid hours, we can next transcribe and edit the interviews, perhaps ultimately into a continuous narrative. The way in which the recordings are further processed depends on both the resources available and the use to which the material will be put.

The easiest and least expensive method is to develop a running summary of *each* tape. As a matter of course, if more than one interview is recorded with a single individual, it is a good idea to listen and to take notes on each interview before proceeding with the next. This is both to make sure that nothing has been missed—particularly new avenues hinted at—and to continually appraise our methods and sharpen our skills. Since the tapes should be reviewed anyway, it does not require much more time to keep a running summary while listening to them. Properly done, this summary can then be used as a basis for indexing the entire group of interviews with a single individual. (For a description and sample of the method that we use in the Feminist History Research Project, see Appendix B.)

This simple system allows the use of the material for any of several purposes, including extraction of specific segments for presentation as evidence, and development of audio or audio-visual presentations. In other words, this system allows for easy retrieval of the material which can then be selectively transcribed as needed. Though it might take a bit longer to locate the material on a tape and listen to it than it would to scan quickly the printed page, the material *is available* for scholarly use, nevertheless. Furthermore, because of subtle communication patterns that cannot be captured on the printed page, listening to the segments might be considerably more revealing than merely reading a passage.

This is not to argue against transcribing the tapes if it is possible to do so, and if the resources are available. However, we should bear in mind that the enormous amounts of time and money required to transcribe an interview (an average of five to eight hours per interview hour) might be better utilized in collecting more oral histories from those older women whose numbers are rapidly diminishing.

If the tapes are transcribed, there are then several different methods of treating the literal transcription. Minimally, it is edited for clarity, punctuation, and correct spelling of names and places. The resulting "edited transcript" is usually placed on a library shelf, to be used primarily by scholars. More extensive editing of the transcripts might be done, when sufficient funds are available, as is the practice of the Regional Oral History Office of the Bancroft Library (University of California, Berkeley). The transcript is edited for smooth flow and continuity, which means that similar material from different portions of the interview is pulled together and organized into coherent sections with headings and subheadings. After a review of the transcript by the interviewee, the interviewer/editor writes an introduction and indexes the volume. Photographs and other documents might be included selectively in the final bound volume, which is deposited at Berkeley and UCLA and is available for purchase by other libraries. The resulting volume is more readable and certainly more accessible and usable than a simple, minimally edited transcript. However, it is quite costly to produce.

Another form of editing, usually in preparation for wider publication, involves all the other prior steps discussed above *and* editing the question/answer format into a continuous narrative, removing the interviewer's questions and comments. Once the questions are removed, transitional passages might be missing. We don't want to put words into the interviewee's mouth, yet we want the materials to flow smoothly and to preserve her unique syntax. We must work the material in ways that will render the written form the most authentic rendition of her oral account. This does not necessarily mean the most literal. When the spoken word is translated into the printed word, a great deal is lost—particularly when we are interviewing women unaccustomed to articulating their ideas or to revealing themselves publicly, especially working-class women. The subtle nuances of the spoken word, or the posturing and gesturing that accompany it, often more effectively communicate emotional tone than do the words themselves. The sensitivity of the interviewer to the interviewee will largely determine many of the editorial choices that will be made. Ultimately, this kind of editing entails what can only be described as literary judgment, though it certainly does not require a writer to make these judgments.

No matter how we process the recorded interview, we must remember that we have created a unique "document," one that above all is oral/aural. There is no one method for best creating this new source or for best processing the raw materials. Each of us must develop the style that best suits her and the women she interviews. With our foremothers we are creating a new kind of women's history, a new kind of women's literature. To this task we should bring the sensitivity, respect, tremendous joy, and excitement that come from the awareness that we are not only creating new materials, but that we are also validating the lives of the women who preceded us and are forging direct links with our own past.

NOTES

1. Allan Nevins, "Oral History: How and Why It Was Born," *Wilson Library Bulletin*, 40 (March 1966), 600–601.

2. Gerda Lerner, *The Female Experience: An American Documentary* (Indianapolis: Bobbs-Merrill, 1977), xvi–xviii.

3. A good account of the use of oral history in the study of slavery, beginning with the work at Southern and Fisk Universities in the 1920s, is to be found in Ken Lawrence, "Oral History of Slavery," *Southern Exposure* 1 (Winter 1974), 84–86.

4. Alex Haley, "Black History, Oral History, and Genealogy," *Oral History Review* (1973), 1–25.

5. Interviews with women who have undergone hysterectomies have been conducted by Susanne Morgan of the Feminist History Research Project.

6. Willa Baum, *Oral History for the Local Historical Society*, 2nd ed. (Nashville: American Association for State and Local History, 1975); Norman Hoyle, "Oral History," *Library Trends* (July 1972), 60–81.

7. Yvonne Tixier y Vigil and Nan Elsasser found that in interviews with Hispanic women there was a greater willingness to discuss sex with the Anglo interviewer than with the Chicana interviewer. On the other hand, topics associated with discrimination were more likely to be discussed openly with the Chicana than with the Anglo. See Tixier y Vigil and Elsasser, "The Effects of the Ethnicity of the Interviewer on Conversation: A Study of Chicana Women," in *Sociology of the Language of American Women*, ed. Betty L. DuBois and Isabel Crouch (San Antonio: Trinity University Press, 1976), 161–70.

8. There are several free booklets on the care of tapes that are available from 3M

Company, St. Paul, Minnesota 55101. Generally it is a good idea to make duplicate copies of your tapes, preferably on a high speed copier (which is available at the audio-visual centers of most schools). To avoid accidentally recording over your taped interview, the tabs at the back of the cassette should be punched out. Should you, for some reason, later wish to record on the tape, it is possible to do so by taping over the empty space created where the tab was punched out. For storage of tapes, a moderate temperature is recommended. Some sources recommend rewinding and winding the tapes at least once a year.

Appendix A

Recommendations on Equipment

Many oral history projects use reel-to-reel tape recorders, since the sound quality of these machines is reputed to be better than that of cassette recorders. A cassette recorder, used with a good microphone, can produce a relatively high quality recording. Whatever kind of machine you choose, it is important that an external microphone be used, preferably a lapel style. Though the sound reproduced by this type of microphone is somewhat more "bass" than that from a directional microphone placed on a stand near the interviewee, the advantage is that the interviewee's voice will not have to be boosted as much, and thus extraneous noises will be less. (Most machines have automatic gain controls that will boost the volume of all sounds, not only the voice of the interviewee.) A lapel microphone is also less obtrusive.

The advantages of a cassette tape recorder, in addition to lower cost, are that it is less obtrusive, simpler to operate, and easier to change tapes than in a reel-to-reel machine. No matter what brand you choose, the lowest priced models usually do not have some features that are important. They also seem to have more system noise than the more expensive machines.

A modulation needle on the machine is crucial. It allows you to check that you are, indeed, recording. Since you have no means of knowing whether you are recording or not until you play back the tape, this is an essential feature. Though the digital counter is not essential, it certainly is helpful both in monitoring the approaching end of the tape and in making your task of logging the tape easier.

Perhaps even more important than the brand of the machine or the type of microphone, is the quality of the cassette itself. Cheap cassettes should not be used under any circumstance. Not only do they create more mechanical noise, which is evident on the recordings themselves, but also they are more likely to jam in the machine and are certain to jam on fast copying machines. This does not mean that the highest priced cassette must be used. It is often possible to buy good quality cassettes such as Memorex in large quantities. Though I have successfully used ninety-minute cassettes, I have heard complaints from others that they have had problems with jamming, particularly when transcribing. Certainly, no cassette longer than the c-90 should be used.

During recording, an AC adaptor plug should be used. (The interviewer should always remember to carry an extension cord, too.) Unless it is impossible to use an electrical outlet, or unless there is a fully-charged cadmium battery in the recorder, it is unwise to use the tape recorder on battery power. It is impossible to know what the battery level is, and as it wears down, the machine runs slower and slower. Then, on normal playback, the interview plays back in a necessarily speeded-up version, and the interviewee sounds like Minnie Mouse.

If a directional microphone is used rather than the lapel style, it is important not to place the microphone on the same surface as the tape recorder; the microphone will pick up the vibrations from the machine. Also, the microphone should be placed as close as possible to the interviewee, preferably on some sort of stand.

Appendix B

Summarizing and Indexing the Tape

The Feminist History Research Project (FHRP) uses a relatively simple method for summarizing and indexing our tapes. Each tape is broken down into fifteen three-minute segments (for a forty-five-minute side of a C-90), and each segment is assigned a number continuous from one to fifteen. It is easy enough to sit down with a stop watch and note the number on the digital counter of the tape recorder at each three-minute interval. It is crucial to do this for each tape recorder, since the digital counters vary from machine to machine—even on the same model. Once done, you merely have to watch the digital counter as you make the running summary. Once each three-minute segment has been assigned a number, these would be used as would the number of a printed page.

When you begin to record, make sure the tape counter is set at zero. Once you start to record, check to see that the tape is running and that the needle is modulating. Though nothing should happen in the course of that side, once you have begun it is a good idea to glance down and double check periodically.

Though it is not always possible, it is best to design a break before the end of the tape rather than risk the tape running out in the middle of a sentence. Some machines even have a buzzer that sounds when the tape is nearing the end. I usually use the digital counter to determine when to start listening for an appropriate break. It takes but a second to flip the tape over or to start a new tape. Be sure, once again, to check that all systems are working at the beginning of each new side. After you have completed the recording it is a good idea to punch out the tabs at the back of the tape so that you will not inadvertently record on this tape again (see Note 8 above).

Following is a sample tape summary and a sample index page.

Rebecca August— The Chicago Years

TAPE SECTION	TIME SEGMENT	CONTENT
Side A 1	0'1 to 2'59	Tape identification
		London—work experience, conditions
2	3' to 5'59	Cont. Work experience in London as child
3	6'	London—living conditions
		schooling
4	9'	London—work conditions
		Emigration to U.S. 1904
5	12'	First knowledge unionism
		Story re: price cuts buttonholes and protest
6	15'	Cont. story re: protest over price cut; fired; blacklisted
		Association with Jane Addams begins efforts to organize Hebrew Trades Union (Council)
		R.A. goes to women of men on strike to enlist their support;
		wives of cigar-makers and bakers.
7	18'	Cont. re: organizing wives
		1906 strike incident; arrest, trial
8	21'	Cont. 1906 incident
9	24'	Discussion trial by jury
10	27'	1930s incident; fired for talking unionism
11	30'	Association with Jane Addams
		Jane Addams called "the garbage lady"—efforts to clean up garbage
		Rebecca August's help enlisted—sent to wives of bakers and cigar-makers
12	33'	Cont.
		R.A. could speak to wives in Yiddish
		Formation of Ladies Branch of Workmen's Circle, with assistance from Jane Addams
13	36'	Cont. formation of Ladies Branch of Workmen's Circle
		Jane Addams speaks at first meeting, only 14 women attend
14	39'	Involvement with anarchists and socialists

Socialists too mild, joined anarchists
Attitude towards marriage, free love
Discussion common-law marriage recognition in
    Washington;
Home Colony: Children of common-law
    marriages at Home Colony
Cont. re: offspring Home Colony common-law
    marriages
Anarchist associations, ideology
Rent strike in Chicago, led by Ben Reitman
Incident with Ben Reitman re: free love

15   42'

TAPE INDEX
Rebecca August— Cumulative Index: Tapes I, II, III

Abramovitch, Bessie,
    IIB 10

Addams, Jane,
    IA 2–3, 9
    IIA 6–7, 11–13
    IIB 11
    see also Hebrew Trades Council Workmen's Circle

Amalgamated Clothing Workers (ACWA),
    IB 1, 3; IIIB 3, 5

anarchists,
    beliefs of, IIA 14; IIB 1, 6
    involvement with, IA 10; IIA 14; IIB 1
    rent strike, IIA 15; IIB 5
    see also Home Colony
            marriage
            Reitman

arrests, IA 4; IIIA 8

birth control, IIIA 2, 11

education, IIA 3

feminism, IIIA 12; IIB 11–14

Hebrew Trade Council, IIA 6, 7

Home Colony, IA 15; IB 4; IIA 14; IIIA 9–11

Hull House, IIA 11; IIB 11

immigration,
> experience, IIA 4
> hearing for deportation, IA 5

I.W.W., IA, 6, 11; IB 11; IIIA 5, 8

Jewish Home for the Aged, IB 4–6

Labor Council (Seattle), IA 7; IIIA 5–6, 8

living conditions,
> Chicago, IIA 11
> London, IIA 3

marriage,
> attitude towards, IIA 14; IIIA 3
> common-law, IIA 14–15
> free love, IIA 14–15; IIB 6
> relationship to first husband, IB 3, 6
> rel. to second husband, IIIA 9; IIIB 8, 9

nursing training, IIB 2

Reitman, Ben, IIA 15; IIB 5

Frontiers 2:2 (1977): 3–14.

Women's Oral History

Resource Section

Topical Guide for Oral History Interviews with Women, developed by Sherna Gluck for the Feminist History Research Project, Topanga, California

The best interview allows for the flow of material in a natural manner, within the interviewee's own framework. This topical guide should be used only to sensitize the interviewer to areas that might be considered in the development of an interview outline tailored to the individual interviewee. For each interviewee it is the interviewer's responsibility to research those areas that specifically affect her life, and to place these general suggestions within that specific framework.

The following are only suggestions based on my own work and should be continually revised, added to, and changed.

I. Basic Background Information

A. Family history:

Trace family history beginning with grandparents: background; when they settled in the community in which interviewee's parents were born; what they did; their values. Include any special interest material (e.g., abolition, Civil War involvement, slave experiences, pogram experiences, immigration, etc.).

Relationship of interviewee to grandparents.

Parents (including family names): birthplace; approximate dates of birth; how parents met, married; educational background; work/occupation; general values; attitudes toward women; community involvement; political beliefs.

Interviewee's birth date, place, and circumstances. Siblings, birth order.

B. Description of social environment, family life, early years:

Size and sense of community; family position within it.

Description of family dwelling, including the members of the household; the size and arrangement of the rooms (include sufficient details to be able to assess family circumstances, e.g., how many shared a room, a bed, was there running water, plumbing, etc.).

Household responsibilities, including decision-making areas of mother and father.

Family relationships: relationship to mother, father, siblings, other family members living in household. How did the family spend time together? Were there family holidays, reunions? Did the family eat together? Which meals? What was the pattern of seating, conversation during meals?

Recollections of births, weddings, deaths? Traditions surrounding these events.

Role of religion in home/family life.

II. Childhood and Adolescence

A. Education:

Recollections of school, teachers. Trace schooling, including level attained, type of curriculum, interests, expectations, school activities.

Parents' attitudes toward education; different expectations for male and female children.

Other forms of schooling, including night school, union classes, and so on. Special training, preparation for job, career.

B. Social relationships:

Who were childhood companions? Relationships? What kind of games were played? With whom? Rules? Equipment?

Teenage associations: relationship to boys, girls. Activities. Dating and courtship patterns.

How homogeneous was the social group (e.g., ethnic, religious, racial)?

C. Family relationships and responsibilities in the home:

What kind of responsibilities were held in the home? Differences between boys and girls.

How did the family spend time with each other?

Who disciplined the children? How?

Were there disagreements with parents? Over what? How resolved?

D. Puberty and sex education:

Preparation for menstruation: by whom? When? First menstrual experience: feelings: what kind of materials/devices used? How handled?

Knowledge about sex: by whom? When? How? If appropriate, early sexual activity.

E. Miscellaneous:

General description of reading materials, clothing, physical activities, hair styles can help to reveal values. Explore these kinds of areas in general and inquire about conflicts with parents over these issues.

III. Early Adulthood

A. Expectations about future: direction, expectations about marriage, family, work.

B. Work history:

How was first job obtained? Trace work career in terms of places, positions, conditions, wages, numbers of men/women, differentials in wages and conditions, union involvement.

C. Social relationships, community/group involvement:

Who were associates? Importance of work associates? Community groups? Religious/social or political groups? Trace involvement in any of these groups/organizations.

Relationships to men/women; patterns of relationship, how time spent, when, under what circumstances? To whom turned when had a problem?

D. Living arrangements.

E. Control over earnings? How spent.

IV. Adult Roles/Life

Married or single? For each, trace expectations, pressures and attitudes toward work/career/marriage/family. And, for each explore a typical day at various points in her life.

A. Married women:

How met husband; decision to marry? Describe wedding, including special traditions/customs/beliefs. What were expectations about the relationship; work outside the home; the role inside the home; children?

What was brought into the marriage (money, property), and how was it handled? Description of husband, including education, occupation, and so on.

Description of daily life, before and after birth of children: how was time spent in the home? What kinds of reading materials. Appliances in the home.

Relationship to husband: How was time spent together? With other couples? What was his attitude toward the role of woman/wife? How were disagreements/conflicts handled? What was the source of disagreements? How close was the relationship? How were decisions made?

Relationship to other women: under what circumstances; nature of relationships; shared "women's talk"? Confide in each other?

Children/family planning: What were plans, expectations about raising a family? Was first pregnancy planned? What were feelings about pregnancy?

Embarrassment about being seen publicly? How dressed? Husband's attitudes?

Any knowledge of birth control? What? From where? Discussed with other women? Methods, if any, used? Effectiveness? Explore in detail where obtained.

Abortions? How many? By whom? Cost? Techniques? Self-induced abortions? "Premature births"? "Miscarriages"?

Childbirth: prenatal and maternity care; birth experiences, including description of circumstances, who attended, difficulties.

Child rearing: who made decisions? Amount of time spent with children how? Role imposed on children? Expectations? Any kinds of child guidance/rearing guides used?

Social life, activities outside the home: with whom? Activities? Political/social concerns: community service, women's clubs, PTA, suffrage, radical-reform movements.

If worked outside the home, how were family/work responsibilities handled? What kind of help was received? From whom? How was time divided? Describe routines. Any resentments about load of work?

Life after children left home.

Note: Within the sequence, be sure to get information about the environment in which the family functioned; type of housing; standards of living; changes in occupation; mobility; effect on individual and family life of various economic, political, and social events.

B. If separated, divorced, or widowed, explore the reasons, feelings; how family was supported; difficulties of one-parent family situation; ways in which life changed.

C. Single women (much of the focus will be on work history and experiences and social relationships): expectations, attitudes toward marriage. Pressures to marry? Attitudes of others toward unmarried women?

Living arrangements?

Life of a single woman: problems in housing; social life; economic pressures.

Social life and experiences during the 1920s: clothing; meaning of the so-called revolution in manners and morals; relationships to men; sexuality.

Social relationships with men/women: kinds of relationships, kinds of activities, generated by whom.

Work/career: satisfaction of; importance of in social life; relationship to other workers. Obtain full work history, including mobility, opportunities, problems as a woman, sexual politics of workplaces.

Political/social consciousness, and involvements; reform organizations; women's organizations; professional organizations; community groups; union. Obtain full history.

Attitudes about women, women's issues.

V. Later Years

A. For married women: activities, interests, feelings in later life, after children are grown, after husband's death.

B. For all working women: retirement—feelings about; life and activities since.

C. For all women: menopause—feelings about; physiological problems; responses; effect on work life or home life. Hysterectomy?

VI. General

A. Reflecting on life: What was happiest time, most fulfilling? Most unhappy time? What would do differently?

B. Reflections on changing role, position of women: comparison to own youth; attitudes toward Women's Movement today; role of women.

C. Within the context of each period discussed, be sure to explore the effects of various events, movements on her life, such as suffrage movement, WW I, Depression, WW II, any local events of significance in the area where she lived and/or worked.

Interview Guide for "The Twentieth Century Trade Union Woman:
Vehicle for Social Change," developed by the Project at the University
of Michigan, Ann Arbor, Michigan

I. Family Background

Do you remember your grandparents? Do you remember your mother talking about her parents? Do you remember things your father said about his
parents?

What did your father tell you about his boyhood? Where was he born? At
what age did he begin to work?

What did your mother tell you about her childhood? Where was she born?
Did she work outside the home as a child? As a young woman? What kinds
of responsibilities or chores did she do around the house as a child?

What did you like to do with your mother?

What did you like to do with your father?

What did your mother do most of her life? Did she work outside the home
after she married? Was she working at any time when you were growing up?
What were her hopes for herself? What were her hopes for her children?
For you in particular? How much schooling did she have? Did she take an
interest in her community? In politics? What were her views?

Was your father's background similar to your mother's? How much schooling did he have? What did he do for a living? How did his job affect the
family? Did he take an interest in politics? What were his views? Did he talk
with your mother about these things? What were his hopes for himself? For
his children? For you?

Were you closer to one parent than the other? Which parent did you admire
more? As a child, did you want to live a life like your parents' when you
grew up?

How many years did you live in the house/apartment where you were born?
What was that house like? The neighborhood? The town? How did you feel
about the place? Who lived with you when you were growing up (grandparents, boarders, how many people)?

Who were your companions as a child? Did you have brothers and sisters (birth order, spacing)? What was your relationship to your brothers and sisters? Whom were you closest to?

What chores or responsibilities did you have as a child? Did you ever think boys had an easier time?

What did you daydream about becoming when you grew up?

Was religion important to you as a child? In what way?

What kinds of arguments were there in your family? Was your family in any way different than the neighbors in your community? How did you feel about that?

II. Education

What did you think of school? What subjects did you like? Did you have any favorite teachers?

What did your family think about school? Did they have different ideas for boys than for girls?

Were your classmates from the same background as you (ethnic, socioeconomic, religious)? What about the teachers?

When did you stop going to formal school? Why? Did you ever wish you had gone further?

Were you ever involved in other kinds of school such as settlement house classes, union, YWCA, or other workers' education classes? What did you think of those experiences? What did you think of the teachers?

Did students ever talk about political events of the times among themselves? Often? Did you participate in this?

Is there anything special about your early schooling that may have contributed to your later union activism?

III. Community Political Background

Describe the community in which you first lived. Did neighbors get together informally? Were you ever active in community organizations?

Did you belong to any religious, social, or political groups as a young girl? In later life? (Construct history of involvement.)

What was the first political group you ever joined? Were you aware of any splits in that group over different positions? Did you take sides?

How did your political views change over the years?

IV. Work Experience

How did you get your first job? What did the work involve? How old were you? Did you expect to keep it a long time? How much did you earn? What did you do with the money? Did you work among women or mixed sexes? Were your bosses women or men? What did you think of your coworkers? Of your boss? Did you make any friends on that first job? Did you socialize with them outside of work? Why did you stop working there? What was the worst thing about that job?

Did you have a plan about future jobs? Did you think you would stop working when you got married? How did you get your next job?

Did you ever have a job where it was possible to move up to more money or more interesting work? What was the best job you ever had? What was the worst job? (Construct job history.)

Have you ever stopped working since you began? For what reasons?

What did you usually do when you came home from work (chores as a young girl, domestic responsibilities later)?

(If applicable) How did your husband feel about your working? What kinds of child care arrangements did you make through the years? Was this an important part of your responsibilities?

During wars, women were often encouraged to work and then discouraged after the soldiers came home. Did you ever feel that pressure?

How do you think your work experiences would have been different if you were a man?

Have you ever been refused a job or a promotion because you weren't friendly enough to a male boss?

If you had a choice of all the jobs in the world and could get the right training, looking back, what kind of work would you choose to do?

V. Start of Union Activism

Where were you working when you got involved in union activities? How did you first get involved?

Was going to union meetings a source of conflict in your family? When you first got involved, were there many other women active?

Who was your first union connection, the first person you knew who was involved? What did you think of him/her?

How popular were unions in your neighborhood, in the newspapers, when you first got started?

Were you active right from the beginning? What was your first official position in the union? Appointed or elected? Who encouraged you to become more active?

How did being part of the union affect your private life at first? Did you go to any other union activities, such as schools or conventions?

When you had your first union position, what were your responsibilities? Were there many women in similar positions? Did women go to meetings?

(If first position was steward): What kinds of problems tended to come up? What were most of the grievances that you remember? Were there any particular to women? How did they get settled?

(If first position was organizer): What were your approaches in getting women involved? What kinds of problems did you encounter? Did you get support from ministers, community leaders? How did you relate to women in other unions? Were they ever helpful? From whom did you learn specific things about organizing skills?

Did you expect to continue active union work? Were there other things that competed for your time (social, political, religious activities, private life)?

VI. Women's Participation in the Life of Their Union

When you first got involved in the union, did you think you would ever have a leadership role? Did you think being a woman made any difference?

Have you ever been discouraged from running for union office?

Did you ever do much traveling in your union work? If so, did you travel alone or with groups? Was traveling with men a problem? Did hotels ever refuse to put you on the same floor with the men you worked with? Was your personal life ever criticized?

Think back to women in your local who were active and then dropped out—why did they, and why did you remain?

How was your union structured? How did you fit into that? Were there informal lines of power that differed from the formal positions? Did you ever feel left out of informal caucusing or decision-making over drinks?

At what periods in your life was union responsibility heaviest? How did you juggle the rest of your life at those times? Did you have any energy left for nonwork and nonunion interests? What are some of the sacrifices you made in order to be active?

What is the highest position a woman ever reached in your union?

When you were most active, did you ever devote much energy to "women's" issues? Were you particularly interested in planning any special programs for women workers? What was the support and opposition like in these cases? Were you involved with protective legislation concerns?

How were your union and industry affected by national issues such as price and wage controls? What happened to your industry during and after the wars? What stand did your union take on workers being laid off? Did you agree with them?

What was the effect of the Depression and the New Deal on your industry/union?

What type of community support did you receive (in the 1920s, 1930s, 1940s) from groups such as the National Consumers League, Y's, churches, settlement houses? Which was most effective?

While you were active in the union, were you ever active in any community or political groups? How did the two relate?

Was there a special kind of camaraderie that developed among union activists? Was it especially strong during certain time periods? Was this usually a mixed or same-sex group? Have you stayed in touch with some of these people? Who were you closest to during your active union years?

What was involved in being a steward/organizer/local recording secretary (all positions she has had; probe for autonomy, policy-making power)?

How many of the employees in the plants you worked with were women?

What were the lifestyles of the women you organized/served as steward? Were you asked, or did you ever help with community and family related problems? How different was your life from the lives of the women you worked with (marriage/children/living alone/with roommates)?

How did various strikes and organizing campaigns affect the women workers? Were there special barriers to their participation? Were there any issues in campaigns of particular interest to women?

VII. General

What was the most exciting part of your life? If you could relive any part of your life, when would it be?

(If you had) a daughter, would you want her to live through your experiences? What parts would you want her to avoid?

Have you been generally more comfortable working with women or men? Which have you worked with most? In what ways?

Were you active in getting women the vote (or other nonunion feminist issues)?

Do you remember reading anything, or seeing a movie, or meeting someone special that influenced your life dramatically?

Do you support the ERA? Do you think organized labor responds to women's needs?

Do you think women working within the labor movement were generally more or less effective because they were female?

What was the most frustrating part of your work within unions? Most satisfying? When did you feel that it wasn't worth it?

If you could be sixteen years old again, how would you relive your life? Would you still be involved with unions (marry/change number of children/ education/travel)?

Interview Guide for Obtaining Family Histories, developed by Joan Jensen

"Women living around us carry the past within them."

A. I would like each person in the class to write a family history of the oldest woman in his or her family. There are several reasons for this assignment. The major one is that the history of these women has not been written, and we can learn much about change in the lives of women from them. A second is that it will enable study of the lives of your foremothers. In addition, you will learn some of the basic skills of gathering oral and family history. People need to be their own historians to really understand what the process of writing history is like, and this project will give you a chance to experience that process yourselves.

If you do not have an older relative with whom you can work on this project, you may select a younger relative or a friend, or you may select an alternative project, with my approval. The alternative project should be geared to some aspect of history in twentieth-century women's history and must be approved by me.

B. Reading for the project. Everyone should read Alex Haley, "Search for an Ancestor," in *American Vistas, 1607–1877,* ed. Leonard Dinnerstein and Kenneth T. Jackson (New York: Oxford University Press, 1975), pp. 221–331, and any one chapter in Sherna Gluck, ed., *From Parlor to Prison* (New York: Vintage, 1976), to get some perspective on the quest for family history and how the lives of women unfold. Read them as early as possible in the semester.

We will devote one session to discussing the process of conducting oral interviews and writing family history and three sessions at the end of the semester to exchanging our histories with other members of the class.

C. Questions. The following questions have been suggested by social historians dealing with the history of the family and can provide a good starting point for thinking about women's lives. While many of the best interviews flow with relatively few specific questions, thinking about these aspects of family life will enable you to better evaluate the woman's narrative and to encourage discussion of particular kinds of information.

I. Internal Experience of the Family

1. Dwelling and organization of family life. Did family members other than parents and their children live in the same apartment, house, or building, along the same street, in the same neighborhood? Did married daughters or sons continue to live with their parents? Did aging parents live in their children's households, in their own dwellings, in retirement communities, or in old-age homes? How did the family organize its living space? How crowded was the household? Who slept in what room? Were there servants or boarders living with the family?

2. Social organization and family activities. What were the daily schedules of family members? How did they spend their time at home and their holidays? Who visited whom, how frequently, and over what periods of time? What kind of family celebrations were held? Were family reunions held? How were weddings, baptisms, funerals, and other ceremonies held? Who attended? Where were they held? What community activities did they participate in?

3. Decision-making and status in the family. How were decisions on daily family business (budgeting, housekeeping, etc.) made? Who disciplined the children and by what means? Did adults other than parents participate in disciplining children? Did grandparents or other adults participate in rearing children? Was there conflict in the family, and how did members respond? Were some members treated as "black sheep," and how did this affect their relationship to other family members? How were members ranked (sex, age, ability, occupation, success) in terms of privileges and obligations? What were mealtimes like?

4. Aid and responsibility. At what age did sons and daughters leave home to begin careers? Did parents help children in college or business? Did older sons and daughters support their aging parents? Who cared for sick or dependent family members? Who helped in times of crisis?

5. Family and property. Who owned property in the family and how did they manage it? What were the inheritance patterns? How did well-to-do members relate to those of lesser means? How was the property held by women and men before the marriage handled?

6. Careers and opportunity. Did sons follow their fathers' occupations? Did daughters work outside the home? What were the attitudes of the family toward daughters (and mothers) working? Was different emphasis put on

their education or different education selected because of sex? Did grandparents or relatives influence occupational choices? What was considered "success" for different members of the family? What was work like?

7. Life cycle. Were babies born at home or in the hospital? Were there midwives? What did men and women think of midwives? Were there attempts to limit the number of children? What were attitudes toward abortion? How were babies treated in the family? At what age did a child cease to be considered a "child"? Was "adolescence" recognized as a special stage? At what age was a young person expected to take on adult responsibilities? What were the attitudes toward aging? Toward mental or physical illness?

II. External Factors

Ask about "historical events" that might have had an impact on the history of the family such as wars, depressions, prosperity, inflation, immigration policies, employment patterns, welfare services, urban renewal, technological change, transportation, mass media, "Jim Crow" laws, emancipation of slaves, revolutions, women's suffrage, and reform movements.

PART II: RELEASE FORMS

The structure and goals of a project will largely determine what kind of release an interviewee should be asked to sign. If the recordings will be for archival use exclusively, a simple agreement is probably sufficient. If, on the other hand, wider use and possible publication are anticipated, a more complicated form will be necessary.

The two forms reprinted here are only intended to serve as guidelines, and no claims are being made about their legal status.

1. The simple agreement reprinted below was adopted from one used by the Regional Oral History Office, Bancroft Library, Berkeley, California:

> I hereby give to　　　　　　　　(name of project/institution)
> for such scholarly and educational use and purpose as
> the Director of　　　　　　　　(name of project/institution)
> shall determine, the following tapes,
> recorded on:　　　　　　　　(dates)
> Date:　　　　　　　　Signature of interviewee:
> 　　　　　　　　Name, address, and telephone number

2. The more complicated agreement printed below was developed by Sherna Gluck for the Feminist History Research Project and includes those elements that are required by commercial publishers:

The interviewee,   (name), hereby grants, assigns,
and transfers to   (director of project/institution)
the right to publish, duplicate, or otherwise use the tape
and/or transcript of the interview(s)
taped on   (dates)
concerning   (subject).

It is further understood that   (name of project director)
may copyright all or portions of the tape(s) and/or transcribed interview(s) and that the interviewee waives any claims in connection with the use of the material, such as copyright claims, and claims for the invasion of privacy and libel.

In the event that material composed of this (these) interview(s) is sold, the proceeds of such sale will be used solely to cover the costs of production and to further the goals of (name of project)

(Name, director of project/institute), hereby agrees to provide the interviewee with access to the taped interviews.

Dated: Signature of interviewee:
Dated: Signature of Project Director:

Frontiers 2:2 (1977): 89–95.

Doing Oral History as an Outsider

MARGARET STROBEL

Until African women overcome the barriers that separate them from literacy, higher education, money, and power, outsiders will of necessity be an important part of recording their oral history. Theoretically, tape recorders make it possible for nonliterate persons to capture and produce their own oral histories. Realistically, however, educated people will be more likely to collect, process, and disseminate oral history. History departments in African universities have for several years incorporated the gathering of oral history into their curricula. But even in these efforts oral accounts from women rarely have been forthcoming, due to a shortage of women students, a lack of interest in and appreciation for women's contribution to history, or both.[1] Thus emerges the role of outsiders: to create from the lives of African women primary documents that are marked only minimally by interference and direction from the outsider. Hopefully, the outsider's efforts will contribute to creating, along with other primary materials, an interest on the part of Africans themselves in women's recollections.

Several excellent oral histories of African women have been compiled by foreign scholars over the years. Without doubt the most thorough account of a woman's life is *Baba of Karo*, edited and translated by Mary Smith, which tells of Muslim Hausa society in Northern Nigeria.[2] An analysis based on oral histories collected earlier is Marcia Wright's "Women in Peril: A Commentary Upon the Life Stories of Captives in Nineteenth-Century East Africa."[3] Anne Laurentin's "Nzakara Women" details the lives of three women from different classes.[4] Finally, Monica Hunter tells "The Story of Nosente, The Mother of Compassion of the Xhosa Tribe, South Africa."[5] Though not exhaustive, this list suggests the variety of women, in different times and places in Africa, whose life stories have been made available for social historians and others.

Although some problems faced by oral historians are common to all of us to one degree or another, the researcher in an unfamiliar culture meets with certain particular difficulties and benefits. Language, customs, taboos, and assumptions that we carry affect the validity and perceptiveness of our oral history interviews. I would like to discuss some aspects of doing oral history as an outsider, drawing on my experience with Muslim women in Mombasa, Kenya.[6]

Language is the most obvious and most fundamental barrier for the oral historian. If you try to interview directly, without an interpreter, as I did, your initial interviews may turn out to be worthless exercises until your command of the language is adequate to allow free-flowing conversation. Still, one can salvage material even from these fitful beginnings. For my first interview I was introduced to Bi Kaje, an eighty-year-old woman who was blind and slightly hard of hearing. Realizing the need for making concrete the abstraction of what I was studying—"the social history of Swahili women," I explained in my halting Swahili that I was interested in women's customs. Bi Kaje proceeded to talk for an hour in Swahili about weddings, with little prompting (or comprehension) from me. Fortunately, I had taped the conversation, and upon listening to it several times, I discovered endless leads—family names, references to slaves, farms, customs, and women who acted as midwives or ritual leaders. Later, when my mastery of Mombasa's dialect of Swahili had improved, I returned time and again for conversations with Bi Kaje, now able to question her about particular people or events.

Although the technique of interviewing in a language in which you have minimal fluency may seem a poor choice, there are advantages to this approach over the use of an interpreter. As an insider, an interpreter may be able to spot nuances of language and situation that you as a stranger miss. However, as an insider, the interpreter may interfere with your objectives.[7] She may be part of community squabbles about which you are unaware; her class or ethnic subgroup may affect her rapport with your subject; and she may have her own motives for covering up and avoiding areas of discussion in which you are interested. Finally, having an interpreter suggests a formal interview situation, which may not provide the best circumstances under which to obtain women's life histories.

Even when language is not a problem, cultural differences between the interviewer and subject must be addressed. In establishing rapport, the interviewer must deal with individual personality quirks and must not violate that culture's behavior norms for women/guests/younger women/strangers—any of the multitude of roles into which the interviewer fits. In doing my own work, I was extremely polite and unaggressive. Nonetheless, I often wondered if I was too diffident, if my care not to be pushy was perceived as aloofness and lack of interest. Let me offer one anecdote about the difficulty of understanding cultural cues.

I was invited to the midday meal by the first family I met in Mombasa. We arranged that I would come the second day for lunch as well. The third day I went to a restaurant but stopped by to visit at teatime, only to be chastised for staying away at lunch. My politeness and unwillingness to impose on the family had been interpreted as a desire not to spend time with them. They saw me as an adopted daughter coming from America; I was not so immediately able to see myself as part of their family by mere virtue of a letter of introduction.

Cultural differences may also affect the content of interviews as well as the process of establishing a relationship with a subject. Some matters may be taboo for strangers to discuss; these subjects may open up after several interviews and visits. Sometimes the reverse may be true—the interviewer may consider sexual matters to be too private to ask of a stranger, when in fact the subject may consider sex to be a universal fact of female existence, discussible with another female. The best rule of thumb, I found, was to be honest about one's confusion about behavioral norms. Often I would explain how we acted in America to show my friends how I was interpreting a situation and would ask how they expected me to behave.

One's position as an outsider, while it lends ambiguity to behavioral expectations, can make certain people and information accessible. As a neutral party (if you take care to remain neutral) you may become a confidante; or, people with conflicting views may seek you out to insure that each side gets your ear. Or you may be able to talk to people from different class backgrounds about matters that insiders would not be able to discuss. Again, let me draw from my field experience.

Until 1907 Mombasa was a slave society in which upper-class people— often, though not exclusively, of Arab ancestry—owned Africans who had been brought from Central Africa to this east African seaport. Part of my research was to investigate the nature of the interaction between slaves and slave-owners and their descendants. Questions of both slavery and women converged nicely in wedding practices, since dances were performed that were cultural survivals of dances brought by slaves in the nineteenth century. By expressing interest in these wedding dances I met women of slave ancestry. Up until this point my contacts had been with the upper classes, and my elite friends were somewhat surprised at my interest in these women and their subculture, which they saw as retaining the tinge of slave origins. By making contact with these lower-class women directly through their dance associations, I was able to meet them on an equal footing. Had one of them, as the cook of the family of a wealthy friend of mine, been summoned to meet me, our relationship would have been tinged by the class and status system of Mombasa.

Though as an outsider I was not limited in terms of my contacts and associations by the class system, in another very real way, class prejudice, racism, and sexism in Mombasa did affect my research. Women, particularly lower-class women, often do not perceive themselves and their lives as having importance. Even if their activities are important to them, they do not perceive them as significant or interesting to outsiders. Moreover, they may be less familiar with American or European culture and thus less comfortable among Europeans.[8] Unlike their more privileged sisters, these women tend not to have secretarial jobs or to work in the tourist industry where they meet foreigners. All of these factors combine to make the information held by upper-class men more accessible than that held by lower-class women, with upper-class women falling in the middle. Let me illustrate.

One of my earliest interviews was with a former judge who decided questions of Muslim personal law such as marriage and divorce. We had a brief but fruitful interview. He had been a teacher and thus had experience explaining material. He had talked with Europeans and so knew how to simplify his Swahili, quite naturally, to make me understand without appearing to be condescending. His position as a judge gave us a specific topic of conversation—Muslim law as it affects relations between men and women. Since the law had been recorded, I was familiar with the subject matter. As an older, wealthy man, he had no household tasks to draw him away from our interview. And, his home had a telephone, so that setting up and confirming the interview was easy.

In contrast were my interviews with Ma Mishi, whose grandparents were slaves. Ma Mishi, too, held a position of authority—she was a leader of an association that conducted puberty rites for girls. These rites, which had been brought by slaves to Mombasa and formed a slave subculture in the city, are secret. Everyone knows of their performance, but only those initiated into the association are privy to the content and meaning of the rituals. I was interested in discussing Ma Mishi's background, her family, and her participation in the puberty rites associations. Despite my joining the association, our interviews never proceeded as successfully as my discussion with the man mentioned above or with upper-class women. First, it is possible that Ma Mishi had never talked to a white person as an equal or superior, although she had worked as a cook for a Kenyan white settler and was thus not completely unfamiliar with white people. It was difficult to find a period of peace and quiet for an interview because Ma Mishi could not afford a servant to help her with domestic chores. She lived with her crippled daughter and during the day took care of her great-grandson while his mother worked at a garment factory. Our talks proceeded while Ma Mishi cooked meals or during the child's naps, and their progress was affected accordingly.

Ma Mishi had not been interviewed before; and although she had explained the puberty rites to hundreds of Swahili girls in her lifetime, she had never had occasion to explain them to a stranger who did not share her system of metaphysics. Moreover, because women's experiences have rarely been recorded, I had no background reading to acquaint me with the rites in Mombasa. To a certain extent she was embarrassed about her ancestry and for that reason, I suspect, was not keen to elaborate about the lives and activities of her grandparents. Moreover, because she could not afford a telephone, she could not call ahead to cancel appointments. Instead, if she were called away to assist some family member, or to bury a young child, or to sit with a sick relative, she would leave a message for me when I arrived for the expected interview.

The effect of this constellation of factors based on Ma Mishi's sex and class was to make her story more difficult to obtain. Difficult, but not impossible. Those who are interested in doing the history of women, of the poor, and of others who have been excluded from history must recognize and creatively solve the problems of obtaining their stories.

One factor that mitigates the difficulty of obtaining information from women and lower-class people in general is that storytelling need not be restricted by class or sex. Even though oral traditions in nonliterate societies are often the province of specialists within that society, many people can tell stories. Bi Kaje's knack for storytelling provided rich material on Swahili society, on relationships between classes and between men and women. Although she would often, without prompting, bring up topics of interest to herself, which revealed her own priorities and values, my experience in eliciting the following story also points to the need for persistence on the part of the interviewer and for the establishment of trust. For Bi Kaje only revealed this incident in her life on my second trip to Kenya and after many hours of visiting.

As background, let me explain that Bi Kaje was born to a poor but freeborn Swahili man and his concubine about 1890. Raised as a freeborn child following the legal status of her father, Bi Kaje was secluded by Muslim custom. Seclusion, or *purdah*, entailed wearing a veil and segregating oneself from the company of men who were not kinfolk. Secluded women of higher status generally had less physical mobility than did slave women who could travel about without compromising their already low social status. As Bi Kaje recounts:

My first husband, Mohamadi wa Mwenye Hija wa Ngao, was related to me: His maternal grandfather and my father's maternal grandfather were brothers, having the same father but different mothers. . . . We lived with my grandmother in her house. . . .

Mohamadi was a self-employed businessman; he did not work for Europeans or Indians. He sent people into the bush to cut firewood and took it to the port where he sold it. Our first child, Ahmad, died at eight months. We lived happily for [a] while. Then he stopped working. Or, if he worked, his mother came secretly and said to him, "Give me the money you make." He and his mother ate at his brother's house. I was left alone in our house.

Mohamadi had a slave, Tabia, who took pity on me when she saw that I had been given nothing. She quickly cooked me some rice and broiled a fish and brought these to me. She did not have time even to make the sauce. I ate the food and quickly cleaned up the crumbs so that Mohamadi and his mother would not see them. Tabia told me, "Run away, come to my place and I will take you to your grandmother's home." I did not know the way myself [because I was raised in seclusion].

That night when they had gone to eat, I locked the door and told a neighbor, "I am going to the toilet at Bi Mkubwa's house." I went quickly to [the neighborhood of] Mwembe Tayari, but I could not find our house. I asked someone, "Which way is Ma Sitara's house?" He showed me. I called at the door just as my brother was on his way to the mosque. But my grandmother said, "I cannot harbor a person's wife. Go back home, or go to [the judge's house]. Don't come to my house."

My brother took my hand and we went to [the judge]. . . . He said, "Go to your husband's house and sleep there." I told him, "I refuse to go." He replied, "Then go to his brother's house." So I slept there. Mohamadi did not go to our house, he came to where I was staying and started cursing me. We argued and abused one another all night long. At dawn I went back to my grandmother's house along the roads that now were familiar to me. Badhadhiki [the slave who had raised me] was there, and she took me back to the judge. He decreed that Mohamadi must provide me with food every day and little money.

The first day he gave it to me, the second, but the third day he ran away. I sent my uncle to the judge saying, "He has not come since the day before yesterday." At home

I opened the door and sat, waiting for Mohamadi's return. When he came, he asked, "Why is the door wide open?" I answered, "It means the wind is whistling through my stomach." He told me to close it, but I refused. [I was not really starving, my grandmother fed me. She sent me a basket of food, which I hid in the attic. When no one was around I would lower it on a rope and eat, then return it to the attic.] I told Mohamadi, "I do not want to, I want a divorce." So he divorced me.

In addition to portraying vividly Bi Kaje's personality, this fragment of her life points out important aspects of women's lives in Swahili society. The intimate interaction and solidarity between slave and freeborn women, and the latters' dependence on the former, is seen in the characters of Tabia and Badhadhiki. Both of these slave women are more familiar with the geography of Mombasa than Bi Kaje because they had not lived segregated from men and secluded from the bustle of street life. Both seem to care about Bi Kaje. Tabia, though a slave belonging to Bi Kaje's husband, was even willing to help her run away. Also, women's dependence on men is clear in various parts of this incident. Unable to support herself financially, Bi Kaje relies on her husband for her daily sustenance. When that is not forthcoming, she must go to the male judge for a decision against him. And, to present her case she is accompanied by her brother. Finally, this episode discloses how women maneuvered through the patriarchal structures of Swahili society. Bi Kaje's grandmother upheld the rule that grants a husband authority over his wife by refusing to shelter Bi Kaje. But she undermined Mohamadi's power by sending food to her granddaughter behind his back. Similarly, Bi Kaje does not challenge the Muslim law that denies her the right to initiate divorce proceedings.[9] Instead, she manipulated the situation—by running away, by refusing to return to live with her husband, by reporting the delinquent husband to the Muslim judge, by sneaking food into her home while charging her husband with failure to provide household money as was his responsibility, by chastising him metaphorically, and by forcing him to divorce her. Such are the strategies of women around the world.

Bi Kaje and Ma Mishi's life histories help illuminate in greater fullness the complexity of Swahili society, composed as it was of slave and freeborn persons. Interviews with other women indicate more directly the nature and intensity of colonialism as it affected women in particular. Taken together, their stories will reveal to people of Mombasa as well as to historians and social scientists elsewhere the attitudes and experiences of those who were not in the colonial limelight of Kenya.

NOTES

1. For example, *Modern Tanzanians: A Volume of Biographies*, ed. John Iliffe (Nairobi: East African Publishing House, 1973), contains the life stories of thirteen men, collected by undergraduates at the University of Dar es Salaam, Tanzania. In his introduction Iliffe notes the lack of women's experience recorded in the work.

2. Mary Smith, *Baba of Karo: A Woman in the Muslim Hausa* (New York: Philosophical Library, 1955).

3. Marcia Wright, "Women in Peril: A Commentary upon the Life Stories of Captives in Nineteenth-Century East Africa," *African Social Research*, 20 (December 1975), 800–819.

4. Anne Laurentin, "Nzakara Women," in *Women of Tropical Africa*, ed. Denise Paulme (Berkeley: University of California Press, 1971), 121–78.

5. Monica Hunter, "The Story of Nosente, The Mother of Compassion of the Xhosa Tribe, South Africa," in *Ten Africans*, ed. Margery Perham (London: Faber and Faber, 1936), 121–37.

6. This research was undertaken with the assistance of a Fulbright-Hays Doctoral Research Abroad Fellowship and a Woodrow Wilson Doctoral Dissertation Fellowship in Women's Studies. The results of this research are in my doctoral dissertation, "Muslim Women in Mombasa, Kenya, 1890–1973," (Ph.D. diss., UCLA, 1975). Some of the material has been published in Margaret Strobel, "From *Lelemama* to Lobbying: Women's Associations in Mombasa, Kenya," in *Women in Africa: Studies in Social and Economic Change*, ed. Nancy J. Hafkin and Edna G. Bay (Stanford: Stanford University Press, 1976); and Margaret Strobel, "Women's Wedding Celebrations in Mombasa, Kenya," *African Studies Review* 18:3 (December 1975): 35–45.

7. Andrew Roberts discusses these difficulties and others in "The Use of Oral Sources for African History," *Oral History* (University of Essex) 4:1 (1976): 47.

8. Margaret Jean Hay makes a similar point in "African Women and American Researchers: A Personal Note," *Ufahamu*, 6:1 (1975): 62.

9. Under Muslim law men do not have to provide grounds for divorcing their wives. Under Mombasa's school of law a woman cannot initiate divorce but can obtain a divorce through the judge if her husband has not provided necessary food and clothing. Bi Kaje apparently chose to manipulate her husband into divorcing her rather than to ask the judge for a divorce. Perhaps she sensed resistance on the part of the judge, whom she had already visited twice, only to be ordered back home to her husband.

Frontiers 2:2 (1977): 54–57.

Digging beneath the Surface

Oral History Techniques

SHERRY THOMAS

I set out on a long cross-country trip to talk to women who had been actively engaged in farming, and I set out wanting to cover basically every region of America in some form or another. My book, *We Didn't Have Much, but We Sure Had Plenty*, is a selection of interviews with those older farm women from all over America.

I had no pretense of social science authenticity, and I was panicked about not having social science authenticity, so I made sure I had at least two Native Americans, two Chicanas, seventeen black women, and women from every class. And I do not mean that superficially. I was really aware that I wanted to present an image of a generation of women in its broadest scope, both in terms of commonalities and differences. I tried to include women of different races, of different classes, and women who had done all kinds of agricultural labor in terms of region, types of farms, and mechanized and nonmechanized labor. I wanted to talk to women who were both landowners and women who had been tenants or field hands without land at all.

When I set out on the trip, I had spent about six months collecting names, contacts, and connections all over the country that would give me the diversity I sought. Often, talking to one woman led to another, so that the trip changed constantly while I was on the road. One of the things that surprised me was that, given how much diversity I found, I also found a tremendous amount of commonality in the stories that arose. That was not something that I had expected, and I felt that the commonalities were genuine to the material itself. For a while I worried that I had skewed my sample somehow, that I was finding only one type of woman, because I was getting common statements over and over, again in tremendously diverse circumstances. I am talking about the daughter of a slave who had been told about enslavement and had worked for twenty cents a day most of her life in the South and a Midwestern grain farmer who owned five hundred acres of land and who was saying very similar things. After I had completed fifty-two interviews, I began to believe that I was hearing similar things because there were threads about that type of life and women in that age range that were surprisingly common despite the diversity.

In the end, only twelve of the initial fifty-two interviews were published in the book. I drove ten thousand miles one way across America doing the interviews, zigzagging up and down, and covering every part of the country. Then I sat in Atlanta for three weeks and thought, "Oh, my god, what do I do with this material?" I reviewed what I had before I started back across the country to re-interview the women whose interviews would eventually end up in the book. It was a maniacal journey, and I realize that part of what was behind it was a sense that I desperately and personally needed to know the stories of the women who had come before me.

I had been a farmer for ten years and during that time had never met any women in farming who were not part of the back-to-the-land movement. My intuition told me that women had been vitally active in agriculture forever, yet there was no body of information to tell me anything about who the women were or what they had done. The stereotypical image that I had received was that there were farmers and there were farm wives, and farm wives were something other than farmers. Even within my own family, which came from an agricultural background, there were no personal stories that offered me any kind of support for what I was trying to do with my life. The personal quest is a good way to start oral history because it is a way to build connections with the people whom you are interviewing. The passion for wanting to know is part of what makes oral history happen in a way that brings it alive in the end.

I set out with a prepared list of questions that I thought I wanted to ask people, but by the third interview, I threw it out, and I did not use it again. Nevertheless, I certainly knew what I was looking for. I wanted to know what kind of work women had done. I wanted to know what was expected of them by their families and communities. I wanted to know how their lives had changed as society had become more materialistic and more mechanized. I wanted to know how they had felt about what they had done in their lives. I wanted to know what regrets or what satisfactions they had. I was dealing only with women aged fifty to one hundred because I wanted to look at a broad spectrum of American experience at a particular time in history, when families had control over their own agriculture and before widespread agribusiness and large-scale farming.

The first thing that became really clear—which sounds obvious and yet nowhere had I read or heard it said before I did the interviews—was that women are *farmers*; they are not farm wives. They were actively engaged in doing the work that sustained the family, bringing cash income into the family. And there was not a significant division of labor in most parts of the country during most of these women's working lives. That wasn't so easy to find out—and this is something I often come back to—because the first thing women told me was, "Well, *really*, I only helped out on the farm." By about the third interview I realized that I needed to find out what that phrase meant, because either I was wrong in what I intuited about these women and work, or something else was going on. So I started asking questions like: Tell me what you did in 1926 in a typical day. Tell me what it was like during the Depression in a typical day. How did it change in the forties? What did you do from six in the morning on? "Helping out" meant getting up at five in the morning, milking as many as twenty-four cows by hand, separating cream and preserving the milk, running a poultry herd, selling the eggs (which was a significant part of the cash income), producing all of the vegetables and fruit for the family, *and* doing up a half of all the field crop work for the family, as well as doing all the housework, all the cooking, all the food preservation, and all the child care. Their husbands did half of the field crop work and some of the animal husbandry, although not as much as the women. That was called "helping," and that is typical of what happens when you ask a question and get a socially accepted response. When interviewing, it is important *not* to stop with the socially accepted response, but to keep going until you find out what the reality of her situation is—not what she thinks you want to hear is the reality of her situation, not how it has always been described, and not what makes the local community or family structure more comfortable. During the questioning process it is often necessary to go back to the nitty-gritty, to talk about the day-to-day experiences that then bring out the much deeper information.

I was thoroughly surprised by the issues that came up in conversations with these women. I had expected to discuss motherhood, child-rearing, and pregnancy, maybe even sexuality. What I did not expect was the frequency of conversations about wife battering, incest, and lesbianism from middle-aged and elderly women from mainstream America. What became clear to me was that if you get women to really talk about what is going on in their lives, and if, statistically, one out of three women is battered at some time in her life in America, then one out of ten of your oral history subjects will have experienced battering. If one out of ten is an incest victim, then one out of twenty of your oral history interviewees can be expected to talk to you about being an incest victim. I think it is important for the questioner to be aware of these kinds of issues and to be comfortable keeping that conversation going, because it is some of the most powerful material that is going to surface. The battering statistics never meant much to me until little old ladies in flower-sprigged dresses told me about being brutally battered in their marriages when they also said they had a happy marriage. I believe that women naturally talk so deeply out of their own experience that when they open up to a stranger, they really open up. I was astounded that as a young woman from California, I could have these in-depth conversations and be welcomed back the second time, because women were surprised when they realized how much they had said into a tape recorder. However, in terms of doing oral history interviews, there seems to be something encouraging about a stranger saying, "You're important, you matter, and I want to know about the meaning of your experience" that elicits material that is difficult to get in any other way. That interest might never come from a woman's family or community in such a way that validates her experience and encourages her to communicate it. The quality of the material that comes from this process is astounding.

Other emerging themes involved tremendous change in America over the first half of the twentieth century in terms of what farmers produced or made and what they purchased. Women explained that when you created the things you needed, then life depended on you, and that self-sufficiency was the reality. When you could buy and consume the material things you needed or wanted, it produced a much more passive way of life.

"I only helped out" came up over and over again in every situation and among women in every class. Likewise, almost every one of my interviewees said, "I was a man. I should've been a man. I was really my daddy's boy. I was a boyish person." It took me a long time to figure out that, again, we were dealing with cultural expectations and a failure of available language to describe women's experience. Because women could "only help out," but they also knew that they had not merely "only helped," then somehow that meant that they were not womanly. As a result, their description of who they were implied that they were something other than women. Digging into what that meant and what it felt like was an important issue. It took me a while to understand it because it was sometimes said in a single sentence, but it came up in interview after interview.

After I had completed the interviews, I struggled with how to transcribe them in a way that was faithful to the language of the person and that created a sense of voice. It became quite clear to me that if you do not re-create the voice, you distort the material. In fact, the material can absolutely lie, depending on the sentence structure and the spelling of the words, even if every word is exact.

Transcribing was a problem I did not know I was going to have until I was well into the process. I was in Atlanta with my tapes, trying to decide how to shape the book and which interviews to include. I was reading Robert and Jane Coles's *Women of Crisis*, which is a classic oral history, when I suddenly realized that I was reading about a black itinerant farmworker for thirty or forty pages while picturing a white, university-educated woman. I absolutely could not believe that she was black. The authors had transcribed the language while taking away the reality of the woman's experience. Having identified the problem in my reading, I thought I could remedy the problem in my own book. In fact, late in the process of editing my book, I got pressed for time and sent some tapes out to an experienced transcriber. What I got back was absolutely useless. Since the transcriber was word-for-word correct, the problem is clearly more than a matter of how accurately the words are captured from the tape. There are dialect problems, and there is the matter of the spelling of words: How much Standard English do you want to use to be accessible to your reader? How much is Standard English a distortion of the spoken language? Sentence structure also makes a tremendous difference. When you start putting in those g's and adding prepositions that are not there, you start changing the sense of who is talking and their reality, because in conversation we do not speak in sentences, we speak in rushes. You can structure interviews rigidly with very short, proper sentences and get a different sense of who is speaking than if you run words together and have phrases that go on and on. I found that I often had to play a phrase over on the tape four or five times before I could decide how to structure it as a sentence in a way that seemed to reflect the voice. Sometimes I would experiment with writing paragraphs—paragraphs that do not exist in spoken language—three or four ways until I thought I had it down accurately, and that was simply taking the same words in the same order and punctuating them differently.

I did not write the book in a straight question-and-answer format, although the first time through I transcribed it that way. I am also a fiction writer, and that adds to my approach to transcription. There are many pauses, there is a lot of inflection, there is a lot of emphasis, there is a lot of laughter, and there are tears in spoken language. The first time through I put all of that in parentheses and later decided how to work with it. Sometimes, by spacing words out on a page, by capitalizing whole words, by dots and dashes, by leaving space between sentences, I could indicate the rhythm of the speech or the inflection pattern. I never figured out what to do with laughter, and I ended up taking it out, which I felt was a tremendous loss, because if you don't know that someone's laughing when they're saying something, you get only part of the impact of the sentence.

Silence is also terribly important, and the significance of a sentence changes if you leave the pauses and the silences in. If you set something apart as it was set apart in speech, the meaning of it becomes clear in a way that is not clear when it is written in a paragraph. There is an entire poetry to transcribing language that I never read or heard about before I did my interviews and transcribed them. And it takes a long time; an hour of tape can take four or five hours to transcribe accurately.

When I did the interviews, I got permission to tape-record, and I tried to be very clear with people that everything they were saying was being recorded. It was quite clear to me that women were very sophisticated about it, because the best information was never on the tapes. I learned a lot by the end of the project about leaving the tape recorder running when it all seemed to be over, because that is when the really important material was shared. Almost inevitably, when I turned the recorder off, then something that I really wanted to have was lost. I got people to sign blanket releases—I used the one in the *Frontiers* first oral history issue, which is a good one in terms of legal coverage. And then I said, "I meant it. I have this release from you. I have permission to use this material. I'm gonna go ahead and do it. If you have any problems please let me know." A *few* people wrote back and said they had to see the material before they could do that, and in two cases we had to change all names and all town identifications, but I refused to change the material. In one case an elderly couple who was lesbian had developed a story, which was a lie, to cover up their relationship. They had been using it for years. Although that story does not even appear in the book, they were so frightened that they could not allow their names to appear in the book in any form whatsoever. Another woman, who talked very deeply and honestly about being battered, would not let me use the interview without changing all the names. There were a few cases where people never even let me turn on the tape recorder in the first place, and that *will* happen. There were also several people whom I interviewed who did not know what a tape recorder was or what it did.

The big issue for me was accountability to the material. Given what I was doing with the transcription — given that I was severely editing the interviews and that I was taking myself out so that every interview appeared to be a first-person statement instead of a question-and-answer format — was I being faithful to the voice and to the content of the material? Could I really take four sentences from here and put them at the end of another whole section and still to be faithful to the flow, to the content, and to the mood and the tone of the piece? I felt a tremendous seriousness about these matters and ended up having to say that I *had* to trust myself, my sense of that person, my sense of the connection out of those long talks, and my sense of what they were trying to convey about their lives. Almost all the women liked what I did, but they did not see what I had done until the book was finished.

Regarding how to ask questions: A woman in Minnesota turned on me about eleven o'clock one night and said, "And now I'm going to interview you." We were up until two in the morning, and it was a very healthy experience. It sounds obvious, but if you accept cultural stereotypes at face value and do not go beneath them because your own expectations are already set up to accept them, you are not going to get at the truth of the situation. And whether there is an objective truth or not, I think there is a truth that is beyond the conventions of our culture. For me, it was a matter of not taking generalized assessments but rather digging down into a particular period of time, a particular feeling, trying to go beneath the surface. Sometimes it lies in the value of asking a stupid question, because some of the best responses come from making mistakes — so it is worth sticking your neck out in terms of your questions. The woman who told me the clearest battering story said her husband had gone off and left her with two little kids. I was somewhat tuned out at the time and said, "Oh, wasn't that a shame!" She looked at me and said, "It was the best thing that ever happened in my life," and she talked for the next three hours. I think that if I had not been smiling and nodding I might never have gotten that material.

I cannot advocate being a fool on purpose, but, in fact, some of the best material I got was in what I call an antagonistic interview. I had left my editor's office in New York, driven to Vermont for an interview, and had gotten bad information about the situation I was walking into. I walked in dressed too, too New York. She took one look at me and was sure I had never done any work in my life. For the next five hours, she proceeded to tell me about what it was like to work. She *hated* me, and she gave me *wonderful* information in that interview. I could not have predicted it. So sometimes being in situations where you are not perceived as being friendly or supportive can get you a good interview, but you are going to have to build a relationship with that person if you want to use the material.

The other important matter in asking questions is how to become invisible. In a sense, the process was to ask questions in such an unobtrusive way that the woman did not know I had asked them. When that happened she could sometimes talk for an hour or two without interruption, and the conversation could be guided to keep her going simply with a phrase. At that the point, my job was to get her to tell me her story and to facilitate her telling her story by not imposing myself on the interview. For me, that was a very lonely process, and it was personally hard to be out on the road for four months being invisible all the time. That is something to take into account because it affects subsequent interviews. Silence is terribly important, and because I'm fast-paced, I had to learn to keep my mouth shut and keep my tape recorder running for long periods of time. People need time to assess, to think. The answer to a question from fifteen minutes earlier comes in the next hour if you will let the silence drag on. That is probably the most important thing, to figure out how to keep quiet enough.

Know your own prejudices. For me, for instance, I found that I am much more of a prude about bodies than I thought I was. I publish my sex life in feminist journals, but I am a prude when I sit in front of an eighty-year-old woman and she starts to tell me about hers. That was a shock, and I had to realize that I had to be careful to not stiffen my back or make my face freeze, or she would stop giving me information that she was quite willing to give. All of us have those prejudices, and you are going to have to work with your own inhibitions, because women are willing to give you material that you may not be willing to accept.

I made a very particular decision, which I feel good about, but it presented problems. I was using a cassette with a built-in microphone—which you are absolutely not supposed to use—with hour-long tapes. I bought the highest quality tapes I could, and I tested a lot of cassettes with some accuracy from a ten-foot range with a built-in microphone. I started with an around-the-neck microphone and quit after the first interview because it made people freeze. A table microphone also made people freeze, and what I was trying to do was to get them to forget that the tape recorder was in the room. It was tremendously important to me to break through that barrier because tape recorders frightened them. I did not take any notes in my interviews for the same reason: I was trying to build up as much of a sense of a conversation as I possibly could. I liked what happened because of my approach, and I knew I was on the right track for the kind of book I was doing. However, it made transcribing very difficult: The tapes are not clear, they are not radio quality, and people have asked me many times to produce some of the material for radio. Because there is wonderful material on those tapes, and because I have fifty-two women on tape and only twelve in the book, it is a shame that the material is not very accessible. The problem with inaccessibility resulted from the decision to make the tapes the way I did.

As soon as the first interview was done and before I left for the day, when we were feeling comfortable with each other, I would say, "Now I'd like you to sign a form that will give me permission to put this in my book, and this is what it means." If I waited too long, I had a hard time getting it; if I had to go back, I had a hard time getting it. Because I was asking for a blanket release, I had to tell them that they were signing away their rights to all of that material. People revealed much more than they had any idea they were going to reveal, and they do have to have a right to have some control over that. I think it is immoral, in a sense, to ask them to sign a release before an interview.

Before an interview I told people that I had been a farmer, but none of them believed that, so that did not do me any good at all. I told them that I wanted to know what women like them had done with their lives, and I wanted to know how they felt about what they had done with their lives. I told them that I thought that farm life was disappearing in America and so it was very important to capture their stories. Every single woman I interviewed said, "You don't want to talk to me, I'm not important." And every one of those people talked, did repeat interviews, and had a lot to say, but there is a sense that the individual is not important and that they are not important. You have to break through that diffidence. I did not try to convince them that they, personally, were important. I simply said, "I'm collecting a whole lot of interviews from women like you, and I'd like your story, too."

I really believe that those stories are important. I believe that without the history of ordinary people we are denied the most basic information about our culture and our lives. Because I am committed and believe the stories are important, I feel I have a right to use the material, but women still astonished me with their openness. Even in Maine, where they do not talk to strangers, I got wonderful connections with people. Nowhere did the stereotypes of women being closed hold up. The best interviews I had with black women I had through family connections. I am not sure I could have bridged the gap in the rural South without that kind of personal connection, but, in general, openness was the norm. You cannot tell before you go into an interview which is going to be a good one and which is not. Women who had phenomenal stories in terms of what they had done with their lives sometimes could not talk, sometimes they were doers not talkers, and sometimes they were not introspective. One woman whose story was incredible kept saying to me, "I only remember the good times." She could not remember fifteen years of her life! And I am not exaggerating; she had no memories from that period of time, so the interview was a bust as far as I was concerned. I found that I could not predict a successful interview ahead of time; I just had to be willing to go into place after place after place, because I did not know what was going to turn out to be spectacular. By spectacular I do not mean extraordinary. I simply mean that someone was able to convey the reality of ordinary experience very clearly.

I think using real names is part of doing oral history. I changed names when I had to, but when I did I also felt like I had lost a small piece that matters to me a lot. Absolutely ordinary people matter and count, their stories are important, and we need all of their stories. When you start changing the names, you take away some of that basic commitment.

This is an abridged version of the transcription of a talk that was published in *Frontiers* 7:1 (1983): 50–55.

The Next Step

SUSAN H. ARMITAGE

I discuss the simple reality of going home at night, of washing one's body, looking out the window with a woman's eyes. We must learn our common symbols, preen them, and share them with the world.

Ntozake Shange

In fall 1977, *Frontiers* published its pathbreaking "Women's Oral History" issue. That issue combined direct teaching with a variety of articles illustrating uses of the new women's oral history. It was an issue full of discoveries.

After that beginning, many of us continued to do women's oral history. Soon we realized that we had taken the next step, beyond discovery. We faced perplexing questions about the use of the material we had gathered so blithely: problems of project design, of analysis, and of intent.

The purpose of the second oral history issue was to explore the new ground that lay beyond the surprise and euphoria of discovery. What does it mean to look "out the window with a woman's eyes," and how do we explain and analyze it?

There will always be a place for personal discovery, especially in the classroom. Oral history is a wonderful teaching tool. Students are usually excited and frequently amazed by the women they interview. When women "speak for themselves" about the activities and concerns of their own lives, they usually talk freely and fully, revealing lives of purpose and significance. Yet, because our historical understanding of women's lives is still so poor, and the disparagement of women's activities runs so deep, we are surprised and awed by these lives. We say, "Golly, gee whiz!" We tend to write up our discoveries in ways that emphasize their uniqueness. That is a natural place to start. It *is* important to celebrate the compelling stories that women tell about their lives. But the truth is that those lives are not unusual; we just thought they were! Furthermore, we can do much more than simply illuminate neglected lives. We can push ahead to the harder job of analysis and connection. To move from the single story to the whole picture requires that we be systematic and critical—while remaining caring and appreciative. We need to move ahead without losing touch with the personal and meaningful discoveries of women's oral history.

Not all of the questions discussed in this article are unique to women's oral history. Many are shared by grassroots historians working with racial, ethnic, and regional groups. But people concerned with women's oral history have raised these questions with the most urgency, and by and large these questions have not yet been answered by the established experts in the field of oral history. The new women's oral history does not fit the older pattern of elite interviewing with self-confident, articulate, middle-class white males. To some extent, therefore, we need to make our own guidelines.[1]

WHAT ARE WE DOING?

Women's oral history is not necessarily the same thing as an oral interview with a woman, as local history projects with old settlers sadly illustrate. Because women live longer, these collections contain many interviews with women, but they are usually tremendously disappointing. The women talk about the activities of their fathers, brothers, husbands, and sons. They do that because they believe that history was made by men. That is, after all, what their history books told them. Usually, the interviewers do not contradict them. The result is that most old settler local oral history projects tell us very little about women. As long as interviewers share this sexist bias, alive, active, thinking women continue to be historically invisible.

Women's oral histories *are* different, primarily because the interviewers wish to make women historically visible. Those of us engaged in women's oral history share a belief in the importance to women of autonomy and self-definition, both today and in the past. We ask women to speak for and about themselves—about their own work and their own lives, rather than about "history" or the activities of their fathers, husbands, and sons.

Oral history is a basic tool in women's history because the lives, activities, and feelings of so many women have been overlooked and unrecorded. Traditional historical sources such as newspapers and manuscripts generally reflect the lives of middle- and upper-class urban women, and tell us almost nothing about the lives of working-class, rural, and ethnic women. Because so much of recorded, official history is written by and about males, women themselves are the major source for information about women.

Interviewing women has another significance, because the female subculture has often been a defense against, and a critique of, male dominance. The very act of focusing on women and asking them to "speak for themselves" is a challenge to traditional male-centered history. We, the interviewers, make that challenge explicit by articulating the values we find in our interviews, and by locating them in an historical context.

What that means is that we do two things. First, we work with the woman we interview to discover and explore her life, often joyfully, sometimes painfully. Second, we step back and ask questions about meaning, about comparability, about context. These *are* two steps, but they must connect. If we stop at the first, we have not realized the full potential of women's history; if we do the second carelessly, we misrepresent the women we have interviewed.

At its best, women's oral history seeks to re-create the lives and feelings of an earlier generation of American women. We want to know about women's private lives and about their emotions. But why should they tell us? Why should they relive sometimes painful memories with an almost total stranger? This, indeed, both personally and professionally, is the core question we need to answer.

Women talk to us because we have convinced them that we want to know about their lives, that their lives have historical meaning, and that they can trust us to use their information appropriately. For these reasons, I believe that we have a deep obligation to the women who are willing to share parts of their lives with us.

Usually, we interview women who are unaccustomed to public speaking and to easy self-presentation in formal or public settings. We need to pay particular attention to the dynamics of the interview. What is our responsibility for the emotions—of grief, pain, and loss, as well as joy and pleasure—that our questions provoke? That is not a sentimental question but a real problem we face in interviews. As engaged interviewers, we are responsible for our role in the human transaction that the interview represents. What matters? There are choices to be made. The only choice that I can see that is compatible with feminism—a belief in female autonomy and self-definition—is one that respects the privacy and the emotional integrity of the narrator.

I want the woman I interview to be actively responsible for what she says, so at the very beginning I tell her that the interview will be a public document, not a private conversation. I also want her to determine the shape she gives to her life. Within a chronological framework I use interview techniques that give her control over the structure of the interview: I hardly ever interrupt, and I do a great deal of active listening. I handle emotional topics carefully, and I am very respectful and slow moving. I do not confront, and I do not probe: I wait for mutual trust. For me, rapport and genuine openness come slowly, as the result of many interviews. Although this technique is slow, it fits my personal style. However, I also insistently teach this technique to my students, regardless of their personal style, because I know that novice interviewers sometimes treat their narrators insensitively and hurt their feelings. I am more concerned about the quality of the interview for the narrator than I am about "getting" every last fact. Sometimes there is a loss of historical information with this technique, but that seems to me acceptable. As you will see from articles in this collection, there are other answers to some of these questions; these are the ones that, after much thought, feel right for me.

Surely this is where analysis must begin: with awareness of our own motivations, beliefs, and personal styles as interviewers. These personal qualities are usually the least obvious parts of any published study or article. It is rare to read a description of the interaction between interviewer and narrator, yet everything really depends on it. In some fields, such as anthropology, the life history method assumes the objectivity of the interviewer as a basic premise. I fundamentally do not believe in that idea. It is simply untrue to describe oneself as a neutral, anonymous observer when, in fact, one has invested so much emotional effort and honesty in achieving rapport in the interview. The bond between us and our narrators is close and meaningful, and ought to be acknowledged — professionally as well as personally.

What Jacquelyn Dowd Hall has called "the often inaccessible emotional realities of women's lives" *are* accessible through sensitive and informed oral history interviewing.[2] But it is crucial to recognize that our eagerness to learn about feelings and emotions affects the structure of the interview. Our choices frequently determine the quality of what we learn — not just simple things like whether we get long or short answers to questions, but more important things, such as the real value to the narrator of the topics we ask them to discuss.

These questions about purpose, personal style, and responsibility to our narrators must be addressed at the very beginning. They are the important methodological questions; they are not merely technical concerns about how to get "good answers."

It is essential that women become historically visible, but only on terms that they themselves have fully and consciously accepted. If this principle is ignored, women remain historical objects—just as they have been in the past. If we do not respect the autonomy and authenticity of the women we interview, how can we then turn around and use our information to illustrate the historical validity and importance of those same principles?

LISTENING

Once the fundamental methodological questions have been answered, we can move on to questions about content. What can we expect to learn in women's oral history interviews?

We are just at the beginning of knowing what has really been important to women. We will learn what we want to know only by listening to people who are not accustomed to talking. It seems strange to say that about women—the stereotypic gossips and talkers. But in the sense of talking seriously and thoughtfully to a listening audience, most women have been deprived.

There is an entire range of topics accessible through oral history, among them ignored activities like housework, private feelings, informal public activities, and a sense of how women shaped their lives.

Housework, that despised contemporary activity, is a gold mine of historical information. Historically, housework has been "hidden in the household" and regarded as private and unimportant. But the work we do is central to our own sense of self; surely this is as true for women as for men. Dorothy Smith, the Canadian sociologist, has suggested that the major task of feminist scholars is to demonstrate how the everyday world is experienced and described by women. A sociology *for* women (rather than of women) would begin, Smith suggests, with an understanding of what housewives do in the home.[3]

Nineteenth-century letters and diaries are very reticent about sexuality, birth control, pregnancy, and other reproductive matters, but it does not follow that women were silent about them in private. Reproductive issues and child rearing seem to be the main topics of the female oral tradition that continues (though in much weakened fashion) today. We cannot ask nineteenth-century women about these matters, but we can ask their descendants. Interviewers need to overcome their discomfort at sexuality, for that discomfort contributes to historical misrepresentation. Biology may not be destiny, but it is too important to pretend it does not exist.

The history of child rearing is still almost completely unexplored. That history cannot be written from prescriptive literature, although some male historians are still trying. A fact as obvious as that women combine child rearing with household tasks has so far escaped historical notice. Only through oral histories are we going to be able to find out how women really raised children. To assume—as has been the case—that mothers are simple transmitters of patriarchal values is unwarranted.

Women's community activities are another important topic. Because women have been defined—by men—as private persons, their public activities have been ignored, denied, and omitted from the historical record. There is a strong pattern of informal female activity in which many community projects are begun, lobbied, and arranged. When the moment of formal organization comes, the women step back; men are elected as officials and often given public credit for the entire enterprise. Because newspapers report official rather than unofficial events, the historian who relies on them can be genuinely oblivious to the activities of women.

For all of the topics mentioned above, written material—diaries, letters, reminiscences, fictional accounts, club and organization records—exist and have been used by historians of women. But these written sources are limited by number, by economic class or race, and by customary reticence. Because of this, oral history is an *essential* component of research on women's lives. What we learn from women's oral histories, above all, are feelings, priorities, and values. Our best chance of seeing women's lives as they truly were lies in using written and oral sources together.

To make that combination work, we must be clear about the strengths and weaknesses of the kinds of evidence we use. For written materials, guide-books already exist. We also need to know the ways in which the oral history format itself affects the information obtained in an interview. The field of oral history has been notoriously slow to analyze itself: only recently, as a result of the interest in grassroots history, has such self-examination begun to occur.[4]

Four specific characteristics of oral history all arise from the fact that the "voice" in an interview is individual and self-focused. These are questions of form that are boringly familiar to literary critics, but are new to most historians.

If we ask a woman to tell us about her life, the spontaneous and unprompted account will contain few, if any, historical landmarks. Events of great significance to the historian may pass unremarked, either because other, more immediate events were more important or because the narrator does not understand how larger events affected her life. She often feels unconnected to "official" history. Probably women feel less connected than do men, but the difference may not be very great. The important point is that oral histories provide access to private experience, not to public events. Authors who choose to re-create a public event through compilation of private experiences, as Cornelius Ryan did by interviewing hundreds of men for his book about the D-day landing in Normandy, find themselves overwhelmed by personal, often contradictory recollections.

Another characteristic concerns chronology. Many women date events in an interview by family milestones: "Let's see, that happened the year that Amy was born. That must have been 1970." Oral histories are *not* the place to look for specifics about dates, times, and places. This chronological uncertainty is one of the most difficult hurdles for new interviewers. The tendency to jump in and say, "Now what year was that?" can be irresistible, but almost always fatal. It stops the narrator short. *She* knows where she is, even if the interviewer does not. Too much attention to chronological detail distracts her from her narrative flow.

The reason why interruption is bad is that it prevents the narrator from giving her own shape to the account of her life. It is obvious that people shape their life reminiscences in different ways. Some narrators spend much time on their childhoods, others almost none, and so on. As a student of mine once asked, "Where does she live in her memories?" The answer will differ by narrator. Does it also differ by sex? At the moment, no one can say.

A related question is that of emotional weight. In any interview, some parts matter more to the narrator than others. The really important parts—the nuggets, I have come to call them—are complete, finished stories of their own. They stand apart. On the tape, you can *hear* the difference in the narrator's voice—she is emotional, engaged. (I note in passing that no one has yet devised a way to transfer that emotional impact to a written transcript—so much is lost in translation.) Regardless of our agenda in the interview, we must recognize these nuggets as the things that matter most to the narrator.

There is one final characteristic which *is* female. Nancy Cott has identified three different perspectives on woman's sphere: victimization, rationalization, and positive affirmation. The more personal the document, the more positive the affirmation.[5] A woman's oral history is a personal document, indeed, a personal statement. The women I have interviewed (mostly rural, western women) have felt positively about their lives and activities even in the face of poverty and sexism. In my experience, then, women's oral histories are strong and affirmative statements; I have never interviewed anyone like Agnes Smedley whose rage at sexism and economic exploitation shapes her autobiographical novel, *Daughter of Earth*.[6] The question then arises: What is the relationship between the reality of sexism and a woman's personal reality? The answer lies in the notion of the female subculture. It may provide the link: Is there really a female subculture in all times and places, and does it really function as a defense against male dominance? Most historians of women believe that, but we need more evidence than we presently have about how female values shape women's lives before we can be certain. Through women's oral history, we can find out how women shaped their lives. If we listen carefully, we will hear meanings that will allow us to reconstruct the world of the female subculture.

PROJECT QUESTIONS: THE PROCESS SHAPES THE PRODUCT

When the conventional historian works with archival sources, census data, old newspapers, or government documents, she uses her historical skills to sort, organize, and analyze existing material. In contrast, an oral historian actually creates new documents: The information she elicits from a narrator is a new contribution to history that would probably not exist otherwise. Clearly, the making of history is a much more decisive role than the conventional sifting. We need to be self-conscious about what we are doing.

At first, any oral history project is faced with a series of seemingly endless questions: Why are we interviewing? Who? How? What have we learned? How do we use the information we have learned? How accessible and available is it to others? What next? All these questions must be answered, at least in a rough sort of way, for a project to be coherent—which is the overriding problem every project faces. Collecting interviews is the easy part compared to keeping it all together.

Furthermore, decisions on these questions force us to take the next step beyond discovery. A single interview, sometimes a collection of interviews, can be individually illuminating. But for a group portrait to emerge, there *must* be standards of comparability. Methodology matters. We must locate our narrators in their context. To carry forward the simile, a group of undated and unlabeled snapshots is no good to anyone but the photographers who took them. Accurate labeling turns them into useful and accessible documents. So, in a similar way, we must use some of the methodologies of the social sciences to make our oral histories useful and, in particular, to make it possible to compare our findings to those of other historical sources. Different projects have answered the basic questions in a variety of ways, as you will discover when you read the articles in this collection. Some general guidelines are possible all the same.

Why?

A single person embarking on a series of exploratory interviews can sometimes afford to be vague about this, but as the organizer of a group project you can save yourself a lot of grief by agreeing on basic goals before you begin. In any case, the incredible growth of publications in women's history makes background research and reading obligatory. It is a waste of everybody's time and effort to go out and do unresearched exploratory interviews when there is published work on the topic. The most serious accusation against all grassroots history (including women's oral history) is that interviewers keep recording the same old uncritical nostalgia over and over.

On the other hand, too rigid a set of expectations leads to closed minds and the failure to hear new points of view, an especially serious matter in women's oral history, where so much understanding of values is needed.

Who? And How Many?

This turns out to be a question fraught with professional and personal booby traps. There is a considerable body of literature concerning statistical sampling, size, randomness, and validity. Most of that literature does not fit oral history very well, where by definition we are dealing with the survivors, and only the willing ones at that. However, statistical measures should not just be ignored. Properly understood, statistics focus on important questions of representativeness and comparability. You must be aware of these issues. Save yourself some time and find a friendly sociologist or political scientist who has already struggled with these questions and can translate for you.

The greatest single criticism of oral history projects is that they are simply collections of individual interviews lacking a context. This criticism is completely valid. We can greatly strengthen the validity of our interviews by paying attention to factors of class, race, age, and location when we select our narrators.[7]

The personal issue is really quite simple: We all have a bias for the articulate, the optimistic, the copers, the willing. There will always be more of them in any group of narrators. I can only suggest that we recognize that fact and try not to play favorites. The problem becomes acute when the end product is a slide-tape show or film where articulateness and the quick, apt phrase are desired. Collaboration with technical people who are not full project participants can fragment over these points. The only answer is a clear statement of project values—and a willingness to fight to protect those values.

How?

Everyone must resolve the ethical questions already mentioned. Usually a few beginning interview experiences will make the need to address them painfully obvious. In addition, group projects with multiple interviewers must agree, as far as possible, on a common interview approach and topical focus. Adopting the rigid schedule of questions that sociologists are taught is not oral history, but common agreement about basic questions is essential.

What?

Group projects need to consult constantly about what they are learning, or members may end up learning vastly different things. So many things happen in an interview that we always have to pick and choose. I think that is why some conservative historians are uncomfortable with oral history: They dislike the complexity of reality!

My students often feel overwhelmed by individual detail and helpless to decide "what's important." When they turn to me for help, my answer is annoyingly mystical. I tell them that learning is an incremental process. The more interviews they do, the larger their "data bank" becomes, the clearer their appreciation both of overall framework and of idiosyncratic detail. There is no "right answer," just a general vague shape of what is important.

Of course specific questions, including very private attitudinal ones, can be asked in oral history. Assessment of the honesty of the answer requires a great deal of the interviewer because she must consider personal factors, such as whether she was successful in establishing an open and honest relationship with the narrator. It is also true that interviewers can "lead" narrators and encourage them to say at least some of the things the interviewers most want to hear. Much of this bias is completely unconscious.

There are several techniques for dealing with this sort of bias. One is to ask the opinion of a friendly, informed, outside consultant midway through a project. Another is to make a firm commitment to group criticism of interviews. Usually, because of time pressures or politeness, the latter does not happen. Yet writers submit themselves to the pain of being critiqued by their peers. We need to see oral history, like writing, as a "work in progress" that we are shaping. Then the helpfulness of friendly criticism becomes obvious.

Use.

Some decisions about the end product need to be made immediately. Slide-tape shows, films, dramatic performances, collections of edited interviews — all impose different requirements on projects and may be more shaping than we realize. We tend to look for what we know we need.

To date, most oral history projects have had very short lives. They fulfill their original purpose and then simply gather dust in the archives because no one else uses them. Although the Oral History Association has urged interviewers to be as comprehensive as possible in their questioning, the fact is that most projects are severely limited by their original intent, which is all the more reason to know what that intent is from the beginning. The long-term answer, of course, is to design truly representative projects that will have lasting value. That is beginning to happen.

Accessibility.

A number of articles in this collection stress the importance of returning the information to its source: sharing with the narrators by dramatic performance, film, or a form of the written word the material they have given us. I think that this action is basic to everything we do. After all, the narrators own the interview until they sign a release form giving us permission to use it. They deserve to see what use we have made of their honesty and sharing. Also, they ought to be our frankest and most valued critics.

Other kinds of accessibility are equally important. There is no substitute for complete transcription, which is very unfortunate because it is so expensive and so few projects have enough money. The next best alternative is careful and informative indexing and cross-indexing. All three of these will help immensely in making oral history collections useful to others beyond the project members. Original tapes should, of course, be placed in archives instead of being tucked away in old file drawers. This is a matter not only of courtesy but of honesty. Historians working with archival material know that no matter how obscure their source, another historian may check up on them. But many oral historians work without that safeguard because their tapes are not available to others. This is not good practice and tends to make us sloppy.

What Next?

Most oral history projects are not stable and permanent, but are one-shot, specially funded efforts. Often such projects end with a set of unanswered questions spawned by ideas that surfaced late in the project, tentative comparisons, or incomplete hypotheses. Usually, these questions die with the project as group members move on to other activities. This is unfortunate and ought to be recognized and prevented where possible. An informal network of western oral historians has shared some of these concerns, but because so much of our work has been first-stage discovery, the need for sharing has only recently become apparent. The most valuable result of a finished project may be a half-substantiated hunch we pass on to someone else. A field grows by sharing and comparing. It is time for women's oral history to find ways to do just that.

This section has focused on the plasticity of oral history and on the ways in which the values we bring to our projects shape our conclusions, often without our realizing it. Obviously, part of analysis is to understand the ways in which these basic decisions have affected the information we have gathered.

SHARING WOMEN'S SYMBOLS

What matters in women's lives? Interviewing for the Washington Women's Heritage Project,[8] we heard about the importance of connections between women beyond the nuclear and patriarchal family. Rural women talked about the opportunity to visit with other women. Urban women, asked about employment, talked less about what they did than with whom they did it. As a result of the Heritage Project, we became aware, as we had not been before, of the importance of personal relationships in women's work, both inside and outside the home. Our project is over, but more questions need to be asked to illuminate these relationships. We need to pass on our unanswered questions to projects just beginning.

Ideally, the process is circular. If we listen carefully enough to ask the right questions, we will elicit answers from women about implicit, unarticulated values. This is tremendously exciting. It is also difficult. Few of us are sensitive listeners; because of our own values and concerns, we frequently hear only what we want to hear. The possibility of misunderstanding and misrepresentation is real, and we should proceed very carefully. But the prospects for women's oral history are bright. As Ntozake Shange says, when we "learn our common symbols, preen them, and share them with the world," then everyone will know what the world looks like to women. We have taken the next step toward that goal.

NOTES

Grateful thanks to Margot Knight, Kathryn Anderson, Corky Bush, and Betsy Jameson for the conversations that led eventually to this paper. Previous versions of it have appeared in working papers published by sirow (Tucson) and nwcrow (Seattle). Important additions have been made by Joan Jensen and Sherna Gluck.

1. There are, of course, exceptions. Two of the most useful to me have been Michael Frisch, "Quality in History Programs: From Celebration to Exploration of Values," in *What Portion in the World: New Essays on Public Uses of the Humanities*, ed. Cynthia Buckingham, Michael Sherman, and Steven Weiland (Minneapolis: National Federation of State Humanities Councils, 1982), 10–14; and Robert A. Georges and Michael O. Jones, *People Studying People: The Human Element in Fieldwork* (Berkeley: University of California Press, 1980).

2. Jacquelyn Dowd Hall, *Revolt Against Chivalry* (New York: Columbia University Press, 1979), xi.

3. Dorothy Smith, quoted in Nona Glazer, "Housework: Review Article," *Signs* 1:4 (1976): 920–22.

4. Barbara Allen and Lynwood Mandell, *From Memory to History* (Nashville, Tenn.: American Association for State and Local History, 1981), 26–28.

5. Nancy Cott, *The Bonds of Womanhood* (New Haven: Yale University Press, 1977), 197–99.

6. Agnes Smedley, *Daughter of Earth* (New York: The Feminist Press, 1973).

7. The decision by Mary Rothschild, the director of the Arizona Women's Oral History Project, to make their sample fit a demographic profile should be a model to us all.

For the use of census data, see Richard Jensen, "Oral History, Quantification and the New Social History," *Oral History Review* 9 (1981): 13–25.

8. The WWHP produced a traveling photographic exhibit, a slide-tape show, and many local programs. Funded in part by a grant from the National Endowment for the Humanities, it was a collaborative effort by Fairhaven College and the Women Studies Programs of Western Washington University, Washington State University, the University of Washington, and the University of Puget Sound.

Frontiers 7:1 (1983): 3–8.

Reflections on Women's Oral History

An Exchange

SUSAN H. ARMITAGE AND SHERNA BERGER GLUCK

In 1977, Sherna Berger Gluck opened the first *Frontiers* issue on women's oral history with an article about the interview process, "What's So Special about Women? Women's Oral History." In 1983, in the second *Frontiers* issue on women's oral history, Sue Armitage wrote "The Next Step" about oral history projects.[1] This issue of *Frontiers* offered them an opportunity to consider current issues in women's oral history, which they did in the following electronic exchange.

ARMITAGE: OPENING COMMENTS AND QUESTIONS

In preparation for this electronic dialogue, I reread the two earlier *Frontiers* issues on women's oral history (2:2 [1977] and 7:1 [1983]). I still think your 1977 article, "What's So Special about Women? Women's Oral History," is the best of all possible starting places. I think you write sensitively and thoroughly about the interpersonal aspects of the interview. For beginners, it is a great introduction. As you know from your own work with students, they commonly experience precisely the four goals you articulate: discovery, affirmation, communication, and continuity. My first direct question to you, then, is whether you would substantially change anything either in the article or in the interview guide in the light of your subsequent experience?

In 1983, as both you and I noted in our articles in that issue, those of us who had been interviewing for a while were beginning to sense that the oral history interview might be more complex than we had realized. And in my article "The Next Step" I tried to lay out some of the issues involved in large projects and the hopes that I had then for the larger insights or generalizations that we might gain from group projects. Those hopes are still unfulfilled. What actually happened in the 1980s was that funding for large projects dried up and researchers' energies waned as the second wave of the Women's Movement ran into backlash. Today we have very little sense of what we might learn from larger projects because there have been so few of them since the early eighties, and there have been so few experienced practitioners who have stayed active. You are one of that small handful, so my second direct question to you is what you now think about the potential in large projects. What does your experience tell us about what we can learn and how we can learn it?

My larger feeling (and the place where I think we may disagree) is that we missed a huge opportunity in the 1980s. The reality today is that women's oral history is used in the classroom as a valuable discovery tool. Even when, as in my own case, a substantial number of student interviews have been done and archived, they are all just beginnings with no follow-through.[2] The other principal form of women's oral history is done by doctoral students as part of dissertation research. Usually the number of people interviewed is small, the interviewers are beginners, and the research is conducted under the time and other constraints of dissertation pressure. And because so much work is academic and is shaped by current academic styles, the emphasis is sometimes more on the interviewing interaction and its difficulties than on what the narrator actually says. I realize I'm on tricky ground here, but what I see in a lot of work looks a whole lot like academic self-absorption to me. In saying this I don't mean in any way to deny the importance of difference, nor even to dispute the serious difficulties of representation and the real perils of appropriation—but is that all? Isn't there still a forest out there that we're missing because we're so focused on the trees?

GLUCK: INTRODUCTION AND DIALOGUE

It is almost exactly twenty-seven years since I plunked my tape recorder down and interviewed Sylvie Thygeson, the 102-year-old suffragist and birth control activist from St. Paul, Minnesota.[3] That interview remains one of my most profound oral history experiences. There I was facing one hundred years of U.S. history, captured in her poignant vignettes, like how she was named after the daughter of a runaway slave family that her father helped on the underground railway. As this centenarian spoke in incredibly measured words and elegant language, bingo numbers were being called out in the background to convalescent home residents who were three-quarters her age. I often refer to this first interview experience, trying to generate the kind of enthusiasm I had then about oral history. I rely on the anecdote about that experience because I don't want my subsequent, more critical questions about oral history to dampen my students' enthusiasm. In fact, as I looked at the students in my oral history methods class at our first class session this fall, I was thrown into a quandary once again. How do I strike a balance between the somewhat naive faith of the first-year college students in the class with the more sophisticated historiographic concerns of the graduate student members? The dilemma posed by the disparate composition of my class echoes the confusion with which I have been beset and the contradictions with which I have grappled for the past decade—and which, oftentimes, make me regret the loss of innocence that marked my earlier work, including the initial methodological essay that I penned for *Frontiers* in 1977.

These contradictory impulses, so evident in the volume on the feminist practice of oral history that Daphne Patai and I coedited almost ten years ago, get played out in a host of arenas.[4] At Oral History Association meetings I find myself avoiding the sessions where presenters focus uncritically on the narratives they have gathered, whether they present them as unmediated reflections or lay claim to a host of historical generalizations. On the other hand, as interested as I am in some of the more theoretical questions about memory, meaning, and representation, I also get impatient with what sometimes verges on navel-gazing—especially since I remain committed to the idea that oral history can be both a scholarly and an activist enterprise, that it can advance our knowledge but also empower people and contribute to social change.

Beset by this dilemma, for several years I drifted toward writing more methodological essays. Recently, however, I have returned to using excerpts from narratives in my own work, but using them to answer a very different set of questions than those with which many of us started. For instance, in an article that I wrote in collaboration with several former students, "Whose Feminism, Whose History? Reflections on Excavating the History of (the) U.S. Women's Movement(s)," we discuss how our interviews with women who were involved in the Asian American, Chicano, American Indian, and welfare rights movements reveal that they were forging what we might now define as varieties of "feminisms."[5] We argue that this reinterpretation of their activism should place them squarely in the history of the contemporary Women's Movement. On the other hand, by questioning our interpretations of their narratives, we raise questions about the legitimacy and appropriateness of such conclusions. Pushing beyond our roles as historical interpreters, however, we engaged in dialogue with at least some of the narrators about our analysis and conclusions, and thus were able to explore the validity (for them) of our arguments.

In other words, this was exploration of meaning and a discussion of interpretive authority but at the same time it put some meat on the query with the use of narrative excerpts to illustrate the kinds of activities in which the women engaged and the ways in which they seem to express a feminist consciousness. So at the same time that we were grappling with these questions, we were providing important new source material for others to ponder and use.

Although I also explored meaning in the narratives from the earlier, larger scale, more systematic project of WWII women aircraft workers (Rosie the Riveter Revisited), in that instance I was imposing my interpretation of the meaning of their experience for them, with little hesitation about the validity of my interpretation. In other words, I was playing the role of the conventional historian. I did try to engage the women in dialogue after I wrote my interpretive essays in order to register their reactions to my interpretation of their narratives. However, these working-class women saw me as the "expert" and were reluctant to do much more than express trepidation about some of their revelations.

To conclude these preliminary remarks, I want to focus a bit on a recent paper I wrote that relied on several other sources of Palestinian women's narratives besides my own. In separate research projects focusing on the Women's Movement in Palestine, three of us interviewed some of the same members of the women's committees at different times. And although all of our interviews were conducted over a ten-year span, they have to be contextualized in very different historical moments. In some instances, both before, during, and after the Intifada, there was a fair amount of unity among different political factions with which the women's committees were aligned, and the espousal of a strong feminist consciousness, I argue, is tied directly to variations in the pressure for nationalist political conformity.[6] As a result, when I compared the different narratives recounting the founding meeting of the first women's committee in 1978, as well as the other expressions of concern about women, I had to revise my earlier conclusions about the evolving feminist consciousness of women activists, which were based on my own repeated interviews with the same group of women over a five-year period. Indeed, the changes that I thought were evident in 1991, in contrast to the discourse of 1989–90, were reflections of consciousness that some of the very same people had expressed some five years earlier in interviews with Joost Hiltermann.[7] In other words, what had changed was not their consciousness but the political environment in which it was revealed.

These preliminary comments on the current state of my thinking and the direction that my work has taken in the fifteen years since the "Women's Oral History Two" (1983) issue of *Frontiers* was published lay the foundation for my side of our dialogue. Indeed, my responses to your comments and questions probably can be predicted based on these reflections.

DIALOGUE: GLUCK TO ARMITAGE (1)

You ask if I would substantially change anything in the original "What's So Special about Women? Women's Oral History" article. Given what I have said above and the criticism of our uncritical celebration of women's oral narratives in the early days of women's oral history, I am terribly embarrassed by the naive assumptions of gender solidarity that mark this article, much as they did a lot of our political and scholarly work in the early 1970s. Yet, when it comes to introducing new students to women's oral history, I would stand by much of the advice I gave in that article, including the topical outline appended to it. However, I wouldn't use the article by itself but would supplement it with more sensitive pieces that force the interviewer to be more self-reflexive. The advice about interviewing that you proffer in "Women's Oral History Two" is precisely what I would add and, in fact, mirrors much of what I tell students, as does the piece by Kathryn Anderson and Dana Jack in *Women's Words.*[8]

In other words, most of my criticism of that early advice is based more on some of the political assumptions than on the practical tips. For instance, the complex and shifting relationship between interviewer and narrator cannot be captured in simplistic assumptions about "insiderness." In fact, sometimes the insider is severely disadvantaged, both by the assumptions she makes of shared meaning and by the assumptions that the narrator makes about her. The realization that any oral history narrative is only a partial history also leads to the recognition that each interviewer will get different partial truths, given her or his positionality. I would put considerably more faith in the ability of some of my male colleagues in oral history to apply what we have often referred to as feminist principles than I would some women who are more bound by race, class, gender, and sexual orientation.

So, when it comes down to the interview process, there is not a lot I would change, except to advise that we be aware of the complexity of the relationship and the interview moment and that, among other things, we attend to the performative aspects of the interview situation. It is when we move to the next step, using and/or presenting the narrative, that my advice would be different, as I alluded to earlier, and may well diverge from yours.

As you point out, by 1983 we were moving beyond the discovery phase and beginning to come to grips with the complexity of the oral history interview. In your 1983 advice about project design, however, I detect some of the same assumptions that guided us earlier about interpretation and use.

The Rosie the Riveter Revisited Project, initiated in 1979, is one of those larger scale, systematic projects to which you allude.[9] My own background in sociology came into play here, and the attempt to reflect a similar composition in our narrator pool to that of the women defense workers did, indeed, give me confidence in interpreting the interviews. I detected certain patterns as I tried to make sense of what the experience meant to different groups of women. And the regular discussion in which the three interviewers on the project engaged involved us in a continuous process: rethinking some of our early ideas, stimulating each other to ask new questions, and so on. The analyses resulting from this more systematic project focused on the meaning of the experience to the women who had worked in the aircraft industry, exploring how it affected their lives. Perhaps of even greater importance is that, regardless of my own analysis, we created a body of interviews that have been used widely and in different ways by a host of others. So my experience with this project does confirm for me the value of more systematic designs.

However, I don't think this is the only way to go, and I believe that I did not pay sufficient attention to exploring the meaning of the historical moment in which the interviews were collected. In other words, even with a more systematic design, much more historicizing about the interviews themselves is necessary. Conversely, as I hope I made clear in my initial remarks, even with a smaller number of interviews perhaps there is a way to both create accounts that yield insights yet simultaneously challenge the assumptions and interpretations we make about them. And while some of the self-reflexive discussions of oral history might do more of the latter, I do believe there is a way—and a need—to do both. Among other things, as I mentioned in talking about the attempt to write various forms of activism

of women of color into the history of the contemporary feminist movement, don't we stand on shaky ground imposing our interpretations of the
meaning of women's experiences if we are not in dialogue with them about
it? This one is really tricky, and I must admit my own ambivalence. Am I
willing to give up my analysis if the narrator doesn't agree with it? What is
my responsibility to her? To scholarship? What do you think about this?

DIALOGUE: ARMITAGE TO GLUCK

Let's see where we are: We agree about interviewing, the need for sensitivity and self-awareness but also on that sense of discovery and connection
that really does happen sometimes, even across race and class lines. So we
know how to start, how to do frequently excellent interviews that capture
individual voices—and that are a pleasure to read almost in a literary sense,
for the individuality of the voice. But I think we need to go beyond that.
We live in a society that is a cacophony of individual voices and individu-
alism. The collective, related ways we think and act, and the meanings that
women (presumably men, too) draw from those connections is getting lost.
Women's history is built on the notion of groups, of collective experience, of
the ways in which women in similar but different ways have been kept subordinate. Oral history is the best method I know for understanding women's
consciousness and their coping strategies. Besides, it provides access to huge
populations of women from whom we would otherwise not hear. Surely
there are meanings that go beyond individual coping strategies that we can
understand. But—and this is what you asked—how and on whose terms?

We agree that there is no such thing as a transparent interview. The interaction and the "positionality" (as we say) of both interviewer and narrator
are a fundamental part of the process. We also agree that the interviewer,
as historian or sociologist, can't simply lay her interpretation on what she's
heard. This is the postmodern heart of it: We have to be faithful to the meanings the narrators give to their lives. But once we have, by whatever means,
done our best to understand their lives in their terms, can we go beyond to
deal with larger context?

The question I want to get to is what are the legitimate ways to draw
meanings and generalizations from interviews. If, as you argue, they ought
to be collaborative, how do you do it? One well-known way is the life history
interview—a long series of interviews with the same person. The woman
who does this best is Fran Leeper Buss.[10] She does, I think, arrive at what

you might call a collaborative meaning because she gets to know the woman she interviews so very well. In group projects, I'm convinced that multiple interviewers are best, and the process you describe of frequent consultations among interviewers is essential. Differences in interpretation among the interviewers ought to keep everyone aware of biases—their own and others. The harder part is collaboration with the women who have been interviewed. I think that, as you point out, much of the effort to "take it back to the community" or to the narrators has been superficial or condescending. We academic women are more formidable than we think!

Finally, this exchange has made me realize that the issue for me is still discovery/recovery. There is a world (and I do mean a global one) of women out there, and we've heard from very few of them. Our job is to get out there and find out what women say about their lives as sensitively as we can. I don't want postmodern cautions and concerns to stop us from interviewing women we haven't encountered before. I want the kind of shock and necessity to accept difference and the multitude of voices that have characterized international women's conferences, and I want to do it with tape recorder and video recorder.

So to summarize where I think we are: Women's oral history is well established in the classroom as a discovery/connective tool. However, especially among longtime practitioners, the difficulties of interviewing are much better understood as a result of postmodernism and the recognition of the importance of difference. As a result, interviewers are much more self-conscious and narrators more wary. On the whole, this is a good thing and has led to more careful representation and much more cautious conclusions and generalizations. The biggest danger is academic navel-gazing, that is, the tendency for the interviewer to grab center stage.

We are still stuck with problems around meaning:

1. We don't really know how collaborative meaning-making might occur because we don't do it. This is what got lost when we threw out "sisterhood is powerful." We don't think that we can achieve agreed meanings, or we don't know how to do it.

2. Because few recent projects have been very large, the issue of generalization, the search for patterns, has receded from view. But surely the search for what in 1977 you called "the rhythms of women's lives" is one we should continue.

3. There is the really big problem of what all the interviews we've already done mean. Shouldn't we be thinking about what we can learn from all the archived tapes? Or is this a problem we should leave to future historians?

DIALOGUE: GLUCK TO ARMITAGE (2)

Despite my own more critical self-reflexive stance and the changes in how I use oral history, I agree that we must still "recover, recover, recover." In fact, as suggested by the title of my recent essay on the history of contemporary women's movements, I think we still need to excavate. There are lots of stories out there—all over the world. Indeed, oral history is the major venue for women who have not had a formal education and/or who don't have access to channels of communication to have their voices heard. And it continues to empower women. Moreover, I still love reading a good oral narrative, though I am increasingly concerned about the authenticity of the voice as edited by the interviewer. So, I think we agree that collection is as urgent as ever. Furthermore, regardless of how we use the narratives ourselves—or today—the recorded interviews are invaluable primary documents.

The questions I have are more about use and interpretation. Perhaps because of my original background in sociology, I am not sold on the notion that large-scale projects offer such a good solution. The problem is that our oral history narrators, for the most part, as we observed early on, are the survivors. They are the women who found what you refer to as "coping strategies" that worked, the women whose families "allow" them to speak, the women who are still alive. Those that have been battered, killed, silenced, or who have gone insane aren't around to tell us their stories. At a less dramatic level, the ones who don't volunteer, that is, agree to be interviewed, might also be among those whose coping skills didn't work.

What I am leading to, I guess, is that though we—and our narrators— might be uplifted by the hearing and telling of their successes, their ingenious coping mechanisms, and especially by their acts of daily resistance, is this really what women's history is about? It is a part of it, and an important part. But I still struggle with trying to achieve that balance about which I worried when I first began to teach women's history: How do we simultaneously understand and document women's subordination and resistance? This is where the issue of the larger context comes in, the need for the "scholar" to historicize the narrative. By this I mean not only the conditions of women's lives but also the political and social contexts in which the narrative is collected, as well as the specific conditions relating to the narrator and the recording. Realizing that even a life history is only a partial truth, it is critical that we spell out the latter conditions to help us understand that partialness. That includes the question of performance, especially among women from cultures where the oral tradition, with all its drama, is still strong. I began to recognize the significance of understanding performance when I interviewed older Palestinian women. Where I had assumed that shifts in emotional tone among narrators in our culture might denote some special meaning for them, among these older Palestinian women these emotional high points did not necessarily reflect their individual state of mind but rather the cultural prescriptions for storytelling.

The construction of meaning is perhaps the most difficult challenge we face, and I guess we just all muddle along in our own way. I think what Daphne and I were trying to say in the afterword to *Women's Words* is that we should continue to muddle along and encourage others to do the same, regardless of all our doubts and questions. Nevertheless, we somehow have to try to figure out ways to collaborate with the narrators about meaning. Part of this requires that we do a lot of soul-searching, too. Are we willing to give up our interpretive authority? What if Katherine Borland's grandmother hadn't finally agreed with Borland's feminist interpretation of her narrative?[11] What if one of my Palestinian narrators—a woman in whose home I stayed repeatedly—had told me what she meant when she responded to a question of mine about what would change in a future Palestinian state? In 1989, when I asked her, she laughed and then said, "Mahmoud [her husband] would be free to take another wife." Unfortunately, for a host of reasons, I never had the opportunity to follow up and ask her what she meant by this, and years later she probably didn't remember the exchange. But because I stayed in their house repeatedly and saw her workload and his lack of domestic responsibility, I interpreted her earlier remark to mean, quite cynically, that perhaps she'd get more help, as co-wives in polygamous households often do.

Is our best advice to try and dialogue about meaning and, if we can't, at least explain the basis for our attribution of meaning? Some might still say, "Let them speak for themselves." But increasingly I find this a disingenuous stance. If we believe that the narrative is a partial story, is a representation, and is governed by a host of complicated determinants, then I think we have an obligation to historicize and contextualize.

This brings me to another point that you raised once again, as you did several years ago: What do we do about all of those archived tapes? Do we just leave them for future historians? Again, I am concerned about our ability to use all these archived tapes if we can't historicize the narratives themselves, that is, the personal as well as social and historical conditions under which they were collected. With the example I gave earlier about the use of some other Palestinian narratives, all of these were collected within a decade, and both the original interviewers and I were able to contextualize them. However, I don't believe that enough of this has been done with the interviews that have been collected and archived. At best, we have some interviewer notes. So perhaps we need to go beyond our earlier agreement that we should still be "collecting, collecting, collecting." Perhaps even the process of collecting requires more than our own self-consciousness and reflexivity, and interviewers need to go further in problematizing and historicizing the narratives they record.

GLUCK: SOME CLOSING THOUGHTS

Inveterate editor that I am, as I looked over our exchange, I was tempted to do some reorganizing so that it "flowed" better—exactly what publishers always try to get us to do with our oral history narratives and what we resist. It occurred to me that in some ways the quick, more spontaneous messages that we write and exchange in our e-mails (probably what has made many of us who are not letter writers become e-mail correspondents) reproduce some of the spontaneity of the oral history interview and pose some of the same questions about presentation to which we have alluded here. So, in keeping with that spirit, I have tried to do what we ask of our narrators—to leave the conversational tone intact.

NOTES

1. Sherna Gluck, "What's So Special About Women? Women's Oral History," *Frontiers: A Journal of Women Studies* 2:2 (1977): 3–17; and Susan H. Armitage, "The Next Step," *Frontiers: A Journal of Women Studies* 2:1 (1983): 3–8.

2. Since 1979, I have deposited oral histories done by students in my women's history classes at Washington State University in the library archives. There are several hundred interviews in the collection, which is titled "Women's Oral History Project, Washington State University."

3. Sherna Gluck, ed., *From Parlor to Prison: Five American Suffragists Talk about Their Lives* (New York: Vintage Books, 1976).

4. Sherna Berger Gluck and Daphne Patai, eds., *Women's Words: The Feminist Practice of Oral History* (New York: Routledge, 1991).

5. Sherna Berger Gluck in collaboration with Maylei Blackwell, Sharon Cotrell, and Karen S. Harper, "Whose Feminism, Whose History? Reflections on Excavating

the History of (the) U.S. Women's Movement(s)," in *Community Activism and Feminist Politics: Organizing Across Race, Class, and Gender*, ed. Nancy A. Naples (New York: Routledge, 1998), 31–56.

6. It was Ted Swedenborg's framing of his interviews on the 1936–39 revolt that inspired me to reexamine my earlier interviews and conclusions and to pay more attention to the varying environments of political pluralism and conformism.

7. Joost R. Hiltermann, "Before the Uprising: The Organization and Mobilization of Palestinian Workers and Women in the Israeli-Occupied West Bank and Gaza Strip" (Ph.D. diss., University of California, Santa Cruz, 1988).

8. Armitage, "The Next Step"; and Kathryn Anderson and Dana C. Jack, "Learning to Listen: Interview Techniques and Analyses," in Gluck and Patai, *Women's Words*, 11–26. An earlier version of the latter article, with comments about large-scale projects and generalization by Sue Armitage and July Wittner, "Beginning Where We Are: Feminist Methodology in Oral History," appeared in *Oral History Review* 15 (1987): 103–27, and was reprinted in *Feminist Research Methods: Exemplary Readings in the Social Sciences*, ed. Joyce McCarl Nielsen (Boulder, Colo.: Westview Press, 1990), 94–112.

9. Sherna Berger Gluck, *Rosie the Riveter Revisited: Women, the War, and Social Change* (Boston: Twayne Publishers, 1987).

10. Fran Leeper Buss, *La Partera: Story of a Midwife* (Ann Arbor: University of Michigan Press, 1980), and *Forged under the Sun/Forjado bajo el Sol: The Life of Maria Elena Luca* (Ann Arbor: University of Michigan Press, 1993).

11. Katherine Borland, "'That's Not What I Said': Interpretive Conflict in Oral Narrative Research," in Gluck and Patai, *Women's Words*, 63–75.

Frontiers 19:3 (1998): 1–11.

Giving Voice to Chinese American Women

JUDY YUNG

Oral history has been central from the beginning in my efforts to reclaim my history as a Chinese American woman and to integrate that history into our collective memory as a multicultural nation. Given the paucity of writings by Chinese women themselves and their invisibility or distortions in the public record, I relied on oral history to help me reconstruct their lives and express their worldviews in all my work, from *Island* (1980) to *Chinese Women of America* (1986), *Unbound Feet* (1995), and *Unbound Voices* (1999).[1] That is because oral history allows ordinary people like my subjects to speak for themselves, fill historiographical gaps, and challenge stereotypes as well as validate their lives. For too long Chinese women have silently borne the maligned images imposed upon them by the dominant culture—the exotic China Doll, erotic Suzy Wong, and diabolical Dragon Lady. They have rarely been asked to speak for themselves about their lives, aspirations, struggles, and accomplishments. I felt it was time for America to begin to listen to their histories, and I wanted to be the conduit that would make this happen.

Much of this essay on the difficulties and rewards of conducting oral histories with Chinese American women draws from the interviews I did for *Unbound Feet* and *Unbound Voices*.[2] How did I go about giving voice to these women and what did I learn in the process about oral history methodology, ethics, memory, narrative form, and analysis that may be useful and applicable to other oral history projects? Let me begin by saying that every good oral historian knows that planning and preparation are crucial ingredients to a fruitful harvest.[3] Moreover, oral histories cannot stand alone as evidence but need to be substantiated and contextualized with archival research. Conversely, historical data alone, without human voices and stories, would be equally incomplete, a skeleton without any flesh. Combined, these two approaches to research allowed me to paint a fuller picture of Chinese American women's history.

Thus, as I began my research, poring over manuscript censuses, immigration documents, and microfilmed newspapers for any information on Chinese American women, I simultaneously mapped out the purpose and scope of my oral history project and lined up women to interview. I knew I wanted full profiles of the women, from their birth and childhood to adulthood, and broad coverage of different aspects of their lives, including immigration, work, family, and community. I also wanted to explore how race, class, and gender dynamics as well as culture, personality, and history have shaped their lives. Most important, I wanted to hear explicitly and understand implicitly what life in America has meant to them. I came up with a consent form and two lists of questions that covered these topics, one for immigrant women and the second for American-born women (see addendum).[4] As expected, I never got to ask all the questions on the list, but they served to lend focus and structure to my interviews and helped me stay on track in covering the essential topics. Within this structure I tried to be flexible about allowing women I interviewed to pursue their interests and story lines. At the same time I looked for opportunities to follow up on unexpected turns in the conversations that might lead to new information and insights into their history.

Being an insider, a Chinese American woman born and raised in San Francisco and bilingual in Chinese and English, had its advantages. It also helped that I was from a working-class background and was regarded in the community as a respectable scholar. Thus, it was relatively easy for me to find both immigrant and American-born Chinese women to interview, to establish trust and rapport with them in their familiar surroundings (usually their homes), and to ask them personal questions about gender roles and relations, sexuality, discrimination, and social change in their lives. However, there were also disadvantages to being an insider. My interviewees tended to omit information or gloss over details, assuming that I already knew them, or hide their true feelings and views for fear of my disapproval or further disclosure.

How did I find the women I interviewed? Most of them were either relatives or longtime acquaintances of mine, referrals from friends and organizations I contacted, or names I had come across in my research. For example, I interviewed my own mother, aunts, and cousins. I found *sau saang gwa* ("grass widows," in this case, women in China whose husbands lived overseas) through my contacts in the Overseas Chinese Bureau in Guangdong Province, and WACS (Women's Army Corps) by writing the Chinatown Post of Veterans of Foreign Wars. I was less successful finding ex-prostitutes and *mui tsai* (domestic slave girls), probably because no one wanted to be identified as such or there were few women still alive to talk about that experience. In one instance, after a great deal of trouble, I finally tracked down the author of an oral history paper on a *mui tsai* that I had found in a university library, only to be told she wanted to hold on to her grandmother's story and develop it into a book someday. Although I had developed a long list of women who had been involved in the war effort from the Chinese-language newspapers, I had a difficult time finding anyone to interview.[5] When I finally located the three Chinese women holding the banner and leading a parade in the front cover photo of *Unbound Feet,* all three declined to be interviewed, saying that they had been coaxed into participating in the parade to welcome Madame Chiang Kai-shek to San Francisco in 1941 and that they really had nothing to add about women's contributions to the war effort. Even when I found an interview that had been done with one of the key leaders, she seemed reluctant to talk about that period of her life or to take credit for her many long hours of volunteer work. I suspect this reluctance has something to do with Chinese women's socialized behavior to be self-effacing, to downplay their political activities and emphasize instead their role in the family.[6]

Ultimately, I interviewed thirty-three of the forty-eight women cited in *Unbound Feet.*[7] Six of the interviews were conducted in Cantonese Chinese. Each interview took me about two hours to complete. In a few instances, I went back for a second interview. I always brought a gift with me, usually something sweet to eat, as is customary when you visit a Chinese home. I tried to engage in casual conversation, inquiring about the family members or remarking on the surroundings, to take the tension out of being interviewed. Before actually starting the interview, I would ask permission to tape the interview, explaining that I wanted to record their story as accurately as possible. Although I wish I had videotaped them, it was easier and less intrusive to do audio recordings. In hindsight, I regret that I had not taken immediate notes about the surroundings, my impressions of each interviewee, and the ways we interacted because my memory usually failed me when it came time to write up the interview, sometimes months later. I made my goals clear from the start: to learn about the experiences of Chinese women like themselves so that I could record them as history lessons for future generations.

I chose to pose my questions in a chronological order to allow for a life history flow, beginning with where and when they were born, their family background, their childhood, and so on. Although feminist scholars now recommend an interactive, dialogical approach in which the interviewer and narrator are put on an equal footing, exchanging views and sharing research goals and analyses, I preferred to play the role of the attentive listener as this approach seemed to work best with the Chinese women I interviewed, all of whom were my seniors.[8] However, I never hesitated to give my opinions when asked. At times I would ask if my analysis made sense to them—that the lives of Chinese women changed dramatically in the early twentieth century partly due to the influential roles of Christian organizations and Chinese nationalism. Interestingly enough, regardless of their own religious and political views, most women agreed with my assessment, bringing forth different examples to support this view.

Sometimes I would inadvertently hit some raw spots. During one interview a woman broke down in tears when I brought up the subject of her brother. Evidently, he had been kidnapped while visiting in China, and the family was unable to send the ransom money in time. He died tragically. In another instance, a woman began talking about how as a baby she was left at the doorsteps of a mission home and then regretted having revealed the secret. Both times, I stopped the interview and waited for the women to regain their composure before continuing. Whenever I encountered uncomfortable lapses of silence, I tried to hold my tongue, but in most cases further prodding and probing on my part did more to elicit responses than waiting it out. At the end of the interview, I always asked to see family photographs, scrapbooks, writings, and any memorabilia. This is how I found many of the photographs and unpublished writings that are included in *Unbound Feet* and *Unbound Voices*. It was also at the conclusion of the interview that I would ask the person to sign the consent form. By then, they knew what had been covered in the interview and whether they could trust me with their stories. No one ever refused to give me her consent.

Due to time constraints I decided to take the shortcut of doing index summaries instead of full transcripts of all the interviews. With the help of a transcriber, this process involves listening to the interview and summarizing its contents by topic in the order in which the conversation evolved. Along the way I would transcribe verbatim any portion of an interview that I thought I might quote later. Because I intended *Unbound Feet* to be a synthesis of Chinese American women's history based on a variety of secondary and primary sources, I could not include anyone's full life story, interesting and significant as that story might be. Instead, I selected excerpts from different interviews to make certain interpretative points about their collective history. In the process of interspersing my analysis with excerpts from the interviews, it was inevitable that I would end up cutting people off and omitting the natural flow and interactions of the interviews.

With my next book, *Unbound Voices*, an anthology of primary writings and interviews of Chinese American women, I wanted to use the oral histories differently. This time my intention was to bring together a diverse range of individual life stories and reproduce them as fully as possible without any interruption on my part. By so doing, I hoped to remove my partiality and allow a range of voices and viewpoints to emerge.[9] I began by reviewing all the interviews used in *Unbound Feet* for possible inclusion in this second volume. In my selection I tried to strike a balance in terms of generation, class, and coverage of topics. In addition, I wanted the oral histories to complement and not duplicate the contents and perspectives of the writings (letters, poems, essays, speeches, and editorials) that were also a part of the anthology. I finally settled on twelve interviews, which included a *sau saang gwa*, immigrant wives, second-generation daughters, social activists, labor organizers, a shipyard worker, and a WAC. Together, their voices were to represent the lived experiences of Chinese women in San Francisco from the gold rush through World War II.

I was particularly attracted to strong women who were articulate, candid, and vibrant storytellers such as Kwong King You, the *sau saang gwa* whom I interviewed in China and whose interview appears at the end of this article. In many ways she represents the many wives left behind in China by Chinese immigrants in America as well as the other half of the story of transnational migration that has seldom been told. Kwong King You's story was especially striking because she had such a vivid memory, strong voice, and colorful way of speaking. She also required little prodding. Indeed, it seemed as if she had been waiting her whole life for someone like me to come along to record her story.

Although an onerous task, I did not mind going back to transcribe and edit the twelve interviews. It gave me a chance to listen more carefully to each interview, do a closer transcription and translation, analyze the subtexts and silences, organize the text, and shape the story as I saw fit.[10] To allow for a narrative flow and to minimize interruptions, I deliberately eliminated most of my questions as well as any redundancies and false starts, keeping my comments and impressions to the introductions and footnotes. When the interview was in English, I would rearrange segments of the taped interview for clarity and an organized flow, but never change the actual words used. When the interview was in Chinese, I had more flexibility with the choice of words and sentence construction in the translation. I tried to stay true to the meaning of the spoken word, but I usually had to sacrifice the manner of speech and the full impact of Chinese colloquialisms, proverbs, and metaphors in the process. For example, such translated phrases as "A bamboo door should be paired with a bamboo door, a wooden door with a wooden door" and "If your head has enough hair, you can put up with a lot of fleas" just do not convey the same powerful meaning and flavor as in the original Chinese.[11]

Rather than interject my voice into their stories, I resorted to using footnotes to clarify cultural and historical references as well as to note any discrepancies or contradictions. Keeping in mind that all forms of recorded history are biased and need to be critically evaluated, I looked for internal coherence and contradictions in the responses of my subjects.[12] Whenever necessary I corroborated what they told me with other interviews and documentary evidence within the context of the broader social history. For example, in one of her interviews with me, my mother said she was detained at the Angel Island Immigration Station. But she arrived in 1941, after the station was destroyed in a fire, so this would not have been possible. When I checked her immigration file at the National Archives, I discovered that she was detained at temporary facilities at 801 Silver Avenue in San Francisco. Evidently, she had heard me talk so much about Angel Island in conjunction with my earlier research that she had assumed she must have been detained there as well. As Alessandro Portelli notes in *The Death of Luigi Trastulli and Other Stories*, "Memory is not a passive depository of facts, but an active process of creation of meanings. . . . These changes reveal the narrators' effort to make sense of the past and to give a form to their lives and set the interview and the narrative in their historical context."[13] My mother had shifted the place of her detention to Angel Island in order to give meaning to a crucial event in her life in relation to Chinese American history.

To add context and meaning to the interviews, I prefaced each interview with an introduction that provided biographical background on the person, the circumstances of the interview, and an analysis of the individual's testimony. For example, in the case of Kwong King You, I discussed how I came to interview her in China, my impressions and interactions with her, and why she was willing to wait a lifetime for her husband to return home, even though she knew he had remarried in the United States. The point was that women such as Kwong King You, who became virtual widows because of restrictive immigration laws and patriarchal practices, found ways to survive and cope with the long separations. In exchange for a life of widowhood, they enjoyed economic comforts and social prestige in the village, but only as long as they remained faithful to their husbands overseas.

After I completed each interview, I would send a copy to the interviewee or a family member for corrections and permission to publish. For those narrators who did not read English, I had to rely on the cooperation and judgment of their children. I was relieved to know that except for a few minor corrections, everyone seemed satisfied with my rendering of her life story. I planned to eventually transcribe all the interviews, send them to the parties involved for approval, and deposit the tape recordings and transcripts in the Chinese Historical Society of America.

To be self-reflexive about the process, I admit I went into the interviews with my own biases and agenda, which in turn slanted the outcome of the interviews.[14] For example, in my line of questioning I tended to overemphasize racism and sexism. This became obvious when I went back to listen and transcribe the interviews. I just would not accept "no discrimination" for an answer but pursued the question in different guises: "Growing up, were you treated differently from your brothers? Were you treated differently at work because you were Chinese or female? Did the white staff at Angel Island mistreat you in any way? Did you see any evidence of discrimination in the shipyards? Did you ever wish you were not female?" Listening to the taped recordings later, I came to the conclusion that there were different degrees of discrimination and that most women did not experience blatant discrimination. Furthermore, if they had encountered subtle forms of discrimination, they might still choose to suppress it. For example, a shipyard worker told me, "I have never really experienced discrimination. If there was, it didn't bother me because . . . I've never let it deter me from doing anything." Others made it clear that certain situations did not spell discrimination as I seemed to suspect. In my interview with a labor organizer, I remember pressing her to admit that there was a gendered division of labor in the National Dollar Stores sewing factory where she worked and that the male-dominated jobs drew higher pay. Why else was it that all the cutters were men? Exasperated with my persistence, she finally said, "Well, because the women can't do that type of work. They have to lift these heavy bolts of material and push those knives through material piled that high on the table [raises her arm about six inches above the table]. Like white muslin, starched, do you know how heavy those are? The cutter would have to lift that and put it on the machine. It's heavy!"

Quite obviously, most of my subjects did not like dwelling on the negative aspects of their lives, preferring instead to focus on the positive. Immigrant women chose to emphasize how they overcame hardships for the sake of their children. In their views and experiences, the cultural baggage they brought from China sustained more than constrained their lives in America. My aunt, for example, stuck to a bad marriage in keeping with her father's admonition not to disgrace the Wong family's name by divorcing her husband. Not only did her strong sense of honor give her the strength to endure the marriage but it also helped her withstand the Great Depression. Many second-generation women talked to me about the "good old days" growing up in Chinatown and their positive interactions with white Americans. Contrary to Marcus Lee Hansen's acculturation theory, second-generation women I interviewed did not simply reject and replace the old Chinese ways with Western values and practices.[15] Rather, they operated within a broad continuum of responses to cultural conflict and discrimination in America—from acquiescing to accommodating and rebelling.

Upon reflection, I know the power to shape my interviewees' stories resided with me.[16] After all, I was the one who got to choose the storyteller, ask the questions, edit their answers, decide what to include and exclude in the final story as well as interpret their stories. For example, as an atheist and feminist I tended to downplay the role of religion and to emphasize social agency in the lives of my subjects. Yet, it was evident from the transcripts that many of the women I interviewed had relied on Christianity or Chinese folk religion to help them survive and overcome hardships. My mother, who is a devout Baptist, took every opportunity in her interview to *gin jing*, or give testimony to her faith in God, although you would not know it from reading her story in *Unbound Voices*. At one point in the interview, when I asked her whether she got along with her coworkers in the sewing factory where she worked, she told me the story about how she went to pray in the bathroom one day after an argument broke out. When she came out of the bathroom, one worker had quit of her own accord and peace had been restored. "Even the boss said I was powerful," she said as she broke out in her favorite religious hymn. Other women I interviewed said they depended on *tin wong* (literally, "king in heaven") to get them through the hard times. While I did not totally ignore the important role of religion in their lives, I chose to highlight acts of social agency often by reading between the lines. Kwong King You said she accepted her fate as a *sau saang gwa*, but she also sought ways to be economically self-sufficient by becoming a midwife. My mother relied on prayer to help her through adversities, but she also went to relatives and social agencies for help when things got out of hand. Immigrant wives I interviewed were indeed the obedient wives they said they were, but I could also see that they often wore the pants in the house.

Ultimately, my subjects had their say, but it was I who shaped, interpreted, and presented their life stories. The decisions I made as to what to include or exclude in their stories were greatly influenced by my narrative goal of showing how women responded to racial and gender discrimination in effecting social change in their lives. Considering that my interviewees approved the final story, I believe I have done an honorable job of staying faithful to their voices and to the substance of their testimonies.

Listening to Chinese American women tell their stories has always been a humbling, vicarious, and learning experience for me. As feminists, we may consider their lives oppressive, but they see them as fulfilling. Karl Marx once said, "Men [and women] make their own history . . . but they do not make it under circumstances chosen by themselves."[17] Given the social constraints of their time and place, Chinese women have always had to be inventive in order to survive, adapt, and contribute to the well-being of their families, community, and country. My job as an oral historian has been to record and give voice to their life stories, to lend context and significance to their history so that we as a nation might learn to bridge our differences and come to terms with our collective past—how we got to be the way we are and how we can make it better. It is for this purpose that I have dedicated my life to collecting oral histories of Chinese American women.

I met and interviewed Kwong King You in her home in the village of Nanshan, Doumen County, during a research trip to Guangdong Province, China, in 1982.[18] She was a spry, seventy-five-year-old *sau saang gwa* married to a *gam saan haak* ("guest of Gold Mountain").[19] Separated from her husband, Ah Fook, for over forty years, she was still hoping for his return someday, even though she had heard rumors that he had remarried in the United States. I was introduced to Kwong King You by Chan Gum, a staff member of the Doumen Overseas Chinese Bureau, who knew of my interest in overseas Chinese connections to the homeland, particularly the stories of *sau saang gwa*.

Throughout my travels in Guangdong Province, I visited villages where more than half of the population had relatives who had gone overseas. Usually, it was the able-bodied men who had left to make a better livelihood in Southeast Asia, the West Indies, or North America. Restrictive immigration laws, financial considerations, and cultural mores had dictated that wives and families be left behind, creating a "split-household family" arrangement where husbands working overseas would send remittances home to support the family.[20] In most cases, these emigrant families were better off than other villagers so that it was considered desirable for a young woman to marry a *gam saan haak* and become a *gam saan poh* ("wife of a Gold Mountain man"). If the woman were fortunate, her husband would send letters and remittances home regularly, return for a visit every few years, and eventually come home to stay a wealthy man. Thus, being a *gam saan poh* meant economic comfort and social prestige. But often it also meant a long separation. In the worst scenario, the woman might never hear from or see her husband again. Yet she was expected to remain chaste and single, suffer the ridicule of people in her village, and somehow find a way to support herself and her family. I heard many sad stories about *sau saang gwa* who had sold their children to survive or who had gone insane because of an irresponsible husband.[21]

Like many other Gold Mountain wives, Kwong King You felt lucky to be arranged in marriage to a *gam saan haak* in 1927. During the interview she emphasized how well she got along with her husband, Ah Fook, during the first two years of their marriage. Then he left to work as a seaman for an American shipping line, visiting her in Hong Kong every forty-two days. But after the Japanese occupied Hong Kong in 1942, communications broke off and Kwong King You never saw him again. Yet she remained faithful to him, telling me she had no regrets.

Like many other separated couples, Kwong King You's marriage endured because the partners kept their obligations to each other. Her husband continued sending remittances home, and she remained faithful to him. As Madeline Hsu notes in her study of transnational families, while legal and economic conditions kept Chinese families apart, principles and flexible practices of family life enabled wives in China to sustain long-term, long-distance relationships with their husbands overseas.[22] Believing that a good woman must remain faithful to her husband, Kwong King You accepted her fate and role as a *sau saang gwa*. She never questioned the double standards at play.[23] She was also able to withstand the long separation because of the strong support she received from classmates, colleagues, and close relatives, especially her father-in-law and adopted children.[24] Moreover, she was driven to prove her worth to an envious sister-in-law. "I had to stand up for myself," she told me emphatically a number of times. "You can't let people get away with looking down at you."

Kwong King You appeared small and frail to me, but her penetrating eyes and forceful tone of voice told me otherwise: She was invincible. As I listened to her story of woe, I couldn't help comparing this old woman to the pictures of a youthful Kwong King You and handsome Ah Fook, dressed in a Western suit and necktie, that hung in a picture frame on the wall directly above and behind her. I had come from across the ocean to hear her story and she was more than ready to leave her legacy as a good example of a *yin chai leung mo* (a virtuous wife and benevolent mother), someone who had more than proven her worth to her vindictive sister-in-law, the whole village, and her husband overseas. In the old days, the imperial government would have erected a memorial stone arch in her honor. Kwong King You had so much to tell that she required little prodding from me or the government official, Chan Gum, who also participated in the interview.[25]

"LUCKY TO BE MARRIED TO A *GAM SAAN HAAK*."

"My *sum* [aunt], who was related to both sides of the family, introduced us. She got a matchmaker to speak to my future father-in-law, saying that I was a good woman, and he agreed to the proposal. Ah Fook came to Siu How Chung [village], hoping to see me, but I was at school so he didn't get to see me.[26] He chose to believe my *sum*, and that was how it happened. I can't remember the date but I was twenty years old. Yes, [I was considered lucky to be married to a *gam saan haak*].[27]

"He was home for twenty-seven months. Then he returned to America. I had one more year of schooling left. He wrote and told me to go to Sister Chow Yung's [midwife] school for the admittance exams.[28] He said that if I had a medical degree I could get into the United States faster. At that time, it was fashionable for married women to go to school, so I followed the girls to school. After I graduated, I went out to practice.

"EVERY FORTY-TWO DAYS"

"At the beginning, he sent money home for my education. But after he became a seaman on the *President Coolidge* line, he had an operation, and the doctor told him to rest for three months. He asked someone to write me that he was unemployed and could not send any more money. I almost had to quit school in Canton. But my classmates were good to me. They noticed I wasn't as playful as usual. 'Sister Kwong, you look like you have problems. You're not too talkative. Are you all right?' they asked. So I said, 'I can't continue with school. I have to leave.' I showed the letter to them. They didn't

Ah Fook and Kwong King You soon after their marriage in 1927.

believe I was married until they read the letter. One schoolmate who was the class president said, 'Don't be discouraged. There are three hundred of us students. If we each give you one dollar, you'll have three hundred dollars.' She asked if I had any relatives there. I said, 'Yes, there's Dr. Chan.' So I went to discuss the matter with Sister Chow Yung. She told me, 'Don't be afraid. Go ask Fourth Granduncle because even if he doesn't have the money, his *gam saan jongg* ["Gold Mountain firm"] does. And if he can't lend you the money, I will.' I had already finished one year of school, so I was reluctant to descend from the mountain [to give up her training to become a doctor].

"Finally, Fourth Granduncle personally brought me three hundred dollars so that I could continue until I graduated. At the end of the year, Ah Fook wanted to come visit, but I told him not to return because it would disturb my studies. I was close to finishing, and I couldn't leave Canton to be with him in the village. At that time, that was how we felt about our studies. If you're going to study, then you have to keep at it until you're finished. So although he wanted to return, I told him not to. He didn't come again until March of the next year. He continued working as a seaman, and over the next five years while I was in Hong Kong, he would dock there every forty-two days. If the shipment were large, he would stay two nights; if not, one night. Then he would go out to sea another forty-two days before coming back. However, after Hong Kong was bombed by the Japanese [in 1942], he couldn't return because his ship couldn't dock. I was afraid to stay in Hong Kong and took our two adopted children, a son and a daughter, back to Nanshan on the last refugee boat. He wrote and told me not to worry and that the next time his ship docked in Hong Kong he would notify me so that I could meet him there. But he quit working on the ships and did not return after that. Then he stopped writing and sending money home because communications were broken off.

"LIFE WAS HARD AFTER THAT"

"After we came back from Hong Kong, life was hard after that. If I didn't have some skill, we three would have died. I worked as a midwife to support my children. Even so, I had to sell our clothes, even my undershirts, to put food on the table. And not even rice, just *juk* [rice gruel]. How I suffered, selling my comforters and blankets to buy eight pigs to raise. Three died and I sold the other five. With the money I was able to buy medicine and set up my practice. People in the village were good to me; otherwise, I would have left for Hong Kong. Every day my table was full of rice and beans [payment from patients]. I was making money then and I used it all on my children's education. Gee Duk [son] went to Jom Gong for school, and Gee Geen [daughter] went to Fat Shan for school. That cost plenty. So whenever I cooked rice, I always threw a handful back. That's how frugal I was until I realized my goals. Fortunately my children were good to me. They were very respectful. Even when we had no rice, just *juk*, they wanted me to eat first. My father-in-law was good to us. He swore to heaven that as long as he lived, he would support me. He sent us money twice a year, and whatever my sister-in-law got, I got.

"I heard people say Ah Fook had died. Others said that after the war started, he remarried in America and had children. Even Second Granduncle said so when he came back from America with two hundred dollars and some medicine from Ah Fook. I said to my father-in-law, 'I heard people say that Ah Fook's ship was bombed and he died. Is it true?' My *mo* [sister-in-law], who was trying to aggravate me, said, 'Second sister-in-law, you don't have anyone anymore. The ship was bombed and he's dead.' I knew she wanted me to leave so that she could take our share of the land. I had to struggle on no matter what. (My father-in-law never got along with her. Called her the Empress Dowager.) She shouldn't have said that to me, to wish ill of my family. She was that jealous of me. I stood my ground and smilingly said to her, 'First, you are born. Second, you die. That's life. As a doctor I can support my children.' I was young then and knew how to stand up for myself. As they say, 'Time will reveal another person's true heart.'

"Ah Fook never told me he remarried in America. You Heung told Ah Go and Ah Go told me, 'Second Sister-in-Law, Second Brother didn't die. I heard people say he remarried.' So I came back and asked my father-in-law if it was true. He said, 'That's what kinsmen have been saying, that Ah Fook has remarried. People saw him with children in the streets.' Ah Go was trying to comfort me, that he was still alive. I said, 'It's better that he's remarried rather than dead.' Today, we talk about monogamy. Before, it was, 'Three wives and four concubines; if your head has enough hair, you can put up with a lot of fleas.'[29] There are so few people in this family anyway. It won't bother me if he had eight or ten wives. He has his life and I have mine.

"Now that he had remarried, all my colleagues were telling me to remarry. They wanted to introduce me to some doctor. But because of what my *mo* had said to aggravate me, 'He's dead,' I was willing to sacrifice my entire future and stick it out in Nanshan. You have to stand up for yourself. You can't let people drive you away by looking down at you. So I wrote Ah Fook. He should have sent for me by then. He was probably afraid I would cause trouble. He used to be afraid of me, always consulted me before he did anything. But because I had written and asked him if he had remarried, he was afraid to write me back. And as long as he didn't write back, I wasn't going to waste money going to Hong Kong to wait for him. I had to make a living at home.

"Ah Fook continued to send money through Second Granduncle. Sometimes more, sometimes less, but he always sent something. He was a good person but maybe because he had remarried and had children, he had less money to spend. (People said that he had three sons and that my son, Gee Duk, was older than his son by one year.) It [the money] was like rain from heaven. No letter, no return address. Maybe he didn't want his other wife to know. People said it was because he was breaking the law. If he put down his address and I wrote him, people would know he had another wife and he would be breaking the law. Second Granduncle told me he couldn't go both ways [be with two wives].

"I DON'T REGRET MARRYING HIM"

"When he first left, I was very upset and wanted revenge, at least until I reached the age of forty-five. My colleagues kept telling me not to be stupid.

If he remarried, I should remarry. I used to cry tears from my eyes down to my toes. It's been such a hard life. It was because of my *mo*'s words that I struggled on. She crossed me for a few *mou* ["acres"] of land and that made me determined to stick it out in the Chan family. I kept saying, 'Alive, I belong to the Chan family. When I die, my ghost will belong to the Chan family.'

"Although ours was an arranged marriage, we got along well. I don't regret marrying him. Every personal possession I had—rouge, powder, perfume, even sanitary napkins, he bought for me. So he was good to me. He bought all the soap and household items as well. I'm just bitter that I haven't seen him for so long. For the sake of the children, I didn't remarry. There's always hope that he might change his mind and come home. That's happened before to many others who remarried. My hope is that he will someday return. I will always welcome him back. My mind would be put to rest if I could just see him one more time.

"I know he's still in America. Because some kinsmen scolded him [for remarrying], he moved away from San Francisco to the countryside. He still sends money, but he won't write me. Before, he would send it through one of our relatives. Now he writes to my daughter, Gee Geen. I just received one hundred Hong Kong dollars from him. Gee Duk, my hardheaded son, said to return the money to him. 'It wouldn't cost him anything more to enclose a letter,' he said. Gee Geen said, 'Let's write him.' He refused, but Gee Geen went ahead.

"I RETIRED SEVEN YEARS AGO"

"I retired seven years ago, although I'm not the retiring type. I enjoyed working. Everyone at the hospital was good to me. Nobody wanted me to retire but my children. Gee Duk used to scold me and say, 'You want to work until you die?' Before, time passed quickly, and I didn't even have to cook. There's no fun staying home and doing housework. It's boring at home. I sit until my butt hurts. So Gee Geen knitted this cushion for me [pulls seat cushion from under her to show me].

"I know time is running out. I just go day by day. If there's something good to eat, I'll enjoy myself. I'm spending my money as fast as I can. My pension is $44.20 a month. That's enough for an old lady like me. Besides, my children always buy me food whenever they visit. They buy me ginseng twice a month [because] when my appetite isn't good or I'm not sleeping well, it helps to take ginseng. Actually, everyone tells me that as long as my

Kwong King You in the doorway of her home in Nanshan village when I interviewed her in 1985.

voice is strong and loud, I wouldn't die yet [laughs]. I only take ginseng to extend my life so I can look after this house my son had built for me two years ago. The old house is up there [points in the direction behind her]. My son said it was too inconvenient so he had this house built. I have my own well. It's considered a good house in this village. My son is a doctor in Macao and my daughter is a doctor at the People's Hospital in Jian On, where my grandson attends school. I usually have two girls stay with me. If I live to be one hundred years old, I know the government will take care of me. I'm not an extravagant person. I live a pretty simple life."[30]

After an hour of talking nonstop, Kwong King You did not seem a bit tired. I asked if I could take some photographs of her and the framed pictures on the wall behind her. She consented without hesitation. I last saw her standing in front of her doorway, waving good-bye to me. I had promised to try and locate her husband for her. Upon my return to San Francisco, I learned from relatives that he was alive and living in Oakland, California. He had remarried and had no plans of returning to China. I did not have the heart to write and tell Kwong King You. In 1991, without ever seeing her husband again, she died at the age of eighty-four.

CHINESE WOMEN IN SAN FRANCISCO — CONSENT FORM

After being provided with a description of this research project and its benefits and possible risks, I consent to be interviewed and agree to the following use of my interview (please check):

☐ Use of tape recording and transcript by Judy Yung only
☐ Use of tape recording and transcript by other researchers
☐ Use my true identity
☐ Do not use my true identity
☐ Other stipulations:

_____

_____

_____

I understand that information from this interview may be used in Judy Yung's research and its eventual publication on Chinese women in San Francisco, but only under the above provisos. Should I decide to withdraw from this study at any time, I will write to Prof. Judy Yung at Oakes College, University of California, Santa Cruz, CA 95064, at which time the interview tape and transcript will be destroyed.

Print Name:
Sign Name: Date:
Agreed: Date:

CHINESE WOMEN IN SAN FRANCISCO INTERVIEW
QUESTIONS—IMMIGRANT WOMEN

Life in China:

1. Where and when were you born? How large was your family? What did your parents do for a living?

2. Describe your daily life and living conditions (responsibilities at home, schooling, work, and social life).

3. How were you regarded and treated as a female in China as compared to a male (relationship with parents, gender roles, responsibilities at home, education preparatory to adulthood, freedom of movement, sex education and conduct, work choice and wages, choice of marital partner and marital role, social life, political and legal rights)?

Immigration to the United States:

4. When did you come to the United States (age and year)? Why and how (immigration status)? With whom?

5. Describe the voyage and the immigration process upon arrival.

6. What were your expectations and initial impressions of life in the United States?

Life After Arrival:

7. What was life like after you settled down in San Francisco? Describe your living conditions, schooling, occupation, family life, and social activities.

8. If married in the United States, how did you meet your husband and decide to marry him? If married in China and separated for a period of time, how did the separation affect you and your marriage?

9. Describe your role as a wife, mother, and homemaker relative to your husband. Who controlled reproduction? What were your household, religious, and cultural duties? Who was responsible for childcare and rearing? Who held the purse strings? What difficulties, if any, did you experience? How were you able to resolve them?

10. What kind of work did you do for a living? How did you like the job? Describe the wages and working conditions. How did it compare to your husband's? What difficulties, if any, did you experience? How were you able to resolve them?

11. Describe your social and political life as compared to your husband's (organizations, social activities, political involvement, interactions with other races).

12. How were you regarded in the community where you lived? Did you experience any discrimination because you were Chinese or a woman? How did you deal with it?

13. What, if any, differences were there in being a woman in China and the United States?

Observations of Life in San Francisco, 1900–1945:

14. What was life like for Chinese women in San Francisco during this period? Any more footbinding or prostitution? When did women start going out and why? What kind of educational and work opportunities were available to them? What kind of organizations did they belong to? How involved were women in politics?

15. How were the Chinese regarded and treated by other races? How were Chinese women regarded and treated?

16. Who were some of the prominent women then?

17. My thesis is that the years 1900 to 1945 were a liberating period for Chinese American women. Do you agree or disagree? If you agree, what do you think were the causes?

18. Which historical events had the greatest impact on you and other Chinese women (1911 Revolution, World War I, May Fourth Movement, World's Fair in 1915 and 1939, Immigration Act of 1924, Communist-Nationalist civil war, Great Depression, National Dollar Stores strike in 1938, World War II)?

19. How influential were Christianity and Chinese nationalism on the lives of Chinese women in San Francisco? How about the women's emancipation movement in China and the women's suffrage movement in the United States?

Reflections:

20. Have your expectations of life in America been fulfilled? Any regrets?

21. How have you raised your children differently from the way you were raised? Are you satisfied with the outcome of your children?

22. What things do you cherish most about America? What things, if any, do you not like about America?

23. Do you have any favorite family stories you can share with me?

24. Do you have any photographs, letters, writings, or memorabilia I can use in my book?

CHINESE WOMEN IN SAN FRANCISCO INTERVIEW
QUESTIONS — SECOND GENERATION

Family Background, Childhood, Youth:

1. Describe your parents' background (year and place of birth, life in China, educational background, occupation, immigration, life in the United States).

2. Where and when were you born? How large was your family?

3. Describe your daily life and living conditions growing up (responsibilities at home, schooling, social life).

4. How were you regarded and treated as a daughter compared to your brothers (relationship with parents, gender roles, responsibilities at home, education preparatory to adulthood, freedom of movement, sex education and conduct, social life)?

5. How much education did you receive? How did you choose your major or field of study? Did you experience any difficulties in school? How were you able to resolve them?

6. If you worked, what kind of job did you have? How did you find the job? Describe the wages and working conditions.

7. Describe your social life (organizations, social activities, interracial interactions).

8. What did your parents expect of you? Did you experience any generation gap or cultural conflict at home? How were you able to resolve them?

9. What were your aspirations? Who were your role models? Who influenced you the most (parents, friends, school, church, popular media)?

10. Did you experience any discrimination because you were Chinese or female? How did you deal with it?

Adulthood:

11. What did you do for a living? How did you find the job? Describe the wages and working conditions. What difficulties, if any, did you experience? How were you able to resolve them?

12. How did you meet and marry your husband? Would you regard your relationship to him as his superior, subordinate, or equal? What was the division of responsibilities? What difficulties did you experience in your marriage and how were you able to resolve them?

13. How many children did you have? Did you practice birth control? What were the conditions during childbirth? Who raised the children? How did you raise them differently than the way you were raised? What cultural traditions did you try to continue? Did you have any difficulties as a mother and how were you able to resolve them?

14. Describe your social and political life as compared to your husband's (organizations, social activities, political involvement, interactions with other races).

15. How were you regarded in the community where you lived? Did you experience any discrimination because you were Chinese or female? How did you deal with it?

Observations of Life in San Francisco, 1900–1945:

16. What was life like for Chinese immigrant women as compared to second-generation women during this period? What kind of educational and work opportunities were available to them? How involved were they in community activities or politics?

17. How were Chinese regarded and treated by other races? How were Chinese women regarded and treated?

18. Who were some of the prominent women then?

19. My thesis is that the years 1900 to 1945 were a liberating period for Chinese American women. Do you agree or disagree? If you agree, what do you think were the causes?

20. Which historical events had the greatest impact on you and other Chinese women (1906 earthquake, 1911 Revolution, World War I, May Fourth Movement, World's Fair in 1915 and 1939, Immigration Act of 1924, Communist-Nationalist civil war, Great Depression, National Dollar Stores strike in 1938, World War II)?

21. How influential were Christianity and Chinese nationalism on the lives of Chinese women in San Francisco? How about the women's emancipation movement in China and the women's suffrage movement in the United States?

22. What was the impact of social institutions on the self-perceptions of second-generation women (public school, Chinese school, religious organization, women's organization, popular media)?

23. Do you have any favorite family stories you can share with me?

24. Do you have any photographs, letters, writings, or memorabilia I can use in my book?

My thanks to students in my oral history classes, the Gender Cluster of the History Department at the University of California, Santa Cruz, and the editors of *Frontiers* for their helpful suggestions in the writing of this article.

NOTES

1. Him Mark Lai, Genny Lim, and Judy Yung, eds., *Island: Poetry and History of Chinese Immigrants on Angel Island, 1910–1940* (Seattle: University of Washington Press, 1980, 1991); and Judy Yung, *Chinese Women of America: A Pictorial History* (Seattle: University of Washington Press, 1986), *Unbound Feet: A Social History of Chinese Women in San Francisco* (Los Angeles and Berkeley: University of California Press, 1995), and *Unbound Voices: A Documentary History of Chinese Women in San Francisco* (Los Angeles and Berkeley: University of California Press, 1999).

2. *Unbound Feet* documents social change in the lives of Chinese women—both the immigrant and American-born generations—as they made a place for themselves in San Francisco from the gold rush through World War II. *Unbound Voices* is an anthology of primary writings and oral histories of Chinese women in San Francisco covering the same period.

3. The following works on oral history were especially useful to me: Willa K. Baum, *Oral History for the Local Historical Society* (Walnut Creek, Calif.: Alta Mira Press, 1967, 1995); Sherna Gluck, "What's So Special About Women? Women's Oral History," in *Frontiers: A Journal of Women Studies* 2:2 (1977): 3–14; Ronald J. Grele, *Envelopes of Sound: The Art of Oral History* (New York: Praeger, 1991); Sherna Berger Gluck and Daphne Patai, eds., *Women's Words: The Feminist Practice of Oral History* (New York: Routledge, 1991); and Valerie Raleigh Yow, *Recording Oral History: A Practical Guide for Social Scientists* (Thousand Oaks, Calif.: Sage, 1994).

4. The consent form and interview questions were based on University of California's Human Subjects Protocol and suggestions from Gluck, "What's So Special About Women?"

5. This is in reference to World War II, which for the Chinese began in 1931, when the Japanese army invaded and occupied Manchuria and northeastern China. As documented in *Unbound Feet*, all walks of Chinese American women actively engaged in fund-raising, propaganda, and Red Cross work in support of the war effort in China and the United States.

6. A number of feminist scholars have noted that women often remember the past in different ways than men, that women are less likely to put themselves at the center of public events or boast of their personal accomplishments. See Joan Sangster, "Telling Our Stories: Feminist Debates and the Use of Oral History," in *The Oral History Reader*, ed. Robert Perks and Alistair Thomson (London and New York: Routledge, 1998), 89.

7. The remaining fifteen interviews cited in *Unbound Feet* were conducted by staff of the Survey of Race Relations Research Project in the 1920s, the Chinese Historical Society of America in the 1970s, and the Chinese Women of America Research Project in the early 1980s.

8. See Ruth Frankenberg, *White Women, Race Matters: The Social Construction of Whiteness* (Minneapolis: University of Minnesota Press, 1993), chapter 2; Ann Oakley, "Interviewing Women: A Contradiction in Terms," in *Doing Feminist Research*, ed. Helen Roberts (London and Boston: Routledge and Kegan Paul, 1981), 30–61; and Kristina Minister, "A Feminist Frame for the Oral History Interview," in Gluck and Patai, *Women's Words*, 27–41.

9. As Robert F. Berkhofer Jr. notes, "The more nearly the artifact or text is reproduced as a whole, the less chance there is that the editor's or other intervener's selection and interpretation will enter the mimetic process" (*Beyond the Great Story: History as Text and Discourse* [Cambridge: Harvard University Press, 1995], 148).

10. This is in keeping with the practice of listening to the silences, the meta-statements, and the logic of the narrative for different levels of meaning. See Grele, *Envelopes of Sound*; Kathryn Anderson and Dana C. Jack, "Learning to Listen: Interview Techniques and Analyses," in Gluck and Patai, *Women's Words*, 11–26; and Frankenberg, *White Women, Race Matters*, 35–42.

11. The first phrase is taken from my mother's interview in reference to class compatibility in arranged marriages. The second saying comes from the interview with *sau saang gwa* Kwong King You and means that if a man is wealthy enough, he can have as many wives as he wants.

12. I always keep in mind what my colleague Paul Skenazy and oral historian Valerie Yow have to say on this subject: "Oral history is always reliable, always unreliable. It does not provide an account of an event so much as the experience, recollected, of an event" (Paul Skenazy, "Oral History: Some Guidelines and Comments," unpublished essay, 13). In *Recording Oral History*, Yow reminds us that diaries, letters, and official documents can be just as biased and slanted as oral histories. She writes, "History is what the people who lived it make of it and what the others who observe the participants or listen to them or study their records make of it" (22).

13. Alessandro Portelli, *The Death of Luigi Trastulli and Other Stories: Form and Meaning in Oral History* (Albany: State University of New York Press, 1991), 52.

14. Here I am reminded of what Ruth Frankenberg said in *White Women, Race Matters*: "An interview is not, in any simple sense, the telling of a life so much as it is an incomplete story angled toward my questions and each woman's ever-changing sense of self and of how the world works" (41). Similarly, Paul Skenazy wrote in his essay on oral history guidelines, "Oral history is an oblique reflection of the meeting of interviewer and interviewee. The material of the oral history is shaped by who it is delivered to and what that person chooses to hear, ask more about, respond to with face and body" ("Oral History," 13).

15. According to Marcus Lee Hansen, the first generation holds on to their culture, the second generation rejects the old for the new, and the third generation reclaims their cultural heritage. See Marcus Lee Hansen, *The Problem of the Third Generation Immigrant* (Rock Island, Ill.: Augustana Historical Society, 1938).

16. For a discussion of how power is tipped in favor of the interviewer, see Yow, *Recording Oral History*, 105–9; and Frankenberg, *White Women, Race Matters*, 29–42.

17. Karl Marx, "The Eighteenth Brumaire of Louis Bonaparte," in *The Marx—Engels Reader*, ed. Robert C. Tucker (New York: W. W. Norton, 1972), 437. I am indebted to Ann Lane for this citation.

18. I was visiting relatives in Nanshan village, the birthplace of my maternal great-grandfather Chin Lung. For a report on my trip, see Judy Yung, "Visit to Guangdong Province: Chinese American Roots," *East/West*, May 11, 1983, 8.

19. The term, *sau saang gwa*, literally means "a widow with a living husband." For a comparable description of life overseas for the husband or "married bachelor," see Paul Siu, *The Chinese Laundryman: A Study of Social Isolation* (New York: New York University Press, 1987).

20. The term "split-household family" is taken from Evelyn Nakano Glenn's "Split Household, Small Producer and Dual Wage Earner: An Analysis of Chinese-American Family Strategies," *Journal of Marriage and Family* 45:1 (1983): 35–48, in which she describes the early Chinese American family arrangement as being a "split household," with production (wage-earning) separated from other family functions and carried out by the husband overseas while reproduction, socialization, and family consumption (supported by the husband's remittances) were carried out by the wife or other relatives in the home village.

21. Abandoned wives who became destitute could remarry, and, in all fairness, there are stories with happy endings as well. See Madeline Hsu, " 'Living Abroad and Faring Well': Migration and Transnationalism in Taishan County, Guangdong, 1904–1939" (Ph.D. diss., Yale University, 1996), chapter 4.

22. Hsu, "Living Abroad and Faring Well," chapter 4; see also, Siu, *Chinese Laundryman*, chapter 9.

23. Although wives in China were ostracized and punished if they did not remain

chaste and faithful, their overseas husbands were allowed to frequent brothels and have second wives in America (Siu, *Chinese Laundryman*, 167).

24. Because of the long separations that made procreation difficult, it was not uncommon for *sau saang gwa* to adopt children to carry on the family line, ensure financial stability, and care for them in their old age. See Hsu, "Living Abroad and Faring Well," 172–74; and Siu, *Chinese Laundryman*, 159–63.

25. Chan Gum guided and followed me throughout my visit in Doumen County in 1982. He was a native of the county and a sympathetic listener. I believe his presence at this interview accounts for some of Kwong King You's comments about the war years, her pension, and her determination to wait for her husband's return.

26. Kwong King You came from a wealthy family. Her father sent remittances from Cuba, where he had a produce store, to support her education.

27. Ah Fook left for the United States with his grandaunt when he was six years old. He returned to Nanshan village in 1927 for schooling and to get married.

28. According to Chan Gum, Chan Chow Yung refused an arranged marriage so that she could become a doctor and support all her brothers and sisters through school.

29. Common sayings that refer to the practice of polygyny among the wealthy class.

30. Kwong King You, interview with author in Chinese, Nanshan village, Doumen County, Guangdong Province, December 15, 1982.

Frontiers 19:3 (1998): 130–56.

Oral History Applications 2

Oral History as a Biographical Tool

SALLY ROESCH WAGNER

Although Matilda Joslyn Gage was an important theoretician and activist in the radical wing of the nineteenth-century American Women's Movement, she has received only passing mention in histories of the suffrage movement. With Elizabeth Cady Stanton, she authored the major documents of the National Woman Suffrage Association, including the "Declaration of Rights of Women of 1876" and the first three volumes of the *History of Woman Suffrage*.[1] Gage held offices in the NWSA roughly parallel to those of Susan B. Anthony's.[2] In addition, she edited and published the official journal of the organization for four years.[3]

In 1889, when the executive committee of the NWSA voted to merge with the more conservative American Woman's Suffrage Association, Gage bitterly fought this move. She saw it as a takeover by a "cabal" of the conservative suffrage-focused forces in the NWSA, led by Anthony, which would ultimately lead to the death of the woman's rights movement.[4] Unable to mobilize sufficient strength to prevent the merger, and convinced that female enfranchisement was no longer a critical issue (since women had gained many legal rights without it), she left the organized suffrage movement and in 1890 formed the Woman's National Liberal Union. The sole function of this group was to fight the church, which Gage viewed as the primary source of woman's oppression.[5]

Susan B. Anthony, furious at Gage's "secession,"[6] seems to have made deliberate attempts to write Gage out of suffrage history.[7] The resulting history has generally been focused on "superhuman" leaders involved in an undeviating quest for the suffrage goal. Such an incomplete picture not only distorts the past, but also denies us insights with which to develop and evaluate our present movement. Through studying the lives of the dropouts and sup-posed "losers" of the earlier women's movement, like Gage, we can, perhaps, correct past historical accounts as well as help direct our own present move-ment with a deeper understanding of the mistakes made during the first wave of feminism. With both these goals in mind, I began to research the life of Matilda Joslyn Gage to write the first biography of her.

Matilda Joslyn Gage's only living grandchild, and namesake, Matilda Jewell Gage, was ninety-one years old.[8] Despite failing eyesight and a hip injury that required her to walk with a cane, she lived alone in her museum-like home in Aberdeen, South Dakota. Raised with the knowledge that her grandmother had been slighted by history, and convinced of her grand-mother's importance, Matilda carefully preserved all of Gage's letters to her son, Thomas Clarkson Gage, as well as Gage's scrapbooks, unpublished manuscripts, and all other items that came into her hands. Not only had she assembled—in an upstairs closet—the largest collection of Gage's papers in existence, but she had also—just as deliberately—gathered family stories about her grandmother. Matilda's home was alive with memories of her grandmother; photographs of her, as well as her furniture and art work, surrounded Matilda.

Matilda Jewell Gage was an old family friend, and for four summers we worked together reconstructing her grandmother's life. I read to her the letters and papers from her grandmother's collection—which her failing eyesight prevented her from reading. Matilda's memory, however, was ex-cellent, and she shared with me her detailed knowledge of family history: births, deaths, marriages, trips, moves—events that I could keep straight only with the help of charts, time lines, and note cards. The tape recorder was our constant companion in both our informal discussions and in the more structured recounting of anecdotes about her grandmother.

One evening early in our working relationship, I told Matilda that the next morning I wanted her to do a tape of the family stories about her grand-mother, and she agreed. That night I wrote an outline of the proposed tape, with the questions I would ask. The next morning I arrived at Matilda's to discover that she, too, had made an outline and was prepared to do the tape alone. I set up the recorder and she began, pausing only to collect her thoughts, occasionally ask my advice, and check her outline. The result was a highly entertaining, coherent, and polished collection of reminiscences about Matilda Joslyn Gage, recounted in a conversational style by her grand-daughter. Subsequently, we added several new family story tapes with each summer, but we also retaped the old stories, as several different recordings of the same story allow a choice of versions to use. Some of these stories, transcribed word-for-word from the tapes, appear in the biography.

Family stories are an extremely rich biographical source, in several ways. For one thing, the kinds of anecdotes a family repeats about its members may say something about the way in which that family works. Though there are innumerable instances in each person's daily life that could be enshrined in story form, to be retold at intervals, only certain events are selected to become family stories. Those that do become so enshrined are chosen, at least in part, because of the function these stories serve in maintaining the cohesiveness of the family unit. They may create a sort of mythology about a person, serving to reinforce, explain, contain, or make acceptable certain aspects of a person's behavior to other family members. For example, my teenage son delightedly recounted (with great encouragement from me) stories about my teaching classes wearing flannel nightgowns and knee-high boots, which I had not taken time to tie. My behavior was a source of pain and humiliation for him, as he went through this terribly conservative period of his life. Yet our ability to laugh together about past instances of my nonconformity served as a safety valve in our relationship. It gave me a feeling of validation and it allowed him a means of circumscribing my behavior in an acceptable (though limited) way, while providing a gentle avenue of criticism.

Similarly, Gage's hot temper was institutionalized in the family as the "Joslyn temper." It was said to have originated with Gage's father, Hezekiah Joslyn, and been inherited by his daughter, who then passed it on to at least some of the children. The explanatory fiction of inheritance (in keeping with nineteenth-century genetic beliefs) relegated Gage's passionate outbursts to the same area of biological inevitability as her blue eyes. Naming the behavior gave its existence public acknowledgment within the family and among close friends. The following family story, told by her granddaughter, illustrates Matilda Joslyn's famous behavior.[9]

THE GREEN TOMATO PIE STORY

It's true that grandmother in that day and age, always had help in the kitchen. I don't know how much cooking grandmother did from time to time, but one time she heard about making a pie out of green tomatoes. She thought that would be something that might be very unusual and very nice to serve. Well, one evening she had some quite prominent people in for dinner, at night apparently. So grand-mother thought that she would make a green tomato pie, so she went out in the kitchen and did this. It was something quite unusual for her to do. Well, the man and his wife came and were, of course, seated at the table, and the dinner was served and then for dessert was brought on this green tomato pie. And with great pleasure, grandmother served it to everyone there. Well, she expected some questions would be asked or some praise would be given for such an unusual dessert, and such a deli-cious one. Nothing was said. Grandmother was a bit crestfallen. Nobody mentioned how good this unusual dessert was. Well, a rather pleasant evening followed and finally, this guest and his wife were taking their leave. Grandmother accompanied them to the front door, and was graciously saying "good evening" to them. But she was a little wondering what kind of thanks they were going to give her. I think they probably told her what a nice time they had had. The started to leave and got part way out on the front porch, and grandmother couldn't stand it any longer. That was just too much. And so she said, "And by the way, how did you like my green tomato pie?" At that, the man, the guest, turned and said, "Well, I didn't like it." Well, with that, grandmother took the front door and simply slammed it in his face, she was so upset that she got no praise for her green tomato pie!

Some family stories, or mythologies, are shared by all family members. But the unique way in which each person experiences every other person in the family finds its reflection in separate family stories. Sometimes iden-tifying the source of an anecdote yields as much information about family relationships as the story itself. For example, Thomas Clarkson Gage ap-pears to have been a shy and somewhat self-conscious child, and the sto-ries about his mother that he passed on to his own daughter, Matilda, are all marked by the common theme of intimidation. His sister Maud, on the other hand, was the only one of Gage's children who was not afraid of their mother, and it was Maud whom they always coerced into representing their interests to her. Not surprisingly, one of the major stories passed down by Maud portrays an "I will"–"You won't" battle of the wills between her and her mother following Maud's announcement of plans to marry "that itin-erant actor," L. Frank Baum.[10] Maud firmly declared that she would elope if her mother disapproved of the marriage. At this point, the story goes, they looked at each other and burst out laughing, in sudden awareness of their evenly matched power. Maud had her wedding.

To her son, Matilda Joslyn Gage at times must have appeared domi-nant, opinionated, and outspoken. These same qualities came through to others as independence, strength of conviction, and willingness to defend her views. One such person was her niece, Blanche Weaver Baxter, who was a favorite of her aunt's, and spent a good deal of time in the Gage home. Gage's qualities that created fear in Thomas Clarkson were greeted with enthusiastic admiration by Blanche. It comes as no surprise, then, that the "uppity woman" stories about Gage—such as the Green Tomato Pie story—celebrating her strengths, survived through Blanche. Matilda heard these stories directly from Blanche and also from Blanche's daughter, Ramona.[11]

In addition to providing an invaluable tool for reconstructing family dynamics, family stories can also shed light on personal dynamics and the implications for political interaction. The current feminist principle that "the personal is political" has contributed to our analysis of modern feminism by leading us to examine the connections between political ideology and personal lifestyle and relationships. If we apply this twentieth-century principle to the nineteenth-century Women's Movement, then new avenues for exploration might be opened. Stories that reveal behavioral characteristics of the women involved in that earlier movement take on a far greater importance than mere anecdotal interludes. They can shed light on the particular tone or style of the women's political behavior, as well, and might even help to unravel the intricate personal dynamics among the women. These personal dynamics led to the creation of affinity groups, factional splits, anger, hurt feelings, and lifelong allegiances—all of which shaped and were shaped by the women's political ideologies and actions.

In my forthcoming Gage biography, the relationship between personal qualities and political behavior will be illustrated with a series of vignettes, having as their basis the family stories about Matilda Joslyn Gage. The examples that follow show how her "Joslyn temper" (seen first in the Green Tomato Pie story) affected the tone of her political interaction.

This quality of quick-tempered aggression found political expression in a scathing attack Gage launched against Anthony Comstock when he threatened to bring legal action against any school board that placed her book, *Woman, Church, and State*, in its library. She said, in part:

I look upon him as a man who is mentally and morally unbalanced, not knowing right from wrong, or the facts of history from "tales of lust." Being intellectually weak, Anthony Comstock misrepresents all works upon which he presumes to pass judgment, and is as dangerous to liberty of speech and of the press as were the old inquisitors, whom he somewhat resembles. A fool as a press censor is more to be feared than a knave, and Comstock seems to be a union of both fool and knave.

Buddha declared the only sin to be ignorance. If this be true, Anthony Comstock is a great sinner.[12]

"Quick to anger, quick to forget," is the way Matilda described the "Joslyn temper," which seems accurately to portray a blow-up by Gage toward her close friend and political ally, Harriet H. Robinson in 1890.[13] Robinson and her daughter, Harriette R. Shattuck, were on the executive committee of the NWSA in 1889 and voted against the merger with the AWSA. Both were furious at the manner in which the decision was forced through the executive committee, and Robinson repeatedly pressured Gage to write a protest to the action.[14] Gage corresponded extensively with other NWSA dissidents, to fully understand the situation and together figure out a course of action. As time went on that year, it looked as though the merger could not be stopped, and that a great many feminists were disenchanted with the suffrage struggle. She also discovered a great deal of concern about confronting the primary role of the church in creating and maintaining woman's oppression, as well as fear of the trend toward a great unification of church and state, an idea being pushed by religious people both within and outside the suffrage movement. And so she began the herculean task of organizing an alternative feminist body, the Woman's National Liberal Union, that would address itself to these political concerns. The Union was to hold its founding convention immediately after that of the merged suffrage organization (the National American Woman Suffrage Association). Exhausted in her overwork, she finally yielded to Robinson's insistent pleas and wrote a protest against the merger because it looked like no one else was going to do it. She worked from letters received from Olympia Brown, Clara Colby, Stanton, Robinson, and Shattuck (among others) and sent a copy of the draft to Robinson for changes. Time was running short; the first convention of the NAWSA was less than a month off. Robinson returned the draft without comment and apparently without her signature. Gage was furious and fired off the following letter:

My Dear Mrs. Robinson:
I think you are perfectly incomprehensible. . . . Why, let me ask, have you not yourself—now, or long since, written what you thought to be right and not laid the burden on me amid all my other overwhelming . . . work? Why did you not *now* write such form of protest as you wished? Why did you ever ask and urge me to write it? Well, well.
Goodbye
Matilda Joslyn Gage[15]

Shattuck and Robinson tardily sent their relatively timid comments, which Gage added as an addendum to the printed protest.[16] But her next letter to Robinson, after the hubbub of the NAWSA and WNUL conventions in February, is warm, newsy, and signed, "As ever."[17]

This example of clear, direct anger—expressed and then forgotten—demonstrates a rather remarkable quality in a nineteenth-century feminist. Correspondence among movement women contains many instances of anger toward someone expressed to a third person, but seldom did these women directly confront the person who had created the anger. Lingering bitterness resulted from these unspoken feelings and adversely affected the women's working relationships. No doubt Gage's ability to express direct anger was assisted by the "Joslyn temper" mythology, which justified her deviation from the prescribed role of placid passivity assigned to nineteenth-century women.

Written sources alone can produce a very one-dimensional, public image of a person. Virginia Woolf suggested, "Biography will enlarge its scope by hanging-up looking glasses at odd corners."[18] The oral tradition of family stories selected by persons who stand in a variety of relationships to the subject may add this richness of perspective. For example, Gage's writings and speeches show her to have been very critical of Lincoln's foot-dragging approach to Emancipation, but she amazed her son, who ran from the village with word of Lincoln's assassination, when she became so distraught at the news that she required a doctor's care. Family stories present a portrait of Gage as a woman who "always went towards her ends with a certain impatience to reach them," to the point of rushing teacups—precariously balanced on saucers—into waiting hands with a "Hurry, hurry, take it, take it!"[19] But, a story told to her daughter by an old family friend shows how this restive characteristic was tempered by other concerns:

When she was living here [Fayetteville, New York] in her later years and was one day about to start for Syracuse by one of the only two trains in the day by which we could go to town for errands and had already locked her door and left the house, a man—not a professional tramp evidently—asked her for food, saying he was in need and hungry. She turned back, unlocked her door and built up a fire in the range and prepared a meal for him, giving up her journey for that day at great inconvenience to herself.[20]

Obviously, one can do biography without the use of a tape recorder and oral history techniques. I came to use them as a means of satisfying pragmatic research needs: I could not take notes fast enough in discussion sessions with Matilda and was losing a great deal of information. Above all, it was important to obtain the family stories as told in Matilda's own words. The picture obtained by this means of tapping the family's oral history provided information about Gage's personality and the dynamics of her family relationships, which created a full and complex personal context in which to place her previously unacknowledged feminist activism.

NOTES

For a brief biographical sketch of Gage, see the article by Elizabeth Warbasse in *Notable American Women, 1607–1950: A Biographical Dictionary*, ed. Edward T. James and Janet Wilson James, 3 vols. (Cambridge: Harvard University Press, 1971). Gage's main work was *Woman, Church, and State*, published in 1893.

1. Susan B. Anthony, listed along with Gage and Stanton as coauthor, did none of the writing.

2. Gage was chairman of the executive committee during Anthony's presidencies in the 1870s; Anthony served in that position during Gage's one presidential term. Both filled various vice presidencies during Stanton's unbroken presidency in the 1880s.

3. The NWSA had a complicated history of official and unofficial journals, but from 1871 to 1881 Gage's publication, *The National Citizen and Ballot Box*, was the official journal of communication.

4. The NWSA and its members fearlessly addressed a multitude of issues related to the oppression of women: the legal slavery of women in marriages, rape, prostitution, child abuse, women in prison, working conditions, and wages—most of the issues that have been raised by the present wave of feminism. They worked for suffrage, too, through a constitutional amendment; and they were separatists. The AWSA included men as members and officers, worked for suffrage state-by-state, and shied away from looking at the unladylike issues of feminism. Gage correctly predicted that the merger of these two groups (which actually assimilated the NWSA into the AWSA structure) would result in the ascendancy of the AWSA's politics. After 1890 all other feminist issues were virtually dropped by the new organization; the suffrage movement emerged, and the woman's rights movement no longer existed. Further, the merger brought with it the Women's Christian Temperance Union, in the persons of AWSA members Frances Willard, Mary Livermore, and others, who were trying in a number of ways to effect a union between church and state.

5. Gage's analysis was twofold: the foundation of the church is the oppression of women; and, the basic institutional and ideological source of women's oppression is the church.

6. Susan B. Anthony to Elizabeth Wright Osbourne, February 5, 1890, Garrison Collection, Sophia Smith Collection (Women's History Archive), Smith College, Northampton, Massachusetts.

7. To be documented and explored at length in my biography of Matilda Joslyn Gage.

8. Matilda Jewell Gage will be referred to as Matilda hereafter.

9. In an attempt to be complete in my research, I baked a green tomato pie, which was really very tasty. Use a green apple pie recipe and substitute green tomatoes.

10. L. Frank Baum went on to write the Oz stories. There is an obvious relationship to be explored between these stories—replete with amazons, matriarchies, and strong female characters—and the influence on the author of a feminist wife and mother-in-law.

11. One summer I had the good fortune of being able to tape Ramona Baxter Bowden telling some of her mother's stories about Matilda Joslyn Gage.

12. *Fayetteville* (N.Y.) *Weekly Recorder*, August 23, 1895.

13. Author of *Loom and Spindle or Life among the Early Mill Girls*, reprinted by Press Pacifica.

14. The decision to merge took place in a midnight session of the executive committee, with no previous announcement that the question was to be voted on. (Gage, who was chairman of the executive committee and unable to be at the convention, was not even informed.) Anthony's "ring" successfully defeated a motion to have the decision put to the full membership; the meeting was packed, and absent members were not allowed to vote. Earlier in the convention, a new constitution was pushed through, which subordinated the national idea to that of the state's, by requiring for the first time that all delegates be sent from state auxiliaries, which disfranchised many of the old pioneers and brought previously autonomous state work under the control of the national organization.

15. Matilda Joslyn Gage to Harriet H. Robinson, January 25, 1890, Robinson Collection, Schlesinger Library, Radcliffe College, Cambridge, Massachusetts.

16. "A Statement of Facts. Private. To Members of the National Woman Suffrage Association only," reads the heading on the protest, signed by Olympia Brown, Charlotte F. Daley, Marietta M. Bones, and Matilda Joslyn Gage. Gage Collection, Aberdeen, South Dakota.

17. Matilda Joslyn Gage to Harriet H. Robinson, March 11, 1890, Robinson Collection, Schlesinger Library, Radcliffe College, Cambridge, Massachusetts.

18. Virginia Woolf, "The Art of Biography," *The Atlantic*, May 1939.

19. Will Thompson to Julia Gage Carpenter, May 4, 1890, Gage Collection, Aberdeen, South Dakota.

20. Thompson to Carpenter, May 4, 1890.

Frontiers 2:2 (1977): 70–74.

"I Give the Best Part of My Life to the Mill"

An Oral History of Icy Norman

MARY MURPHY

Bounded by the fall line and the coastal plain on the southeast and the Appalachian Mountains on the northwest lies the southern Piedmont, the first part of the South to undergo industrialization. By 1880, southern farmers were leaving the land for the new textile, tobacco, and furniture factories springing up on the banks of the region's rivers and the outskirts of dusty market towns. By the eve of World War II, the country's tobacco and textile industries had concentrated in the South, and southern workers looked more often to the factory than the farm for their livelihood.

The timing of southern industrialization presented a unique opportunity to record the experiences of men and women who left behind the working rhythms of sun and seasons to live by the mill bell and the time clock. In 1978, the Southern Oral History Program at the University of North Carolina at Chapel Hill received a grant from the National Endowment for the Humanities to study the industrialization of the Piedmont. At the end of two years, approximately 250 interviews had been conducted with tobacco, furniture, cotton, hosiery, and glove workers in five core communities in North and South Carolina.[1]

Icy Norman was one of those workers; she lived in Alamance County, North Carolina, in the Piedmont Heights mill village of the town of Burlington. Alamance County was the site of some of the South's pioneer cotton mills, the earliest built in 1837. Nearly a century later, Alamance witnessed the birth of Burlington Industries, now the world's largest textile company. Alamance County textile workers not only knew the shift from farm to factory, but they also suffered the transformation that took place on the shop floor when water-driven, family-owned mills gave way to corporate-controlled factories that stressed scientific management and employed technologies that stretched the endurance of mill workers. J. Spencer Love, who founded Burlington Industries in 1923, was the prototype of the "new mill men" who emerged after World War I, leading the southern textile industry in rationalized mill management.[2]

When Icy Norman retired from Burlington Industries in 1976, she had worked for the company longer than any other employee, nearly fifty years. She was unusual in remaining at one mill for so long; the southern textile labor force as a whole was highly mobile. But Icy had the common experience of moving from farm to factory, and she lived through the technological and managerial revolutions of the twentieth-century textile industry.

Icy never married, and her brothers and sister left Burlington. She lives alone in a small, neat mill house, but Icy by no means considers herself lonely. She uses the simile "like a family" to describe her relationship with her fellow workers and bosses. The phrase "like a family" cropped up in dozens of interviews. Workers used this image not to invoke a picture of Norman Rockwell family life, but to encompass the complexity and density of the family dynamic that pervaded mill life. In many cases, family was literal. Southern mills encouraged the migration of whole families to mill villages. Mothers taught daughters how to spin, fathers and sons worked side by side. But the bonds of family extended beyond blood kin. Interdependence, warmth, and tolerance, as well as arbitrary authority, competition, and disagreements, knit together the men, women, and children who peopled the South's mills and mill villages. Icy Norman's story is, in more than one way, a family history.

I was born in Coalwood, West Virginia, in 1911, the thirteenth of April. It was on Easter Sunday—snow, Mama said, was knee deep. See, Mama has been married twice, and she had five children by her first husband. So my daddy, he helped raise them five children. Then she had three by my daddy. Barney and me and Florence, she's the baby.

We left from Coalwood and went to Wilkes County, North Carolina, up in the mountains. My daddy, I think he put out two crops. Then we went to Schoolfield [Schoolfield, Virginia, now a part of Danville, was the site of the Dan River Mills]. Stayed there fifteen years and he worked one job fifteen years. My mother worked some in Schoolfield. My baby sister, she was a just a little baby. They had a nursery. They would take me and my brother and my baby sister—she wasn't four months old—to the nursery. They had trained nurses, real nurses. I mean they had a degree. It was a big nursery that the company had. They would keep tiny babies, year-olds, two years on up, until they was sixteen years old. They checked when you went in that nursery—they changed your clothes, they put their clothes on you. They had a big round table with little chairs for them little young ones to sit there and eat. Then they had a place for the bigger children. It was a huge place, you know. They had doctors to come in once a week to check each child. If any one of the children was running a temperature they would send for its mother to come to the nursery to take that child home.

Then they built a huge Hilton Hall. Oh, that was a huge building. It was eight stories high, counting the two ground floors, counting the basement. People could go there that worked in the mill and have a boarding place. They served your meals and everything. They didn't charge but so much a week. All they had to do was cross the railroad and ride into the mill. Then they built that YMCA. Then they put a movie in there. They had a huge city park. That was the most beautifulest park you ever seen. It was then, I don't know how it is now. I ain't been over there in years. The mill just run all of Schoolfield.

They had swimming pools there [Hilton Hall]. They had exercise rooms, a gym. A huge gym. Once a week us school children we'd go swimming there. One day out of the week we'd go to the gym. One day out of the week we'd go learn to cook. One day out of the week we'd go learn to sew, the girls would. They had something else for the boys, too. But I never did learn how to swim. I still don't know how to swim. It would just tickle us to death to go over to that Hilton Hall. It was so pretty. We'd go over to that gym, we'd play. They had all kinds of swings and things. Now they never did have no seesaw. When we went into that gym we had to have our white tennis shoes on and our white socks. That floor was just like a looking glass. We'd go over there and have plays over there. It was just wonderful.

Mama worked three or six months, I can't say. One morning there my daddy told her, "I didn't marry you to work. You got all the work you need at home and your children. It's not a wife's place to work. If a man can't make a living for his wife and children, he ain't no business marrying. Now if you going to work, I'll quit and come home and tend to our children." He says, "I'm not dragging these little young ones out in the cold carrying them to that nursery of a morning. Your place is at home and that's where you're going to be." So Mama go in and worked her notice and come home.

Daddy's health got bad. Back then doctors was good doctors, but they really didn't know then what they do now. He got to the place he just wasn't able to work. He wanted to go back to the mountains so he could die there. So we moved back to the mountains in 1927, the fourteenth of February.

Back on the farm Icy and her older brother Dewey put out a crop, and Icy got a job in a shoe factory several miles away in Elkin, North Carolina.

One Sunday night, my Aunt Leotta, my daddy's baby sister, she stayed all night at our house. She told Mama, she says, "Let Icy go with me down there. I'll take her over to the shoe factory and it will be a treat for her." It tickled me to death. I wasn't but a young one. I wanted to go see it. Mama says, "Well now, we got a big washing to do. If she'll get back in time to help me start that washing, she can go."

I got up next morning and went with Aunt Leotta. She was showing me over the plant, how they cut out shoes and how they sewed them. She sewed, that's what she done. She showed me where they put the bottoms in the heels. She showed me where they smoothed them off and polished them, ready to ship out. That just tickled me to death. We started back up the steps and ran into Fred Knees.

He says, "Who is that little girl you got with you?"

She says, "That's my niece. That's my brother's daughter."

He says, "Does she want a job?"

Before I could say, "No," Aunt Leotta says, "Yes, she wants a job." Well, scared me to death.

I says, "No, I don't want a job neither."

Aunt Leotta says, "Yes, she does, too! Put her to work, Fred."

"All right," he says, "You come along with me, little girl." I was scared for death. I didn't go for no job. I just went to see it. He carried me over there and he told me to stay with Aunt Leotta. She showed me everything about it. Well, I could sew on a paddle sewing machine, but these here was electric. Anyway, I reckon it was electric, too, because you just mash a paddle and the thing would just flap. He put me out by myself. He put me on the leather part, he put me out making the linings. Well, I messed up I don't know how many. That machine would go so fast and I was scared to death, too.

Well, I didn't go home and did Mama throw a fit. She told Dewey, "You get in that car and you go down there after that young one. She's not going to go to work."

Dewey says, "Mama, I can't. She's already at work."

Well, you know, I just enjoyed that after I got the hang of it. It didn't take me over a day to get the hang of the machine. I made five dollars and a half a week for five days and a half. Saturday I went home and Mama just had a fit. My daddy says, "Charity, now just hush. Let that young one work if she wants to. She don't have to work. If she likes it, let her work a while."

Well, I went back. I was really liking my job. Of course, I didn't make nothing, but I thought that I was rich when I got that five dollars and a half. You know, they didn't take nothing out of it. Then they would pay you in a little brown envelope about that long, and it was sealed up and would tell how much was in that envelope. I never opened my envelope. On Saturday Dewey brought my daddy to the doctor down there. While my daddy was in the doctor's office he come up there and get me and Aunt Leotta. We got back home, my daddy had to lay down and rest a little while. I went in there and I says, "Papa, here's my money. Look and see how much I draw." He looked and he says, "I'm tickled for you. It's yours."

I says, "It's yours."

He says, "I don't want it. That's your money."

I says, "Uh-huh. It's yours."

He says, "You take this and do with it whatever you want to do with it."

I says, "No, Papa, I want you to have it."

You know, as long as he live, I give him my money. He go to Elkin, he'd go sometime through the week. He would surprise me when I went home on Saturday. About once a month he'd have me the prettiest outfit you ever seen. He was the best somebody to buy clothes. I know one Easter he bought me a new dress and a new pair of shoes and he got me a hat and he bought me a spring coat. First spring coat I ever remember seeing. Oh, I thought it was the prettiest thing I ever seen.

Well, Fred Knees come and told me one Saturday, "You tell Dewey to come in. I need a hand in the cutting room." I says, "Goody. Goody. Goody. I get to go home every night." So I told Dewey. And Dewey, he went to work. Well, we had the crop planted and it was coming up. We would work. We'd have to work until six o'clock. We'd get home and soon as we eat, we'd take off to the field. He would plow and I'd hoe. We worked that way and raised our crop.

Back then you couldn't go to the store and buy vegetables. You had to raise anything you'd eat through the winter. We raised wheat for flour. Of course, that wasn't no trouble. All you done, you sowed your wheat in the fall. That's all you had to do to it until you threshed it. Then a man come around with a wheat thresher and with a crew of men, and they'd thresh a big field of wheat in a day. We would always raise potatoes. I've often wondered why people can't do that this day and time. Back then we would raise potatoes anywhere from seventy-five to a hundred bushels of Irish potatoes. Then Mama would always can all of our beans and make her jelly and canned all of her fruit. You didn't know what it was to go to the store and buy something because they didn't have it. All you could find in the store would be this green coffee, and even then you had to parch it. You could buy sugar and salt. We had our hogs. We had our chickens. We raised everything we eat, you know. They take the wheat and had it ground up in flour. We'd take our corn and have it ground up for corn bread. We had plenty of milk and butter. What more do you need?

When the crop was laid by, me and Dewey would come and hand-pull fodder, bundles of fodder by the moonlight. By the time we got home then, it was dark. We'd eat supper and we'd take off to the fields. That's the only time my daddy would let me wear a pair of overalls, would be when I was cutting tops or pulling fodder. He'd let me wear a pair of Barney's overalls and tie them around the ankles on account of snakes. We maybe have ten or fifteen acres in corn. We'd pull all that fodder and go back and cut all them tops and tie them. Shuck them, stack them up.

Then we'd go back and pull our corn, and we'd have a corn shucking. Now, that's when you'd have a good time. They'd have a pile of corn bigger than this house. People would come in and help shuck your corn and throw it in the crib. Maybe the next neighbor would have his ready, and we'd all go to his house. That's the way they done until everybody got their corn shucked and put away in the smokehouse. The mothers would always cook dinner, if it was dinnertime. At suppertime another neighbor would cook supper. Then after the corn shucking they'd give us young people a dance. That was a lot of fun.

Then they'd have quilting. People would gather and have quilting at different houses. It would be the same way. They'd cook a big dinner, a big supper. And after that was through, the eating and everything, they'd pull everything back and the young people would have a little square dance. Different ones would make music. My daddy never would let no dancing going on. We'd go to dances at some of the rest of the homes. But we had to be home from that dance by ten thirty, at the latest. No later. If we was later than ten thirty, we didn't get to go no more for a while. All of us boys and girls go together. We all growed up together. We just had a big time. I reckon when you been with somebody like that and then you go into a textile mill, go to working, well, it come natural that you want fellowship with your coworkers. You want to be acquainted with them, to be friends with them.

At school they'd have a supper. They'd call it a box supper. The teenagers, the young ones, they'd fix it. Well, if we was going to have supper tonight at the school, well, you would cook something yourself. And you'd fix you a box, and you'd wrap it real pretty. But you'd fix your box so you knowed it from the others. You didn't put your name on it. They would give that box off. The one that bid the highest, well, you had to eat supper with the boy. That was a lot of fun. We would have ice-cream suppers and we'd have parties. You know, the neighbors there lived a half a mile, maybe a mile apart. Some of them two miles. We'd take a circle, and we'd visit everybody, they'd take a circle until they'd visited everybody. And everybody just had a good time.

In early 1929, Icy's father died and the shoe factory shut down. Like many widows in the Piedmont South, Charity Norman left the farm and took her family to the mills. The Normans first went to Lynchburg, Virginia, where Icy got a job in a cotton mill.

Barney and Dewey didn't get no work, period. I was the only one that was a-working. Then I'd work a week and be off two weeks. You know, back then you didn't draw no unemployment. So the two weeks that the mill stood, Mama told Dewey and Barney, "We can't live here like that. You don't know, the thing may shut down for good. We're going to hunt us a job, hunt you all a job." So we got in my daddy's old T-model. The whole two weeks that the mill stood there, we was on the road hunting jobs. We went everywhere. Back then the Depression was starting. Mills was closing down. So you just couldn't get a job. Every freight train that you seen pass was loaded down with people going from town to town, hoboing.

Mama said, "Being we're this close, let's just go on to Durham [North Carolina] and see Don." That was Mama's oldest boy by her first. So we went down there and spent the night. And Don says, "Mama, while you're this close, don't go home tomorrow." That was Sunday. Says, "Go up to Burlington. Somebody told me that they was hiring help. You might get on up there." And Mama says, "Well, we ain't tried there."

And so we come. Back then, they didn't have no fence. There was a little old bitty mill; it was a little old wooden mill, two rooms, and they had everything in it. They had a few frames of spinning, and they had two slashers, and then they had, I forget how many dobby-headed looms. It wasn't many. And then they had spooling, and they had spinning. It was all in that little two-room building.

And so we drove up, and Dewey and Barney got out. You know, anybody could go in, any time day or night that they wanted to. There was a little old bitty machine shop, it wasn't as big as this porch. I can just see that little old shop now. And they didn't have but two hands a-working in it. And so

Barney asked that man, "Can you tell us how to find Mr. Copland?" And he says, "Yeah, he's right down yonder. You can't miss him, he's down there helping us get that slasher going." They went down there, and he had his sleeves rolled up, and he was greasy as a hog from his elbows on down. And he seen Barney and Dewey, and he just had a fit. He says, "Well, where in the world is your mama and my little girl?" My daddy worked for him there in Schoolfield, and he'd come every Sunday evening and spend the evening with my daddy after he got to the place he couldn't work. He thought the world of my daddy. And Dewey says, "They're out there in the car." And boy, here he come. He grabbed up a piece of old cloth, and here's the way he was coming, just like this, a-wiping it off. He come out there, and he was just tickled to death. And he told Mama, he says, "Well, I promised the last time I seen Mr. Norman — I take it he's gone." And Mama says, "Yes." And he says, "I promised Mr. Norman that if you ever needed any help and I could give you all a job, that I wanted you to come to me. I reckon that's why you all have come, ain't you?" And Mama says, "Yes, we've been everywhere hunting a job." And he says, "Well, you don't have to hunt no farther. You've got a job. We're tearing out the cotton and putting in all rayon."

And he says, "When can you move?" Mama says, "Well, if you'll give Icy a job, we can move any time." So he called up a moving van. And Mama told Barney, "You take Rosetta [Dewey's wife], Mary [Barney's wife], and the baby," — Gilbert, that was Barney's little baby — "and Icy back to Don's, and me and Dewey will go with the transfer, and we'll be back tomorrow evening." We went back, and it just tickled Don to death.

We left Don's and come on back. We had the key to the house. We went on in and took our suitcases in. All at once, Gilbert started screaming and a-crying. We couldn't get him to shut up, and instead of getting sweet milk, Barney got buttermilk. And Gilbert was on the bottle. It was right funny. You laugh at it now, but Lord, it just worried me to death. That young'un screamed. And there was two big old pear trees out there. Well, there we was. We didn't have a bit to eat, no way to cook nothing, and so we sat there. And so Mary says, "I'm going out there and get me one of them pears. I'm about to starve." So we went out there and got us some of them pears and eat them pears. And poor little Gilbert. We'd carry that baby and we would give him water, and we'd try to give him that buttermilk, and that give him the colic. And we had a time. And so there was a big old house right across on the same side, and that woman come over there and says, "What's the matter with that baby?" And Mary says, "He's hungry, and Barney got buttermilk instead of sweet milk, and he's wanting his bottle." She says, "You come home with me. Bring his bottles, and I'll fill his bottles up with milk, and we'll fix that little feller something to eat."

And so we went over there and she says, "Have you all had anything to eat?" I was bashful. I never opened my mouth. And Mary says, "No, we ain't eat nothing since we left Uncle Don's house in Durham." And she says, "Well, we'll fix that. We'll fix you all something to eat." And oh, she was the nicest somebody and a sweet woman, but I was bashful. I was starved to death, but I wouldn't eat but just a bite or two. Oh, Lord have mercy, I could eat a whole cow. And so she fixed six bottles for Gilbert. Gilbert was happy as a coon when he got it, and the little old feller, he took that bottle and he sucked that bottle, and he went to sleep. We fixed him in the car. And it was hot, and Barney run the car up under that pear tree under the shade.

Well, it went on, and poor old Mama and them, they didn't get there, it was nine o'clock that night. Back then you didn't have no electricity; you had to use lamps. We didn't have no light. Mama and the truck and Dewey come in. Gilbert woke screaming again, wanting his bottle. The little feller was just hungry. And Mary stuck one of them bottles in his mouth; we didn't have no way to warm it. Mary says, "I'm not going back over to that lady and ask her to heat that milk for me. He can suck that or do without." And so he took it. Well, we was all getting hungry again. They unloaded the furniture, and we put the beds up and fixed our beds where we'd have something to sleep on. Mama brought some kerosene oil with her. We lit the old oil stove. We rambled around in a box, and we found a ham. We was already eating on the shoulder. Mama wasn't going to let us cut our ham until we eat all of our shoulders up. And that's what we was hunting for. And I just couldn't wait to get a piece of it. I was so hungry. And so Dewey says, "Mama, here's a ham. I can't find that shoulder we was eating on." Mama says, "I don't care. Cut it, I'm getting weak." So he got the lamp lit, and he cut. He just went right down to the heart of that ham, and he sliced it. And Mama and Mary and Rosetta all was in there, and we had on two frying pans full. We fried a platter that long and that high of that ham. And Mama went and fried some eggs. We had a big old pan. It was that wide and that square—it just fit in the bakery of the stove—she made that thing full of biscuits. Made some hot coffee. We set down there, and we ate every bite of that platter of ham. She made a big bowl of milk gravy. And boy, was that good. That was the best stuff. And we sat there and we ate. There was Rosetta and there was Dewey and there was Barney and there was Mary and there was me and there was Mama and there was Florence. That was seven of us, and it didn't take long for that platter of ham to get gone. And it didn't take long for that bowl of cream gravy to get gone. We ate that big old square pan of biscuits. And I have never in my life eaten no ham that I thought was as good.

Me and Barney and Dewey went to work Monday morning. That was the twentieth day of September, 1929. I was so green, I didn't ask Mr. Copland would I make any money. And come to find out, anybody that didn't know nothing had to go in and learn the job, and if you learnt the job, and they was satisfied with you, they'd give you a job. Now in this day and time, people would laugh at you if you said, "Well, I'll give you a job if you want to learn it. After you got learnt I'll pay you." They wouldn't do it. No way could you get nobody to do that this day and time. Then, that was the only way you got a job with the Burlington Mill, if you didn't already know how to do. If you went in there to learn, you learnt for nothing. And I really learnt for nothing.

They carried me over there to Dewey McBride. He was weighting up yarn. Mr. Copland told Dewey, "I want you to fix a place for this little girl; she's going to learn to wind. Give her two spools of thread and show her how to tie the weaver's knot." I sat over on that old box all day long tying old weaver's knots. I thought, I'll never make it. Jim Copland come by and Old Man Smith [M. B. Smith was president of the Burlington Mill], they come by and they sat down there. Jim says, "How's my little girl doing?" I says, "Mr. Copland, I ain't doing. I can't tie that knot." And he sat there and watched me. The more they watched me, the scareder I got.

When I started home, Dewey McBride give me two spools of thread with just a little bit of rayon on it. Says, "You take this home, and you practice this tonight." And I said, "Well, I'll take it, but I'll never tie that knot. Why can't you tie a knot like this?" He says, "You can't do that, Icy. It's got to be a weaver's knot. It can't be no chickenhead knot." Well, I went home and I set down there and I started after supper. I told Mama, "Mama, I've had to do this all day long. I can't tie it." Well, Mama showed me how to tie it. She worked in a woolen mill after her first husband died. She could just shut her eyes and tie them just as fast. You know, you're supposed to tie a weaver's knot on that middle finger and the thumb, and hold it with this finger. I couldn't do that.

Next day, on the old box I sat. Well, I sat there. The more I studied about that thing, the more I hated that. Oh, I hated that mill. Ooh, how I hated it! And I thought, "Well, if this is all they got for me to do, I don't want it." I went home and I was crying. Mama says, "What are you crying about?" I says, "Because I can't tie that old knot." And she says, "I've told you how to tie it, and I've showed you how to tie it. That's the only way you can tie a weaver's knot."

I set down there. She said, "I want you to hush up that crying." I says, "Mama, I wisht I was back in Lynchburg. I hate it up there." So she says, "Sometimes I think we might have made a mistake. But things are going to work out. It's got to get better." And Mama was a good Christian woman, and she says, "You just forget about it. I have prayed about it, and I've left it in the Lord's hands. And the Lord ain't going to make no mistakes, and the Lord is going to look after us. We might not have the best; we're not promised nothing but bread and water. You read the Bible, it says the Lord promised us bread and water. And I'm looking to Him. I don't have no doubts."

I couldn't figure it out, and I just cried and I just cried. Well, I went ahead, and you know, one day there on that box, I was doing my best to do like the bossman told me, and that thing would slide out with me every time. So all at once something come to me just like it spoke: tie it on your forefinger. And I looked down at that forefinger, and I fixed that thread just like I fixed it on you. Instead of taking this finger and holding that down like that, I took *this* finger and held it down. And you know one thing? I'd tie them things as fast as you could wink an eye. And there come Jim Copland and Old Man Smith. And I thought, "Lord, I better not let them see me do that." Well, I went back. Oh, Lordy. I hated it; I hated it so bad. Jim Copland says, "Well, how's my little girl doing? You can tie that knot now, can't you?" I says, "If you'll let me tie it the way I want to tie it, I can tie it." He looked at me, and he said, "What do you mean? It has got to be absolutely a weaver's knot." And I says, "Well, let me show you how. . . . Something told me to tie it like this." He looked at me so funny. He says, "Something told you!" I said, "Yes. Something told me to tie it on my forefinger." He said, "Well, let me see what you're talking about." I'd put that thing down there and I'd just tie them and I'd just tie them, and he looked at that knot, and he said, "Do it slow." I got so I could do it just as fast. And I did.

Icy mastered the weaver's knot, but there were more tasks ahead. She was still learning, and learning for nothing.

I was getting paid for what little I done. That wasn't much. I think I made a quarter one day and one day I made fifteen cents. Anyway, I didn't draw but a dollar. And I just cried. I told Mama, I says, "I wish I was back in Lynchburg. I was making two dollars a day. I ain't making nothing here. I won't ever make a winder." All of them girls, they was on piecework, they'd make anywhere from twelve, fourteen, fifteen dollars a week. I knowed I never could. So I'd just cry about it. And poor Mr. Copland would come and sit and talk to me. Well, every one of them was so nice to me. They didn't talk hateful to me. If they had, I'd a-went running out of that mill.

One day, Mr. Love, he come by and he sit down. He says, "Well, little girl, how you doing?" When he first sit down, I didn't know who he was. I didn't know he owned that mill. Him and his daddy, you know. He was good looking. He was young, then. He says, "You look like you been crying." I sat down and I says, "You know, I hate this place." And I started crying. He put his arm around my neck. He says, "Don't cry. We all have to go through this." I says, "Yeah. I got a mama and a little sister to take care of. I ain't making nothing." He says, "Them's the ones that make the best hands. Honey, don't cry. You'll catch on to it." Oh, all the rest of them was just working up a storm and making money and me doing nothing.

Finally I go to the place I'd keep my side up pretty good. The first big check—it wasn't a check, it was money in a little envelope—I drawed five dollars. I thought, well, that's better than drawing a dollar. I went home, but I was still crying. Because I knowed what was on me; there was Mama and Florence and myself. I was so disheartened.

Mama says, "If you going to work there, the Lord's going to help you. He's going to be with you. I have prayed that the Lord's going to help you." I says, "I ain't getting no help now." Back then I was a sinner, you know. My poor mama, she was a good Christian woman, her and my daddy both. So I kept on working. First thing you know, they had a board. They'd put each day—where your name was—how many pounds you run, a production sheet, and that's what they called it. Well, I never would look at mine because mine was so pitiful. Everybody else, they was it. And I felt I was nothing. I think that was one reason I cried so, because I couldn't compete with them. So one day it seemed just like something spoke to me: "You can do it. Get in there and do it." Just as plain. I thought, "Well, there's all of them girls working, making good money. If they can do it, I can, too!" I don't know what it was, but it just seemed like something just spoke: "You can do it. Get in there and do it!" I looked around, and I didn't see nobody. Well, that got me. I thought, "Well, maybe I can do it." I went to work, and I worked, oh brother, I worked just fight and far. I got so I could put the yarn on real good. It would go just a-flying. First thing you know, I run two packs of yarn that day. I was so tickled because I hadn't been running sometimes a half a pack a day. I run two packs. Dewey McBride says, "You getting a little better, ain't you?" Next day I worked just as hard as I could work. Next day I run my two packs. I went down to the scales and I said, "Dewey, I want another pack of yarn."

He says, "WHAT?" just like that.

I says, "I want another pack of yarn."

He says, "What have you done with the other one, put it in the waste can?"

I says, "No, I run every skein of it." He give me another pack and I run half of it. That was two packs and a half. Well, I was a little bit better in another two days. I kept on going, but I never would go on over and look at that production sheet.

Here come Mr. Love and his daddy. They sit down there and got to talking. Spence says, "Come on over here. I want my daddy to talk to you." I drawed up. I knowed he owned the mill, him and Spence together. I'd been talking to Spence, but I didn't know that was his name. I just talked plain to him. Then I find out him and his daddy owned that mill. You could have pushed me over with a feather when I found it out. I looked up at him and I says, "Are you all Mr. Loves? Lord, mercy, here I've been talking to your boy, telling him all my troubles and a-crying. Telling him how bad I hated my job. And he owned the mill. I apologize. But I do hate it."

He says, "Little girl, you're doing fine. Mr. Copland is real proud of you."

I says, "Mr. Copland's been knowing me ever since I was a baby." Him and his daddy sat there and talked with me. Every time they'd come through the mill—we'd have boxes at the back of us to put our yarn in—they'd sit down there. They'd say, "Come here, I want to talk to you a little bit." If they hadn't encouraged me like they did, and Mr. Copland, I wouldn't have stayed in that mill. I hated it.

On payday, them men, especially on second shift, and a lot of them on daytime, they'd slip out, they'd bring the stuff in there and get started drinking and they wouldn't know one end for the other. I never seen a woman up there drink, but the men would. I don't know what it was they drunk or nothing about it. They would have something they'd get drunk on. They'd get so drunk they'd pass out. Them machines running. It was a lot of waste.

After they put that fence around there that stopped the drinking. They couldn't run out and get it all during the night and day. Jim Copland, he would fire them if he seen any of them drinking. I don't see how the poor fellow stayed awake. He'd come through there of a night every two hours. Now, if he liked you, he liked you. That's the kind of man he was. He was a regular old tyrant if you made him mad. And Old Man Smith, now he was a fair old scratch. I've seen him pick his hat off. He'd had great big old chewing tobacco that big, him and Old Man Spivey, too. I've seen them get mad. They'd pull their old hat off, throw it down and spit in it and jump on that hat and stomp it. Yeah, Mr. Copland, he was a bird if he was mad. And boy, he was strict. But he never did say one harm word, what I mean, like he was mad at me or anything.

After I got to where I got up to drawing ten dollars a week I was well satisfied. I took an interest in my job. And I'd study to see which I thought would be best for the company. I tried to keep my job up. I stayed with them. A lot of them would try to get me to quit when the work was slack and go other places. I wouldn't do it. I stayed right on with them. I know work was getting so bad, Spence Love come down there and he look like he was so down and out. I said, "Mr. Love, you look like you're mighty low this morning."

He says, "I am. I'm just on rock bottom. I don't know which way to do for the best. I'm going to have to close the place down."

I says, "Well, there's always a brighter day a-coming. My mama told me that when I come here and I told you how bad I hated this place. But I really love to work here now. It will be a brighter day."

He says, "You really think so?"

I says, "Yes. It will be a brighter day. I'll stick with you through thick and thin. If you sink, I'll go down with you." I laughed and he got to laughing.

He says, "You just beat all I've ever seen."

Then it wasn't too long until that strike, they walked out. I think they was out a week or two weeks. Some of them signed the union and some of them didn't. I never did sign it. I don't know. I just heard so much about the union, I thought, "I don't know whether it would pay or not." I read the paper about people being out for months and months on strike. I just didn't believe in it. If you was working and was making money all that time you was out on strike, you would come out in the end a whole lot better than you would be laying out, maybe three and four months at a time. I'd tell them I wasn't interested in it, and they'd go on and leave me alone. I didn't know whether it was good or bad, so I didn't mess with it. Something I don't know nothing about, I don't like to mess with. So I never did sign it.

One thing I want to tell you about. Wilma Clemmons, she was running the front of the warp mill. Well, on that warp mill it didn't have no stop motion. If the end broke down, she had to stop it all. I was creeling up there in the corner of the mill. Wilma was over there. All at once I hear someone scream out. I turned to Mary Dell and said, "What was that?"

She says, "It's somebody pranking."

About that time I heard them scream again. I looked and I said, "Lord have mercy, something's happened to Wilma." I flew under the end and I flew to her. That roller was taking her whole arm up. She had one of them great old big thick wedding bands, real thick. She had that on. That mashed that wedding band as flat as a platter, and it tore every speck of the meat off of this hand. She didn't have no meat on there. I run to her. I didn't know how to stop it all, not that one. Had it been one of the others I could have stopped it.

I screamed to Buster, "Buster, run here quick and stop this mill." For I knowed it was going to take her whole arm. He run over there and he stopped it. About that time the boss men come. They went running to the machine shop and they got some orange poles that was bent flat on one end. They had two of them things on the front prying that roller and two at the back, with men, two on each one of them, doing their best to pry that roller up. And there she stood.

Shirley, she come running. "Shirley," I says, "Wilma is going to pass out. Run and get her some ammonia." She run and got some ammonia. By the time she got back and give her that ammonia, they got that roller up enough that they could slide her hand up. It wasn't nothing but bones there. Oh Lord, it made me so sick. They grabbed her, called the ambulance, and rushed her to the hospital. You know, today she can't use that hand. She ain't got no feeling. You can feel of that hand and it's like a chunk of ice. They kept her over there a long time, I forget how many weeks. Then they sent her to Chapel Hill. She can't hold a broom to sweep her floor. When she come back to work, they put her out there in the cloth room, something that she can pull the cloth with one hand. Since then they went around and put them stop guards on all the machines.

Oh, yes, it's much safer. I know I was creeling, helping them change the high speeds. They had a stool just like that but it was this high. Them high speeds is higher than this house. I couldn't reach the top. Lunchtime, Lena got down and says, "Icy, let's wash our hands. It's time to eat." I said, "Lena, I didn't know it was that late. Time sure did fly." We had all the yarn took out of the mill. The mill was empty with them spindles sticking out. I went to come down off of that high stool. My foot slid on the second step and I just went right down between the middle of that mill. It hurt this arm. By the time I got up my arm was as black as a nigger. It hurt me so bad. I didn't

Icy Norman, with a photograph of her mother, 1982.

know whether I broke a bone or not. Lena turned around and looked and I was crying and holding my arm. Instead of going to the bathroom to wash, I went on up there to the first-aid room. Pat was working on somebody's eyes. She turned around to me and says, "Icy, what in the world happened?"

I says, "I fell off that stool. I started down that high stool and I missed the second step and I fell down between the warp mill." Well, she run over there and she checked it. She says, "There ain't no bones broke." She went to putting ice on it.

They was all working and I still hadn't eaten no dinner. She kept that ice on me there about two hours. Then she rubbed some kind of medicine on it and she wrapped my whole arm in that wide bandage that you wrap your leg or something in. It hurt me so bad. Milton, the warping boss, says, "Icy, you can go home if you want to."

I says, "No, I'll stay and do what I could." I didn't lose no time.

I stayed with the Burlington Mill. I did everything they ever asked me to do. I always got along with every boss man. I seen overseers, bosses, and second hands go and come. I always got along with every one of them. I never did have one say a short word to me because I always went and done what they would tell me to do. I do my work as near right as I know how. And so I swung with them for forty-seven years.

The first time they ever give a supper, they give a five-year pin. They give it up here at the old Army hall. I think they tore that building down. Well, Spence and his daddy and his mama and his wife, a lot of them big shots you know, was there. They made a talk. They had tables set and had your name at your place. I wound up with Mack Freeman sitting beside me. They made the talk, how proud they were that they could fix a supper for the ones that had been with them five years. They had a little present for us and a little pin, a five-year pin. They had a wonderful supper. You know, that Mack Freeman was so drunk, he layed on the table right beside me. That about killed me. He never heard one word they said. I said to—I believe Lottie Adams was sitting next to me on the other side—I said, "Lottie, how come you couldn't have got beside of him?" I says, "Of all things, I had to sit by that thing."

Icy retired in 1976, having worked longer for Burlington Industries than any other employee—forty-seven years. Retirement at sixty-five was mandatory, and she was forced to stop working just months before fulfilling the terms of a profit-sharing plan. She begged the company to let her work out the term, and her boss-men and the mill superintendent supported her request. But corporate policy was immutable.

When I retired, they fixed a dinner. On Wednesday, Milton come told me, "Icy, they're going to take you to Greensboro tomorrow." [Greensboro, North Carolina, is the site of Burlington Industries' southern headquarters.] I went up there to that main office. They carried me all over that thing. I met everybody. Each floor had different color carpet, different design, different furniture. I went clean to the top. You know what they had in the top? They had the prettiest white rug. It was a beautiful thing. Beautiful furniture. Everything was white.

I says, "They went all the way out with this, didn't they?" This girl that took us a tour, she says, "Do you know what this room is, Icy?"

I says, "No, but it is something." That was the prettiest place I ever seen.

She says, "This is where the big shots come. This is where they have their meetings when the gather from New York."

I says, "What?"

She says, "You going to meet all of them."

I says, "No, I ain't neither. I'm going home."

Personnel man laughed, and said, "You won't go home until I take you home." First thing you know, all them big shots from New York, twenty-five of them. There was poor little me, scrooched up with all them men. They got to talking to me, asking questions. They asked me how long I'd been with the company. Some of them says, "That's amazing. She's the oldest hand the Burlington Mill has got anywhere." I'd been the company longer, that's what I mean. They talked, they took pictures. Well, they asked me everything in the book.

After they got to talking they said they already knowed me from the way Spence Love talked [J. Spencer Love had died in 1962]. "You know one thing, you are the one hand that Spence Love said went through thick and thin with them. You have made the Burlington Industries. Your part and your faithfulness to the Burlington Industries, you have got a part in all the mills that the Burlington Mills owns."

I says, "I feel like that I'm a part of it. I wasn't nothing but a young one there and I growed up with them." And they laughed.

I begged them to let me work on but they wouldn't. They knowed it was in the making. They could have let me work on until January. Then I could have got that big profit sharing they all get now. I feel like I was part in making the Burlington Industries, because I come there and stayed with them, I went with them through thick and thin. In other words, I give the best part of my life to the Burlington Industries. It kind of hurt me to think that as long as I stayed there and as faithful as I worked and all, that I didn't get none of that profit.

I said I didn't have no family in Burlington. In the other sense of the word, I've got a big family, because I try to fellowship with the other fellow. If they need something, I try to help them. If I can do them a favor, I'm there to do it. I think that there is a lot of joy to me. Of course, some people may think that ain't no joy in doing that. But it is. You just come right down to it, you get more joy out of doing some little something than anything in the world.

You know, money can't buy happiness. Money can't buy joy. That's why I said I enjoyed working on my job. I got a pleasure out of it, and it made me happy to do my job. When I come out of that mill, I know that I done the very best I could. Somewhere along the way I felt a peaceable mind. It's wonderful to feel that way.

We had good years, we had bad years. I reckon that goes with life. Everybody seemed to get along and everybody seemed like they enjoyed working with one another. Just like I said, everybody up there in the room I worked in felt like just one family. We just laugh and joke. We'd play anything. We didn't think nothing about what we said to one another because nobody paid no mind. We'd all work together and tried to pull together. I think that's the main thing on the job, especially where it's a group of people. If they all work together.

When I left the Burlington Mill, I left my family. They all felt like my brothers and sisters. I worked with some of them so long. I was the oldest one in the Pioneer Plant, the oldest hand they had. When those others come along, I got acquainted with them, I growed to love them. And I growed to fellowship with them. We'd all laugh and have fun together. It was just like leaving one of my family. I couldn't help but cry. I said all the time I wasn't going to cry. When I went out and started home, I did cry, but they didn't notice.

NOTES

1. Interview tapes and transcripts from the Southern Oral History program's industrialization project are deposited in the Southern Historical Collection at the Louis Round Wilson Library at the University of North Carolina, Chapel Hill. The interview with Icy Norman was conducted by Mary Murphy on April 6 and April 30, 1979, at Norman's home in Burlington, North Carolina.

2. Further discussion of these issues is found in *"Like A Family": The Making of a Southern Cotton Mill World* (Chapel Hill: University of North Carolina Press, 1987). The book is based on the interviews completed by the industrialization project staff, and is a collaborative effort by Christopher Daly, Jacquelyn Dowd Hall, Lu Ann Jones, Robert Korstad, James Leloudis, and Mary Murphy.

Frontiers 9:3 (1987): 83–90.

Looking Inward, Looking Backward

Reminiscence and the Life Review

HARRIET WRYE AND JACQUELINE CHURILLA

The process of looking inward and looking backward over time at the life one has lived is a natural and healthful integrative process of aging. Life review and oral reminiscence are sources of heroic myth and legend. In the *Odyssey*, Demodocus, old and blind like Homer himself, the "sacred minstrel / To whom the gods have given power / To gladden us with song," sang or chanted each evening in the great hall before young and old, servant and master, the deeds of those who had lived before.[1] The epic song served as a kind of communal ritual to pass on the dreams and sorrows of a culture from one generation to the next.

But, in addition to serving as a mode of transmission of culture, of providing historical continuity, life review also serves important functions for the individual reviewer. As Florida Scott-Maxwell has said:

A notebook might be the very thing for all the old who wave away crossword puzzles, painting, petit point, and knitting. It is more restful than conversation and for me, it has become a companion, more a confessional. It cannot shrive me, but knowing my self better comes near to that.[2]

Life review and reminiscence have double significance: They are valuable to the individual older person who reminisces, as well as to the immediate listener(s), readers, and the broader culture.

Reminiscence or life review may take a number of forms, formal and informal, alone or in the presence of others, recorded or unrecorded, silent and internal, oral or written. It may range from the relatively random and haphazard flashes of unbidden memory to a structured process. It is experienced to some degree by all people throughout their lives, beginning in childhood, when one first develops a repertoire of memories to look back upon. Reminiscence, like dreaming, may be said to focus on issues of symbolic and emotional significance for the individual: unresolved conflicts, satisfactory and pleasurable accomplishments, guilt, attachments, and losses. There are also sensory memories of particular meaning—the smell of a dusty road after a rain, the sound of a familiar car in the driveway, the sight of grandmother's skin—wrinkled, freckled, slightly furry and soft, or the touch of one's bare feet on the grass. Oral histories collected on tape by researchers may be categorized as the more formal and structured life reviews of individuals whose lives are deemed to have some particular interest to historians, anthropologists, and others.

LIFE REVIEW AS A NORMAL DEVELOPMENTAL PROCESS

Although the life review process usually increases with age, and with the awareness of approaching death, its function throughout the life cycle is integrative and adaptive, and it is often naturally stimulated by such social events as anniversaries, reunions, retirement dinners, "rites of passage," year-end events, and family holidays. It is often jogged by major life transitions such as moves, job changes, divorces, children's graduations, and the like. In one study of 357 respondents, 67 percent reported that they reminisced silently about their lives often or occasionally, recalling people, events, thoughts, and feelings. Seventy-nine percent said they reminisced when they were together with spouse, friends, relatives, and associates. A correlation between reminiscence and good morale suggests that life review serves a positive adaptive function in the aging process.[3]

Paul Rhudick and Arthur McMahon reached a similar conclusion after they interviewed a rather remarkable group of veterans of the Spanish-American War. Their average age was eighty-one, already fourteen years beyond the current life expectancy. They all lived outside of institutions and were being studied to determine why they appeared to have aged so successfully. Immediately noting that the veterans seemed preoccupied with the past and frequently reminisced, Rhudick and McMahon wondered if the increase of reminiscing in these men signified a coping behavior, and if so, how it facilitated adaptation.

Contrary to popular mythology, reminiscence in this group was not correlated with a decline of intellectual functioning (as measured on the Wechsler-Bellevue Intelligence Test). Further, a negative correlation was found between depression and the degree and frequency of reminiscence.

In other words, the depressed subjects showed a tendency to reminisce *less* than the nondepressed subjects. Finally, the depressed subjects survived for a shorter period of time than the nondepressed subjects.[4]

Erik Erikson's model of the eight stages of man posits that the developmental task of the last stage of life before death is to resolve a struggle between "Ego Integrity [and] Despair." Ego integrity involves the acceptance of one's own life cycle, a feeling of some world order and spiritual sense, and an emotional integration that allows acceptance of both leadership and secondary roles. In contrast, a lack of ego integrity is revealed by a great fear of death and a despair that the time is too short to attempt to start another life or try alternative roads to ego integrity.[5]

Although resignation, despair, and fear of death are always possible outcomes of the life-review process, Robert Butler and Myrna Lewis remind us that until the moment of death, all the significant emotional options remain available—love, hate, forgiveness, reconciliation, self-assertion, and self-esteem.[6] Most people do have the capacity to reconcile their own lives, confront old guilt feelings and bitterness, and see their lives as meaningful and deserving of acceptance, especially if they are supported and accepted by others.

The life-review process functions to accomplish this developmental task in a number of ways. Simply summing up one's life can enhance pride and self-esteem; elderly people who are not active in the present often gain pleasure in recalling what they have accomplished in the past. The life review may serve to restore a sense of ethnic identity, since individuals sometimes lose sight of their cultural and ethnic heritage in the press of daily life. Reminiscence can reweave these lost threads of the past. The review process can also function as a gift to society, carrying with it the gratification and sheer pleasure of being a storyteller to a younger audience who wants to listen. Such a review can provide an opportunity for people who have a particularly strong need to justify their lives. For some the use of fantasy about the glories of the past can have positive adaptive elements; like dreaming, fantasy can serve to ease the conflicts of waking life.

Most important, reminiscence meets another major need of the aged, given the fact that old age is a time beset by losses of all kinds—loss of spouse, friends, roles, jobs, physical capabilities, income, and the approaching loss of one's own life, as well. In "Mourning and Melancholia" Sigmund Freud describes mourning as the working through of personal loss. It involves a time-limited and decreasing preoccupation with the past as it is associated with the lost love object or role. Unlike melancholia, mourning is an adaptive and healthy process of relinquishing the lost object, role, or capacity, rather than a loss of personal self-esteem.[7] Reminiscing can assist in the working through of this adaptive process. The finding that depressed subjects both reminisced less and died sooner is an example of a melancholic response to loss.[8]

Closely related to this mourning function is the role reminiscing plays in meeting the narcissistic needs of the elderly. With the loss of significant objects and roles, the individual tends to turn inward. Reminiscing thus provides the kind of self-gratification that was formerly experienced through relations with other people, places, and things.[9]

Life review thus aids normal development in old age. Though it may be facilitated and encouraged by others, it usually occurs spontaneously, fairly frequently, and may take many different forms including silent musing, mirror gazing, looking at old photographs or letters, attending reunions, and visiting with old friends and family members. Many people keep diaries or journals as a form of life review. Usually these remain private, although occasionally, individuals are persuaded to publish their journals, and we are able to see the value of the life-review process at work. Anaïs Nin described her diary as

my kief, hasish, and opium pipe. This is my drug and my vice. Instead of writing a novel, I lie back with this book and pen, and dream and indulge in refractions and defractions. . . . I just relive my life in the dream. The dream is my only life . . . I see the echoes and reverberations, the transfigurations which alone keep wonder pure. Otherwise all magic is lost. Otherwise life shows its deformities and the homeliness becomes rust. . . . All matter must be fused this way through the lens of my vice or the rust of living would slow down my rhythm to a sob . . . I only regret that everybody wants to deprive me of the journal, which is the only steadfast friend I have, the only one that makes my life bearable, because my happiness with human beings is so precarious, my confiding moods so rare, and the least sign of noninterest is enough to silence me. In the journal I am at ease.[10]

Anaïs Nin's diary is remarkable for the depth of its introspection and the poignancy of its sensory imagery. Frequently artists and writers keep their own journals; it is possible that the kind of person who would be inclined to create a personal journal without prompting might also tend to have a more active inner life. Robert Havighurst and Richard Glasser tested the hypothesis that persons who have a more vivid and inner-directed life would reminisce more frequently and with more mental imagery, and found a remarkably high correlation.

Some journals are inner voyages, as is the case in Anaïs Nin's *Diaries*. Others, such as Alex Haley's *Roots*, are voyages backward to establish identity. And still others, like psychologist Joanna Field's journal, are self-conscious attempts at self-analysis and personal introspection.

Sometimes the meaning of an experience would only begin to dawn on me years afterward, and even then I often had to go over the same ground again and again, with intervals of years between. In fact, I came to the conclusion that the growth of understanding follows an ascending spiral rather than a straight line.[11]

Florida Scott-Maxwell, born in 1883, was a writer and suffragist who at fifty began training under Carl Jung for a career as an analytical psychologist. At eighty-two she began a private notebook in which she recorded her feelings about being old and at variance with her times. Her diary is a treasure for those interested in the subjective life experience of the aged, for she is an articulate, witty, and profoundly introspective writer.

I do not know what I believe about life after death; if it exists then I burn with interest, if not — well, I am tired. . . . If there are more lives to be lived, I believe . . . I should experience what I have made others experience. It belongs to me and I should learn from it.

. . . the most important thing in my life was the rich experience of the unconscious. This was a gift life gave me and I only had the sense to honor and serve it. . . . It taught me that we are fed by great forces, and I know that I am in the hands of what seemed immortal. It hardly matters whether I am mortal or not since I have experienced the mortal.

. . . At my age I care to my roots about the quality of woman, and I care because I know how important her quality is. . . . One can improve one's character to the very end, and no one is too young in these days to put the old right.

. . . My kitchen linoleum is so black and shiny that I waltz while I wait for the kettle to boil. This pleasure is for the old who live alone. The others must vanish into their expected role.[12]

Throughout her diary we find expressions of a remarkable and adaptive old woman — a woman whose journal implicitly reflects her struggle to achieve ego integrity, as opposed to despair. Unafraid of death, fully immersed in the richness of her own inner life, concerned still about the women's movement, and active as a writer, Florida Scott-Maxwell also personifies the qualities of successful aging (reported as findings in the Kansas City Study of Adult Life), namely, activity modulated by adaptation and disengagement.[13] For example, Scott-Maxwell's description of her delight in waltzing alone offers a striking image of each of these three qualities of successful aging. That this is expressed in her journal is a testament to the integrative value of the journal process.

LIFE REVIEW AS A THERAPEUTIC TOOL WITH THE AGED

When aging is not progressing smoothly and adaptively, life review can be encouraged by a trained clinician and can be highly therapeutic. Frequently life review is the central core of psychotherapy. The process of reviewing one's life in the supportive company of a therapist enables one to re-examine unresolved conflicts from a new perspective. According to Butler and Lewis: "In individual psychotherapy, the life review obviously is not a process initiated by the therapist. Rather the therapist taps into the already ongoing self-analysis and participates in it with the older person."[14]

Most of the work on life review as a therapeutic tool focuses on either the use of reminiscence as a diagnostic indictor or the importance of helping the client make constructive use of reminiscence. Since a tendency to reminisce seems to be related to good mental health in aging, its absence may be a clue that something is amiss. Conversely, an excessive amount of reminiscing may be due to a lack of sources of gratification in the aged person's current environment. The content of reminiscences provides important information about the client's functioning in a variety of areas—self-concept, quality of interpersonal relationships, and adaptability. The kinds of experiences a person either omits or emphasizes in reviewing his or her life are a clue to important areas of conflict.

The elderly—from feelings of inadequacy, a sense of the disapprobation of the young, or awareness of the stereotype of the old who live only in the past—are sometimes reluctant to engage in the process. Therapists working with the elderly may need to help free their clients and significant people around them from these inhibitions. A major therapeutic benefit is often derived from simply re-educating the client and those close to him or her as to the acceptability and value of reminiscing. The therapist can assist the client in his or her struggle to form a positive identity as an elderly person, to accept shortcomings, and to derive a sense of meaning from his or her life. For example, a woman who previously had seen herself as an unattractive, wrinkled, and useless old person saw that despite physical changes, she was the same person who also had been cheerful, productive, and important. The therapist also can foster self-esteem in clients by encouraging them to share their reminiscences with those who would be most likely to enjoy them, such as children.

But life review is not a therapeutic panacea. Every person who engages in life review will experience some negative feelings, and it is the integration of both positive and negative experiences that is therapeutic. Some, however, will feel that their lives were useless and bad, and will regret major decisions that they have made in their lives. The life review may reveal a clear pattern of character disorder and pathology that requires longer and more intensive therapy sessions. Considerable clinical skill and discretion is required in working with those elderly persons who are deeply depressed or show evidence of other serious disturbance, and anyone who engages in life review with an older person must be sensitive to the possible dangers inherent in the process. Those who are inexperienced should engage in the process only when they have access to good clinical supervision. More severe affective and behavioral consequences such as panic, intense guilt, severe depression, or obsessional ruminations seem more likely to occur, however, only when the life review proceeds in isolation, and with those older people who have suffered disruptive, unresolved losses, failures, and discontinuities (including such psychosocial disruptions as forced retirement).

Usually aged persons view their lives negatively when they believe they have failed to achieve certain goals. In the context of supportive therapy, life review usually enables them to realize how far they have come given the limitations of their background (e.g., lack of money, education, good role models) and they develop a new perspective. In this context, it is helpful to encourage the elderly to compare themselves with their cohorts, people who started with many of the same cultural restrictions and limitations that they did, rather than with those much younger, who tend to be more sophisticated and educated as a result of overall societal advances.

The therapeutic use of reminiscing has thus far been primarily offered as an adjunct to intensive therapy. It also can be used effectively in short-term and group therapy. Groups are especially helpful in decreasing the sense of isolation and uselessness felt by many elderly people. As one group member said, "My life is so 'daily.' I love to share the adventures of others."[15] Groups provide the opportunity for the old to learn how and when to use their life experiences to serve as significant models for others. In a mixed age group, the presence of older people carries with it the sense of life's flow from birth through old age.

Short-term individual therapy involves anywhere from four to fifteen sessions, during which the client relates his or her life story. Afterward, the therapist can help to integrate a former lifestyle and personality with the present situation, understand the meaning of one's life, and work through conflictual areas uncovered by the life review.

In order to explore the ramifications of life-review therapy with normal elderly persons, Jacqueline Churilla worked with an eighty-seven-year-old woman in life-review therapy for five one-and-one-half-hour sessions. With the exception of a few questions aimed at clarification, the client was allowed to tell her story uninterrupted. She had finished by the end of the third session, so during the fourth session, she was asked to tell about the happiest moments or experiences of her life, important people and events, her spare time activities, and the books, magazines, movies, television programs, and art that had been most influential in shaping her life. These broad, open-ended queries were intended to generate further reminiscence and thus help the client focus on the positive aspects of her life, as well as become aware of the things that had been most meaningful to her.

There were two aspects of her life that she recounted with obvious enjoyment. One was her activity in the Communist Party during the Depression. The other was the time she had hitchhiked across the country from New York to California. She realized with surprise that, because of the interesting conversations she had had on this trip, it had been one of the most significant experiences of her life. In both cases, the interviewer got the impression that this was the first time in her life that she had realized how much she had enjoyed these experiences.

Although it is difficult to assess objectively the effectiveness of the five therapy sessions, a "Degree of Life Satisfaction" questionnaire, which the client had completed both before and after therapy, indicated that afterwards she viewed some aspects of her life more positively and others more negatively. But the life review did seem to provide her with the opportunity to reconcile and accept some of her negative feelings. Whereas when she was first approached to participate in the life-review process, she said immediately, "I feel that my whole life has been a failure," during the interviews she was able to recognize an aspect of her personality that gave her considerable pride. Several times during the sessions she said, "I was really gutsy, wasn't I?" she also took one statement from the questionnaire and incorporated it into her own thinking several times throughout the sessions, "I feel that I've done the best I could with what I've had to work with."

LIFE HISTORY AS A VEHICLE FOR TRAINING AND RESEARCH IN GERONTOLOGY

Life review clearly offers personal and professional benefits to the clinician or social worker who takes the geriatric patient through the process. It can also lead the researcher to develop important insights for further research. Inexperienced therapists often fear that engaging an elderly person in life review may be depressing. This fear probably stems from the younger therapist's own unresolved fears of aging and death. Recognition of these conflicts about aging and dying is an essential step in the personal growth of the future clinician: Experience in taking life histories with the elderly makes the issues of aging more real than academic. Unfortunately, because our society typically isolates the elderly, therapists have had little daily contact with the aged. Direct clinical experience with children is a common part of most clinical training programs because it is recognized that adult conflicts and pathologies usually originate in childhood. Rarely, however, is the value of clinical study of the "denouement" of these conflicts at the end of the life cycle appreciated.

In addition to clinical training, the life-review process provides a highly accessible and pragmatically feasible data source that can be used to generate hypotheses and research designs. One interested, trained interviewer working alone with a tape recorder and/or notebook can gather a set of life histories from a small sample of people selected according to the interests of the researcher. Harriet Wrye recently completed a research study that generated a hypothesis on the beliefs of women with breast cancer.[16] With a sample of sixteen women, Wrye conducted journal-writing workshops in which the women wrote their life histories. Using the journals as data, Wrye looked for the most specific statements that were common in all the journals, refining and focusing the statements until a hypothesis was reached.[17]

The paucity of research on the particular strengths and needs of women in their old age underscores the need for researchable hypotheses, and the value they would have. Tish Sommers argues for sweeping changes in the Social Security system, and laws concerning the rights of older women. She builds a strong case portraying the compounded inequities of sexism on women as they age. She notes that little attention has been given to the unique plight of elderly women by gerontological research, the feminist movement, or the general public.[18]

Women live longer than men and generally marry men older than themselves; because of increasing life spans, women can thus anticipate that they will spend a long period of time both old and unmarried. The Women's Movement has ignored the needs of older women, and it is an especially disturbing exclusion, since the older women who have been ignored include among their ranks the very women who fought for women's suffrage.[19]

For example, analysis of existing life history documents such as those of the five elderly suffragist women interviewed by Sherna Gluck can be used to develop preliminary research hypotheses about aging, adaptability, and the significance of feminist consciousness to elderly women.[20] These women, from a wide range of family backgrounds, all shared a pride and feminist consciousness, an idealism tempered by realistic political pragmatism, a commitment to political activism, and a long history of independent and autonomous activity beyond their roles as support for their husband and children. Only one of the five women appeared clearly depressed in her old age, and she appears to have exhibited a depressive character throughout her life, using the feminist and other social movements to try to give meaning to a life that she felt was empty and deprived at the core.

Since activity, autonomy, and self-esteem appear to be important attributes in successful aging, it would be valuable to develop a research design that compared a sample of widowed women who had spent their lives in traditional support of their families with a group of more independent widows such as the suffragists mentioned above.[21] It would be possible to ascertain if there were, indeed, any correlation between successful aging and such a variable as a history of independence associated with feminist activism. If such a correlation were found, we might then propose that consciousness-raising sessions for women during their middle years might stimulate for them a more positive old age.

LIFE REVIEW AS A MEANS OF COMMUNICATION BETWEEN GENERATIONS

It is not only the clinicians and the researchers who can learn a great deal from life review. Students in an anthropology class and an English class were assigned the task of locating and interviewing an old person, often a grandparent, neighbor, or housemother. They attempted to reach an understanding of the inner meaning of the old persons' lives through their reminiscences, and a review of old photos and documents. The students were asked to write life-history papers, reviewing them with their subjects until the paper met the subjects' approval as a viable document of their life. The teachers, Barbara Myerhoff and Virginia Tufte, report:

It was a major encounter with history as a meaningful concern in human terms for the students. Countries, wars, social changes, became more than mere names and dates. They saw something of the life of people whose preoccupations were outside their experience: the old people described struggles to assure mere subsistence and safety for their families, coping with hardships and adjusting to a new country in the hope of finding religious freedom for their progeny.[22]

With the popular success of the television version of *Roots*, some high schools and colleges are now offering classes that encourage students to explore their own "roots" by interviewing their grandparents and aunts and uncles about their lives. In addition they are encouraged to study the historical periods and cultures of their family's past.[23]

In another learning situation, high school students interested in careers in social work, psychology, and education worked as volunteers in a home for the elderly, listening to life stories and then writing a journal of their own feelings and responses to the elderly person's experiences.[24] For many of these teenagers, this was their first close encounter with aging. Some were initially fearful and threatened, but through the process came to appreciate the vitality and range of experience of these elderly people and to perceive old age as much more complex and interesting than their initial stereotypes had led them to expect.

Anthropologists and historians, as well as clinicians, have long used the autobiographical record as a primary source in gathering data. Historians traditionally have worked from extant autobiographies to develop a sense of an historical period, and anthropologists have gone to the field to collect their own life histories from people whose lives represent a unique, culturally significant experience. Such an account is *Mountain Wolf Woman: The Autobiography of a Winnebago Indian*, a unique and unforgettable history taped by anthropologist Nancy Lurie as a document of a dying tribal culture and a study, from the first-person point of view, of a woman shaman.[25] With the development of oral history, historians, like anthropologists, are taping life histories of women in an effort to document women's experience.

Life review can be a valuable developmental process that normally occurs spontaneously and naturally from childhood to old age. In order to foster a healthy old age that integrates both positive and negative feelings about past experiences, life review and reminiscence should be encouraged. And, when there are unresolved conflicts and adaptive difficulties, life review is an excellent addition to personal therapy with the aged.

The benefits accrue not only to the individual who looks inward and backward over his or her life. Clinicians and social workers also benefit from taking life histories with the elderly; their understanding of the human life cycle is enhanced. Life review also offers excellent material for work in the growing field of gerontology. And, as has been known since Homer's time, it is through the process of sharing tales of deeds done and lives lived, that culture is transmitted from one generation to the next.

NOTES

1. Homer, *Odyssey* (New York: McGraw Hill, 1957), 57.

2. Florida Scott-Maxwell, *The Measure of My Days* (New York: Alfred Knopf, 1972), excerpted in *Revelations: Diaries of Women*, ed. Mary Jane Moffat and Charlotte Painter (New York: Vintage, 1974), 363–64.

3. Robert J. Havighurst and Richard Glasser, "An Exploratory Study of Reminiscence," *Journal of Gerontology* 27 (1972): 245–53.

4. Arthur W. McMahon and Paul J. Rhudick, "Reminiscing: Adaptational Significance in the Aged," *Archives of General Psychiatry* 10 (1964): 292–98.

5. Erik Erikson, *Childhood and Society* (New York: Norton, 1963).

6. Robert Butler and Myrna Lewis, "Life Review Therapy," *Geriatrics* 29 (1974): 165–73.

7. Sigmund Freud, "Mourning and Melancholia," *A General Selection from the Works of Sigmund Freud*, ed. J. Rickman (Garden City: Doubleday/Anchor Books, 1957).

8. McMahon and Rhudick, "Reminiscing."

9. Therese Benedek, "The Psychosomatic Implications of the Primary Unit: Mother-Child," *American Journal of Orthopsychiatry* 19 (1949): 642–53.

10. Anaïs Nin, *The Diary of Anaïs Nin, 1931–1934*, ed. G. Sthulman (New York: Harcourt Brace, 1966), ix.

11. Joanna Field, quoted by Charlotte Painter in "Psychic Bisexuality," in Moffat and Painter, eds., *Revelations*, 393.

12. Scott-Maxwell, *Measure of My Days*, 363–68.

13. Havighurst and Glasser, "An Exploratory Study."

14. Butler and Lewis, "Life Review Therapy," 168.

15. Butler and Lewis, "Life Review Therapy," 173.

16. Harriet Wrye, "The Belief Systems of Women with Breast Cancer," (Ph.D. diss., The Wright Institute, Los Angeles, 1977).

17. William S. Robinson, "The Logical Structure of Analytic Induction," *American Sociological Review* 16 (1951): 812–18.

18. Tish Sommers, "The Compounding Impact of Age on Sex," *Civil Rights Digest* 7 (1974): 2–9.

19. Evelyn Kahana, "The Older Woman: Implications for Research for Social Policy," paper presented at the American Sociological Association meeting, New York, 1976.

20. Sherna Gluck, ed. *From Parlor to Prison: Five American Suffragists Talk About Their Lives* (New York: Vintage, 1976).

21. Havighurst and Glasser, "An Exploratory Study."

22. Barbara Myerhoff and Virginia Tufte, "Life History as Integration: An Essay on an Experimental Model" *The Gerontologist* (1975): 541.

23. See Joan Jensen, Beverly Baca, and Barbara Bolin, "Family History and Oral History," *Frontiers: A Journal of Women Studies* 2:2 (1977): 75–78.

24. Wrye, "Exploring Careers in Human Development," unpublished report of the Regional Occupational Program (for students in Los Angeles high schools), Los Angeles, Calif., n.d.

25. Nancy Lurie, *Mountain Wolf Woman: The Autobiography of a Winnebago Indian* (Ann Arbor: University of Michigan Press, 1961).

Frontiers 2:2 (1977): 79–84.

Good Work, Sister!

The Making of an Oral History Production

AMY KESSELMAN, TINA TAU, AND KAREN WICKRE

The Northwest Women's History Project was founded in Portland, Oregon, in 1978 by a group of women brought together by our common interest in oral history. We each brought skills to the group in a variety of fields, including social work, teaching, book distribution, office work, and planning. Only two of us perceive ourselves as professional historians, but we all have felt a need to seek out and record the firsthand accounts of women's lives. Over a period of four years, we found ourselves committing increasing amounts of time, energy, and money to develop and complete a media production using women's oral histories. At the beginning of our project, none of us envisioned just how great our commitment would become: During the last half of 1981, we collectively devoted 100 hours a week to the project, and the product of our work became the focus of considerable excitement in the Portland, Oregon–Vancouver, Washington, community.[1]

Like many other oral history projects, ours focused on an event within the memory of numbers of people, one that was significant in the history of our region. The topic we chose grew out of a women's history class at a local college taught by one of our members. She was intrigued by the interviews students had done with women who worked in the shipyards during World War II. The story of the women war workers quickly captured the imagination of the Northwest Women's History Project. We were drawn to the issues and concerns the wartime and postwar periods raise about women in the workforce. Few of us had grown up in Portland; we did not fully understand the significance of the shipyard experience or the war years in the history of the area. We learned that the wartime shipbuilding boom had been a watershed for Portland and its neighbor city across the Columbia River, Vancouver, Washington.

In 1940, both Portland and Vancouver were small, semirural towns in which less than one-sixth of the population was industrially employed. By the end of the war, the population had grown 30 percent, and half of the area's workforce was employed by industry. The number of black people in Portland grew from about 2,000 to 22,000 (after the war, it declined again to 11,000.[2] Three small shipyards in Portland expanded rapidly as they obtained government contracts. Kaiser Corporation built three large shipyards, two in Portland and one in Vancouver, and recruited workers from all over the country. The massive influx of workers and their families strained the area's resources as the demand for labor continued. Seeking to tap a local source of labor, the shipyards began to hire women to do production work (in addition to clerical work). By 1944, there were over 40,000 women working in the six shipyards. Approximately three-quarters of these women were production workers, doing jobs that few women had done before.

As they did in other war industries in the United States, women played a key role in the rapid and efficient production of ships.[3] Similarly, after the war ended, the Portland story was not unique: Women were among the first to be laid off as the shipyards slowed production. Our women interviewees echoed what we had learned from archival material. Edna Hopkins, a former welder, relates the story of her last day of work:

The foreman came in and he said, "The war's over," and everybody stopped work and gathered around him, you know, to hear the news. They just kept standing around, and I had a pipe going in my booth, and I decided that I'd go back and work on my pipe. So then the boss, he comes over and he says, "Shorty, what are you doing working on that pipe?" He said, "You can do that tomorrow," he says, "There's nobody working but you." And I said, "Well, I want to finish this pipe." I said, "This is the last pipe I'll ever weld." And he laughed, you know, and he said, "Oh, you're kidding, Shorty." He said, "You'll be here tomorrow." I said, "You want to bet?" He walked away, and I went ahead and finished my pipe, and that was the last pipe I welded. They laid me off the next day. The women in the pipe shop were all laid off.[4]

After the shipyards closed, the women found themselves unwelcome in the trades they had learned during the war. As narrator Reva Baker comments:

When the war was over, the Boilermakers did not want the women in the union, they did not want them working in men's jobs, they didn't feel that women were qualified for men's jobs, even though we had been doing it all during the war; they were trying to protect the men and their jobs.

In the postwar world, women once again provided the low-paid labor force in occupations such as textile, cannery, sales, service, and office work, as well as in the home. While the women war workers had been hailed as patriotic heroines during the war, they faded into obscurity when the media once again glorified domesticity as the fulfillment of female destiny. Knowing that women had contributed to the war effort, and that their feelings about subsequent work experiences were undocumented, we wanted to reclaim this dimension of Portland-Vancouver history and to add to our understanding of the process by which women were first included in and then excluded from the traditionally male-dominated world of skilled industrial work. We felt certain that personal accounts would illuminate this episode in women's history.

The Northwest Women's History Project was an independent group that had no formal affiliation with any academic or research institution. Our autonomy—the result of carefully considered choices—was cherished, but it presented certain problems. We had no easy access to equipment, supplies, offices, or meeting rooms. We met and maintained files in group members' homes, and were forced to limit our copying and mailing. We soon discovered that we needed funding to do any substantial historical project. We did qualify for, and receive, tax exempt status, and this designation was very important in our funding efforts.

Because we settled on a regional focus for our project, and because of our commitment to and interest in oral history, the most likely funding source for us was the Orgeon Committee for the Humanities. The OCH, a state office under the National Endowment for the Humanities, funds projects that bring a variety of educational topics, in a variety of formats, to audiences throughout Oregon. In 1980, we applied for and received a $6,000 grant to interview women who had been shipyard workers, and to create a slide-tape show based on their interviews. The grant also provided for a series of free public showings accompanied by panel discussions about issues raised in the show. It is important to note that few oral history projects are funded without providing for some sort of vehicle to bring the material to the public. Collecting interviews with no public final product in sight is not philosophically or financially desirable to most funding agencies.

We proposed a slide-tape show because it required somewhat less technical assistance than a film and less time than a book. It also lends itself more easily to collective decision making. Copies can be duplicated inexpensively for wide distribution. None of us had ever produced a slide-tape

"Good Work, Sister" (National Archives Poster).

show, but we were willing to learn and felt confident that people with particular technical skills would help. We were not disappointed. Through our wide network of contacts, we were able to find people to meet a variety of research and production needs. The assistance and support we received from people outside the group improved the quality of our production immeasurably. Group members also learned new skills. Over the various phases of the project—research, interviewing, scriptwriting, selection of visual material, publicity—different women in the group demonstrated their interest in and ability to take on new tasks.

The purpose of a humanities grant is to disseminate historical, literary, philosophical, and aesthetic interpretations and viewpoints, generally through people who have graduate degrees in some field of the humanities. We employed a number of these, including two of our own group members, to offer workshops on such topics as oral history techniques, women's history, local labor history, and sociology of women's work. We also asked a former shipbuilder to explain shipbuilding terminology and techniques. Some of the humanists did research and provided fact sheets and bibliographies to the group. Although these workshops and materials were very helpful, we were frustrated by the stipulation in our grant that we pay only "humanists" and technical consultants for their contributions. Most of the expertise we drew on was volunteered, and the division between compensated and uncompensated work often seemed arbitrary and unfair. In retrospect, we feel that we may have interpreted the constraints of our grant too literally.

We were committed to working as collectively as possible. The limits imposed by our other jobs certainly presented difficulties, and yet they also created opportunities for sharing and rotating responsibilities. Having a group of ten allowed some of us to step back when necessary and others to take over. Certainly no collective effort is ideal, however, and as deadline pressures mounted, we experienced the tension and frustration any project-by-committee can expect. Despite these, as the time to complete the interviews, perfect the script, select photographs and music came to a close, we were struck by the willingness and determination of the group to follow through and complete the task at hand. Determination, of course, was not enough to carry us through the process. We also were very conscious about our collective process, making sure we took time to work through tensions, and to play as well as work together.

It is also important to note that in addition to acting collectively, we had a project director as a stipulation of our grant. She served as a repository

Counselor, scaler, and leadwoman at the Commercial Iron Works, Portland, Oregon, 1944 (Photo courtesy of the Oregon Historical Society).

of information for the group (an especially important function since we had no central office) and coordinated simultaneous tasks. She was also liaison to our funding source and other public contacts when necessary. We had very real questions throughout the project about such a role within a democratic group. The position was intended to be nominal, and yet did entail extra responsibilities and afforded a small salary. We struggled to find a comfortable balance between sharing responsibilities and acknowledging that one person felt more liable and responsible.

How does an oral history project, dealing with a subject that involved thousands of people, find and select "narrators"? (We have chosen this word for the women we interviewed.) For some topics, historical records may be available that make it possible to track people down. In our case, we had only random names collected from newspaper stories; locating women initially proved difficult. Many women's names had changed; many had moved or died. In addition, wartime shipyard records were not available from the succeeding companies. We decided to publicize the project in order to recruit volunteer narrators. We arranged for extensive local newspaper and radio coverage, and distributed hundreds of brochures describing our project to senior centers, neighborhood associations, and unions in Portland, Vancouver, and adjacent areas. Simultaneously, we collected names through our own personal contacts. The response to this publicity drive was very positive. For several weeks we were inundated by letters and phone calls, and within three months we had collected over 200 names. It was clear that many women were eager to talk about their shipyard years. Of course, two key groups of women were underrepresented from the beginning: those who were over thirty-five during the war, many of whom had died; and those who had left the area after the war, since our funding limited us to local interviews.

There are advantages and disadvantages to using a self-selected group of narrators. The women who contacted us generally saw the shipyard years as significant in their lives, and had positive feelings about them. They were enthusiastic and provided us with fascinating material, which had clearly been kept alive in their memories by a conviction that their shipyard work was an important experience. They often had pictures and memorabilia, which were useful in triggering memories of the times and as visual material for the show. On the other hand, the self-chosen character of the narrators skewed our sample in many ways—some obvious and others subtle. Who did a self-selected group exclude? Were they women who felt that their experiences did

"Grandmother Crew," composed of older women shipyard workers, Portland, Oregon, 1944 (Photo courtesy of the Oregon Historical Society).

not "match" the story the project was seeking, did not think that their experiences were significant, were too busy with other concerns, or had negative feelings about the war years that they did not wish to relive or make public? It is important to emphasize to potential narrators how integral a part of history their experiences are. In women's history in particular, we must be open to hearing stories that traditional history has negated or ignored.[5]

There were obvious results of the self-selection of our sample: women who achieved journeyman status (mostly welders) were overrepresented; we also had to do a good deal of searching to contact black women, who were a significant minority of women workers. Because of the discriminatory practices of the craft unions in the shipyards, they worked in predominantly unskilled jobs. In addition, all of the project members were white and had relatively few contacts in the black community.

Unfortunately, we had the resources to interview fewer than one-quarter of the women who called us. We had to devise a method for narrowing down the number. On the basis of our research, we developed a rough sense of the relative proportion of women in the local wartime work force for different age groups, prewar and postwar work experiences, race, and marital status. Following the example of Sherna Gluck's project on World War II women aircraft industry workers in Los Angeles, we devised a telephone questionnaire with which to interview each of the 200 women for about twenty minutes. These conversations, which we summarized on forms, provided us with basic demographic information as well as some sense of each woman's prewar, wartime, and postwar experiences. We then spent a very difficult month selecting our sample of narrators, weighting a variety of factors in choosing them. It was at this point that we first noticed how a slide-tape production would affect the oral history process. If we were to create an effective show, we needed narrators who were fairly articulate, had presence, and came across well on tape. We also found ourselves remembering and preferring women who told distinctive anecdotes, since these would fit the slide-tape format easily.

The forty interviews were conducted over a three-month period by the project members. Each interviewer indexed her tapes, writing a full narrative description of each five-minute segment, and transcribed portions of the tape that she thought would be useful for the slide-tape show. Since we had not yet written the script, the decisions about what should be transcribed depended on the interviewer's own perspective as well as the broad guidelines we had collectively formulated over the previous six months and which enumerated the range of topics we were interested in. We tried to transcribe as much as possible to minimize the effects of individual bias, but were limited by time constraints.

Besides our general enthusiasm and excitement about the project, we also had concerns about the interview process. We wanted to know what women felt about the experience of working in defense jobs and of being excluded from similar work in the postwar period, but we wondered how clearly they could remember how they had felt thirty-five to forty years earlier. Would their feelings have been reinterpreted in terms that were "acceptable" in the 1950s and possibly reinterpreted again in the 1970s? How could we be sure people were telling us what they felt and not what they thought we wanted to hear? What could we find out from these women that we could not find in the archives, in statistics, in newspapers?

The story of women workers in World War II can easily be seen as the manipulation of women in and out of the skilled work force in response to the needs of industry and government. The oral history interviews make it clear that this is only one aspect of the picture. They vividly demonstrate the ways that women workers shaped their own experiences during World War II.

With considerable hesitation and reluctance on the part of industry, government, and labor, the door to industrial work for women was opened a

Tanker crew: These women cleaned out the tanker ships, Portland, Oregon, October 1944 (Photo courtesy of the Oregon Historical Society).

crack during the war.[6] In the interviews we did, the women shipyard workers describe the myriad ways in which they pushed the door open further through their own initiative. The changes that these women made as they took advantage of new opportunities have reverberated throughout their lives, changing the way they related to husbands and families, and changing their views of themselves.

These dynamics reveal themselves in the interviews with the women on a variety of levels, beginning with the decision to take work in the shipyards. For example, here is Rosa Dickson's story about her husband's reaction to her desire to go to work:

When I said I wanted to work in the shipyards, he said, "Oh, no, you cannot work down there in the shipyards. They're too rough, and the language is bad," and all of these kinds of things of which I was not used to. I tried Ward's, I tried lots of other places. You know what they paid? Seventy-six cents an hour. That was about the average base pay Meier and Frank [a Portland department store], anybody had at that time. And I said, "Well, I'm not going to take a job like that, because the shipyards are paying the big money."

Another worker recalled her husband's opposition to her shipyard work and his initial unwillingness to set foot inside the house she bought with her shipyard wages. "My husband," she commented, "was from Kentucky. He didn't think women knew anything—so I showed him."

Women pushed against both the upper and lower age limits that were imposed, but that were later modified as the labor shortage became more acute. The youngest former shipyard worker present had been fourteen when she was hired at the yards. At the shipyard workers' reunion in January 1982 (discussed below), she was asked how she did it, and she called out, "I lied!" A burst of applause came from the audience; the image of defiance, of pushing against the limits, struck a responsive chord in the other women.

As Karen Beck Skold points out in her study of the Portland shipyards, occupational segregation by sex was not eliminated under the wartime labor pressure. Barriers were lowered or they shifted; they did not disappear.[7] A majority of the women hired in the shipyards were hired as helpers or laborers or clerical workers. The only skilled trade in which significant numbers of women became journeymen was welding, the craft in which there was the most severe labor shortage. Women did, however, penetrate other skilled crafts. Through the oral history interviews we gained insights into ways in which women were pushing against the limits and expanding their options. Where the written material tends to emphasize the enduring presence of sex segregation in the shipyards, the interviews began to turn our attention to the number of skilled crafts into which women did push their way.

JoAnn Hudlicky, for example, was working in the clearance office when she first got hired at the shipyard. Because all workers who were leaving the job passed through the office, she learned that production pay was much higher than office pay. So she hired out as a helper in the duplicating shop, but did not like it very much.

And I saw the cranes, so I grabbed my boss and said, "How do you get a job running a crane?" And he said, "Well, you have to talk to the man who hires for that," and he said, "I'll show you who it is." Well, evidently he told him that I asked, because the next day he came around and he said, "I hear you'd like to run a crane." And I said, "I sure would," and he said, "Do you think you can do that?" and I said, "Well, I don't know why not, other people are doing it!" And the very next day, he came after me.

Hudlicky did get a crane operating job and loved it.

Most of the women we talked to seemed to have found their wartime jobs satisfying and rewarding. Some accepted the idea of their work as temporary and expected to return to the world of "female work" after the war. Some would have liked to stay in the metal trades, but recognized that the effort was futile, and found other work. As Kay Baker relates,

"You'd better find a niche," says I to me. I thought there wouldn't be any soldier boys lining up to be grocery clerks, and so that's what I decided to be.

Still other women tried to stay in some kind of industrial work, and their stories indicate a hidden pocket of resistance and struggle that has been invisible. For example, Nona Pool asserts that the shipyard experience "made an industrial worker out of me." After she was laid off from her welding job at Oregon Ship, she changed jobs nineteen times trying to find industrial work that would pay her decently and would approach the satisfaction of her wartime welding job. She tried several times throughout the 1950s and early 1960s to get back into welding:

I went to work for Freightliner, and I kept telling them that I wanted to weld. "No way, no way, you're too dumb, women don't weld." You know, the funny thing was, I went to them a long time ago and I said, "Hey, how about giving me a job welding?" And the guy, he turned around and looked at me and kind of laughed, and he says, "I wouldn't doubt you're a good welder, but we don't have facilities for women." I says, "I'll bring my own potty, just bring me a curtain!"

Finally, after equal employment legislation reopened skilled industrial work for women in 1974, Nona Pool took additional training at the local community college and became the first woman welder the company had ever hired. She expressed the spirit that sustained her:

What you've got to do is say, "I'm this wide, and I'm gonna push a hole in there just the right size for me, and if you don't like it, that's tough stuff."

Scriptwriting was done by a rotating group of project members over a six-month period. The script was based on the taped excerpts, with narrative bridges written by us. Determined to produce the most effective script possible, we went through ten drafts altogether. Although scriptwriting by committee slowed the process, constant revisions by more than one person honed and refined the ideas we wished to convey.

While we were creating the show, we held several preliminary screenings to get feedback from different groups of critics. One of these was for the shipyard workers featured in the show. The production was, and is, an expression of our values, politics, and perspective—a perspective that was significantly affected by what we learned from the interviews. We wanted very much to know what the women thought of the way we presented their experiences and were encouraged by their positive responses.

As the script took shape, it became clear that we could not present interview segments in their unedited form and create an exciting slide-tape show. We trimmed excerpts, removed words, and connected statements from different portions of interviews. We tried at all times to retain the intent of the statements, and did not use segments of an interview if we thought the context was not clear. In an early draft, for example, there was a series of quotations about women taking initiative to learn new skills, and their competence on the job. One woman asked that she be put on a drilling crew. The foreman was reluctant; she would be the only woman on the crew. After a time on the job, however, the foreman acknowledged that despite her being the only woman, she was the only one never to drill a hole in the wrong place. Our excerpt ended there. In her interview, however, she went on to say that the next day she did drill a hole in the wrong place—an amusing recollection to her, but one which would alter the point we wished to make. Rather than end the story too early, we dropped it altogether in the interest of presenting material in its full context.

We were warned by media consultants that it was inadvisable to produce a slide show longer than twenty minutes—some even felt fifteen minutes was too long. The task of compressing our material into a maximum of twenty minutes often seemed overwhelming. Not only had we collected about seventy hours of interview material, but we wanted to deal with complex issues and had encountered a wide variety of attitudes and perspectives that we did not want to oversimplify. In the end we had to sacrifice parts of our story, such as the housing problem during the war, for the sake of brevity and clarity. Given a wealth of visual material to put with the tape, we now feel that the twenty-minute rule may not always be appropriate for oral history material if it is handled carefully. Many of our audiences have been hungry for more when the show is over. This is one advantage film or videotape has over slide-tape.

We generally feel pleased with our product and believe we have conveyed both strong feminist messages and a sense of the variety of women's responses to historical forces. We titled the production *Good Work, Sister!* a phrase drawn from a postwar poster that patronized women war workers by having a male worker say, "We never figured you could do a man-size job!" We wanted to use the phrase to affirm the value of the work the women did.

Purists among oral historians have long questioned editorial license taken with interviews. More practically, however, we became increasingly aware of public interest in our final product, which is, in fact, meant to be entertaining as well as educational. The show reaches a far greater number of people than our "pure" research material (tapes, indexes, and transcripts). This kind of project, then, becomes the compromise—and the challenge—of a vehicle for oral history interviews: to preserve significant experiences in some form, highlight the dominant themes in historical development, and whet the audience's appetites for more information still to be gleaned from both documents and people.

When *Good Work, Sister!* was finished, as a reward to ourselves and our narrators, and to involve the many women we did not interview, we organized a reunion of Portland-area women shipyard workers, and they were our first audience. The reunion, cohosted by a local department store, was widely publicized. On an unusually wintery day in January of 1982, 250 women between the ages of fifty-five and eighty-nine found their way to the store's large dining room and watched the show with excitement. The enthusiasm at the reunion was moving in many ways. Women were eager to locate coworkers they had not seen for thirty-five years. Most were unable to find their lost friends, but two sets of women reunited, and they hugged each other tearfully as the rest of us clapped and cheered. Perhaps the most profound aspect of the reunion was the evident craving for recognition on the part of the ex-shipyard workers. In part this need was generated by the contrast between the wartime fanfare and the postwar obscurity that the shipyard workers experienced. It also reminded us that most working people, particularly women, feel unrecognized and unvalued. As one of the shipyard workers, Helen Berggren, exclaimed that day, "Thank you *so* much for doing this—I thought I'd *die* before someone remembered us!"

NOTES

1. We are grateful for the suggestions made by the whole Northwest Women's History Project that helped to formulate this article. Over four years, the project has had thirteen members. The ten most actively involved in this production were Sarah Cook, Susan Feldman, Barbara Gundle, Amy Kesselman, Madeline Moore, Sandy Polishuk, Tina Tau, Lynn Taylor, Barbara Whittlesey-Hayes, and Karen Wickre. It is important to note that this article was written just as we completed this first major project in 1982. Our discoveries about the material, our procedures, and our process were new; with time, new understandings will emerge.

2. E. Kimbark MacColl, *The Growth of a City: Power and Politics in Portland, Oregon, 1915–1950* (Portland: Georgian Press, 1979), 584.

3. Frederick Chapin Lane, *Ships for Victory: A History of Shipbuilding under the U.S. Maritime Commission in World War II* (Baltimore: Johns Hopkins University Press, 1951). Lane describes the impressive achievements of Kaiser Corporation's shipbuilding efforts. In the article "The Job He Left Behind: American Women in the Shipyards During World War II," (*Women, War and Revolution,* ed. Carol Berkin and Clara Lovett [New York: Holmes and Meier, 1980], 55–75, Karen Beck Skold summarizes the variety of industrial jobs women took.

4. Hopkins's words and subsequent excerpts from taped interviews are taken from the production, *Good Work, Sister!* or from the additional taped material in the files of the Northwest Women's History Project.

5. Susan Armitage explores concisely some of these same questions in her paper, "Private Lives and the Public Record: Some Questions in Women's Oral History," delivered at the 1980 Oral History Association Colloquium, Durango, Colorado.

6. See Eleanor Straub, "U.S. Government Policy Towards Civilian Women During World War II," *Prologue* 5 (1973): 240–54, for a description of the ambivalence of the federal government toward women in industry.

7. Skold, "The Job He Left Behind," 60–66. For a detailed description of sex segregation in the Kaiser shipyards, see also Karen Beck Skold, "Women Workers and Childcare During World War II: A Case Study of Portland, Oregon Shipyards," (Ph.D. diss., University of Oregon, 1981).

Frontiers 7:1 (1983): 64–70.

Filming Nana

Some Dilemmas of Oral History on Film

CONNIE BROUGHTON

My husband talked for years about interviewing my grandmother, Anne Dunphy Magnuson, for a film he was working on about Burke, Idaho, the mining boomtown where she was born in 1898.[1] He was fascinated by her stories about Burke, which had been, unquestionably, a colorful town. Beginning in 1885, some of the richest and deepest silver mines in the world were worked in a canyon so narrow that the creek and the road together nearly covered the canyon floor, so narrow, as a Burke resident in the finished film says, that the dogs were forced to wag their tails up and down. Though many familiar frontier characters were part of the Burke story, the narrowness of the canyon and the depth of the mines put life in Burke on a different perspective than other western boomtowns.

That perspective was what interested my husband, Irv, especially since people who had lived in Burke during its heyday were still alive and could still be interviewed. His preference as a filmmaker is for the talking head— the live person speaking his or her own words. He wanted me to research and write the script for the film, but I resisted the idea of a film about Burke. For one thing, the history of Burke was not exotic to me, and public interest in my birthplace has always seemed to be limited to its semi-open prostitution and single stoplight, so I wasn't sure a film on Burke would find an audience. More significantly, Irv saw my grandmother as the central character of the film, and I couldn't imagine basing a film on my grandmother talking in front of a camera. I didn't think she would speak on film at all, and, if she did speak, I didn't expect her necessarily to tell the truth.

But Irv persisted. He badgered my grandmother, whom we called Nana. She responded with snorts and unladylike remarks. One day in 1975 he filmed her with me (in stylish wide-legged pants) on the site of her mother's long-gone boardinghouse in Burke. Ten years later he announced that our holiday trip to Wallace, Idaho, the town where my parents lived, seven miles down the canyon from Burke, would also be a film trip. Nana had agreed to be interviewed on film.

I helped him load the film gear, telling him with every heavy metal case we heaved into the car that he was sadly mistaken if he thought Nana would behave for his camera. When we got to Wallace, my parents and brothers and sisters were equally negative. No one believed Nana would actually speak on film. She had been approached many times by reporters and producers to talk about Burke or about the early days of the Coeur d'Alene mining district, and she had always refused, saying they always messed things up and wouldn't use her words right. Everyone but Irv was dumbfounded when we dumped the equipment in the entrance to Nana's retirement apartment and found her waiting in a chair, hair done, makeup on, and dressed in a film-friendly pink blouse. We set up, and my sister Jan was designated interviewer with a list of questions Irv had prepared. Irv turned on the camera. Nana looked straight into its lens and began to speak.

Jan asked her about when her parents came to Burke from Newfoundland. Nana told about how her father and uncle had come first and then sent for her mother, her mother's mother, and her older brother and sisters. She told how when her mother arrived, Burke was nothing more than a small circle of cabins. The family came by train, then steamboat, then by wagon. She told us that my great-great-grandmother had announced, when they headed up the seven-mile canyon to Burke, that they were headed straight to hell. She told us how the women made bread and did laundry for the single miners there. At first they wouldn't take any money, so the miners would give the children gold pieces. At some point the women decided to go into business and built the boardinghouse where Nana was born.

Except for an annoying click of her dentures, Nana was terrific. Her stories were lucid, detailed, believable. I should have been thrilled. As her granddaughter I *was* thrilled to have her on film. But now I was going to be the writer of a film on Burke, and as a budding historian I was worried. For one thing, on film Nana had changed some details of these old familiar stories. For instance, she had a juicy story about an Irish waitress who had been impregnated by an influential Wallace man. The story I remembered was replete with names and details. On film, she left out the names and seemed to be very confused about the details. Part of me was glad for that, thinking her self-editing meant she was telling only the truth, not gossip.

But another part of me wondered if she had always been telling the truth and was now self-editing in order to present a cleaner image of the area. Ultimately, that story wasn't a part of the finished film, so I could leave my questions with the film on the cutting room floor.

Making a film using oral history provides plenty of problems in itself, but what happens when the subject of the film is not only someone you love, but also someone you know doesn't have a strong attachment to the truth? For all the scholarly discussion about the crisis of objectivity, people who watch a documentary film expect the facts to be right, and the people who are filmed expect their words to be used as they were meant.[2] So I approached this film with these great fears. First, even though I don't believe in objectivity, I do believe that the appearance of objectivity is what gives projects like a film on Burke, Idaho, their weight. A documentary is supposed to be "true." How was I to write a film that appears to be objective without merely pretending to be objective? Second, even if objectivity is impossible, an oral historian has a responsibility to try for the truth the person interviewed intended. So how was I to use other people's words and lives respectfully? And third, how do I mediate among my family's feelings, my own feelings, and my job, which was to write, more or less, the film my husband felt he wanted to make and at the same time write it like a historian (which I was only learning how to be).

With none of these questions answered for me, we began the film. Irv's method is to interview people he thinks will be interesting and to film images that he thinks will fit in somewhere. After critical mass is reached, someone, in this case me, tries to find some large order out of all the bits and pieces. Then he films more people and images to fill out the frame. The finished film is made up of former Burke residents talking about Burke. Their stories are illustrated and punctuated by contemporary footage of Burke and wonderful black-and-white still photographs. This is a good and respected method of filmmaking, but it is not efficient, and it means the finished film is not so much "built" as it is "discovered."

Funding for this film came from our local public television station, KSPS, and from the Idaho Humanities Council. Irv was asked by the funders more than once to make a film "like *The Civil War*." The implication that in making his documentary series on the Civil War, Ken Burns somehow invented documentary film or is the only exemplary documentary filmmaker is always hard to take, especially since our goal was to get people on film before they died. The greatness of Burns's film on the Civil War, I think, comes from the voices from the grave, so to speak, the letters and diaries. Furthermore,

Anne Dunphy Magnuson, the author's grandmother, as a young woman.

Burns is a fine filmmaker, but he certainly did not invent documentary film. What people who suggested we make a film like his really meant, I suspect, is that they would like a film as *successful* as *The Civil War*. Ironically, in 1993, just when I was *unsuccessfully* trying to write the first draft of the Burke film, I heard Ken Burns speak at a conference in Boston.[3] The conference was called "Telling the Story: The Media, the Public, and American History," a project of the New England Foundation for the Humanities in association with the Massachusetts Cultural Council and with support from the National Endowment for the Humanities. It was a huge conference, very crowded, and attended by big important historians like Alan Brinkley and big important filmmakers like Ken Burns, and little aspiring filmmakers and little aspiring historians like us. The program was devoted to the question of whether it is possible to make good history and good film at the same time, but the little aspiring filmmakers kept changing the focus to how they could get the same kind of financial support Ken Burns has gotten. Burns, to his credit, said he got his money by wearing a red dress slit up to here, pointing to his thigh. I came away with the impression that the real answer was to move to Washington DC or New York, because real money wasn't coming to Spokane, Washington. That's really another issue, but it is germane to a film on Burke, Idaho. Film is a medium where money counts. The more money you have, the better the film can be. A really good one-hour film on Burke should cost just as much as a really good one-hour film on the Civil War, but a film on Burke would be pretty hard to sell to Mobil.

Finances aside, the discussion between filmmakers and historians was timely for me. Burns pointed out that film is less like the essay a historian might write and more like music. He pointed out, essentially, that history was sung before it was footnoted, and Burns means his films to be like song. But historians were critical of Burns's *The Civil War*. Daniel Walkowitz criticized the film, among other reasons, because it did not tell the *contested story*. The film was criticized for giving an impression rather than giving an argument. There was, of course, a lot more to the discussion, but this argument mirrored my dilemma. Should the Burke film give an impression or give an argument? Did a "historical" film have to contest something?

In a limited market for documentary film, the success of a film like *The Civil War* weights it with far more importance than it can bear. Somehow Ken Burns's vision of the Civil War becomes *the* vision of the Civil War. Well, that's wrong, and if there were more films by more people with as much money as Ken Burns had to make that film, we would see that his is just one vision, one story. But as things are, the historian has to criticize the film not just for its limitations but for its success. The success is that Burns made exactly the film he wanted to make; that's not easy, and it is not the film a historian or anyone else, including me, would make. I was sympathetic to Burns because the director of a film has to make his own film if it is to work. But I was also sympathetic to the historians because historians know that, because of the power of film, whatever film Ken Burns makes *becomes history*.

Because there isn't likely going to be another film on Burke, Idaho, I was about to—for better or worse—write a film that would define Burke. Knowing that other filmmakers and other historians and other film writers struggled with the same tensions I was struggling with was some comfort, but it gave me no answers. Which side was I on—the historians or the filmmakers? For the Burke film, I was supposed to be the scholar, the historian; I was supposed to be the one telling the contested story. But I was only the writer. If you know anything about filmmaking, you know that being the writer doesn't mean much. It is a director's medium, and the director's job is to make the film work, and a film works by impressions, by images, by sounds and colors. Those were the things Irv was thinking about, and, just like the historians at that conference, in making the Burke film I was resisting the kind of film that the filmmaker was making because I was thinking about the structure and balance and accuracy that would make the argument and not necessarily the images and sounds that would make the song.

This conflict between argument and impression was not the only thing that made constructing the film so difficult. We had a mass of materials including straight history, newspapers, wonderful old photographs, and much oral history, and it all covered Burke from 1885 to 1997. The inclination in ordering material like that would be to follow major events—either in the mining industry or in the larger history of the nation. But we couldn't see how to do that in an hour-long film, so, acting on a suggestion by one of our humanities scholars and advisors, Katherine Aiken, we ordered the material by different aspects of the community: the terrain, the dangers, the mines, the creek, and so on. Even then, my husband's poetic nature conflicted with my need for order, that is, some kind of large frame for the film. The answer came, I think, by accepting the personal nature of the project and putting the narration in his voice. We had always expected him to speak the narration because he is a fine professional narrator, but we eventually wrote the narration in his personal voice. We began, as I began this article, with Irv trying to get Nana to be interviewed and ended with Irv carrying her casket to her grave. We imposed Nana's life on the life of the town, and Nana's life became, in a general sense, the scope of the film. Irv's personal voice also gave us permission to use natural, native historians in the film rather than professional ones. Instead of having a historian say that the development of the automobile was ultimately responsible for the demise of the town of Burke, we had Sophie Armbruster, who had lived there all her life, on film telling us that when people got cars they moved down the canyon to Wallace where the weather was a little better. She didn't study that up or read it somewhere; it was a fact of her life.

But there are problems in using interviews with ordinary people; for one thing, they are not always articulate. We interviewed several people who simply couldn't get the story out straight once the camera was on. And when you're using your grocery money to pay for the film that is going through the gate at one hundred dollars a minute, you can't afford to be patient until they get it right. You don't have the luxury of inexpensive audiotape, where you can sit and let it roll while people think. On the other hand, ordinary people are great in that they know the importance of regular life, and that infuses their stories with perspectives that you might not find written down on paper. One story my grandmother tells is about building the first church in Burke. According to her, they had been having a Sunday mass in the living room of my great-grandmother's boardinghouse. My great-grandmother didn't like that because people would stay around all day, and even stay for dinner (it's a boardinghouse, right?), and my great-grandmother couldn't get her work done. So she made my great-grandfather dig a basement for a church. The rest of the building was done by other people in the community, including carpenters from the mines. I'm sure no newspaper would begin a story about the new church by saying it was built so Mrs. Dunphy could bake her Sunday pies, but that is my grandmother's take on the story, and it is not only as important as any other but probably is more interesting.

Working with oral history was frustrating at times because so much of what we filmed could not be checked. Ever since the film aired, I've been waiting for the letter that tells us all about the dreadful mistake we made, the lie we believed and broadcast. (It hasn't come yet.) But by relying on oral history, the film demanded that we be—not gullible—but at least willing to believe, willing to accept the version of history that came from the people who were there. I had worried so much about how to present both sides of any contested issue, but there was, I thought, a rich, complex consistency in the stories and the impressions people had of life in Burke. I found that using oral history gave me the ability to juxtapose the mining engineer talking about fights in the street and Bill Dunphy talking about the Saturday night drunk train and newspaper articles about Burke's national reputation as a tough town, with Mamie Picard talking about the idyllic nature of her childhood in Burke. She had no fear, no worries, never saw fights, never felt any danger. What Bill Dunphy saw in Burke existed neither more nor less than what Mamie Picard saw, and I don't think their differing memories are confusing to the audience.

One of my mother's friends told her after the film was broadcast, "Irv and Connie can make a film about my family anytime." The film did include my grandmother, my mother, my uncle, my second cousin, and music by another cousin and my daughter. My son ran sound, and my youngest child appears in the credits with a clapstick. My dad's segment was cut after he pulled me aside and said, "I'm counting on you to get me out of this." Philosophically, I see no difference between family history and "real" history, but I worried that a focus too narrow would not find an audience. Narrow focus did not worry Irv in the least. One segment of the finished film is about my great-aunt being hit by a train when she was a child. I saw it as an interesting, and a little maudlin, family story; Irv saw it as a metaphor for the dangers encountered by and nurturance given to children in a mining town. He was the director so he won. He may even have been right. Maybe I was really just worried that viewers would think I thought my family was so important that everyone should know about my great-aunt being hit by a train (and surviving). This argument typified the tension I felt between being a historian privileging accuracy and linearity and being a filmmaker, an artist, privileging motion and emotion.

Another piece Irv wanted to include was my grandmother talking about how federal agents had asked her to tell them which miners were using more than one name when she was working at the post office in Burke as a young girl. Some miners used more than one name because they were avoiding the draft during World War I; some were trying to beat a blacklist against union miners. Irv thought it was funny how innocently and easily she cast herself as a stool pigeon. I never was able to think it was funny. I don't know how much of my distaste for that story comes from not wanting my grandmother to have pointed out those men and how much was from a concern that I not do to her what she had prevented other writers from doing—misusing her words. The question she was asked was, "Did the miners get mail under two or more names?" She said:

Well, that was after they had the mines in Butte. And after they had trouble, they had a big strike in Butte. And they would be blackballed. And they'd had the list of the men who were troublemakers to blackball them. And they would come to Burke, and they would get [unintelligible] many, many years later. And they would come to work, and they'd be getting mail under two or three names. How we knew that they were getting mail under two or three names, that was during World War I, the draft inspection officers came up there and they would ask. And Mr. Harris, the postmaster, said they got men that got mail under more than one name. But they said they were getting their partner's mail that was on a different shift, and they couldn't get down when the post office was open. But he'd stand there in the post office, and if a man asked for mail under more than one name, I'd nod my head. And then he'd go out and investigate him after he'd left the post office. But we weren't allowed to give them any names out of the post office.

It was the last line that Irv thought was so funny: On film it seems as if she didn't realize that a nod of her head was no different from actually giving them names. But I know my grandmother. She was not stupid; she knew. What her words do not make clear to me is whether she thought she was helping to find draft dodgers, or helping to maintain an antiunion blacklist, or simply doing what an officer of the law asked her to do. I didn't want to use this segment without knowing more about her motivations, but she died before I thought to ask her to explain. I thought that without further explanation, using this clip would just make her look stupid without adding any real insight into blacklisting or draft dodging, neither of which we had time to explore anyway. I did not want to ambush my own grandmother (or anyone else in the film) by using her words to give meanings she did not intend. That seems to me to be an important ethic for the documentarian. Nana's little speech on the post office was not edited in, so I won this battle; maybe I was right.

I thought I knew something about making films when I started this project, but what I learned was that I had never learned to see and hear like a filmmaker. My vision for this film had more to do with control and order than it had to do with emotion and song. A friend of mine talks about how scholarship has given her a voice. I can see how a historian gets a voice by processing the voices of others, by taking letters, newspapers, diaries, and business documents and translating them, forming them into some kind of idea. The historian gets power from study and inclusion and method and from contestation. That's what I started the film wanting to do—to delineate some contest of ideas or of differing interpretations. But the Burke film wasn't my film. As the writer, I found the contest was in learning how to think both like a historian and like a filmmaker. And I found that, just like the historian, the filmmaker's technique is to blend the voices, along with sounds and pictures and colors. For this film, the filmmaker wanted to celebrate Burke, to present the people of Burke in their own voices, and in his own voice. The goal, I discovered, was not to determine the "truth" by privileging one voice over another, but to express truthful emotions by respecting the "truth" of as many voices as possible.

NOTES

My thanks to Barbara Williamson for helping me to clarify my ideas.

1. The film, titled *Burke: The Story of a Frontier Mining Town,* took about ten years to complete. It was supported primarily by the production company owned by my husband and myself, Mill Mountain Productions, and the public television station in Spokane, Washington, KSPS. Bill Stanley of KSPS was the executive producer. Additional funding came from a grant from the Idaho Humanities Council, Coeur d'Alene Mines, Hecla Mining Company, Silver Valley Solidarity Committee of the United Steelworkers of America, Don Heidt, and Mary Callahan Zeller. The film was first broadcast in July 1997 on KSPS.

2. Discussed by Peter Novick in *That Noble Dream: The "Objectivity Question" and the American Historical Profession* (Cambridge, England: Cambridge University Press, 1988) and most compellingly for me in an essay by Jane Tompkins, " 'Indians': Textualism, Morality, and the Problem of History," *Critical Inquiry* 13 (1986): 101–19.

3. The conference took place April 23–24, 1993. All references to events of this conference come from my notes.

Frontiers 19:3 (1998): 190–99.

Treading the Traces of Discarded History

Oral History Installations

ALISON MARCHANT

Drawing attention to a conventional, detrimental process whereby history is made and perceived as novelty/nostalgia and emptied of substance, objects and experiences undergo a movement counteracting the stasis of the museum to create a web of interacting forces.

Rochdale Art Gallery Exhibition Catalogue, *Lancashire, England*

Historically, as working-class people, mill and factory workers have been denied access to the writing and representation of our own class histories. The middle classes maintain power over the printed word and our representations, their narrow perspectives remaining exclusive, inexperienced. Within such a context our stories have been distorted, stereotyped, and fragmented. The experiences of mill workers, who are the subjects of the two installations represented here, *Time & Motion* and *Tying the Threads*, are not an issue of the past. Many women are mill workers today, just as many people work in factories; as someone who has worked in such places, I know these realities too well. In conducting the research for these projects, I also feel I am researching a part of my own history as a wider context, broadening my own realizations.

By addressing historical misrepresentations, excavating through a process of critical dialogue, a new space is constructed where people speak for themselves. My work is not nostalgic because in charting our histories we reach the history of the present. Through multimedia installation I attempt to cut through illusions, grounding real associations with the memorabilia. For example, many of the elderly weavers and spinners have bysinnosis, a chronic breathing condition from which women still suffer. Naturally, there is cynicism toward unions who enforce only small concessionary measures and still do not exact compensations.[1]

These installations are like books of images, objects, and voices, opening out into a monumental physical space, inviting and enveloping the viewer. The aim of my oral history installations is to bring contemporary artwork into a wider audience, outside the art gallery as well as in it. Because the making of my installations involves working-class people, they are eager to see the results, although they have often never seen an installation of contemporary artwork before or may have never visited an art gallery. The opening of *Tying the Threads* was crowded with women mill workers, their families and friends. I am interested in changing the social space of the art gallery through my work in order to empower working-class people. Therefore audience engagement and site are important considerations. When the work is sited in locations where there is a substantial working-class audience, there tends to be an uninhibited response to the work, and conversations emerge once again.

TIME & MOTION

Time & Motion is a live art installation commissioned by Rochdale Art Gallery, in Lancashire, England, and the Arts Council of England. The installation evolved from conversations I had had with my relative, Alice Slater, over the years. Alice still lived in a weaver's cottage handed down through her family in Lancashire. Her living-room window looked onto the cotton mill where she spent her working life. When Rochdale Art Gallery invited me to create a new artwork, *Time & Motion* began to take form as a site-specific installation at a Lancashire cotton mill.

The conditions of the Rochdale Art Gallery project were that I create an artwork both in the gallery and in a site-specific context outside the gallery. The site of the cotton mill seemed most appropriate, and so the exhibition organizer, Sarah Edge, approached Barchant Cotton Mill.

In the disused upper floor of Barchant Mill, I suspended a roll of cotton fabric that cascaded to the floor from a central beam. Projected onto the fabric were huge, haunting, grainy images of mill women's faces, whose eyes seemed to stare out, confronting the viewer. The portraits were slide enlargements I had made from formal group portraits loaned by Rochdale Library. As monumental projections from floor to ceiling, the women's faces dominated the factory interior, dissolving from one face to the next. Women weavers still worked on the lower floors, and amid the relentless clatter of the looms still functioning, the projected portraits dissolved like ghosted faintness, suggesting the fragility of human experience. The installation spread out across the floor surrounding the projections as I slowly and carefully retrieved discarded weavers' objects from far corners of the space to construct a complex of discarded clogs, mill workers' clothing, tools, bobbins, oily rags—fragments of past mill activity.

Accompanying the visual aspects of the installation was an audiotape of the Barchant Mill looms interspersed with elements from an interview I recorded with Alice Slater, whose recorded voice was loud and clear, filling the entire factory floor. Alice herself attended the installation opening and watched from the audience as the factory siren was sounded and women left their weaving to enter and view the installation.

I swept dust from the corners into the center of the space. Onto the debris I scattered a pile of pink printed tags labeled "8s Ring Yarn." I uncurled loom belts as if to unwind the past; I dragged a heavy chain from one end of the space to the next, back and forth; and, as I moved, my shadow was cast across the projections. I untangled the threads of discarded cotton reels and positioned them across the floor in relationship to other objects and the projection. I moved slowly and carefully to the sound of Alice's voice, chalking strike and lockout dates on the wooden floor in order to add a further layer to the installation. The humid air of the mill's upper floor caused the chalked words to lift and fade as the humidity rose from beneath, creating a blank space upon which more dates were then inscribed.

Time & Motion illustrates a process of shifting; for example, moving clothing from museums—clothing that carries the imprint of their former wearers—into the disused and desolate work space created an ominous presence, a scene of confrontation. The voice of Alice Slater recalling her memory of millwork added to the installation the reality of the compulsion of wage labor. The archive projections were represented so that the details of faces were drawn out of the posed and formalized photographs to reveal the identities of the women, hinting at possibilities for self-determination and autonomy from the ways lives have been defined by work.

The *Time & Motion* of the title subverts its usual definition—a time and motion study as surveillance of the productivity of individual workers, where the motion of the looms become a monotonous, thundering sound. The installation rejects the confines of these meanings and moves into real time: the struggle for redefinition, where meaningful relationships and connections can be made. *Time & Motion* suspends the moment of exploitation, portraying it as potentially paralyzed, where the only movements are the words spoken and those chalked onto the mill floor, and where the motion of knowledge and experience is defined by the weavers themselves:

I started work when I was fourteen. We had no choice, you knew you were going into the mill, if you were clever, or whatever, it didn't matter, you had to go there.

Well, it was a bit of a shock the first time I went in, the noise and the dirt and the fluff, it was terrible. I thought, oh, I won't be able to stand this, but you did. We used to start at seven in the morning and seven till ten in the morning on Saturdays. I worked in the mill forty years, I left to have my children, then I went back after the war and worked part-time. . . . Nearly everyone went back to work after having their children because they couldn't afford to stay at home. One wage wasn't enough, especially if your husband worked in the mill too.

When I first worked in the mill I was sort of tenting—we had to do the sweeping for a trained weaver who we had to work for. We had to lie on the floor; sweep under the looms, and we got six shillings for doing four looms like that! The fluff was deep, deep, and everywhere was covered in this fluff; it couldn't have been healthy. Those were the conditions at the time and we had no protection. Many people I knew had bronchitis and other ailments later in life, and I'm not surprised because all that was in the air at the time.

There were tattlers, managers, and bosses higher up. It was very strict, the managers were always looking around, walking around to see if they saw you talking, laughing, or minding your work. By talking you did a lot of sign language, so you could talk to someone right across the shed. I think that's why people in Lancashire talk more clearly, because we had to use our lips to pronounce, we could read each others lips.[2]

TYING THE THREADS

Tying the Threads was installed at the Oldham Art Gallery in Lancashire, England, funded by North West Arts. The installation audiotape combined a small selection of excerpts from oral history interviews with spinners from the Oldham Library archive, including Nellie Fitton, Lucy Lees, Annie Mills, Agnes Sutton, and George Wild. These archive interviews were edited in chronological order and interwoven with my own interviews with both retired spinners who remembered the trade and spinners currently working in the trade. These latter sixteen extensive interviews were with local spinners Lillian Hirst, Harriet Berry, Alice Whitehead, Alice Tait, Ivy Scott, Doris Bradbury, Sheila Cartmill, Lily Challinor, Pat Gormley, Alice Hilton, Olive Jones, Maria Maksymowych, Joan Moores, Alice Partington, Edith Taylor, and Ingrid Wilson. Through the interwoven interviews, comparisons could be made about women's experiences at different times. By adding interviews with the sixteen women—some who began in the industry early this century as half-timers and others who started a few years ago—a near complete picture was mapped out over time.

While the Oldham museum paints the usual nostalgic view of life in the industry, *Tying the Threads* portrays a very different reality. Like the representation of Alice Slater's account in *Time & Motion*, the Oldham mill workers are portrayed as the history-makers as opposed to the traditional industrial revolution "pioneers" they are often portrayed to be.

The installation at the Oldham Art Gallery was laid out with dissolving slides projected onto the far wall. As I had done in the *Time & Motion* installation, I rephotographed and enlarged images from the local archive, collaging thread onto the printed archive images that I later produced as slides. Tinting the slides so that some were sepia, faint green, blue, or gray added subtle colors that created an atmosphere connecting the archival time of the photographs to the present reality of the chronological voice recording and the contemporary voices. The gallery space was long and narrow, so from the projections at the far wall I attached threads of cotton that spanned out, crisscrossing from floor to ceiling, back and forth across the space, until the threads themselves formed a scale equivalent to a loom. Interspersed between the threads were objects from the local history museum that were once used by local cotton workers. The threads and objects crisscrossed over the projections and cast shadows as the oral history tape I had compiled with the local Oldham mill workers played throughout the gallery.

Because many early radical suffragists were working-class women and mill workers, a window at the left of the gallery was blocked off by cotton strike dates and the names of suffragists who worked at Lancashire mills. In 1808, *The Times* reported, "The women mill workers were more turbulent than the men." In 1834, there was the Eight Hour Riot in Oldham, and among those arrested was Sally Whitehead, a cotton worker. At the early Peterloo cotton demonstration in 1819, several banners were inscribed "Universal Suffrage," and sixty-five years later four female Peterloo survivors, who had been cotton workers, demonstrated to the House Of Lords. They were Mary Collins, Cathrine McMurdo, Sussannah Whittaker, and Alice Schofield. Other active suffragists from Lancashire include Sarah Reddish, Mrs. Winbott, Annie Heaton, Annie Kenny (born in Oldham), Cissy Foley, and Selina Cooper.[3] Undoubtedly, there were many more, but none received the recognition given to middle-class women like the Pankhursts. The working classes are constantly denied the power of their own printed words, so little is known of the few women we can name.

Harriet Berry is one of many elderly women I interviewed in Oldham who still suffers from the poor working conditions after retirement. Berry worked in the cotton mills from 1923 to 1937, and, like many mill workers who suffered ill health resulting from industry conditions, she received no compensation:

My job was putting raw cotton in the back of the roller so that it comes out as a coil. It was called "feeding the devil," and I got bysinnosis. The damage was already done. I had chronic bronchitis at seventeen, and I had to go into the hospital because they thought I had consumption.

The union just brought me small food parcels when I had this poisoning. (I don't have much faith in unions.) It's the dust that did it. I could feel the dust going up my nose and in my throat. There were big lumps of dust always flying about. Breathing problems were common; a lot of people I worked with, early on, got bysinnosis. I didn't get compensation because my doctor first identified it as bronchitis. But apart from anything else, it gives you a bad heart. I collapsed last Wednesday, and the nurse said I could collapse anytime because my heart is under strain and is not strong enough to help my circulation. I had to be tested in Manchester, and they asked me to blow [into a measure]. But I couldn't blow into it at all![4]

Lily Challinor was born in 1940 and has worked in the cotton industry since 1958:

I began work in the industry in 1958, and early in the sixties there was a lot of dole, short-time working. When we went in the mills, the mills were higher wages; that's why we went in. Now, even though I have an excellent work record, I've never been on the dole. I get £3 an hour for doing the same job I've done for thirty years.[5]

Maria Maksymowych was born in the Ukraine in 1930. She has worked in the cotton industry since 1955:

I'm a ring spinner. I've been doing my job for thirty-six years, ring spinning. Some people get bysinnosis. When you work for a long time in the mill you have to watch yourself. You always have to wash your hands before you have your meals, wash your mouth out; you have to look after yourself. You have an x-ray every five years, I think. They used to come to the mill in the yard, a special mobile x-ray we used to have so you knew whether you got it or not.

The machinery makes a lot of noise and you have to wear earplugs, because it does affect your hearing if you don't wear them. It's five years since they asked me to wear them. Before we didn't know, nobody was bothering about hearing aids, but now they do.[6]

Bysinnosis and deafness are two common conditions for women who worked in the cotton industry. In addition, "kissing the shuttle," or threading the shuttle, often caused mill workers to lose their teeth from sucking in the dirt, dust, and oil along with the thread.[7] Ingrid Wilson explained that the oil used in the cotton industry caused skin cancer. Ingrid Wilson, born in Austria in 1931, worked in the cotton mills from the 1950s to the 1980s:

When the men did the oiling, they had a certain kind of oil, and when they oiled the spindles, they had little cups and they had to take the spindles out and put the oil in. You had to move because that oil caused skin cancer. That was when I was still working.

There were tapes, and them tapes are turning four speeds, two on this side, two on the other side. Sometimes the tape slips off because beneath the mill you had a big tin roller that went over, and they had to go and check that. They put the machine on, and checked to see that the tape was still on, and the oil splashed. Then they got burnt out, they had marks. The men had marks on their skin and arms, on their legs and around here [indicates stomach and groin area]. They got burnt out, but they didn't make a hole, it just left a skin bite, it never went any deeper, it always left a bite. Little rings and that oil caused skin cancer.[8]

Through their personal and direct experience, the weavers and spinners integrate and overturn the status quo of traditional social historians and powerful history makers. Installation art concerns itself with space and composition of media through space—both *Time & Motion* and *Tying the Threads* realize this formal construct in relation to meaning and metaphor. Both pieces embody a notion of social space, where the viewer listens to voices traditionally marginalized and silenced.

NOTES

1. Alison Marchant, *Renegotiations: Class, Modernity & Photography*, exhibition catalog, ed. John Roberts (Norwich Gallery, England, 1993).

2. Alice Slater (b. 1920), personal interview, Longridge, Lancashire, England, June 1990.

3. Jill Liddington and Jill Norris, *One Hand Tied behind Us* (England: Virago, 1978).

4. Harriet Berry (b. 1909), personal interview, Oldham, Lancashire, England, November 1991.

5. Lily Challinor (b. 1940), personal interview, Oldham, Lancashire, England, November 1991.

6. Maria Maksymowych (b. 1930, Ukraine), personal interview, Oldham, Lanchashire, England, November 1991.

7. Minnie Walkden, recorded interview by Freda Millet, Oldham Local History Library, Lancashire, England.

8. Ingrid Wilson (b. 1931, Austria), personal interview, Oldham, Lanchashire, England, November 1991.

Time & Motion, installation, 1990 (Photo: Patsy Mullan).

Time & Motion, detail, 1990 (Photo: Patsy Mullan).

Time & Motion, detail, 1990 (Photo: Patsy Mullan).

Tying the Threads, installation, 1993.

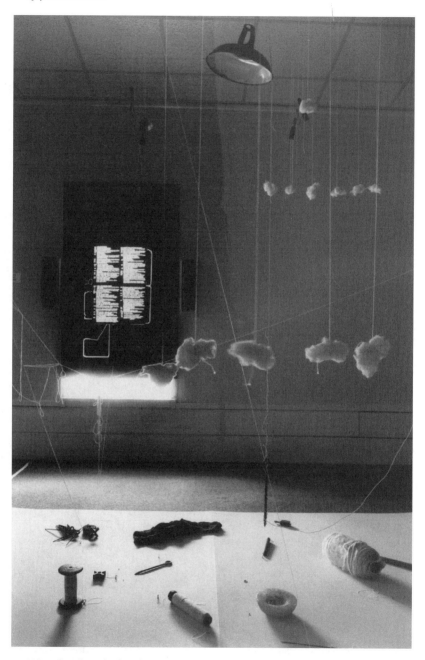

Tying the Threads, detail, 1993.

Tying the Threads, detail, 1993.

Patching the Past

Students and Oral History

ANNE M. BUTLER AND GERRI W. SORENSON

The women's history curriculum, with its many tiers, resonates with intellectual opportunities for both instructor and student. With the addition of an oral history component, especially at the introductory course level, the boundaries of the classroom bend outward and encompass women beyond the academic setting. As a result, all involved have a possibility of learning more about the patterns of womanhood than might be expected from the traditional lecture/discussion course.

My first call to teach women's history came simultaneously from two different institutions—one a Jesuit-owned local college where I did occasional adjunct evening teaching and the other Gallaudet University for the Deaf where I held a full-time position in the history department. The two schools mirrored one another in terms of student interest and ability but differed in matters of pedagogical strategies. Faced with the need to develop somewhat parallel courses, I wanted to maximize my preparations, making them appropriate for both environments while customizing the design to meet the needs of two separate constituencies.

To start, I turned to Gerda Lerner's 1981 pamphlet, *Teaching Women's History*.[1] Lerner's argument that the judicious use of family interview and autobiography assignments could be successfully woven into the fabric of a traditional introductory course persuaded me to include an oral history assignment for my courses.[2] By doing so, I hoped to draw my two groups of students into previously unexplored family arenas that could be illuminated within a historical context; in addition, I believed the narrative form—especially powerful in sign language communication—would serve to bond deaf students to their hearing families.

I began with the premise that the introductory U.S. women's course, while framed around historical eras and significant events, should emphasize the roles of ordinary women in the building of America's heritage. One way to accomplish that was to encourage young college students to talk with older females, preferably family members, to understand the links between their own relatives and national events. Thus, I chose to model my major class activity after that suggested by Ruth Rosen in her University of California, Davis, course, "Society and the Sexes in the Twentieth Century."[3] This course included the requirement that students interview a woman at least twenty years older and use the responses to place the interviewee within a historical context.[4]

In addition to the interview itself, Rosen required students to produce a seven-page paper that analyzed the impact of historical change on the interviewee. The transformation of an oral element into a written assessment fit well with the current emphasis on student writing.[5] Yet, the thought of so much life information about individual women only passing before my eyes seemed to flatten the vitality of the project and prevent the students from learning about many diverse experiences.

From this concern, I constructed a second project element, wherein I divided the class into panels. Each panel assumed responsibility for a full class period to present a summary of its collective interviews. The panels' task came with considerable latitude in choosing themes for the presentations. For example, one group might stress the role of education in the lives of its interviewees, while another might focus on the impact of domestic life, and yet another on the varieties of experience in the paid labor force.

Certain stipulations guided the panels. The presentation had to fit the limits of the class hour, each panel member had to participate actively in the group's project, and some sort of handout had to be distributed to the other students. The inclusion of each student in the presentation and the handout requirement came directly out of my deaf-classroom experience. Of the former, I had learned that deaf students, after years of struggle in hearing classrooms, often showed little inclination to stand before a group. As for the latter requirement, handouts have almost universal appeal for deaf students who find it nearly impossible to watch simultaneously a lecture delivered in sign language and take notes about it. Over time I learned that these strategies proved just as valuable for hearing students. Both groups needed to expand self-confidence in front of an audience, and both relied on the handouts as study guides when preparing for the final examination.

Each year when I introduced this assignment and designated the teams, I sensed the negative tension that ran through the class. Students, who rarely knew each other, glanced around uneasily, read over the instructions, and peered at the suggested questions. Clearly, they did not relish the idea of working with a group of strangers in a situation in which personal initiative might be uneven. Nor did they like the out-of-class time commitment. Not only would the interview consume several hours, but the panels would need planning sessions, probably more than one. Male students, often the most academically aggressive and quick in the larger class discussion, appeared especially uncomfortable; with only one or two on a team, they recognized that the power dynamics had shifted, and they entered an intimate team situation that accentuated their minority status in the class.

I learned that it was important to allow students to raise questions about the interviews over several class meetings. After the first quiet resistance, students began the objections: "My grandmother lives in California. I can't do this over the phone"; "I don't know any deaf adults in this area"; "I work nights and don't have time to meet with my group"; "My mother was only eighteen when I was born"; "I don't know any woman twenty years older who is still alive."

Then there was the thorny problem of how to present the interview material to the class. At the outset, students appeared stymied by the need to organize a full class period. To get them moving, I gave the groups about fifteen minutes to meet in class on the day I announced the panels. I suggested they use the time to exchange names and phone numbers and possibly select a group leader. As they began the process, the concept began to solidify, and they developed more significant questions.

I encouraged students to interview their mothers or grandmothers but stressed there was no requirement to do so.[6] I acknowledged that some family situations—estrangement, mental illness, violence, or alcoholism—might make a student exceedingly uneasy about an interview with a parent. Other circumstances—death or distance—might make the choice of "mother" impractical. The interview process can lead to certain risky intellectual and emotional quagmires with any respondent. Issues of subjectivity, language choices, class and cultural differences, family agendas, generational conflicts, and misrepresentation are only a few of the stumbling blocks, especially for the novice interviewer.[7] Despite these possible problems, I urged students to "take the plunge" and interview their own mothers or another relative, always reminding them they were under no obligation to do so.

Invariably, a few students felt "stuck," removed from family and unfamiliar with the older generation about the campus. In those cases, I directed students to some university workers, women on campus who were delighted to be included. A powerful interview came from a staff secretary who had cancer and died the week after her interviewer movingly spoke about this woman's changed gender perspectives, altered by the force of a terminal illness. In addition, some students enjoyed successful interview experiences by contacting local nursing homes, inquiring if some resident would accept a college student visitor armed with a recorder and many questions. Both the nursing home residents and their caregivers responded enthusiastically to these sessions. As a result of these nonfamily interviews, students often found themselves surprised by the early achievements and attitudes of these elderly women, and their new cross-generational friendships often continued after the project's completion.

As students engaged the interview process and as panels began to design presentations, invariably a mood change overtook the class. Before class, while previously students sat silently engrossed in the school paper, now the classroom buzzed with conversation or sign-language clusters. Students who had ignored each other for weeks or only chatted about campus gossip now grabbed each minute for a quick brainstorming session or the exchange of information.

At some point, dates for the various presentations had to be announced. During the preparation period, I seldom have known the intended themes or the status of a project. Yet, by some simple good fortune—and perhaps a bit of pedagogical observation—for each class I have chosen a well-prepared and interesting first panel. Invariably, other groups, impressed by what they see and hear, immediately rendezvous and plan an emergency meeting to upgrade the quality of their activity. The initial panel serves a critical role as an inspiration, jolting the others to enhance their original program to a level of similar excellence.

Over ten years, my students have presented an amazing array of creative group projects. Each season I think that nothing new can be done with this assignment. Each class shows me that I am wrong. Panels have adopted the personality and dress of the subjects, created displays of their needlework and cooking, designed a women's newspaper using their interviewees for the articles, brought their subjects to trial as offenders of the "cult of domesticity," executed elaborate videotapes, discovered overwhelming accounts of the courage of their deaf mothers and the tenacity of their hearing ones, invited their grandmothers, mothers, spouses, and friends to their presentation, written songs about women and work, and performed a television talk show, complete with a Geraldo-type host. In a particularly moving presentation, one panel uncovered one-by-one huge photographs of their women as children, exploring the common themes permeating the adult lives. The contrast between the expectant faces of the little girls and the gender realities of adulthood created an unusually somber mood among the listeners.

From my adjunct position teaching a class of registered nurses working for bachelor's degrees came diverse accounts of a woman whose retired military officer husband refused to allow her to give the interview unless he sat in the room; of a woman who interviewed her mother-in-law over seven hours as the father-in-law followed the two women from room to room trying to suppress the accounts of forty years of physical violence; and of the student who told of her Puerto Rican mother, who had never heard of New York's Triangle Shirtwaist Factory but who had experienced its horror in a New Jersey camera manufacturing plant in the 1960s (a fire forced the women to flee, but they found all the emergency exits locked and, driven by panic to the one open door, they trampled the incoming firemen to the ground). Finally, there was the senior charge nurse who explained how she agonized about her supervisory responsibility and her relationship with an employee who had neither the time nor the tuition to take the academic courses that would have made her a registered nurse. This licensed practical nurse was always late for work because her drug-addicted sister and brother-in-law had moved home, where she herself had fled to escape an abusive spouse. Lacking sufficient income to rent her own apartment or pay for child care, the LPN dared leave her four-year-old son for only a few hours each day because of the threat of violence in her parents' house. Her erratic work attendance jeopardized the marginal employment she had. "What am I to do? What is she to do?" the supervisor asked over and over, overcome by emotion and frustration.

Clearly, the interviews unleashed powerful information and accounts, they revealed far more than I had anticipated, they touched students in every class, and year after year, they enveloped me. Unfailingly, they underscored the way in which gender, race, class, and disability made an impact on women's lives within the context of American history. Further, students came to perceive that ordinary, unknown American women made social, economic, and political contributions to the shaping of our heritage. In the more than ten years and four universities where I have used this assignment, only one woman surrounded by fame served as the subject of an interview, and she was the daughter of prominent Hollywood celebrities of the 1930s, not a "star" herself.

The presentations have ranged from the humorous to the painful, but each one has always brought a resounding burst of applause at its conclusion. Not one has ever been boring, nor have students lost interest as the presentations stretched over six or seven class days. Never once has a student failed to complete the entire assignment—interview, panel, and paper. Students wrote me notes and thanked me for allowing them to get to know their mothers and grandmothers. Mothers and grandmothers thanked me for the shared moments with their daughters and granddaughters. Deaf students connected with hearing mothers and with other deaf women. Older women especially saw themselves and their subjects as part of America's rich story. As for me, I often felt overwhelmed, saddened, inspired—always further convinced that oral history served to illuminate deep and powerful indicators that women have been crucial to the development of America.

My sense is that this assignment allows for an experience of oral history at its best. Young women and men find themselves immersed in the lives of their own relatives but also excited by the accounts of other interviewees. The students talk to their subjects and then they talk to each other. Of course, when a class includes a range of ethnicity, the results are even more dramatic. Suddenly students confront both the commonalities and disparities in womanhood; they learn from firsthand accounts the ways in which race and class divide American women. While the accounts are highly personal and subjective, they also illuminate historical eras from which the students have felt distanced. The interviewees enjoy the realization that their own lives are held up as examples of American womanhood. It no longer surprises me when at the end of the term, students insist that I retain the interview project for the following year.

In 1989, I moved to Utah State University, bringing with me the women's history course. I worried as never before about how women's history would affect the students. Most came from a religious and social culture that stressed traditional values in their most conservative forms and viewed intellectual subjects concerning women and feminism as threatening and radical. I believed that the students would be courteously receptive to the lectures, but personally removed. I suspected that the response would be, "This lecture stuff is very interesting, but all that work outside the home and political activism does not relate to women here in Utah." Generally, I was correct in that assumption, yet the oral history interview project often dramatically altered students' perceptions of their female relatives and themselves. I realized that in Utah the panel presentations continued the earlier patterns I had seen at other universities, influencing the tone and response of the class. Yet, even with all this experience and sense that the assignment elicits both personal and intellectual benefits for students, I was not prepared for the presentation of the quilt by a panel in my 1997 women's history class at Utah State University. Below, Gerri Sorenson, a group project leader, offers her own and other group members' insights into their panel's quilt project.

THE VOICE OF A STUDENT LEADER

The group project for Anne M. Butler's women and family history class evolved into the telling of our own stories. Exploring the lives of the women interviewed proved a discovery for each student participant. This project, requiring oral interviews of women twenty years older than each student and the group organization of the interviews to be presented, took shape as a multileveled learning experience. As the students within the groups came to know better the women they interviewed, so too did they come to understand the connection we all share within the circle of humanity.

Each group within the class selected a different way to present its finished projects, but the initial consensus of the class toward the assignment seemed to be the same. Everyone agreed that she/he scorned group-related projects. While Professor Butler may or may not have been aware of the great distaste for team activities in a classroom setting, she, nonetheless, presented the project to the class with the highest of expectations. In fact, her enthusiasm was quite annoying, but no one felt bold enough to challenge her plan. At best, however, the class greeted her description of the assignment with reserve; she did not seem to notice.

Remarkably, this project given to Utah State University's "Women and Family in America" history class resulted in stunningly successful evaluations from students. Members of the panel featured in this article agreed that this was not only the first academic group activity that they had enjoyed, but also that this experience revitalized and focused their learning through its many dimensions.

In general, students vacillated about the first step in the assignment, selecting a woman twenty years senior for a respondent. The assignment permitted students to select any woman, but Professor Butler repeatedly encouraged the class to try a family member. As we began to chat informally among ourselves, I noticed the first warming to the assignment as my class-mates talked about the appeal of interviewing a family member. Many students, however, lived away from home and could not find convenient ways to converse with their mothers or grandmothers. Travel expenses and phone costs blocked the way for student budgets. Other students seemed reluctant to involve themselves in such a personal exercise with their maternal relatives. Some class members simply maintained a silence about the whys and wherefores of their choices. We did not press each other to explain these decisions.

Of the seven-member team for which I was the group leader, four interviewed women within the family circle, while three chose nonrelatives. Of the latter three, each expressed an initial desire to interview family. For example, Sheryl Fain-Chance wanted to question her aunt, but the older woman's illness prevented this and so Sheryl turned to a local bartender with whom she had been acquainted for several years. Dean Dominguez, the only male and Hispanic in our group, interviewed a woman he knew through coaching a local high-school swim team. After the project had been completed, he rued that he had not driven home to interview his mother, whose ethnic experience would have expanded our perspective. Luwanna Cook could not meet the twenty-year rule with her mother, so she met with a neighbor woman who had given her assistance and guidance. I faced the same constraints about my mother and so drove to Idaho to see my grand-mother. Brandy Oliver, curious about her personal heritage, also chose her grandmother; with thousands of miles separating the two, the interview had to be conducted by telephone. Tawna Hasty and Natalie Rose interviewed their own mothers because they felt close friendship with these women and hoped to deepen cherished sentiments.

During our team preparations, each student acknowledged that the oral interview changed his or her interaction with the interviewee, regardless of how long the association had existed. Sheryl, a returning student who worked as a nightclub singer, summed up the group feeling when she indicated that prior to the interview she had enjoyed a somewhat superficial acquaintance with her bartender friend, but after their lengthy session the relationship acquired a new intimacy, one difficult to explain. The other panel members agreed, each talking about a fresh perception of his or her subject. I remember saying to my colleagues, "I feel a new connection with my grandmother. I see her as more than my grandma in an apron. . . . It has opened up my eyes toward other women."[8]

The context for women's history given through the class lectures suddenly took on greater texture and larger implications. Our class, generally, began to understand the complexities of individual lives and the way in which each melded with others to create "history." Even further, from these conversations, we began to sense our place and contribution in this process. Students in my group commented that by stretching relationship boundaries, new personal confidence began to emerge. Sheryl spoke for all of us when she said, "We came to know ourselves better and how we related to the world. I had always had this thing . . . I'm not good enough. Watching women go through all that they did gave me an appreciation for all that I am as a woman and a realization that it's okay to be me."[9]

Our group grappled with these feelings as we wrestled with the practicalities of the assignment concerning the class presentation of our interviews. It was one thing to gather the interviews and talk about how moving they had been for us; it was another to figure out what we would do with our class hour. Sharing our interviews with each other proved to be fun and interesting, but we felt overwhelmed about how to convey our findings in an organized manner to the class.

Assembled in my living room one evening in the winter of 1997, our panel represented a cross section of the student body. We six Anglo women and one Hispanic man ranged in age from nineteen to forty-one. No prior friendships or associations helped bridge us to one another. We came together as strangers, selected to be the first group to present a fifty-minute "event" for our classmates. We tried to tell ourselves we had won a lucky spot, for certainly little would be expected of the first presenters. On the other hand, our group felt an obligation to set a high standard for the other students. Later, we laughed when Tawna captured those first sentiments of the group: "We wanted to be the best so that the rest of the class would hate us!"[10]

Although merely strangers thrown together by chance, our group shared a common tone from the outset. We had agreed that by our first meeting the interviews would be completed, and each student met that deadline. From our first discussion about the interviews, we agreed that we had undergone a different process in academic learning, that we all wanted something distinctive for the class. Above all, we thought that our class presentation should reflect favorably on the exceptional women we had interviewed. If their contributions to womanhood had been anonymous for several decades, we set about to correct the oversight.

As we discussed various possibilities, our eyes were drawn to a double wedding ring quilt hanging on my living room wall. The ivory muslin background set off in stunning array the colors and patterns of the varied bits of fabric, all linking to form the ring design. The group began to talk about a quilt as a metaphor by which the lives of the women could be introduced to the class.

This particular quilt, made from scraps donated to an invalid Idaho woman, seemed to capture the message we wanted to convey—small pieces, many textures, combined into a work of art that highlighted the triumph of womanhood. Like the differing fabrics that made up the coverlet, each woman had a life story that blended into a larger mosaic. In addition, drawing inspiration from the labors of a bedridden rural woman underlined the fundamental concept of our class: Ordinary women, through their diverse labors, contributed to America's heritage.

Deciding on an appropriate metaphor for the women we interviewed turned out to be the easy part of our task. We then faced the problem of how to present this quilt comparison to the class. Finally, the group settled on making a quilt that would represent the lives of the women interviewed. The one man among us was aghast; such an undertaking was completely beyond his comprehension. Later he admitted returning to his fraternity house and telling his roommates that he was part of an insane group of women.

Coupled with his reaction, other pressures threatened our project. Four members of the group were scrambling toward spring graduation, and one was recovering from a recent heart attack. The reality of these other demands and a class presentation now only one week away caused the panel to sort through other options, but we kept returning to the idea of using a quilt as the base of our presentation.

Given the constraints of time and responsibility, we decided to make a paper quilt for the class and use it to recount the stories of our interviewees. Almost immediately we realized that constructing a paper model would prove as time-consuming and expensive as an actual quilt. It was during this process of selecting our theme that initial reservations about group work diminished and the cohesiveness of our panel developed. We reached a unanimous decision that a real quilt promised to illuminate the importance and the permanence of the assignment—qualities about the interviews we all now admitted to each other and to ourselves.

It occurred to us that the idea of producing a quilt and other materials for a class presentation within a week was daunting at best. Like the quilting metaphor, however, taken in pieces the project became manageable. Soon every member of the group believed we had defined an attainable goal.

Though Dean Dominguez expressed skepticism about his ability to make even one quilt square, his female copanelists won him over with their convictions about his abilities, and their encouragement carried him through the following week.

Having arrived at a consensus, our next step involved determining the procedures by which we could complete our undertaking. Here the widely differing talents within the team became an asset. Though some knew nothing about sewing, they knew everything about organization, or production, or print materials. The structure of tasks for finishing a quilt lent itself to an easy division of group labor.

Each student assumed responsibility for contributing one page for the class handout and producing two squares for the quilt. Of the two quilt blocks, one was to represent the life of the woman, the other to contain a picture or silhouette of her. Reducing the life of an individual into the space of an eight-by-eleven-inch block meant more than just shaping an artistic projection; the work allowed us time for personal introspection and exchange. Once again, many levels of understanding emerged among us. One group member asked, "If I were going to make a quilt square about my life, what would I include?" This query focused the task at hand, but also heightened our awareness of the life potential we each encompassed.

After many hastily organized meetings and the consumption of much chocolate, both quilt blocks and friendships began to take shape. Meeting time we spent cutting and creating quilt blocks, helping those who lacked access to sewing machines. Although we always began by talking about the women we interviewed, by the end of each evening we had mingled their lives with ours and retold our own histories.

In addition, the importance of each woman spread from her interviewer to all of us; after a time, any of us could recount the life of each woman interviewed by our team. We wept when one member told how from the interview she learned that her grandmother had been the product of a vicious rape. We applauded another woman who, though only five feet tall, loved to play basketball, even through her later life. We grieved for the woman who lost four of her six children through illnesses and accidents.

Shared stories and unique moments forged our unity as the patched pieces came together. Not only did the group assume that Dean lacked any understanding of sewing and quilting, but we also wrongly expected the converse, that all the women would be schooled in at least some aspects of needle and thread. With chagrin we acknowledged that within our group some members shared a common distaste for domestic activity of any kind. Yet, as our quilt—fourteen life blocks pieced together on a floral background and then tie-quilted with yarn—emerged, each member focused on what she or he could bring to the endeavor, and judgments and criticisms never surfaced among us. Completing the quilt revealed our own gender prejudices but did not introduce disharmony as the work progressed. Ultimately, the outcome represented a celebration of differences. From the women interviewed to the members of the group itself, variety—like fibers, colors, weft and warp—contributed to the beauty of the whole.

When the day arrived to present the content of our interviews, the bonds formed among us while quilting made our appearance before the class less threatening. We felt more comfortable handling the information—much of it highly charged with emotion—than we had expected. For example, one student, fearful of public speaking, said she would accomplish this difficult task by focusing on the panel as close friends, gathered for an intimate conversation. Thus, the friendships initiated within our group transformed the class presentation into a quilting bee atmosphere for us, creating yet another level to the larger assignment.

As for the hour, our quilt made an obvious impact on our classmates. They sat riveted as we explained the symbolic meaning of each square, the life of the woman, and the impact of the interviews on each of us. With the exception of one participant, we each brought for display a quilt borrowed from our interviewee, thus enlarging the symbolism of our quilt metaphor. Our classmates felt the power of the accounts, which we explained within the context of such forces as women's employment and educational opportunities during the Great Depression or World War II. One student explained the family response to the illegitimate birth of her grandmother in terms of sexual mores prevalent during her great-grandmother's life. Another described the seemingly misguided educational choices made by her mother in the context of marriage pressures of the 1950s. The audience appeared to appreciate our device for displaying these seven lives and grasped their historical significance because of class lectures devoted to these earlier decades.

Both male and female students responded favorably to Dean, an athlete and swimming coach, for his full participation in the project, while he glowed with obvious pride as he explained his quilt blocks. We knew, too, that we had stunned Professor Butler when at the end of the hour we gave the quilt to her. It will be secure in her care, where it can be shown to other classes pondering the best way to showcase their interviewees.

This class project, intended to illuminate the historical place of individual women, provided us with unexpected benefits. As we explored the stories of the women interviewed, we reconsidered our own lives, in them finding parallel themes and personal potential. The many levels and nuances developed within each of us were best expressed by Natalie Rose. She said, "This group experience will always hold a special place in my heart, as I remember the friendships that we made as we tried to discover a woman's place in history. This assignment made me realize that no one stands alone in this world. We are all connected through a quilting of experiences."

Our desire to do well in the course and to create something with a sense of permanence survived beyond the construction of the quilt and our accounts of women's lives as shaped by gender. Five months after our presentation, late in the summer of 1997, the panel reassembled twice to discuss the ramifications of this assignment. I found it significant that so long after a course had ended, class members would respond with such enthusiasm when given a chance to talk about a homework assignment. And our relationships have not ended. The panel, moved by Dean's assertion, "Now I want to make my own quilt," has agreed to help him do just that. This promises to be another memorable group initiative, but now generated from among ourselves and not out of a course requirement. Below are several student quotes drawn from the second session.[11]

This experience brought me back to life as a student. I miss tangible learning, you can only sit and listen to a lecture for so long.—Tawna

We came to know ourselves better and how we related to the world.—Sheryl

We became friends. That is why the presentation was so good.—Brandy

My husband used to say, "There you go with those feminist ideas again," and I used to back down. Now I say, "You're right!"—Luwanna

These women shared so many of the same struggles. All had trials and tribulations, yet they approached them differently.—Brandy

The main theme which I picked up from the class presentations was that women of all generations are not content to simply sit back and let others shape their lives.—Natalie

I had just known her as my mom; I really didn't know her as more than that. —Luwanna

We are living the product of history as women.—Sheryl

As described by this panel of students, the assignment to conduct an oral history interview produced several results, some of which appear to have survived the course. First, the students came to know and understand their interviewees in ways that heightened the importance of gender. At the same time, students increased their awareness of their own potential and significance as participants in history. Second, the assignment to create a group activity expanded the oral history aspect of the project, as students within a team exchanged their subjects' lives and their own with each other. Thus, the oral history segment acquired a multilayered value. Third, the students linked individual lives of ordinary women to larger historical events. This component, however, required the instructor's attention throughout the course, so that student reports, written and oral, did not degenerate into simplistic romanticized terms that ignored the historical context of a woman's life. Fourth, the assignment helped students to forge peer relationships that extended beyond the duration of the course. Fifth, some questioning of role definitions for women and men occurred within this group because of its project. As the instructor, I hope that sense of inquiry will continue for each individual.

For this panel, the use of oral history as central to a student-generated activity resulted in personal bonding and intellectual understanding. Within the class generally there may have been complex responses to the assignment that were not entirely positive for an individual student or respondent and for which no measure was taken. Written course evaluations, which exceeded the department and college norm, did not appear to indicate that such was the case for students, but such information could have been intentionally withheld. Nonetheless, this assignment, despite its risks, transcends the classroom and suggests that the personal voices of women across generations illuminate gender history in ways that have eluded rigidly traditional instruction.

NOTES

1. Gerda Lerner, *Teaching Women's History* (Washington DC: American Historical Association, 1981).

2. Lerner, *Teaching Women's History*, 23–27, 57–60.

3. I acknowledge my intellectual debt to the many professors who contributed course outlines to Annette K. Baxter's *Women's History: Selected Reading Lists and Course Outlines from American Colleges and Universities* (New York: Marcus Weiner,

1984). The various statements of purpose, course goals, requirements, readings, and projects included in that publication influenced the way in which I shaped my course. The syllabus of Ruth Rosen, winter 1984, is on pages 81–94.

4. Baxter, *Women's History*, 87–90. Rosen provided students with a set of guide questions to facilitate the interview, the answers serving as the basis for a short paper.

5. When Donald A. Ritchie's book, *Doing Oral History* (New York: Twayne) appeared in 1995, I used it to further my understanding of how to guide students toward effective family interviews. By 1996, I had used at different times Jill Ker Conway, ed., *Written by Herself: An Anthology* (New York: Vintage Books, 1992); LaDonna Swan, *Autobiography of a Dakota Woman* (Norman: University of Oklahoma Press, 1991); and Sherna Berger Gluck, *Rosie the Riveter Revisited: Women, the War, and Social Change* (Boston: Twayne, 1987) as class readings to help students conceptualize the value of the autobiography.

6. Lerner, *Teaching Women's History*, 18.

7. For discussion of many of the difficulties that intertwine with the value of women's oral history research and suggestions about how to be alert to these problems, see the essays in *Women's Words: The Feminist Practice of Oral History*, ed. Sherna Berger Gluck and Daphne Patai (New York: Routledge, 1991).

8. Gerri W. Sorenson, group interview, August 7, 1997, Utah State University, Logan, Utah.

9. Sheryl Fain-Chance, group interview, August 7, 1997.

10. Tawna Hasty, group interview, August 7, 1997.

11. Gerri W. Sorenson, interview with panel members: Sheryl Fain-Chance, Luwanna Cook, Dean Dominguez, Tawna Hasty, and Brandy Oliver, August 7, 1997, Utah State University, Logan, Utah. Natalie Rose could not be present but mailed a statement to the team leader. Natalie Rose to Gerri W. Sorenson, August 5, 1997, Logan, Utah.

Frontiers 19:3 (1998): 200–213.

Oral History
Discoveries and Insights

3

Using Oral History to Chart the Course of Illegal Abortions in Montana

DIANE SANDS

Well, in 1969 I was sixteen and I found out that I was pregnant. And, of course, the first thing that I thought of was that I didn't want to be pregnant, and started asking around. Abortion was extremely illegal then. I first went to Dr. ——— here in town, who was my gynecologist, and he said absolutely not, that he saw no medical or psychiatric indications for an abortion. And I said, "Oh, come on, there's something, there must be something you can do." And he just said, "Absolutely not." And so then I went to Dr. ——— and I had sort of rumors that, had heard that somebody in town was doing them, and I couldn't find who it was. So I told my parents that I was pregnant, and they agreed with me that an abortion would have been the best procedure for me, and they talked to Dr. ———. And he referred us to a doctor in Kalispell. And then, I'm pretty sure that that was Dr. ——— and we went up there, and he was real, real nervous and sort of said out of the corner of his mouth, "I'm not doing them right now, but there's a doctor in Shelby who will do it." So we went from Kalispell over to Shelby and located this guy's office. And that was Dr. ——— and he was over the, had an office over the Rexall drug store on the main street in Shelby, Montana.

It seems to me it was $400 in cash, up front. And we went up there and it was just really, really a strange office, you know. There was no receptionist. There was this little old guy, and he just—ancient, way in his eighties—sort of came doddering out of the office. And he looked, I mean at the time I wasn't, I was really young, but I'm pretty sure now he was an alcoholic. You know, he had that sort of, the red nose and the bloodshot eyes, and his hands shook. And he was just filthy. He had food stains dripped down, he was wearing this really old suit and had food stains dripped down the front of this suit. You know, gravy on this tie and all that. And he told us to come back at—several hours later—it seems to me probably after hours, five o'clock or so, and to bring the money. And he was real concerned that, he wanted to make sure that, he didn't examine me, but he was very concerned about when my last period was. He wanted to make sure that I wasn't over whatever specified time limitations he had. He told me to bring a box of sanitary pads and some aspirin and come back. And so I, we, left and we sort of drove around Shelby for a while and came back.

And he took me into his back office, and it was . . . really strange. I'd never seen anything like that, even since. It was not, not any sort of a table. It was a chair where you sat upright, and it had stirrups on it, and you were supposed to be sitting upright. And he told me to take off my panty hose and my underpants and my shoes and sit up in this chair and put my feet up in the stirrups. And I did, and I looked around and, God, it was just, a stainless steel basin right by, right next to the chair with these instruments in it, with this sort of . . . the water was bloody and there was a sort of film of crud over the instruments, and the floor was dirty, and it had, there was blood on the floor, and there was another bowl that had these sort of bloody looking sponges in it, and I was thinking, God, you know, I've heard terrible stories, you know, my mother had told me about, oh, women she knew in the thirties and forties who had abortions, and one woman who had tried to, or had aborted herself with a, with a crochet hook, and how these women just, you know, died. They got infections and they hemorrhaged and they died. And I sat there and I realized, God, this is going to happen to you. I mean, this is just, this is not good. And he sat down and he took out a speculum and inserted that, and then took out what I realize now was probably a uterine catheter, and I looked at it, and, God, his hand was shaking, and I just said, "I've got to leave." So he just took the, oh, he told me, he told me that it was going to be very painful, and, but that if I screamed, that he would immediately stop the procedure, and throw me out. You know, he said, "If you want this, you know, you'd better be quiet." And I said, "Well, what are you going to do?" And he said he was going to dilate my cervix and then pack my uterus with gauze soaked in some sort of chemical, and that when I got back to Missoula, I was supposed to go right to the emergency room at the hospital and tell them what had been done, and that they would take care of it from there, but that this chemical, whatever it was, was going to start the abortion process.

The realities of reproduction, or at least potential reproduction, and the desire to control it are shared by all women. But, in proportion to the importance of these issues to women present and past, relatively little historical examination has occurred. The above quote is from the project entitled, "An Oral History of Illegal Abortion in Montana, 1880–1973," which, as an outgrowth of the Montana Women's History Project, began to examine women's reproductive history.[1] In 1975, the MWHP interviewed elderly women about their lives and contributions to Montana history. As part of those interviews, questions were asked about sexuality and reproduction. In 1980, the Montana Committee for the Humanities funded our project to conduct research into illegal abortion using oral history as the primary methodology.[2] Twenty interviews were conducted: Ten explored the private experience and values of the women—of various ages and backgrounds—who had sought illegal abortions; the other ten interviews concentrated on persons in the public sphere who had knowledge of abortions and the function of abortion in the community.[3]

The project also incorporated traditional research methodology into the history of illegal abortion. We assumed that such sources would be very limited, but this assumption proved incorrect. We knew in advance that material existed from trials of two abortionists, but we expected to find little else. The material we found within legal records, however, was considerable, though more illuminating by its volume than by its depth.

There are many reasons for the lack of historical research into the topic of female reproduction and its control. A primary one is that reproduction has not always been viewed as being within the historical process. Women have babies, have babies, have babies. This is seen as an ahistorical act, relatively unaffected by the events historians traditionally examine. Further, until the rise of the new social history, historians primarily examined events in the public sphere. Generally, reproduction has been viewed as existing totally within the private sphere, within the confines of the family. This study suggests that illegal abortion is to a large degree a "public sphere," or normal, community phenomenon. Finally, perhaps the most basic reason for the lack of historical examination is that female sexuality and reproduction exist within the realm of women's total life experience under patriarchy. In a society that continues to devalue women in all economic, social, and political arenas, it is not surprising to find that few resources have been invested in examining these areas of women's lives. Fortunately, recent emphasis by the Women's Movement on family and women's history has included the study of reproduction.[4]

Women have often been defined in terms of reproductive capacities. Women's contribution in the bearing of children has been extolled as women's primary role. The other side, the underside, of women's contribution is the control of, or limiting of, reproduction. In the interest of a better quality of life for themselves, their children, and their families, women have spent considerable time and energy *not* having children. The overwhelming evidence from the Montana project, as well as from cross-cultural studies conducted by Normal Himes and George Devereux, for example, is that women wanted children when they planned for and were able to provide for them, and sought to limit reproduction when conditions were less than desirable. Women have spent hours talking to husbands and sexual partners about birth control, pregnancy, childbearing, and ideal family size. They have passed endless days waiting and worrying for the late or missing menstrual period. They have read and consulted friends, doctors, and pharmacists about family planning techniques and "female problems." Unplanned and unwanted pregnancies were discussed in cloaked language, and if abortion was opted for, then more energy was required to find an abortionist and obtain the procedure. All this and more occurred within the context of repressive laws and social mores discouraging public discussion and dissemination of information on these topics.

WOMEN'S EXPERIENCE OF ABORTION

Who were the women who had abortions in Montana before 1973? Adding together the women interviewed and the women represented by death certificates and coroners' records, we found over seventy women. Just over half were married, just under one-third were single. The rest were divorced, widowed, or of unknown marital status. Except for three black women from the early part of this century, all were white. The economic status of most is unknown. Several informants have stated that in one town "one abortionist worked on coloreds and immigrants" while another worked "on the respectable women." The relationship of economic and ethnic status to access to competent medical care has been explored in other research and needs to be applied to this topic in future studies.

A case study will serve to illustrate some of the information gained in the interviews:

E.M., the oldest informant, had three abortions in the early 1930s during her first years of married life. The beginning of the Depression and a strong moral sensibility as to the obligations parents owed offspring led her and her husband to delay child rearing for ten years. Attempts at birth control ranged from cold water or turpentine douches to condoms and diaphragms. With the aid of a male family pharmacist, E.M. obtained two abortions from a women in a neighboring city for the sum of $100 each. The informant guessed from several clues that the abortionist was a prostitute. These successful abortions were done with catheterization, followed by sterile packing of the uterus. Her husband accompanied her to the first abortion, but for economic reasons she went alone for the second. A third abortion was obtained with the assistance of a friend, a neighboring ranch woman. This was done with a length of peeled, sharpened slippery elm, sold in most drug stores, which was inserted into the uterus and left for several hours. The slippery elm worked by puncturing the amniotic sac and also by slowly swelling and thereby dilating the mouth of the uterus. All abortions were done without pain killers and were quite painful. Stressing that she had never regretted the abortions, E.M. emphasized that she and her husband had felt it "unethical" to have children for whom they could not provide. In the 1940s, after ten years of marriage, they had two children. She stressed her daughters' successful careers and families, implying a relationship to their upbringing as "planned" children at a time when the family farm was economically strong. Other than her husband, her mother, and the persons directly involved in the abortions, the interviewer was the only person with whom she had ever discussed her abortion experiences.

Most of the women interviewed had tried various birth control techniques, but then as now, most methods were unreliable even when used correctly and regularly. Those who found themselves pregnant and decided on abortion did so primarily for socioeconomic or "quality of life" reasons. For single, divorced, or widowed women, lack of economic resources, as well as the scorn of the community for the unwed mother and her illegitimate child, influenced their decisions. Married women hoped to provide more economic and social resources for their children by having fewer children. Also, many women were aware of the health cost to the mothers of large families. Interestingly, health and safety concerns were seldom mentioned as a major concern in most women's attempts to find an abortionist.

Women who attempted self-induced abortions were likely to use a female network to obtain information about techniques. Crochet hooks, knitting needles, heavy lifting, coat hangers, turpentine drinks, throwing oneself down stairs, lysol or phisophex douches were among techniques reported. From the interviews and the over fifty death certificates showing illegal or self-induced abortion as the cause of death, it is hard to get a clear picture of the relative dangers of self-induced versus professionally induced abortions, but we assumed that professional abortionists had a lower complication rate.

In contrast to what we had expected, most women who sought abortions from "professionals" went through male networks to obtain this information. One could speculate that this is related to the access males have to "public" information on sexuality in our society. Male doctors, pharmacists, boyfriends, and men "who knew about these things" gave women the addresses of abortionists and, in some cases, even made the appointments. Although a community may have had a known abortionist, women tended to go to other towns to ensure privacy.

How did the women feel about the abortion? "Relieved" was the word women used repeatedly. None of the ten expressed excessive guilt over the abortion. Several women commented on the pressure they felt from family and friends to "feel guilty" when instead they either "felt numb" or "relieved." One woman even tired to respond to the cues to feel guilty, being quite conscious that she did not feel that way. For these women there were few people around them who were supportive of their choice or who were even good listeners.

It is very important to remember that ten women is not a large sample and is self-selected in many ways. Those women who had physical complications or emotional distress did not elect to talk to the project. This is, of course, a major methodological problem with oral history. We speak to the survivors and to willing survivors at that.

The abortion experience did have a marked, though varied, effect on the relationships of the women with their families. In cases where the women were married and the abortion was a mutual decision, as in the case study above, the women commented about how the experience brought husband and wife together. In another case, a marriage already in serious trouble was pushed closer to the edge by the experience: "On my first night home, he didn't pick me up at the airport and he had invited two friends to stay overnight in our one-room apartment. . . . It did contribute to our ultimate divorce." In yet another case, a young single woman told her parents she was pregnant. The father said, "You're going to have an abortion. Arrange it and send me the bill," and walked out of the house. He later told her that because of the abortion "no one will ever want to marry you." To prove to her father that this was not so, she married within six months of the abortion.

Men rarely accompanied women to the abortionist. More often a mother, sister, or close female friend went along. In these cases the women spoke very warmly of their feelings. "I wouldn't have gone with anyone else. My mother was the daughter of a physician, and I knew if anything was a little peculiar, mother would pick it up."

Finally, I cite a few examples of the effect of the "illegality" of the procedure on the women as they saw it. Most importantly, illegality made circuitous behavior necessary in obtaining an abortion. Many women felt the need for deception. The trick was to find a competent abortionist before the end of the first trimester of the pregnancy had passed. Secondly, the need for secrecy and deception took its toll; as one interviewee said, "Now I'm aware how demeaning that was, that the whole thing was so shameful. You had to go away, you had to keep it a secret, you had to pretend it never happened. It's just denying such a part of yourself. I tried to do that for years and years and years, and I couldn't do it." Lastly, two of the women were politicized by the experience, becoming feminists in the late 1960s. One started a referral service to assist women in obtaining legal abortions out of Montana; the other assisted a doctor in performing illegal abortions. "I saw myself in that situation as victimized and trapped. When it was over, I just said, 'God, that is never going to happen to me again, ever. If I have anything to do about it, it's never going to happen to anybody that I know ever again.' That's the essence of feminism, it's taking control of your own life and being responsible for your own life instead of being a victim."

ABORTION IN THE COMMUNITY

According to Malcolm Potts, Peter Diggory, and John Peel, "While abortion is an unexpected and irregular event in the life of an individual woman it can be a relatively predictable aspect of fertility control in a community."[5] Using this premise, we looked at illegal abortion as a *normal* part of the community; we presumed its presence and started looking for the documentation that would validate this assumption.

At the beginning of the project we knew of six abortionists and two cases of legal action. Searching the records of eight Montana communities we now suspect over thirty persons of being "professional" abortionists in the period from 1882 to 1973, at which time abortion was legalized as a result of *Roe v Wade*. Only seven abortionists came into the legal arena through a coroner's inquest or trial. Of these, two were convicted of abortion-related crimes. In contrast to our stereotypes of "back alley quacks" this study shows most, but not all, Montana abortionists to be medically trained and reasonably competent, often prominent persons around town, practicing on "Main Street" and retaining full privileges in the major hospitals (Catholic and non-Catholic) of their communities. Every major town in Montana had at least one abortionist. Some towns, such as Missoula, have a traceable series of abortionists from the 1880s straight through to 1973 when abortion became legal.

In the community part of this project, ten persons were interviewed who could shed light on this area of public policy and community life. Among those interviewed were two abortionists, several physicians who did not perform abortions and whose reactions ranged from sympathetic to antagonistic toward the topic, social workers, attorneys on both sides of cases that came to trial, and law enforcement personnel. Much more research needs to be done in this area, and questions can be only tentatively answered — often only with more questions.

Who were the "alleged" or suspected abortionists? The term "alleged" is used because absolute confirmation can only come from the abortionist or a client. If reliable people who worked with the alleged abortionist related the information, we generally assumed it to be the truth. Substantiation often consisted of noting the suspected abortionist's name appearing over and over on death certificates of women who were listed as having died from abortions. A further indication comes from the suspected person's involvement in a coroner's inquest or from having been tried for an abortion-related crime, even if never convicted. We feel strongly that our use of the label "abortionist" is correct about 90 percent of the time, but we acknowledge that in some cases there is a significant margin for error.

For the purposes of this study, the "professional" abortionist is a person who spent a significant percentage of his or her time performing abortions and who was generally known as an illegal abortionist. There are also numerous references to family doctors in the data. These doctors performed abortions for a few regular patients or for another doctor's family members. Often these were done under the guise of cleaning out an incomplete miscarriage or some other medical reason. Though these physicians performed abortions, they were neither labeled nor self-identified as illegal abortionists. While several people interviewed mentioned the family doctor abortionist, none of these doctors was interviewed, and it remains a subject for future research. How many abortions these family physicians are actually responsible for is unknown, and this creates another factor in the difficult assessment of the true number of abortions. It is an educated guess that any deaths resulting from these procedures probably were registered as deaths from some other cause.

Surprisingly, the deaths resulting from procedures of professional abortionists tend not to be disguised. At least there are a sufficient number of death certificates listing abortion as cause of death and the name of the attending physician/abortionist to allow the surmise that in many cases disguise was not necessary. We located nearly sixty death certificates between 1883 and 1973 that we identified as being abortion-related deaths.

Most professional abortionists had some medical training. Many were regular physicians, but there were also large numbers of homeopaths, osteopaths, and chiropractors. There were two with some nursing training. There was even a "magnetic" physician. Some, such as one prostitute, are assumed to have nonprofessional medical training. Only six of the professional abortionists were women. One was an M.D., one a chiropractor, three had nursing backgrounds of a questionable nature, and one was a prostitute.

The relative acceptance of the abortionist in the community by other medical persons and public officials may be one reason it was unnecessary to disguise the cause of abortion-related deaths. Only seven abortionists are known to have had encounters with law enforcement officials. Five were actually tried in abortion-related cases, and two were convicted. The "magnetic" physician, Dr. Elijah Hoyt, was sentenced to two years in the state prison in 1882, after he had been convicted of malpractice, even though his patient had recovered from her abortion. Rose Husted, in 1939, was sentenced to one year in prison for manslaughter. Three of the six women abortionists were involved in legal proceedings (two trials, one conviction), resulting in the termination of their practices.

Remarks from medical people and public officials I interviewed fit into an "abortion as a necessary evil" framework. More than one doctor commented on his own shock as a young doctor entering a community where an abortionist practiced, often sharing privileges in the same hospitals. Two doctors commented that they came to see the medically trained abortionist as preferable to either self-induced abortion or practices of nonmedically trained abortionists. Health and safety were the primary issues in these cases.

There were abortions being performed, and I'm being very honest this time when I say I can't remember the names of a couple that were doing them. And the only cases that I would run into were those that had been botched up, maybe come in with infection, hemorrhage, what-not. That's when I first learned, in that way, that illegal abortions were going on. What did I do about it? First of all, I got all hot and bothered, because this was not the way I was trained, the way I was brought up, and then I found out that the, in a reasonable period of time, that the individual who had been well trained was doing abortions, without any complications, no infections, no deaths, no hemorrhages at all, whereas these others were really being botched up. And, finally as a, oh, you might even call it a growing-up process, I recognized that abortion, an abortionist, even though it was an illegal sort of thing, fulfilled a social need, that was going to be met by a person who was capable of doing it, or a person who was not. And the efforts were made, as best one could, to at least dry up the abortion process by people who were not well trained. Who were doing it in a septic fashion and all.

Doctors said they never spoke directly to the abortionist about his/her practice though they may have practiced in the same town for twenty years.

Yeah, and I'd be at the same parties with him, you know, everything like that. Socially, a very fine person, nice individual. Well, I wasn't going to attack him at a party or anything like that, and I guess this is the sort of attitude that developed.

The few cases where abortionists were prosecuted are suggestive of the way public policy on abortion does not totally prevent but regulates abortion. In four of the seven cases that came under the scrutiny of the law, the abortionist had very questionable medical skills, or little or no training. In one case, a Mrs. Gertrude Pitkanen assumed the abortion practice of her husband, Dr. Gustavus Pitkanen, upon his death in 1936. She often called herself "doctor" and was in the abortion business for over twenty years in Butte. Also, in the cases of Rose Husted and Dr. Elijah Hoyt, medical competency was doubtful.

Another intriguing case is that of the practice of Dr. Edwin Kellogg, 1893–1915, in Helena. In four separate cases he appeared before coroner's juries, and each jury called for his indictment in an abortion-related death. Although Kellogg was tried once, he was not convicted, and questions of jury tampering and other suspicious dealings played a part in all of his legal encounters.

Some abortionists were highly respected members of their communities and their profession. For example, one abortionist was a prominent doctor who served on the Montana Board of Medical Examiners, according to a fellow board member. Another example is Dr. Sadie Linderberg of Miles City, who was a widely known abortionist and who also delivered over eight thousand babies. In 1953 she was named "Woman of the Year" by the Business and Professional Women of Miles City and was later honored by the Montana Medical Association for her long years of service. One client recounted her perception of Dr. Sadie's practice:

Dr. Sadie was like a little old lady doctor and I found it quite remarkable that she was doing what she was doing with such fervor. She described everything that was going to happen, what could happen, and what could not happen. She was very fair about the whole thing. . . . Actually, the person I remember more than Sadie is one of her nurses. She ran the nursing home, and when there were empty beds she brought the abortees in. She was extraordinarily kind and patient, really a lovely, lovely lady. The experience itself was not horrible; if you're going to have an abortion it is probably one of the best ways to do it, with people like that. They were really dedicated to what they were doing. They believed in it. That's why they were doing it.

Most of these cases, and others, are illustrative of the "turn the other way" attitude of most public officials. The law was selectively enforced when they felt that health and safety standards were not being met, or when it suited the purposes of these officials, such as when the state attorney general, in order to "clean up the town," made a statewide sweep against prostitution, gambling, and abortion in 1959. One woman was interviewed who told of being hired by a group of doctors seeking a witness to shut down an abortionist in another town. She pretended to be pregnant, made an appointment, and when the abortion procedure began she claimed to have changed her mind and left. The case was never pressed. Finally, the glaring fact is not the prosecution of cases but the absence of prosecution. Abortion was an unpleasant but necessary community service.

Several interesting questions emerged from the project that will need further research. First, the relationship of abortion to prostitution is intriguing. Several abortionists regularly served prostitutes, especially in Bozeman and Miles City. In fact, in Bozeman a hotel contained both an abortionist and prostitutes, each working separate floors. Further, a Bozeman social worker claimed that one of the Bozeman abortionists owned a hotel noted for prostitution. In what ways are these related occupations? Is there a tendency to "clean up" a town of prostitution and abortion in the same sweep? Do payoffs to officials occur with abortion as with prostitution, as was suggested by several informants? What questions are raised by being both a part of the "underworld" and the "culture of deviance" as the sociologists understand it?

Also, the process of "criminalization" of the abortionists themselves raises some interesting concerns. In some cases, other community professionals seemed to have had a strained relationship with abortionists. What effect did stigmatization have on the abortionists and their families? What effect did being outside of the sanctioning/peer review process have on the quality of work? Were illegal abortionists part of a "subculture of deviance" in the eyes of the community? How did abortionists see themselves? More work needs to be done on the public functioning of abortion within the community setting. Most questions remain unanswered and further work in this area will shed light on these questions.

A final word on methodology. As regards written sources—documents and records—death certificates did, in fact, often list the cause of death as abortion or self-induced abortion. Death certificates also include the name of the attending physician, and certain names turn up over and over again. The length of time attending the deceased and time of any procedure performed are clues as to whether the attending physician performed an abortion or whether the physician was attending a woman who was already aborting from natural or self-induced causes. The argument that the woman was already aborting was used frequently by those few abortionists who found themselves facing a coroner's jury. At least one abortionist routinely required clients to sign a document stating that they were miscarrying before she would touch them.

In the course of the project, other records turned up that included inquests into the deaths of a dozen women, and a coroner's inquest into the disposal of a fetus in the sensational Masonic Temple Furnace case in 1893 in Helena. Missoula's city sanitation records of fetuses in the sewage system, and their subsequent burial in an unmarked area of the cemetery, were also found. There are prison records of those abortionists who served time, and a file in the Catholic diocesan headquarters under the title "abortion" containing letters from parish priests who had absolved women parishioners of sins related to abortion. We were told of the last source by the historian for the diocese, but did not examine the letters because of confidentiality.

As regards the impact of the oral interviews, I believe I was able to achieve a more balanced perspective about the abortion experience because I had been able to talk with women who had survived abortions and in most cases felt positively about them, and I was also able to talk with other public figures involved. My judgment of the abortionist became much more sophisticated as the project developed. For example, as I gained information on each abortionist, I found myself placing them along a continuum of competent to incompetent, based on factors such as perceived sympathy toward patients, "acceptable" death and complication rates, and evidence of alcoholism. Conversely, my research assistant, Sarah McHugh, developed a strongly negative view of illegal abortionists, based on the records and documents that she found. I would like to suggest that the oral histories we conducted as part of the project gave perspective to the whole history of illegal abortion in Montana. Furthermore, information from the interviews often sent us back to sources we had not thought of, for confirmation or for additional information.

Many oral history projects avoid asking sexuality and reproduction questions of women. Perhaps because these issues are considered to be private, we do not feel we can ask about them. Often, as interviewers, we are ourselves uncomfortable in discussing these issues. To interview successfully on these topics or establish the necessary rapport on "sensitive" issues it is imperative that the interviewer be absolutely comfortable with the issues herself. When I first started asking these questions in the context of life review interviews with older women, I found that adding in questions about early sex education and menstruation provided clues about women's willingness to talk about these topics.[6] Body language, laughter, and other verbal and nonverbal clues give fairly clear messages to a sensitive interviewer.

The conceptualization of reproduction and sexuality as functioning primarily in the private sphere has contributed to the invisibility of these important issues. Further examination outside of the paradigm of public/private spheres may prove more fruitful for understanding reproductive choice within a community context. Given the centrality of reproduction and sexuality to contemporary women and to our foremothers, these issues need to be a priority for women's history.

NOTES

1. Tapes, transcripts, and research materials resulting from this project are deposited in the University of Montana Oral History Archives of the Mike Mansfield Library and at the Montana Historical Society. As the Montana Women's History Project is committed to public education, it plans to convert the research into a traveling Chautauqua program for Montana audiences.

2. Research was conducted jointly by myself and Sarah McHugh. I conducted the twenty oral interviews with one exception.

Enormous support and assistance in helping me "see the forest for the trees" came from other women historians of the Northwest, especially Sue Armitage of Washington State University and Corky Bush then of the University of Idaho.

3. Finding people to interview was not as difficult as I had anticipated: Through the use of women's networks and through the presentation of numerous "in progress" reports, we found almost all of the ten women who had had abortions. Referrals and personal contact produced better results than newspaper and newsletter articles in finding informants. We also quickly learned that we should never assume

that people will automatically be shocked or dismayed by a "sensitive" research topic; sources of information may be found where you least expect them. For example, I lunched with a sixty-five-year-old mother of a friend—a devoted Catholic and, for the most part, a conservative. When she asked about the topic of my current research, I told her what I was doing. She brightened and said, "Did I ever tell you about 'Abortion Mary'?"

The study did not include any Native American women; none appeared in the death records or other documents surveyed, and we did not include any in the oral interviews. This does not mean that Native American women did not seek abortions; it probably reflects the fact that they did not enter the white culture's system for handling unwanted pregnancies—they had their own system. There is also good reason to believe that for many Native Americans, the principal reproductive issue of the time period covered by this study has been forced sterilization rather than access to abortion.

4. The work of Linda Gordon (*Woman's Body, Woman's Right: Birth Control in America* [New York: Penguin Books, 1977]) and Carl Degler (*At Odds: Women and the Family from the Revolution to the Present* [London: Oxford University Press, 1981]) were especially helpful in formulating a framework for this study. Other sources consulted were: George Devereux, "A Typological Study of Abortion in 350 Primitive, Ancient, and Pre-Industrial Societies," in *Abortion in America*, ed. H. Rosen (Boston: Beacon, 1967); Norman Himes, *Medical History of Contraception* (1936; New York: Schocken Books, 1970); James Mohr, *Abortion in America* (London: Oxford University Press, 1978); Malcolm Potts, Peter Diggory, and John Peel, *Abortion* (London: Cambridge University Press, 1977).

5. Potts, Diggory, and Peel, *Abortion*, 30.

6. An oral history interviewing technique that worked especially well on this project involved starting the interview with the general statement, "Please go through and tell me your experience with illegal abortion. When you are done, we can go back through your story with any questions I might have." This open-ended question brought responses from ten to thirty-five minutes in length, while I listened, took notes, and did not interrupt. This practice worked especially well for the ten women interviewed who had experienced illegal abortions, but less well in the interviews with the ten public figures because their experiences were not all of a piece, as were those of the abortees.

Frontiers 7:1 (1983): 32–37.

Grassroots Leadership Reconceptualized

Chicana Oral Histories and the 1968 East Los Angeles School Blowouts

DOLORES DELGADO BERNAL

The 1960s was an era of social unrest in American history. Student movements that helped shape larger struggles for social and political equality emerged from street politics and mass protests. A myriad of literature discusses the social and political forces of the 1960s, particularly the liberal and radical student movements. Yet, as Carlos Muñoz Jr. argues, there is a paucity of material on 1960s nonwhite student radicalism and protest.[1] He outlines various explanations that have been provided by white scholars for their failure to incorporate nonwhite student radicalism into their work: that the black student movement was not radical enough and that Mexican students were simply not involved in the struggles of the sixties. However, though Muñoz points to the omission of working-class people of color in the literature on 1960s student movements, he neglects to include a serious analysis of gender in his own examination of the Chicano Movement and the politics of identity.

In 1968 people witnessed student demonstrations in countries such as France, Italy, Mexico, and the United States. In March of that year well over ten thousand students walked out of the mostly Chicano schools in East Los Angeles to protest the inferior quality of their education. This event, which came to be known as the East Los Angeles School Blowouts, has been viewed through a variety of analytical historical perspectives, including those of protest politics, internal colonialism, spontaneous mass demonstrations, the Chicano student movement, and as a political and social development of the wider Chicano Movement. None of these historical accounts, however, include a gender analysis.[2] Indeed, even contemporary depictions, such as the important documentary series *Chicano: A History of the Mexican Amer-*

ican Civil Rights Movement, continue to marginalize women's activism; part three of the series, "Taking Back the Schools," fails to tell the stories of young Chicanas and the roles they filled in the East Los Angeles Blowouts.[3]

As an educational researcher and a Chicana, I am interested in the women's voices that have been omitted from the diverse historical accounts of the Blowouts—particularly those women who were key participants.[4] The Blowouts provide an opportunity to rediscover a history that has been unrecognized and unappreciated. In addition, a historical analysis that focuses on the Blowout participation of women allows us to explore how women offered leadership and how that leadership, while different in form and substance from traditional interpretations, was indeed meaningful and essential.[5]

Hence, my purpose is twofold. Through the oral history data of eight women, I provide an alternative perspective to the historical narratives of the 1968 Blowouts that have thus far only been told by males with a focus on males. At the same time, I will use the oral history data to examine the concept of leadership in community activism. I propose that a paradigmatic shift in the way we view grassroots leadership not only provides an alternative history to the Blowouts, but it also acknowledges Chicanas as important leaders in past and present grassroots movements.

METHODOLOGY

The relationship between a researcher's methodology and his or her theoretical and epistemological orientation is not always explicit, but these elements are inevitably closely connected. To reclaim a history of Chicana activism and leadership, I utilize a theoretical and epistemological perspective grounded in critical feminisms that are strongly influenced by women of color. Critical feminist theories challenge the dominant notion of knowledge and provide legitimacy as well as a logical rationale for the study of working-class women of color. Chandra Talpade Mohanty points to the importance of traditionally excluded groups, such as Chicanas, breaking through dominant ways of thinking and reclaiming history. She discusses the development of alternative histories: "This issue of subjectivity represents a realization of the fact that who we are, how we act, what we think, and what stories we tell become more intelligible within an epistemological framework that begins by recognizing existing hegemonic histories. . . . [Thus,] uncovering and reclaiming of subjugated knowledge is one way to lay claim to alternative histories."[6]

The struggle to reclaim history is a contention over power, meaning, and knowledge. Critical feminisms provide a space within the academy for historically silenced peoples to identify unequal power relations and to take the first steps in constructing alternative histories. In short, my epistemological orientation, which is grounded in critical feminisms, allows for the identification of unequal power relations, the development of alternative histories, and the validation of a methodology based on the lived experiences of Chicanas.

Kenneth Kann writes that there are three types of history: "the kind you live, the kind you hear about, and the kind you read about."[7] The second, when documented as oral history, transforms the first into the third: Lived history becomes written history. In my own attempt to transform lived experiences into written history, my primary method of data collection is the oral history interviews of eight women who as high school or college students participated in the 1968 Blowouts. Oral histories provide a special opportunity to learn the unique perceptions and interpretations of individuals, particularly those from groups whose history has been traditionally excluded or distorted. Oral sources are thus a necessity when studying working-class women of color, though they may be less important when studying topics involving white men of the dominant class who have typically had control over written history and collective memory.[8] Oral histories, grounded in critical feminisms, provide a means of breaking through dominant ways of knowing and reclaiming an alternative history of grassroots activism in the 1968 Blowouts.

The interviews I conducted took place between June 1995 and January 1996 in a place that was most convenient for each woman, usually in her home. Following a network sampling procedure, I interviewed eight women who were identified by other female participants or resource individuals as key participants or leaders in the Blowouts.[9] I followed an interview protocol with open-ended questions in order to elicit multiple levels of data. Though the interview protocol was used as a guide, I realized that as the women spoke of very personal experiences, a less structured approach allowed their voices and ways of knowing to come forth. Although I took interview notes, each interview was also recorded and transcribed, and the full transcription of each interview tape has helped me create a more complete database.

In addition to conducting an oral history interview with each participant, I also conducted a focus group interview that included seven of the eight women together for one interview. The videotaped interview took place at Self-Help Graphics, a community art gallery and studio in East Los Angeles, during February 1996. Focus group interviews incorporate the explicit use of group interaction to produce data and insights that would be less accessible without the interaction.[10] Therefore, my interest in conducting a focus group interview was less on reconstructing the "truth" of what happened than it was on recording the new information, differing viewpoints, and recurring issues that the group communication generated.

To work within critical feminist scholarship, I provided each woman with a transcription of her individual interview so that she had a chance to reflect and comment on her responses to questions. The women were given these transcriptions prior to the focus group interview, allowing them the opportunity to reflect and bring up concerns at the group interview. During the group interview, I also shared my preliminary analysis with the women and asked for their reaction and input to four themes I had identified from their oral history interviews. Their comments have helped me to better understand the roles they played in the Blowouts and the ways in which we might look at grassroots leadership differently.

THE WOMEN

All eight of the women are similar insofar as they are second- or third-generation Chicanas, first-generation college students, and grew up in working-class neighborhoods on the east side of Los Angeles. However, these women are not a homogeneous group, nor does their composite lend itself to a "typical Chicana" leader or activist. Two of the women grew up in single-parent households with only two children, while the other six come from two-parent families with four or more children. Four of the women come from families that had been involved in union organizing or leftist political movements since the 1940s. Three women state that they come from strong Catholic families, while three other women state they were raised in families in which their parent(s) had abandoned the Catholic Church. Though six of the eight women are bilingual in Spanish and English today, only one of the women grew up in a predominantly Spanish-speaking home. Three of the women come from mixed marriages and are half white, Jewish, or Filipina. Finally, during high school, six of the women maintained an exceptional academic and extracurricular record as college-tracked students.

Despite the similarities, the notable differences in the women's family and personal histories reflect the complexity and diversity of Chicanas' experiences in 1968 and today (see table 1). Indeed, there are also similarities and differences in the type of participation and leadership each woman contributed to the East L.A. Blowouts. While this article is an interpretation based on the personal perceptions and experiences of these women, knowing the historical circumstances of the time provides a clearer picture of the 1968 East L.A. School Blowouts.

THE 1968 EAST LOS ANGELES SCHOOL BLOWOUTS

Chicanos' struggle for quality education and the right to include their culture, history, and language in the curriculum is not a phenomenon of the 1960s but instead predates the 1968 Blowouts by a number of decades. In fact, many of the concerns and issues that were voiced by participants and supporters of the 1968 Blowouts—implementation of bilingual and bicultural training for teachers, elimination of tracking based on standardized tests, improvement and replacement of inferior school facilities, removal of racist teachers and administrators, and inclusion of Mexican history and culture into the curriculum—were very similar to those voiced in Mexican communities in the United States since before the turn of the century.[11]

For years, East Los Angeles community members made unsuccessful attempts to create change and improve the education system through the "proper" channels. In the 1950s the education committee of the Council of Mexican-American Affairs, comprised of educated Mexican professionals, addressed the failure of schools to educate Mexican students through mainstream channels. They met with legislators, school officials, and community members and attended hearings, press conferences, and symposia to no avail.[12] In June 1967 Irene Tovar, commissioner of compensatory education for the Los Angeles district, explained to the U.S. Commission on Civil Rights that a long list of recommendations to improve the inferior schooling conditions was presented to the Los Angeles Board of Education in 1963 but that "few of those recommendations were accepted and even fewer reached the community."[13] In the years immediately preceding the Blowouts, students and parents participating in one East L.A. high school's PTA specifically addressed the poor quality of education and requested reforms similar to those demanded by the Blowouts two years later.[14] Nonetheless, formal requests through official channels went unanswered.

In 1963, the Los Angeles County Commission on Human Relations began sponsoring an annual Mexican-American Youth Leadership Conference at Camp Hess Kramer for high school students. These conferences were important to the development of the 1968 Blowouts because a number of

Table 1: Family and Personal History of Blowout Participants.

Name	Two-Parent Home	Strong Catholic Family	Family History of Community or Labor Involvement	Named Mother as Influential Other	Named Influential Others Besides Parent
Cleste Baca			x	x	x
Vickie Castro	x	x	x	x	
Paula Crisostomo	x	x	x	x	
Mita Cuaron	x	x	x*		
Tanya Luna Mount	x		x	x*	
Rosalinda M. Gonzáles	x	x	x	x	
Rachael Ochoa Cervera	x	x		x	
Cassandra Zacarías		x	x		

*Indicates that a focus was placed on both her mother and her father

students who participated in the conference later became organizers in the Blowouts as well as in other progressive movements. Given these outcomes, it is ironic that the camp held an assimilationist perspective, stating that the official goal of the camp was to improve self-image and intergroup relations so that Mexican American students "may be free to develop themselves into the mainstream of Anglo-American life."[15] Students were encouraged to be traditional school leaders, run for school offices, and go on to college. The student participants were selected by either a school, a community person, or an organization based on their ability to contribute to the group as well as on their ability to return and create progress in their own communities.

The weekend camps were held at Camp Hess Kramer in Malibu, California. The student participants were assigned to cabins, and college students served as camp counselors and workshop leaders. Four of the women in my study participated in at least one of the leadership conferences prior to their involvement in the 1968 Blowouts. They remember the camp as a beautiful place where they were given a better framework to understand inequities and where they developed a sense of community and family responsibility. As one woman put it, "These youth conferences were the first time that we began to develop a consciousness." Rachael Ochoa Cervera discusses her memories of the camp: "First of all, it was a nice experience because you'd get away for a whole weekend and the environment, the atmosphere was quite beautiful, very aesthetic. Being by the ocean, yet you felt you were in the mountains. . . . It was very affirmative. That's where you began to have an identity. You weren't with your schoolmates, you could be more open. You could say what you wanted to."[16] While the camp fostered civic responsibility and school leadership, many students felt motivated to organize around more radical and progressive issues. Rosalinda Méndez González describes how the conferences motivated students to organize: "Well, when we started going to these youth conferences, there were older Mexican Americans. Now we were high school kids, so older was probably twenties and early thirties. They would talk to us and explain a lot of things about what was happening, and I remember they were opening up our eyes. After those youth conferences, then we went back and started organizing to raise support for the farmworkers, and things like that."[17]

As a direct result of youth participating at Camp Hess Kramer, the Young Citizens for Community Action (YCCA) was formed. The YCCA (which later became Young Chicanos for Community Action and then evolved into the Brown Berets) surveyed high school students' needs, met with education officials to discuss problems, and endorsed potential candidates for the board of education. YCCA members, still following official channels to bring about improved educational conditions, supported and helped elect the first Chicano school board member, Julian Nava.[18]

Also influential in the development of the Blowouts was the fact that by 1967 a relatively larger number of Chicano students began entering college—though still a small representation of the Chicano population. In that year, one of the first Chicano college student organizations in the Los Angeles area, the Mexican American Student Association (MASA), was formed at East Los Angeles Community College.[19] Student organizations rapidly formed throughout college campuses in California, including United Mexican-American Students (UMAS) at the University of California, Los Angles; California State University, Los Angeles; Occidental College; and Loyola University. The primary issue of these organizations was the lack of Chicano access to quality education.

Historians have also noted the importance of the community activist newspapers *Inside Eastside* and *La Raza* to the rise of the Blowouts.[20] *Inside Eastside* had an emphasis on social, cultural, and political activities relevant to students and for the most part was written and edited by high school students. In fact, two women in this study wrote articles for *Inside Eastside* and *La Raza*. *La Raza*, aimed at the Chicano community as a whole, was concerned with a spectrum of political activities focusing on the schools, police, and electoral politics. The newspapers provided a forum in which students and community members were able to articulate their discontent with the schools, and frequent themes were the poor quality of East Los Angeles schools and the cultural insensitivity of teachers. The newspapers, the increased number of Chicano college students, and events such as the Camp Hess Kramer conferences were all influential in bringing attention to the poor educational conditions of East Los Angeles schools.

During the 1960s, East Los Angeles high schools had an especially deplorable record of educating Chicano students, who had a dropout/pushout rate of well over 50 percent as well as the lowest reading scores in the district. In contrast, according to a survey undertaken by the Los Angeles City School System, two west-side schools, Palisades and Monroe, had dropout rates of 3.1 percent and 2.6 percent respectively in 1965–1966.[21] According to the State Department of Education's racial survey, Mexican American students were also heavily represented in special education classes, including classes for the mentally retarded and the emotionally disturbed.[22] The classrooms were overcrowded, and most teachers lacked sensitivity to or understanding of the Mexican working-class communities in which they taught. Rosalinda Méndez González recalls: "There were teachers who would say, 'You dirty Mexicans, why don't you go back to where you came from?' So there was a lot of racism we encountered in the school. We had severely overcrowded classrooms. We didn't have sufficient books. We had buildings that were barrack-type buildings that had been built as emergency, temporary buildings during World War II, and this was in the late 1960s, and we were still going to school in those buildings."[23]

As a result of the poor educational conditions and the fact that numerous attempts to voice community concerns and school reforms were ignored, school strikes took place during the first week of March 1968. Though the Blowouts were centered at five predominately Chicano high schools located in the general east side of Los Angeles, other schools in the district also participated, including Jefferson High School, which was predominately African American.[24]

The school boycott began on different days during the first week of March and lasted a week and a half, with over ten thousand students protesting the inferior quality of their education. Though there had been weeks of discussions and planning, the first impromptu walkout was prompted by the cancellation of the school play *Barefoot in the Park* by the administration at Wilson High School. Paula Crisostomo, a student organizer at Lincoln High School, comments on the atmosphere at her school preceding the walkout:

"I know tension had heightened, activity had heightened district-wide, a lot of schools were talking about it, everyone knew it was going to happen, everyone was waiting for the sign. But I remember the atmosphere was absolutely tense, I mean it was just electric in school. This had been building for so long, and everyone knew it was going to happen and everyone was just waiting and waiting."[25] Though there was coordination between the schools, the planning and actual implementation of each school walkout took on a distinct character. High school students, college students, Brown Beret members, teachers, and the general community took on different roles and provided different kinds of support.

Vickie Castro, a Roosevelt graduate, was a college student who played a crucial role in organizing and supporting the Blowouts. Vickie recalls that while she was at Roosevelt trying to help organize students, she was recognized by a teacher and escorted to the gate. The teacher told her, "If I see you on campus again, I'll have you arrested." Vickie later used her old Mazda to pull down the chain-link fence that had been locked to prevent high school students from leaving: "I remember having to back my car and put chains on and pull the gates off." In contrast, her key role at Lincoln was to set up a meeting with the principal and detain him while other college students came on campus to encourage high school students to participate in the walkouts. Vickie recalls the strategy she used at Lincoln, pretending to be a job applicant to get an appointment with the principal: "I remember we had a whole strategy planned for Lincoln, how we were going to do it. And who was going to be in the halls to yell 'walkouts' at the various buildings. And my role was to make an appointment with the principal to meet him, to talk to him about either employment or something. I'm in his office and my job is trying to delay him. He kept saying, 'I'll be right with you, I'll be right with you.' So I was to just keep him distracted a little bit. Then when the walkouts came, of course, he said, 'I have to leave.' And then somehow, I don't even recall, I got out of the building too."[26]

Just as the planning and actual implementation of each school walkout took on a distinct character, so did the response by each school administration and by the police. While the student walkouts on other campuses could be characterized as ranging from peaceful to controlled with mild incidents of violence, the students on Roosevelt's campus experienced a great deal of police violence. Police, county sheriffs, and riot squads were called. With a number of students and community members injured and arrested, the student protest turned into a near riot situation. Tanya Luna Mount, a student organizer, points out that even though the students were following the legal requirements of a public demonstration, the situation with the police escalated to the point of senseless beatings with school administrators trying to stop the police:

They [the LAPD] were treating it like we were rioting and tearing everything up, which we weren't. We weren't breaking, destroying anything. Nobody was hanging on school property and tearing it apart. Nothing, nothing like that happened. And we were told to disperse, we had three minutes. Everybody kept yelling that we had a right to be there. . . . All of a sudden they [the riot squad] started coming down this way. They start whacking people. Now they're beating people up, badly, badly beating people up. Now people, administrators are inside yelling, "Stop, my God. What are you doing?" Once you call LAPD, the school no longer has any jurisdiction. They couldn't even open the gate and tell the kids to run inside because the police were telling them, "Remove yourself from the fence and go back, mind your own business." That's when all of a sudden they [the administrators] realized, "My God."[27]

The student strikers, including those at Roosevelt who were subjected to police violence, were not just idly walking out of school. They proposed that their schools be brought up to the same standards as those of other Los Angeles high schools. The students generated a list of grievances and pushed for the board of education to hold a special meeting in which they could present their grievances. The official list of student grievances to be presented to the board of education consisted of thirty-six demands, including smaller class size, bilingual education, more emphasis on Chicano history, and community control of schools.[28] Many of the grievances were educational reforms previously proposed by concerned parents, educators, and community members, and all of the demands were supported by the premise that East Los Angeles schools were not properly educating Chicano students.

The Blowouts generated the formation of the Educational Issues Coordinating Committee (EICC) by parents, various community members, high school students, and UMAS members. With pressure from the EICC and the student strikers, the Blowouts also generated at least two special board of education meetings in which students, the EICC, and supporters were allowed to voice their concerns. By Friday, March 9, the school strikes had not ended, and the board of education scheduled a special meeting to hear the students' proposals. At this meeting it was decided that another meeting would be held at Lincoln High School and that the board would grant amnesty to the thousands of students who had boycotted classes.[29]

Approximately twelve hundred people attended a four-hour board meeting that was held at Lincoln High School, yet the board of education made no commitments. Students walked out of the meeting in response to the board's inaction. The sentiments of the board were captured by an article in the *Los Angeles Times*, stating that "school officials deny any prejudice in allocation of building funds and say that they agree with 99% of the students' demands—but that the district does not have the money to finance the kind of massive changes proposed."[30] At this meeting, the board went on record opposing the discipline of students and teachers who had participated in the boycott. Yet in the late evening of June 2, 1968, thirteen individuals involved in the Blowouts were arrested and imprisoned on conspiracy charges. Though female students were involved in organizing the Blowouts, the "L.A. 13" were all men, including Sal Castro, a teacher from Lincoln High School. With a focus on males, especially those who looked the militant type, females avoided arrest. Though the charges were later dropped and found unconstitutional, Sal Castro was suspended from his teaching position at Lincoln High School. For many months students, community, and EICC members rallied in support of the L.A. 13 and then focused organizing efforts on the reinstatement of Sal Castro.

A RECONCEPTUALIZATION OF LEADERSHIP

In exploring how and when women participated in the Blowouts, it is important to outline a reconceptualization of leadership that places women at the center of analysis and does not separate the task of organizing from leading. The reconceptualization I put forth comes out of a women's studies tradition that in the last twenty years has produced an impressive body of new knowledge and has contributed to the development of new paradigms on leadership. Rather than using traditional paradigms that view leaders as those who occupy a high position in an organization, feminist scholars have developed alternative paradigms that more accurately consider gender in the analysis of leadership.[31]

In the area of science, Thomas Kuhn's influential work *The Structure of Scientific Revolutions* presents a model for a fundamental change in theories and scientific paradigms, arguing that without major paradigm shifts we may never understand certain scientific phenomena. He gives the example of how Joseph Priestley, one of the scientists said to have discovered the gas that was later found to be oxygen, was unable to see what other scientists were able to see as a result of a paradigm revision.[32] Similarly, a paradigm shift in the way that we understand and study leadership allows us to see how women—specifically the women in my study— emerge as leaders. Perhaps there is something faulty in the previous leadership paradigms that have not allowed us to understand and explain the lived experiences of Chicanas.

Karen Brodkin Sacks indicates that the traditional paradigm of leadership implicitly equates public speakers and negotiators with leaders and also identifies organizing and leading as two different tasks.[33] She challenges this notion of leadership by placing working-class women at the center of analysis. Leadership in this perspective is a collective process that includes the mutually important and reinforcing dynamic between both women's and men's roles. Leadership as a process allows us to acknowledge and study a cooperative leadership in "which members of a group are empowered to work together synergistically toward a common goal or vision that will create change, transform institutions, and thus improve the quality of life."[34] This paradigm of cooperative leadership along with the inclusion of women's voices allows an alternative view of the Blowouts and of different dimensions of grassroots leadership to emerge.

Dimensions of Grassroots Leadership

In previous work, I have identified five different types of activities that can be considered dimensions of grassroots leadership in the 1968 Blowouts: networking, organizing, developing consciousness, holding an elected or appointed office, and acting as an official or unofficial spokesperson.[35] The distinction between these activities is not meant to be a rigid and impermeable one, nor are these activities inclusive of all dimensions of grassroots leadership. Not every leader need participate in every dimension of leadership, and I argue that there is no hierarchical order assigned to the different dimensions. The activities can be viewed as locations on a moving carousel, each location being of equal importance. There are many entry points at which one can get on and off, and once on the carousel one is free to move about in different locations (see figure 1).

Writing about black women involved in the Civil Rights movement of the same period, Charlotte Bunch points that "while black male leaders were the ones whom the press called on to be the spokesmen, it was often the black women who made things happen, especially in terms of organizing people at the community level."[36] Likewise, when I initially described my research proposal to a male Chicano colleague of the Movement generation, he sincerely encouraged me to pursue the topic, but unassumingly warned that there were no female leaders in the Blowouts and that few women were involved. Perhaps because he views the Blowouts from a traditional leader-

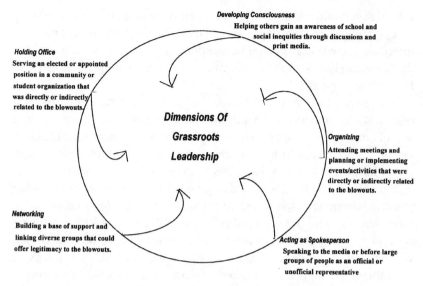

Figure 1: Dimensions of Grassroots Leadership.

ship paradigm, he overlooked Chicanas as leaders and failed to recognize their important contributions to the Blowouts. Yet in distinct ways and to varying degrees, the women I interviewed participated in these different dimensions of leadership. Their participation was vital to the Blowouts, yet because a traditional leadership paradigm does not acknowledge the importance of those who participate in organizing, developing consciousness, and networking, their leadership remains unrecognized and unappreciated by most historians.

In the following sections, I will discuss each of the five identified, interrelated dimensions of leadership, exploring the ways in which the oral histories of the women in this study further our understanding of the Blowouts and of women's activist leadership.

Participation and Implementation of Meetings, Events, and Activities: Organizing

Organizing includes attending meetings and planning or implementing events and activities that were directly or indirectly related to the Blowouts. There were numerous meetings, events, and activities that took place prior to and after the Blowouts in which students, teachers, parents, and community members raised concerns about the quality of education in the East

L.A. high schools. All eight of the women discuss attending and actively participating in PTA meetings, school board meetings, Blowout committee meetings, or community planning meetings that were held in such places as the Cleveland House, the Plaza Community Center, and the home of Tanya Luna Mount's parents.[37]

In an attempt to address and remedy school inequities, activists in these organizations implemented a number of strategies before resorting to a school boycott. For example, Vickie Castro, Paula Crisostomo, and Rachael Ochoa Cervera were intimately involved in YCCA, a community youth group formed by former Camp Hess Kramer participants that took up issues of education. Members of this group met regularly, talked to other youth at government-sponsored Teen Posts, and conducted a needs assessment survey to find out what was going on in the schools. Vickie discusses her and others' organizing efforts in the years prior to the Blowouts: "And we even had like a questionnaire that we had made. I wish we had kept all these things. We wanted to compile complaints and I guess we were trying to develop, even in our simple perspective, like a needs assessment. We would talk to kids, What do you think about your school? Do they help you? Do they push you out? Are you going to college? . . . I know that we compiled quite a bit of complaints and that's where during the walkouts when you hear about the demands, a lot of that was based on these complaints. So we had a process in mind."[38] After the surveys were returned and tallied up, Vickie, Paula, Rachael, and other YCCA members decided to actively support and work on Julian Nava's school board campaign. Paula remembers how their organizing efforts progressed: "So it was interesting when we got it [the surveys] back and we tallied it up and again it strengthened our belief of how inadequate we saw the schools to be. Well, of course, the next question was, 'Okay, now what do we do?' We got involved in a campaign, my first political campaign that I worked in, for Julian Nava, the first Latino to run for school board. It was an at-large position before the board was broken up into districts or regions, and he courted us. We worked with him, we worked for him, thinking that this was the way, this was an answer."[39]

When Tanya Luna Mount speaks of her organizing efforts, they range from the antiwar movement she helped organize at Roosevelt just prior to the Blowouts to the work she did against police brutality in her community. In addition, Tanya remembers participating in the planning of what would be presented in discussions with the board of education: "I was on the committee that would decide what would be said at the board of education meetings. And we'd elect who would do it." She also speaks of the many Blowout organizational meetings that were held at her home and how "we were open all night . . . [and] people would come over to our house during the walkouts." She remembers that her home even made the news when George Putnam, a conservative news commentator, said that there was a house at "126 South Soto Street in East Los Angeles, in Boyle Heights, that is notorious for being commies, rebel rousers, and anti-government."

In fact, an important component of organizing the Blowouts was the active participation in meetings that helped to develop or support the demonstrations. Mita Cuaron remembers actively participating in many community meetings prior to and during the Blowouts in which "we set up a list of demands on various topics and issues that we felt we were being deprived of," and community members decided that these concerns had to be brought before the board of education.[40] Rosalinda Méndez González describes the school board meetings in which she and others protested the suspension of teacher Sal Castro and demanded that the board return him to his teaching position at Lincoln High School. Though the police employed various intimidation techniques, she and others continued to organize and actively participate in these meetings: "I mean there would be so many hundreds of us that would show up, students, elderly people, some professionals, all kinds of people that would show up to these meetings that we couldn't even fit inside the board room. I mean people were out in the courtyard and they had to have the P.A. system. . . . But I remember also at these meetings all of the intimidation. The police were going around literally, aisle by aisle, snapping, snapping, snapping, snapping pictures of everybody who was there. I mean it was pure intimidation. If you're here to testify and you're here to demonstrate, we're going to have you on file."[41]

Without the organizing efforts and persistence of these and other young Chicanas the Blowouts probably would not have taken place, and the attention needed to expose poor educational conditions may not have been garnered. By organizing community people, the women in this study demonstrate the dynamic process and complex set of relationships that comprised the leadership of the 1968 Blowouts. Indeed, this reconceptualization of leadership allows us to consider organizers as leaders in various grassroots movements, including the Chicano Civil Rights Movement.

From behind the Scenes: Developing Consciousness

A second dimension of leadership is developing consciousness, the process of helping others gain awareness of school and social inequities through discussions or print media. Developing the consciousness of individuals is crucial to generating and maintaining the momentum needed for any social movement. Yet just as organizing is separated from the task of leading, consciousness shaping is often overlooked as part of the dynamic process.

Each of the women I talked with participated in raising consciousness through informal dialogues with her peers, family members, or community members. As young women they challenged others to think about and consider the inequities that they confronted on a daily basis. One woman put it bluntly, "You raised consciousness in any way that you could do it, subtly or outright."[42] Often one of the most difficult and least rewarding tasks of leading, developing consciousness requires one to help others see and understand things like they never have before. Cassandra Zacarías reflects on the difficulty of the task: "I was talking to students and trying to explain to them, and I remember that was really hard for me because I was a really shy person at the time. I was a real introverted person and this was really difficult to have people actually say, 'Oh you're nuts. What the hell is wrong with you?' And I remember feeling sometimes, what have I gotten myself into?"[43]

In addition to holding informal discussions about school conditions or social inequities, these women used print media to raise consciousness. Both Tanya Luna Mount and Mita Cuaron's families had mimeograph machines that they used for mass duplication of informational leaflets and flyers that were then distributed throughout the communities and schools. Furthermore, all the women I interviewed were somehow connected to the community activist newspapers *Inside Eastside* and *La Raza*. Celeste Baca worked in the *La Raza* office as a volunteer, Tanya Luna Mount and Paula Crisostomo wrote for and distributed newspapers, and the other women all read and encouraged others to read these newspapers. As high school students, Tanya Luna Mount and Paula Crisostomo contributed to building consciousness by writing articles specifically addressing the poor educational conditions in East Los Angeles schools. Paula recounts her involvement with the community activist newspapers: "I typed and did layouts, and wrote ghost articles about the schools. I would also go to the [Whittier] Boulevard to sell *Chicano Student Movement* or *Inside Eastside*. . . . I would bring a whole stack to school and I would give a few to people, and they would pass them out to their friends. And then the school said we couldn't do it anymore, so I'd get to school early and I'd leave them around the campus. I would go into the bathroom and I would put them in the bathroom, the cafeteria, where I knew kids hung out, and I would tell people where they could find them. People would find them, but I wasn't actually distributing."[44]

Developing consciousness, whether through verbal or written communication, is less public than tasks normally associated with traditional interpretations of leadership. Like organizing and networking, it is work that is done from behind the scenes, often unrecognized and unappreciated. By placing working-class females at the center of analysis, we are able to see this behind-the-scenes work and appreciate its importance in the leadership of the 1968 East L.A. Blowouts.

A Need for a Wide Base of Support: Networking

A third dimension of leadership, networking, refers to activities that link diverse groups in building a base of support. During the time of the Blowouts it was important to have support from community members as well as from those outside of the community who could lend some legitimacy to the students' efforts. Thus, networking involved both transforming community and familial ties into a political force and building a supportive political front by reaching those outside of a comfortable social network. As Brodkin Sacks found in her study of workplace networks at Duke Medical Center, the networks formed during the Blowouts functioned as a sort of "telegraph system, carrying a collective message of protest against unfairness."[45]

Students who were involved in the walkouts were continuously accused of being communist, being organized by outside agitators, or just wanting to skip school. Networking within the community was a way to develop an awareness of the school inequities and develop a political force. Cassandra Zacarías remembers having to defend her own and other students' actions while trying to gain support from teachers, peers, and some family members: "The issue would come up, well, it's all outside agitators, it's all communists coming in and riling up the little Mexicans and these little teenagers and we'd say, 'No it's not. It's within our community.' . . . I remember feeling like most of the kids didn't really like us and they'd say, 'Oh, you know you guys are communists and you're crazy.' . . . I'd tell my family, 'No, I'm not a communist,' and then start to tell them that there's all these inequities in the system."[46] Similarly, Vickie Castro, a college student at the time, comments on how important it was that high school students not cause a disturbance or skip school without understanding the issues: "I remember something that was very important to all of us is that we just didn't want disturbance for disturbance sake. And we were really talking to kids saying, 'We want you to know why you're walking out.' . . . There was a purpose so that we did meet with groups in the park, in the schools, on the corners, and we tried to say, 'This is why we're doing this and we need your support.' "⁴⁷ Cassandra and Vickie's statements exemplify how networking—transforming community ties into a political force—is closely interrelated with raising consciousness—helping others gain awareness of school and social inequities.

During my interview with Sal Castro, he discussed networking strategies that involved the students connecting with individuals outside of the communal or familial social networks. He knew that an endorsement from the church, César Chavez, or politicians would lend legitimacy to the students' cause: "I constantly wanted people of the cloth to support the kids. I was never able to get any support from the Catholic Church. We had to steal a banner of the Our Lady of Guadalupe because we couldn't get any priest."⁴⁸ Finally, after a number of phone calls and some pleading, "a major coup" was set in place: Bobby Kennedy agreed to talk to the students and make a statement of support. Kennedy was on his way back to Washington DC, from a visit with César Chavez in Delano, California. He had to make a stop at the Los Angeles airport, where he agreed to meet with a group of students that included Paula Crisostomo and Cassandra Zacarías. A picture of Kennedy with the students appeared in local East Los Angeles papers, and Kennedy's endorsement proved to be a helpful networking strategy that increased support for the Blowouts.

During the actual week and a half of the Blowouts, Paula Crisostomo was involved with other students who were building a base of support throughout the city with groups such as the Jewish organization B'nai B'rith and Hamilton High School on the west side. Through speaking engagements, students voiced their concerns and discussed school inequities with others who could offer support and advocate on the students' behalf. Crisostomo recalls: "We were also doing speaking engagements. I remember we spoke to the B'nai B'rith in West L.A. And we went to Hamilton and they had a rally for us in a park. During that week we were hot items, and a lot of groups were asking us to come and speak, and we were getting more support, so the board had to [listen]."⁴⁹

In light of the widespread communist and outside agitator accusations, it was especially crucial to develop a network formation of individuals and organizations who could sanction and endorse the students' actions and demands.

Less Focus on More Visibility: Holding Office

Holding an elected or appointed office is a fourth dimension of leadership. Four of the women I talked with held an elected or appointed office in direct or indirect relationship to the Blowouts. Vickie Castro was the first president of YCCA, the youth organization that focused on education and was a precursor to the Blowouts. Shortly after the school walkouts, Mita Cuaron and Cassandra Zacarías were elected student body officers. Their Freedom Candidate slate was made up of Garfield Blowout Committee members and was based on the ideal of "instituting an educational system in our school that is based on *equality, justice,* and *first-rate education for all.*"[50] Months after the Blowouts, Rosalinda Méndez González was one of the youths appointed to the Mexican American Education Commission, which was originally an advisory board to the school board.

Though these positions probably accorded these women slightly more visibility than other young female participants, the positions seemed to be secondary to their other leadership activities. For the most part, women casually mentioned these positions during their interviews. They spent much more time recalling and talking about the more private tasks that I have included under the dimensions of networking, organizing, and developing consciousness. In other words, they seem to identify their role in the Blowouts more in relation to these dimensions of leadership than in the elected or appointed positions that they held. Yet, though these women gave less focus to the more visible and public roles, documenting this dimension of leadership is important in that it demonstrates that young Chicanas also contributed to the Blowouts (and in other social movements) within the more prevalent notion of leadership that equates elected officers and public speakers with leaders.

A More Public Space: Acting as Spokesperson

The fifth dimension of leadership is acting as an official or unofficial spokesperson. During the Blowouts male participants usually took on this role and were found in front of the camera, quoted in the *Los Angeles Times,* or speaking before crowds. However, there were occasions in which a female student who was active in other dimensions of leadership also took on the role of spokesperson. Rosalinda Méndez González and Paula Crisostomo were both asked to act as official spokespersons by providing testimony about Mexican Americans in education based on their experiences as students. Each of them testified before the United States Commission on Civil Rights at hearings held in Los Angeles. As a recent graduate of Lincoln High School, Rosalinda felt that the school curriculum was primarily responsible for the failure of many Chicano students. The following is an excerpt of Rosalinda's comments before the United States Commission on Civil Rights in June of 1967:

From the time we first begin attending school, we hear about how great and wonderful our United States is, about our democratic American heritage, but little about our splendid and magnificent Mexican heritage and culture. What little we do learn about Mexicans is how they mercilessly slaughtered the brave Texans at the Alamo, but we never hear about the child heroes of Mexico who courageously threw themselves from the heights of Chapultepec rather than allow themselves and their flag to be captured by the attacking Americans. . . . We look for others like ourselves in these history books, for something to be proud of for being a Mexican, and all we see in books and magazines, films, and TV shows are stereotypes of a dark, dirty, smelly man with a tequila bottle in one hand, a dripping taco in the other, a serape wrapped around him, and a big sombrero. But we are not the dirty, stinking wino that the Anglo world would like to point out as a Mexican.[51]

In an effort to return Sal Castro to the classroom, Rosalinda also testified before the Los Angeles School Board, as did Vickie Castro and other young Chicanas.

Though most young women involved in the Blowouts did not fill the role of official spokesperson, several of the women I interviewed described instances in which they spontaneously addressed a group of students or the media in relation to the Blowouts. Mita Cuaron reconstructs a situation in which she was an unofficial spokesperson: "It was just so spontaneous. And I remember picking up an orange cone from the street, and began talking about, we are protesting and this is what's happening. And I don't remember exactly what I said, but I remember physically standing on a car and talking out loud. And for two minutes there was quite a group of students not going back into school, and then the police were called and they began to chase us."[52]

Thus, although acting as a spokesperson is a dimension of leadership that was more often filled by males, these examples show that some women did participate in this dimension of leadership while also participating in other dimensions.

THE MULTIDIMENSIONAL INFLUENCE OF GENDER

How is it that these eight women came to participate in the 1968 Blowouts in the ways that they did? What influenced and shaped their participation? This study provides evidence suggesting that the dimensions of leadership are not necessarily gender specific, and the same individual may engage in several dimensions.[53] While young women were more likely to be found participating in the first three dimensions of leadership—networking, organizing, and developing consciousness—it is important to look at the factors that shaped their participation rather than assume that these are gender-specific dimensions of leadership that are only filled by females. In a study of traditional and nontraditional patterns of Chicana and Mexicana activism, Margaret Rose concedes that personalities have shaped female participation in the United Farm Workers of America (UFW).[54] However, she argues that the pattern of participation is more greatly influenced by complex factors such as class, cultural values, social expectations, and the sexual division of labor. Indeed, the eight women I interviewed discuss similar factors that appear to have shaped their participation in the school boycotts. In this final section, I will present the oral history data that speak to the multidimensional influence of gender.

The influence of gender was perceived in a somewhat nebulous way by the women in this study. Women made statements ranging from, "Nobody ever said that you couldn't do this because you were a girl," to "I know that the females were not the leaders," and from, "Being a female was not an issue, it was just a non-issue," to "I'm sure I knew that there was sexism involved . . . but we probably didn't talk about it." This diversity of statements, both within interviews and between interviews, leads to a conclusion that these women held no single distinct and precise viewpoint on the influence of gender. Rather, the women's individual and collective thoughts on gender represent the indeterminate and complex influence of gender within a system of patriarchy—a system of domination and unequal stratification based on gender. Though the way that boys and girls were socialized may have reinforced the gender differences in how they exercised leadership in the school Blowouts, the women's diverse comments reflect the complexity of gender's influence while also attributing their participation in various leadership roles to sexism, role-compatibility, choice, and expectations.

The social, cultural, and temporal milieu all contributed to what was expected of young women in 1968. And though most of these women ventured from these expectations, they were very aware of them. For example, one woman stated, "So I think that my home life, in one sense, brought me up very traditional. And I definitely knew what the female role was supposed to be. And that it wasn't college, and it wasn't this and that."[55] Paula Crisostomo also comments on the way that gender expectations, "how it was then," and her personal agency shaped the ways in which she participated in the Blowouts: "Boys were more outspoken and I think that's just because of, that's how it was then. They were given the interviews more than the girls were. When we would talk about the division of who was going to speak to what group, it was the boys who were chosen and the girls who sort of stayed back. And I think that's just how it was. . . . And I was happy, as I still am today, to be in the background. I'll do what you want me to do, but I'll do it back here. Don't have me stand in front of a mike, or in front of a group of people, I just don't want to do that."[56]

Vickie Castro points out that patriarchy and her own agency were complex forces that interacted to shape her participation. Vickie believes there was a "big gender issue in the family." She grew up in a "traditional" family with a very strong and dominant father who expected her to get married and have children. Her father was an inspiration through his own strength and leadership, yet he often held traditional gender expectations and tried to place limitations on Vickie. On the other hand, her older brothers were always encouraging and supportive, and they urged Vickie to go on to college. Her family's influence gave her the strength to combat the sexism she and other young women found in some of the student organizations: "Maybe my male friends at the time, in the organization, would try to put me in female roles. Like be the secretary, make the sandwiches, do that. But I think that I had such a strong male influence in my household, you know, four brothers and my father, that among my brothers I was equal. So I always challenged. And when I would see that there were no women involved, boom, I made myself right there."[57]

Rosalinda Méndez González also offers comments that demonstrate how the influence of gender interacted with various structures and social systems to offer a multidimensional influence. First, she acknowledges that few people raised the question or offered a critique of patriarchy in the early part of the Chicano Movement (a point with which most of the women concur), yet Rosalinda experienced sexism in a personal relationship. Second, she points to the fact that it was older males involved in Camp Hess Kramer and other organizations, rather than females, who encouraged her and other young women to become involved in Blowout related activities:

I think that when we participated in things initially, there wasn't a consciousness of patriarchy. If you were a young man or young woman and you saw injustice, whether in regards to the farmworkers or in regards to our college, you spoke out and got involved. Now in my case, I very early on began to encounter some patriarchal hostilities from my own boyfriend, who very much criticized me for taking an active role and speaking out. But he didn't convince me nor did he succeed in holding me back. I was just very hurt by it, but I didn't accept his arguments or his reason. I encountered it at a very personal level. At the same time there were a lot of men, older men that were encouraging me to speak out and participate.[58]

Rosalinda explains that after the Blowouts, as the movement began to gain momentum, she encountered increasing evidence of sexism and that women began addressing patriarchy as a system of domination. In fact, she argues that in many cases it was the female students who were at the forefront of the movement and that male students tried to hold young women back and move into the more visible leadership positions.

Though sexist gender expectations were prevalent within the existing patriarchal relations, Vickie Castro also points to how she and other female and male students were conscious of gender stereotypes and used them to their advantage. They would strategize the roles that students would take based on individual characteristics and resources. For her, that meant different things at different times. At one point it meant using her car and a set of chains to pull open the gates around Roosevelt High School; at other times it meant using her "goody-two-shoes image": "So we knew that if we needed someone who didn't look threatening, that looked like a nice person, I was to go in. I was the, you know, I'm a little bit more *güera*. I didn't really dress, I didn't really look *chola*. If we wanted somebody to be aggressive and very vocal then that was David's [Sanchez] role. . . . I always had the look to get out of it. I always looked real strait-laced. And I knew that. And I used it. I never looked the militant type, the *chola* type."[59] In other words, she did not embody what some school officials feared most in Mexican American students. As a fair-complexioned female who dressed "appropriately," she was not threatening to the white mainstream community nor to the older or more conservative Mexicans in her own community. Vickie's physical appearance influenced the type of participation and leadership she offered to the Blowouts, and she used it to gain support for the Blowouts.

Gender interacted with sexism, patriarchal relations, personal agency, and the family to shape the participation and leadership of young women in the Blowouts. And while the women in this study acknowledge the impact gender expectations had on their participation, they link their participation in the Blowouts to the discrimination and oppression of the community as a whole rather than to that of women. One woman stated, "I felt as a whole, in terms of my peers and I, we were being discriminated against, but, personally, as a woman, I didn't feel that there was a differentiation."[60] This echoes the findings of Mary Pardo's study of the Mothers of East L.A. in which she points out that working-class women activists seldom opt to separate themselves from men and their families.[61] As the women in my study reflect back, they too view their participation in the school Blowouts as a struggle for their community and quality education.

The oral history data I present challenges the historical and ideological representation of Chicanas by relocating them to a central position in the historical narrative. Through a cooperative leadership paradigm that recognizes diverse dimensions of grassroots leadership, we are able to move beyond the traditional notion of leadership and identify ways in which women offered leadership to the Blowouts. Though their stories are often excluded in the writing of history, I confirm that Chicanas have been intimately involved with and have offered leadership to the ongoing struggle for educational justice. The experiences of Celeste Baca, Vickie Castro, Paula Crisostomo, Mita Cuaron, Tanya Luna Mount, Rosalinda Méndez González, Rachael Ochoa Cervera, and Cassandra Zacarías rebuke the popular stereotypes of Mexican women as docile, passive, and apathetic, and demonstrate that women's leadership in events like the 1968 East Los Angeles School Blowouts has often been unrecognized and unappreciated.

Through the oral history data of these eight women, I illustrate that looking at grassroots leadership within a cooperative leadership paradigm leads us to an alternative history of the 1968 East Los Angeles School Blowouts—a history that makes the invisible visible. This alternative history of women's participation and leadership also pushes us to consider how we can redefine the categories for studying and participating in community activism. By redefining the leadership paradigm, we may be able to break through dominant ways of thinking and doing and reclaim histories that have been silenced in our communities, as well as shape our future histories to be more inclusive of traditionally silenced voices. Indeed, there is something faulty in previous leadership paradigms that have not allowed us to acknowledge Chicanas as leaders in the 1968 Blowouts, the Chicano Movement, and in other grassroots movements. A cooperative leadership paradigm allows us to address the erroneous absence of Chicanas as participants and leaders in history and contemporary life.[62]

NOTES

I would like to thank the many individuals who provided me with supportive criticism during the different stages of analyzing, conceptualizing, and writing. The completion of this article benefited from the feedback and encouragement of Ramona Maile Cutri, Claudia Ramirez Weideman, Anne Powell, Amy Stuart Wells, Freddy Heredia, Mary Pardo, Danny Solorzano, Octavio Villalpando, and the readers at *Frontiers*, including Vicki Ruiz. A special thanks also to Sal Castro. I am especially indebted to the eight women who allowed me to transform their lived history into a written history—*muchísimas gracias*.

1. Carlos Muñoz Jr., *Youth, Identity, Power: The Chicano Movement* (New York: Verso, 1989).

2. The following scholars have studied the Blowouts from theoretical perspectives: Myron Puckett, "Protest Politics in Education: A Case Study in the Los Angeles Unified School District" (Ph.D. diss., Claremont Graduate School, 1971); Carlos Muñoz Jr., "The Politics of Chicano Urban Protest: A Model of Political Analysis" (Ph.D. diss., Claremont Graduate School, 1972); Louis R. Negrete, "Culture Clash: The Utility of Mass Protest as a Political Response," *The Journal of Comparative Cultures* 1:1 (1972): 25–36; Juan Gómez-Quiñones, *Mexican Students Por La Raza: The Chicano Student Movement in Southern California, 1967–1977* (Santa Barbara, Calif.: Editorial La Causa, 1978); and Gerald Rosen, "The Development of the Chicano Movement in Los Angeles from 1967–1969," *Atzlan* 4:1 (1973): 155–83.

3. Luis Ruiz (executive producer) and Susan Racho (segment producer), "Taking Back the Schools," part 3 of *Chicano: A History of the Mexican American Civil Rights Movement* (Los Angeles: National Latino Communications Center & Galán Productions, Inc., 1996).

4. In this paper "Chicana" is used when referring to female persons of Mexican origin living in the United States—irrespective of generational or immigration status. "Chicano" is used when referring to both male and female persons; I specifically indicate when the term refers only to males. Terms of identification vary according to context and it should be noted that during the period of interest in this paper, 1968, these terms were especially prominent within the student population as conscious political identifiers. The term Chicano was not prominent prior to the 1960s and is therefore used interchangeably with "Mexican" when referring to pre-1960s history.

5. In the last fifteen to twenty years there has been a relative increase in the works that look specifically at the grassroots leadership, community activism, and historical struggles of Chicanas. The following are but a few examples: Adelaida R. Del Castillo, ed., *Between Borders: Essays on Mexicana/Chicana History* (Encino, Calif.: Floricanto Press, 1990); Rosalinda Méndez González, "Chicanas and Mexican Im-

migrant Families, 1920–1940," in *Decades of Discontent: The Women's Movement, 1920–1940*, ed. Lois Scharf and Joan M. Jensen (Wesport, Conn.: Greenwood Press, 1983), 59–83; Magdalena Mora and Adelaida R. Del Castillo, eds., *Mexican Women in the United States: Struggles Past and Present* (Los Angeles: Chicano Studies Research Center Publications, University of California, 1980); Vicki L. Ruiz, *Cannery Women, Cannery Lives: Mexican Women, Unionization, and the California Food Processing Industry, 1930–1950* (Albuquerque: University of New Mexico Press, 1987); Adaljiza Sosa-Riddell, "Chicanas and El Movimiento," *Aztlan* 5:2 (spring and fall 1974): 155–65; Adela de la Torre and Beatriz M. Pesquera, eds., *Building with Our Hands: New Directions in Chicana Studies* (Berkeley: University of California Press, 1993); Mary Pardo, "Identity and Resistance: Mexican American Women and Grassroots Activism in Two Los Angeles Communities" (Ph.D. diss., University of California, Los Angeles, 1990); and Patricia Zavella, "Reflections on Diversity Among Chicanas," *Frontiers: A Journal of Women Studies* 12:2 (1991): 73–85.

6. Chandra Talpade Mohanty, "On Race and Voice: Challenges for Liberal Education in the 1990s," in *Between Borders: Pedagogy and the Politics of Cultural Studies*, ed. Henry A. Giroux and Peter McLaren (New York: Routledge, 1994), 148.

7. Kenneth Kann, "Reconstructing the History of a Community," *International Journal of Oral History* 2:1 (1981): 4.

8. Alessandro Portelli, "The Peculiarities of Oral History," *History Workshop Journal* 12 (1981): 96–107.

9. Patricia Gándara defines a networking sampling procedure, which is sometimes called a "snowball" procedure, as one in which participants identify other potential participants based on an informal social or professional network (*Over the Ivy Walls: The Educational Mobility of Low-Income Chicanos* [Albany: State University of New York Press, 1995]).

10. Richard A. Krueger, *Focus Groups: A Practical Guide for Applied Research* (Thousand Oaks, Calif.: Sage Publications, 1988).

11. For different interpretations of the Blowout demands see Puckett, "Protest Politics in Education"; Rosen, "The Development of the Chicano Movement"; Carlos Muñoz Jr., "The Politics of Protest and Chicano Liberation: A Case Study of Repression and Co-optation," *Aztlan* 5:1/2 (1974): 119–41; and Jack McCurdy, "Frivolous to Fundamental: Demands Made by East Side High School Students Listed," *Los Angeles Times*, March 17, 1968, 1, 4–5. For an overview of educational concerns and issues of Mexicans during the first half of the century, see Gilbert G. González, *Chicano Education in the Era of Segregation* (Philadelphia: Balch Institute Press, 1990), and "The System of Public Education and Its Function within the Chicano Communities, 1910–1950" (Ph.D. diss., University of California, Los Angeles, 1974).

12. Kaye Briegel, "Chicano Student Militancy: The Los Angeles High School Strike

of 1968," in *An Awakened Minority: The Mexican-Americans*, ed. Manuel P. Servín, 2nd ed. (New York: Macmillan, 1974), 215–25.

13. California State Advisory Committee to the United States Commission on Civil Rights, "Education and the Mexican American Community in Los Angeles County," CR 1.2: Ed 8/3 (April 1968), 16.

14. Rosalinda Méndez González, personal interview, October 8, 1995.

15. "Conference Fact Sheet: Fifth Annual Mexican-American Youth Leadership Conference, 1967."

16. Rachael Ochoa Cervera, personal interview, December 10, 1995.

17. Méndez González, interview.

18. Rosen, "The Development of the Chicano Movement."

19. Gómez-Quiñones, *Mexican Students Por La Raza*.

20. Briegel, "Chicano Student Militancy"; and Rosen, "The Development of the Chicano Movement."

21. California State Advisory Committee, "Education and the Mexican American Community."

22. California State Advisory Committee, "Education and the Mexican American Community."

23. Méndez González, interview.

24. Based on the Los Angeles Unified School District's "Historical Racial Ethnic Data 1966–1979," the percentage of "Hispanic" students in each of the five schools in 1968 was as follows: Garfield, 96 percent; Roosevelt, 83 percent; Lincoln, 89 percent; Wilson, 76 percent, and Belmont, 59 percent.

25. Paula Crisostomo, personal interview, November 16, 1995.

26. Victoria Castro, personal interview, June 8, 1995.

27. Tanya Luna Mount, personal interview, January 31, 1996. For a historical analysis of patterns of police brutality in East Los Angeles, see also Armando Morales, *Ando Sangrado/I Am Bleeding: A Study of Mexican American Police Conflict* (La Puente, Calif.: Perspectiva Publications, 1972).

28. McCurdy, "Frivolous to Fundamental."

29. Jack McCurdy, "School Board Yields on Some Student Points," *Los Angeles Times*, March 12, 1968, 1, 3.

30. McCurdy, "Frivolous to Fundamental," 1.

31. Karen Brodkin Sacks, *Caring by the Hour: Women, Work, and Organizing at Duke Medical Center* (Urbana: University of Illinois Press, 1988), and "Gender and Grassroots Leadership," in *Women and the Politics of Empowerment*, ed. Ann Bookman and Sandra Morgen (Philadelphia: Temple University Press, 1988), 77–94. These works have greatly influenced my conceptual analysis of grassroots leadership. See also Helen S. Astin and Carole Leland, *Women of Influence, Women of Vision: A*

Cross-Generational Study of Leaders and Social Change (San Francisco: Jossey-Bass, 1991).

32. Thomas S. Kuhn, *The Structure of Scientific Revolutions*, 2nd ed. (Chicago: University of Chicago Press, 1970).

33. Brodkin Sacks, *Caring by the Hour*, and "Gender and Grassroots Leadership."

34. Astin and Leland, *Women of Influence, Women of Vision*, 8.

35. Dolores Delgado Bernal, "Chicana School Resistance and Grassroots Leadership: Providing an Alternative History of the 1968 East Los Angeles Blowouts" (Ph.D. diss., University of California, Los Angeles, 1997).

36. Charlotte Bunch, foreword, Astin and Leland, *Women of Influence, Women of Vision*, xiii.

37. Tanya Luna Mount's parents had a long history of labor, civil rights, and peace activism. Her mother, Julia Luna Mount, was actively involved in a labor resistance movement at one of the largest food processing plants in Los Angeles that included a massive walkout and a twenty-four-hour picket line to end deplorable working conditions. See Ruiz, *Cannery Women, Cannery Lives*.

38. Castro, interview.

39. Crisostomo, interview.

40. Mita Cuaron, personal interview, January 23, 1996.

41. Méndez González, interview.

42. Ochoa Cervera, interview.

43. Cassandra Zacarías, personal interview, December 7, 1995.

44. Crisostomo, interview.

45. Brodkin Sacks, "Gender and Grassroots Leadership," 81.

46. Zacarías, interview.

47. Castro, interview.

48. Sal Castro, personal interview, February 6, 1996.

49. Crisostomo, interview.

50. Election campaign materials, Garfield Blowout Committee, 1968.

51. California State Advisory Committee to the United States Commission on Civil Rights.

52. Cuaron, interview.

53. See Brodkin Sacks, "Gender and Grassroots Leadership," who suggests that grassroots leadership roles need not be gender specific.

54. Margaret Rose, "Traditional and Nontraditional Patterns of Female Activism in the United Farm Workers of America, 1962 to 1980," *Frontiers: A Journal of Women Studies* 11:1 (1990): 26–32.

55. V. Castro, interview.

56. Crisostomo, interview.

57. V. Castro, interview.

58. Méndez González, interview.

59. V. Castro, interview.

60. Mita Cuaron, interview conducted by Susan Racho, December 3, 1994.

61. Mary Pardo, "Mexican American Women Grassroots Community Activists: 'Mothers of East Los Angeles,'" *Frontiers: A Journal of Women Studies* 11:1 (1990): 1–7.

62. The following provides the reader with a quick snapshot of where the eight women were at the time the article was written:

Today, Celeste Baca lives in Sonoma County, California, with her husband. She holds a Master's in Education from the Claremont Graduate School and a Master's in Computer Technology in Education from California State University, Los Angeles. She has taught elementary school for twenty-four years and currently teaches in a Spanish two-way immersion classroom in Roseland School District. She has been a member of the National Association of Bilingual Education throughout most of her teaching career. In addition, Celeste teaches computer courses as a part-time lecturer in the Mexican American Studies Department at Sonoma State University.

Vickie Castro obtained her bachelor's degree from Cal-State, Los Angeles, her teaching credential from the University of California, Santa Cruz, and a Master of Science in School Management and Administration from Pepperdine University. She has worked as an employee of the Los Angeles Unified School District for twenty-eight years. Throughout her career, Vickie has been very active in the Association of Mexican American Educators (AMAE), serving as the East Los Angeles local chapter president and then the state president in 1981. In 1993, Vickie was elected to the Los Angeles City Board of Education, the second largest school district in the nation. Vickie continues to volunteer as a sponsor or workshop facilitator to various Latino youth leadership conferences in the Los Angeles area. A resident of the Echo Park community, Vickie is mother to an adult daughter and grandmother to a new grandson.

Paula Crisostomo graduated from California State University, Sonoma, with a major in liberal studies. Today she lives with her husband and two teenage children in the Los Angeles area. For a number of years Paula was a fund developer for the National Association for the Advancement of Colored People (NAACP) Legal Defense. For more than five years, she has been working in the field of social marketing—selling public service ideas—and is currently working on public housing and economic development issues for Los Angeles County. Paula continues to participate in various community-based activities and over the years has remained very active in the Mexican

American Youth Leadership Conferences at Camp Hess Kramer. As a member of the nonprofit Educational Issues Coordinating Committee and acting director of the conferences, Paula has been involved in fund-raising to maintain the conferences since 1988.

Mita Cuaron's social activism has often been displayed through her work as a nurse and an artist. Beginning in the late 1970s, she was a member of the "Flying Samaritans," a group of medical professionals who made monthly trips to Baja California, Mexico, to administer free medical care. In the early 1980s, she went to Nicaragua to participate in the International World Health Tour. More recently, Mita has also served as a volunteer nurse for the Mexican American Youth Leadership Conferences at Camp Hess Kramer. She has exhibited her artwork at various sites, including Self-Help Graphics, Plaza de La Raza, and the University of California, Riverside. She recently donated a piece of art to a silent auction benefiting the Rigoberta Menchu Fund. Today Mita continues to reside in the Los Angeles area with her husband and four-year-old son. She works at White Memorial Hospital in East Los Angeles as a registered nurse specializing in the area of psychiatry.

Throughout college and her career as a professor, Rosalinda Méndez González has been active in movements against gender, class, and ethnic/racial oppression. She and another graduate student, Linda Apodaca, created and then co-taught with a third woman the first course in women's studies at the University of California, Irvine, "The History of Women's Oppression." She has conducted and presented research at various regional and national conferences such as the National Association for Chicana and Chicano Studies and the Latin American Studies Association. She was awarded the Woodrow Wilson Fellowship for Women's Studies for her dissertation research, and in 1980 she was invited to be a delegate to the International Conference on Women in Copenhagen, Denmark. Today Rosalinda is a mother of two adult children and is a college professor at Southwestern College in Chula Vista, California. Most recently, she has been very involved in issues of culture and the empowerment that comes from reclaiming family roots and community history; she is currently working with two other historians on a book on the history of Chicanos in San Diego County.

Over the years Tanya Luna Mount has worked and volunteered in various political and social justice movements. In the 1970s she took undergraduate courses at California State University, Los Angeles, and worked as a teaching assistant in the bilingual/ESL program at a junior high in East L.A. She was active in the anti-Vietnam movement, La Raza Unida, and organizing against police brutality. She worked with the Barrio Defense Committee, which was a support and advocacy organization that brought attention to police brutality in East Los Angeles communities. During the 1980s Tanya remained active in developing a third political party through the Peace and Freedom Party. She also worked at the East Los Angeles Health Task Force, which is a multiservice social agency. Today Tanya has an eighteen-year-old daughter and a twenty-one-year-old son and continues to live in the Los Angeles area. She works at a junior high in East Los Angeles as a cafeteria clerk for the Federal Lunch Program. She actively supports the Los Angeles Catholic Worker Brittania House, which is a progressive Catholic social service organization in East Los Angeles.

After graduating from Cal-State, Los Angeles, Rachael Ochoa Cervera attended the Claremont Graduate School to earn her Master's in Education and a Bilingual Specialist Teaching Credential. During her early teaching career she was very involved in the Association of Mexican American Educators (AMAE) and served on its state executive board. Rachael has been teaching elementary school for twenty-four years. She is a bilingual teacher in the Garvey School District and teaches evening adult education classes at the El Monte/Rosemead Adult School. She is active in the California Teachers Association (CTA) and was recently appointed to be a reading recovery specialist and a member of the Mentor-Teacher Selection Committee by her district. She continues to live in the Los Angeles area with her husband and two school-aged children, and over the years she has remained actively involved in Roosevelt High School's Class Reunion Committee.

Cassandra Zacarías attended the Claremont Graduate School while working on her teaching credential. However, after teaching for a short period, she realized teaching was not for her and left the program. She worked for a while outside of the educational field and then returned by attending graduate school and obtaining her master's degree in School Counseling and her Pupil Personnel Services Credential from California State University, Los Angeles. Early in her high school counseling career, Cassandra was involved with the Association of Mexican American Educators (AMAE), attending monthly meetings and participating in scholarship fund-raisers for Latino students. Today, Cassandra is a high school counselor in the Whittier Union High School District. She continues to live in the Los Angeles area with her husband, who is an elementary school administrator, and her elementary school–aged daughter.

Frontiers 19:2 (1998): 113–42.

The Southern Paiute Woman in a Changing Society

LUCILLE JAKE, EVELYN JAMES, AND PAMELA BUNTE

Three women started this oral history project because they were interested in what it was like to be a Southern Paiute woman at the turn of the century. Lucille Jake and Evelyn James are Southern Paiutes (one a Kaibab-Paiute, the other a San Juan Paiute) who grew up hearing about what their grandmothers had done and how they had lived. The project was especially important to them because they wanted the knowledge of the traditional lifeways of these elder Paiutes for their descendants as well as themselves. Pamela Bunte, an anthropologist who has lived with both Kaibab-Paiutes and San Juan Paiutes, shared their interest. She helped coordinate the project and did the writing for this article.

With these goals in mind, the authors arranged to interview the two grandmothers selected for this project, Mabel Drye, a Kaibab-Paiute woman in her nineties, and Marie Lehi, a San Juan Paiute woman in her eighties. Mabel Drye's interview took place in her grandson's home in Kaibab Village. Present, besides Mabel, were Lucille Jake and Pamela Bunte and her husband, Robert Franklin. Lucille Jake has known Mabel Drye all her life and is well liked by her. Pamela Bunte, who speaks Southern Paiute, had talked to her on several previous occasions. While the three women sat around the kitchen table, Robert Franklin sat back a little and took charge of the recording equipment. During the session, several people entered and left the house. The session with Marie Lehi took place at her sheep camp and started in the shade-house with many people sitting around. Because it was a windy day and therefore difficult to obtain a good recording, we moved into an adjacent hogan. During the principal part of the recording only Marie Lehi, Pamela Bunte, and Evelyn James, her granddaughter, were present.

Both women were told that the authors were particularly interested in what it was like to grow up not only as a Paiute but also as a woman. The authors were, in fact, asking the two grandmothers to reminisce about certain aspects of their lives. One of the differences between the two women was in their attitude toward reminiscing. Mabel, who is often alone, had had time to think about the many events in her past life as well as notice and worry about the vast changes taking place in the younger generations. She wanted her story taped so that the knowledge, of whose importance she is aware, is not lost. Marie, although she teaches her grandchildren Paiute traditions and remonstrates them when they do not follow these traditions, is busy herding sheep and making baskets, and seemed to wonder why we were asking her about her life. She is also sometimes shy. She told us at one point, "I think of many things to tell you, but then when I'm here I can't remember them."

As the gathering of these oral histories progressed, the authors found that their attitudes were influenced not only by their goals but also by their relationships with the storyteller and by their feelings about the actual material. An important difference among the authors was how personal the material was to them. Moreover, the participants' attitudes might change during the course of the session, and the change could decide whether there were any interruptions and, if so, of what type. For example, during her interview Marie Lehi began to discuss a topic not directly relevant to the subject. After listening awhile, during a pause one of the authors asked a question designed to bring the discussion back to a previous point. Marie answered the question but returned to her topic which was obviously important to her. Such differing goals had, of course, to be "negotiated" by the participants.

In addition to the attitudes of the individuals involved, the attitudes of their social groups were also important. In Marie Lehi's case the entire Willow Springs community thought the recording of oral history was a good thing. Since they are in the midst of filing a petition to be federally recognized as the San Juan Southern Paiutes, they were certainly aware of the value of such recordings to their tribal goals. At Kaibab, too, the older people are afraid that much of the traditional knowledge will soon be lost. There is, however, no immediate need for this knowledge, and many of the younger people dislike having people interview their relatives. Thus the feeling about oral history was ambivalent, even at the individual level.

The structure of the story and translation was influenced by several factors. Evelyn James, for instance, as the spokesperson of the San Juan Southern Paiutes, has had much practice at oral translation from English to Paiute and from Paiute to English. She has developed a fluent style and knows exactly when she must interrupt and start the translation without losing any of the material. Marie is perfectly aware of Evelyn's style. As a monolingual Paiute speaker, she has often had Evelyn interpret for her. In fact, all three participants had engaged in similar work on several occasions. Mabel, on the other hand, has a very different style; she prefers to talk uninterrupted except for allowing occasional emphatic responses to indicate attentive listening. Part of the reason for this style is that she is hard of hearing, and it is more difficult for her to stop and answer questions. In addition, she is used to talking to Lucille Jake and feels comfortable. Lucille, although an excellent translator, preferred just to listen rather than to interrupt, knowing that the translation could be done later.

In the course of the oral history gathering process the authors learned that while every person telling a story has his or her unique style and interests, the final form of an oral history is influenced not only by the storyteller but also by the audience. The interaction between the interviewer and the interviewee is critically important, as are the political, economic, and historical contexts in which they find themselves. The analysis of oral history is a complicated process.

GEOGRAPHICAL AND HISTORICAL SETTING

In the pre- and early contact period, the Southern Paiutes were loosely organized into territorial bands. The extended family, however, was the group most important in daily activities, especially in economic activities. Although the primary activity of a family would take place within the territory recognized as belonging to a band, the renewal of kinship ties, economic pursuits, social occasions, or any combination of these activities, would take members of one group to adjacent territories. The two Southern Paiute bands relevant to this article are the Kaibab and the San Juan. The Kaibab precontact territory (mainly in Utah and Arizona) was bounded on the east by the Paria River and on the south by the Colorado River.[1] To the north their territory stretched into present-day Utah to the Kolob Plateau. The western boundary began a small distance beyond Kanab Creek Canyon and proceeded north, passing east of Toquerville, Utah, to the Kolob Plateau. Traditional San Juan Southern Paiute land stretched from the east bank of the Colorado River in Arizona, to south of Cameron, west to Kayenta, and north into southern Utah.

Neither group was much bothered by Anglo expansion until the 1850s, when the Mormons began moving to southern Utah and northern Arizona, taking over the Paiutes' springs and the best farming land and bringing cattle to graze on the plants the Paiutes had gathered for food. Subsequently large numbers of Paiutes starved and died.[2] Although the Mormons thoroughly appropriated the Kaibab territory, the invasion in the San Juan region was much more limited; it appears that only the major springs in the Tuba City area were appropriated, and the herds of livestock were relatively small. Also, the Mormons never established themselves securely in the San Juan territory and left the area in the nineteenth century. Some of the springs used by the Mormons reverted to the Paiutes; the others were given to Navajos. Before the Kit Carson roundup of 1864—the so-called Long Walk—very few Navajos lived permanently in the San Juan territory, although they often passed through it, raiding both the San Juan region and the Kaibab region. After the roundup, Navajos gradually moved into the territory to settle permanently. Paiutes became a real minority, however, only after the 1918 flu epidemic, which caused massive depopulation and opened up for exclusive Navajo use many areas that had previously been used by Paiutes.[3]

The San Juan and Kaibab bands had traditionally lived in very similar ways: Both groups had farmed, gathered various kinds of plant foods, and hunted; members of each group had a detailed and sophisticated knowledge of their environment. Culturally, too, they were very similar: They spoke dialects of the same language, performed the same ceremonies, had similar values, and even intermarried to some extent. Although the mothers of both of the women in this study had grown up in this traditional Southern Paiute culture, the world into which Mabel Drye and Marie Lehi were born already contained elements of the substantial changes that were to affect them during their lifetimes.

CHILDHOOD

Mabel Drye was born in the 1880s. As a child, she lived with her grandparents near Cannonville, Utah, which was already established as a Mormon town.[4] Her grandfather had grown up in this area long before any white people lived there: In her words, "It was all Paiute land then and that was before people went to school." Her grandfather hunted in several places, sometimes in the Kaiparowits area farther east in Utah, but also near a mountain that "looked like a face in a circle, *avingkovaxant*.[5] On one side of this mountain there's a grassy place with lots of willows that we used to gather [for basket-making] and a reservoir that the white people call Pine Lake. He also hunted at a place called Eastfork and a nearby mountain, *wunakaiv*. These were my grandfather's hunting grounds." In addition to his hunting grounds he had gardens at Paria. Paiutes, although they traditionally felt a primary tie to a certain "water" or spring, did not stay the entire year there. As we can see from Mabel Drye's story, her grandfather was from Cannonville—not only did he live there, he was buried there—but he moved around to many other areas. Usually a group of closely related families would move around together with the women gathering seeds and plants while the men hunted.

When Mabel was a little girl, she moved around with her family and helped gather plant foods. She possessed a tremendous knowledge of food and medicine plants and their locations, particularly in the northern portion of the traditional Kaibab area, that is, in southern Utah. Her discussion of her early life, however, centered on two principal events that clearly made a strong impression on her: her father's death; and going away to school with her brother and, later on, his death. These events are best recounted in her own words:

When I got a little older, my father, who lived above Kanab, sent a letter to my grandfather asking him to bring me down to visit him. My grandfather had a Mormon read it for him. And then my grandfather said, "You'd better leave now." So then my grandmother and I got ready with the horses. And then we left on the horses. And then arrived at a ranch and then on we went through *sikurumpa* [Johnson Canyon]. We slept there, and I was afraid of the owls when they were crying.[6] We left again in the morning and arrived in Kanab, but they didn't live there. They had recently moved from Long Valley [Utah] to the top of the hill above Kanab above the rodeo ground. So we went to that place and he [Mabel's father] started crying when he saw us and put his arms around us. A little while later my baby brother, Stanley, and I were lying with my father and he had died, but we didn't know it, and then our mother told us to get up because our father was no longer with us.

When we had first gotten to Kanab, Johnny Dick arrived and told us that my father was in a really bad way and then Sara Williams, who was a sister to my father, arrived. She couldn't find the Indian camp, so then we all went together to the Indian camp, and it was after that that he died. Then they buried him up above Kanab. I'm the oldest child in my family, then another girl came after me, then a boy, two of them, and then Stanley, and that's our baby brother: Two girls and three boys, that's how many children my mother had. I'm one of the girls. There were five of us, that's all. And after my father died, then that Sara wanted Stanley to be buried with my father. But another old lady said not to let that happen to him. His uncle also said that he wasn't going to let that happen, so nothing happened to him.

Later on, do you know what happened? A Mormon had dug the grave up. It was the Mormon that has the store in Kanab. This was a long time ago. We were living in Delta, Utah, and I read in the Kane County newspaper that some white man had dug up an Indian grave in the area where my father was buried, and I know that that must have been my father's grave. This was in 1948. I wanted to save that article and show the article when I went back to Kanab to someone who could help me, but my daughter said, "Don't do it. There's no way that you can prove it is your father's grave." I told her that I could trace it, but she said no. After that I lost the clipping. The one that has the museum in Kanab did that.

And then when I got a little older they sent me to school. There was a school going on there in Panguitch. My brother [not Stanley] and I were sent there. I'm telling all about myself and my brother. That's where I spent my days learning to read and write in English. And then every summer we went home. My grandfather used to send the horses so we could come home. Then my brother and I used to ride on one horse. Some of the children had to stay at school all the time and not come home because they kept doing things wrong and acting bad, like kids are doing today. So they stayed there all summer. Now isn't the only time they're doing that running around; they've been doing that a long time but we [my brother and I] always came home. I used to have a picture of the school. I didn't want the whole building in the picture, just the kids. I'm so crazy; I don't know why I didn't want the whole building in it. I felt bad after it had burnt down after I had my kids.

And then he [my brother] grew up. I believe he was ten years old. My brother used to go rabbit hunting. One day they went a little farther up the mountains. There was lots of water in the wash. Joe told him to wait and not go into the swift water and he didn't listen. He covered his mouth when he went under the water, and just the horse came out.

Funerals, although always sad, were and are an occasion when Paiutes who do not live near each other gather from long distances. Friendships are renewed, and even marriages sometimes result. Mabel recounted that at her brother's funeral two couples got married. She continued, "Everyone was laughing at them because it seemed that they went to the funeral to get married. They all came home except the ones who got married."

Later the authorities wanted her to go away to another boarding school in Sherman, California. Her parents had gotten her all ready to go, but her aunt protested, telling her that whenever girls go far away to school they never come home. Her aunt's son, Alec, also told her not to go. Instead they arranged for her to get married, and she did what they told her.

Marie Lehi was born in 1901 at a place now called Pasture Canyon. Marie told us, "My mother went there to pick willows and had the baby around midday. She wrapped me up in some leaves and then came home—with a baby." Although Marie lived with her parents, she spent a lot of time with her grandparents, especially her grandfather, Machukats. When she was still a little girl, she would often ride horses with her grandfather to the fields and other places. She recounted,

When he went places, I would go with him, and he would tell me stories and tell me about hunting, especially about when he would go antelope hunting. He used to be an expert at tracking antelopes and making traps for them. He would make holes in the ground and use special grass to attract them. There was also special medicine to put on the tip of arrows to make them go straight. The Paiutes would never miss antelopes!

Her grandfather, like other Paiute men, also hunted rabbits. Rabbits were important for both food and clothing because the blankets woven out of rabbit pelts kept them warm in the winter. In the summer they wore yucca sandals, but in the winter they wore moccasins of badger skin with the shredded bark of cliff-rose inside for extra insulation. Marie remembers that hers went all the way up to her knees to keep out the snow. Marie's family, like the other San Juan Paiutes of her time, moved around quite a bit. She mentions wintering in different places, although they often returned to Willow Springs at Echo Cliffs and to the plateau area west of Willow Springs called *atatsiv*, Sands, where she now lives. Her family had to work hard to get enough to eat. They hunted and gathered and farmed. Life during winter, especially certain winters, was harder than ever, and Marie speaks of a couple of winters in particular: During one, when they were living near Gap, Arizona, all they had to eat was the corn her mother ground for them; during another, spent in the Coppermine area at a spring called *shaxwaruipats*, her feet were bare and frozen. According to her, because of that she cannot go barefoot at all now.

Paiutes are great visitors. Not only did the San Juan Paiutes have friends and kin in other Paiute groups, whom they would visit at certain times of the year and at funerals, but they also had friends among other Indian groups. Marie's mother told her that Walapais used to come over to Willow Springs to visit and dance together in round dances.[7] They were friends of the Paiutes and would bring roasted *yant*[8] and deer meat for the accompanying feast. According to Marie, Walapai visiting occurred only before she was born. When Marie was a little girl, however, the Hopis had already moved into lower Moencopi. Marie tells about visiting them with her mother who had friends there and who could speak Hopi. The two of them would travel down there on a donkey and sometimes they would trade things.

Another important aspect of Marie's early life was the shamanistic activities of her grandfather, Machukats.

My grandfather used to be a Paiute medicine man [*puaxat*, one who has power]. He used to use the eagle for medicine. He would suck out the evil from the body. This evil was a kind of evil spirit, *ᵾnᵾxakats*. They could talk to these spirits. I used to watch him when he would sing medicine songs over the patient. Another spirit of his was the flying squirrel. He never killed an eagle or flying squirrel but just prayed to them singing, and the people got well. One time my grandfather went to Blanding to sing over some sick people. When he was doing that, a witchdoctor who lived in Blanding tricked him—he stole what he [my grandfather] was using for medicine. He had been putting a witch power on people making them sick. He used to kill young people—he'd go around witching them. A few years after that my grandfather died. I guess that was the end of Paiute doctors, Paiute medicine men. He was an old man when he died, and I was just a young girl then.

Paiute young girls are expected to be helpful, but they are not forced to work. Even today young Paiute girls start practicing certain crafts and cooking skills on their own when they are ready (often at a fairly young age). Marie Lehi told us that when she was a little girl she started making baskets using yucca and copying her mother. She would sharpen a stick for a needle and start making baskets like a toy. In addition, she told us,

I used to help my mother gather seeds and roots, all kinds of seeds and roots. I also helped pick corn and grind it. I still grind it the old way [with a mano and metate]. I sometimes make with the corn a "Navajo cake," a patty of cornmeal, the kind that Navajo girls have to make at the time of their first menstruation. Of course, I didn't do it for mine because at that time we didn't know what Navajos did.

When she was a little girl she knew some Navajos since "there were two families of Navajos on the plateau near us. They were Navajos that the Paiutes had hid when Kit Carson was going around and so they were good friends with the Paiutes. These Navajos that the Paiutes had saved used to have lots of sheep and used to give some to the Paiutes. But there were very few Navajos then." Marie added later, "When I was an older girl there were only six homes of Navajos down in Tuba. Just recently, the Navajos have really been moving in, and now they are overflowing."

Marie's first menstruation was an important time for her, and she discussed with us the teachings she received.

I used to fetch wood and carry it from far away—I was real strong. They used to watch me. I couldn't take a bath by myself or touch my hair with my hands. I had to run as far and as fast as I could to the east to get strong, to stay young, and not to get heavy. At that time, I wouldn't eat meat because I was told that if I ate meat I would lose my teeth before I was old. You weren't supposed to scratch your face or you'd get wrinkles. Women at that time would only eat cornmeal. After I had my first menstruation I would run under the rising sun in the morning. I wasn't supposed to follow any trails or tracks—just run straight east.

At the age of thirteen, Marie was scared of men and boys, but her mother kept telling her that she was reaching the age when she had to think about getting married.

I hardly ever went to any dances, but there were dances by where I lived and my future husband used to come to them.[9] Some people used to go to Kanab [Utah] and Pipesprings [Arizona] to dances there, and they had deer meat, but I never went there. I was too scared to cross the Colorado. Although a lot of them traveled around over by Kanab, I never did. I stayed with my mother and gathered seeds. My mother told me that it was time to get married. But I didn't know what marriage was, so I asked, "What does married mean?" My other answered, "That's when you lay with a man." I told her, "I don't want to lay with a man. You go ahead and lay with him if you want to." I was just too scared. My husband-to-be kept coming around and wanted to get married, but I was too scared. Finally my mother planned it, and we got married when I was fourteen or fifteen. I had had lots of questions about it because I was young and didn't know what it was all about. The moment I found out what marriage was really like, then I was happy!

Mabel's story from birth to marriage took place in the late nineteenth century ending somewhere around the turn of the century. Although her early life was lived in a Paiute context with grandparents who certainly had grown up in very traditional ways, it was severely affected by the Anglo-Mormon culture. She moved around with her family in the traditional way depending on the time of year, but the Mormons had already taken over the best lands and forced the Paiutes into a marginal economic position[10] Mabel cannot remember a time without Anglos and fairly large Mormon towns. Early in life she had to learn to speak English and to read and write at boarding school.

Marie, on the other hand, although she passed through her formative years later than Mabel, from 1901 to 1915, was very little touched, at least directly, by Anglos. In fact, the first time a white man came, she was about six years old. She told us, "They came in a covered wagon, and I was scared. I was watching from a cliff." Obviously Anglo culture and values could have very little direct effect on her life with this kind of contact. She never needed to learn English and never was sent away to school. In her youth even Navajos did not seem to be an important influence. She never felt the need to learn the Navajo ways or language, although her daughter a generation later did need to do so. Her life, however, was not the same as her mother's and grandmother's. Certain things were changing. Sheepherding had been introduced; horses and donkeys were used; and most importantly, the Navajos' increase in numbers resulted in competition for scarce resources.

THE ADULT YEARS

After she was married, Mabel had two sons, Eddie and Theodore, Her husband got sick and soon died; for the next four years she worked to support herself and her children. She worked for Mormons, and she also made baskets and tanned buckskin for money to buy food. In traditional Paiute society a widow did not remain long unmarried. Often the next husband would be a relative of her late husband, often a brother. In Mabel's case, she told us, her late husband's relatives "had been talking about me":

His father said that I should get married to his [her late husband's] brother. So I married him. He's the one that died in Kaibab. Ever since then I've never married again, and I'm still not married. My husband died in 1945. That's thirty-six years. He was working in Hack's Canyon with some Mormons when he got sick. When they were working above Hack's Canyon, they found some Pueblo ruins and bows and arrows, water jugs, and other things. That night a ghost kept bothering him. It was kneeling over him. From then on he was sick.

Way later, after my father died, then my mother married Charlie Bullets. I was in school when she got married. She had three boys and one girl after that. When her daughter was grown up, she died. She had problems with her knees and then she went blind. The doctor [probably a Paiute medicine man] had told her that a man had done that to her. After that her husband died. It was the flu at the time that Dan was a big boy when he was in Houserock.[11] My mother died in May 1932. They had gone to Fish Lake [Utah] and she died there. The Koosharem [in central Utah] who were her relatives didn't want her brought to Kaibab. The relatives were stingy with her. Then later my grandmother died. She died in the summer of yellow fever. I lost my grandmother on this side of Buckskin. Right after this I met a white man at the Two Mile and he asked me how I was. I told him, "Pretty bad," and then asked to use his phone. I said that my brother Dan would call Wes Levi and Joe Pikavit. After that, everyone came for the funeral from Koosharem, Richfield, Kanosh, and Moapa.

Mabel was a young woman when Kaibab was made into a reservation. She lived many years on the reservation and lives there now. Some of the intervening years were spent working in different Mormon towns and on Mormon farms in Utah. Mabel discussed her recollections of the founding of the reservation and some of the trouble they had keeping it:

I remember when Kaibab was made into a reservation. There was a lady and a man, and the lady wasn't married. She was the boss. A man was helping her and was hauling everything, material, flour, and even yarn and needles to make stockings with. It was by the house in Moccasin where they stored all that stuff. There was a whole stack of flour, and stockings, and she was giving us material to make dresses with. Then they gave material to the men to make pants with. They gave us some stuff and our wagon got filled. We loaded all the stuff in our wagon. Also, they gave us bacon, great big thick ones. There wasn't any meat on it. The Indians said it wasn't pig meat, it must be elephant meat—it was too big. The people with more children received more food. They even gave the children bacon, and needles and thread. Then they asked the Mormons to make us stockings.

At that time up on the mountain [Kaibab Plateau] there was no white man, and the Indians used to go hunt deer there. They went up on horses. I used to ride horses with my pots and pans rattling. Then they knew it was me coming. All my pots and pans would be rattling. Now, I would fall off. Later on, after it had become a reservation, then they closed the mountains [the government did not let the Paiutes hunt there anymore].

Later a government man gathered them [the Paiutes] in town to talk to them. The Mormons were there listening. He had gathered to talk to them. He was asking them if they would like to move to an area around Glendale [Utah] or Johnson [Utah] or Kanab [Utah]. The Indian people said that they didn't like Glendale—it was just a big wash—and at Johnson nothing grew good. "And how about Kanab?" he asked. We said, "No." I don't know where we would've been placed. There was one woman who talked and that was Wuri. She said that they were going to send us to San Juan. The government man said that if we didn't like any of these areas, they were going to send us to San Juan. And then a lot of the Mormons got together and talked among themselves and then told the man, "How could they be moved? They are O.K. where they are." Then Wuri said that she wasn't going to move. She was going to stay near her graveyard. Her father, Captain Frank, was buried there.[12] The government man got real mad because he wanted to send them to San Juan, but the Mormons where the ones that prevented him from doing that.

When speaking of her life after she was married, Marie Lehi tended to emphasize the good things that happened. She gave us much insight into the good parts of growing up Paiute and living as a Paiute wife and mother;

When a woman has her first child it's the same as having her first menstruation. My very first child was Anna. I had Anna at Willow Springs. A woman who was about to have a baby was put alone in a little house to become brave. She sat on ashes. The hot ashes were in a hole covered with wet sand and a blanket, and she was given only warm water to drink. After the birth, the woman drank a tea made from medicine plants to heal the inside. This was cedar leaf tea. I always had easy births.

My mother took care of Anna a lot of the time. My husband and I would go jogging together in the morning towards the east. It was the same for a man as for a woman. They couldn't scratch their hair with their fingers and they had to run, too. There's a kind of red powder that you put on your face. It's good for the skin. You can also take it with water for upset stomach, diarrhea, and measles.

Although some of the things such as sheepherding and baking white bread that she taught her children were not traditional in the sense that they would not have been taught to Paiute children in the mid-nineteenth century, Marie taught everything in a traditional way:

I had lots of kids. As they began to know what was going on, I taught them what sheep are, how to take care of them and herd them, to handle a horse, and how to go hunting and cook and make bread and how to make baskets. I never forced my girls to make baskets, but they just started doing it as play when they were in a good mood. Even the breadmaking was like that. When they were willing to do it, they started to, and they would get real interested.

Times were not always good, however; Marie speaks sorrowfully of the "big sickness"—the 1918 worldwide influenza epidemic. She told us of all the Paiutes that died at that time. For instance, she spoke of entering one Paiute community and finding everyone dead except one baby. She also told us about the death of her younger brother and his wife from the flu and about carrying water to sick people.

The San Juan Paiutes today live on only a small part of their traditional range with their principal settlements on the Navajo reservation at Willow

Springs, Arizona, and Navajo Mountain, Utah, as well as on the Ute Mountain reservation at White Mesa, Utah.

Mabel lived on the Kaibab reservation. At the time of these interviews, she was living with one of her grandsons. Although perfectly alert, she did not get around very well because of cataracts, which caused her to lose her sight. Her great-grandchildren kept her up to date on village events; she was always eager to hear news of any type. She was saddened, however, that the children no longer spoke Paiute and that on the reservation much of the old knowledge was being forgotten. Mabel herself, although she knew how to speak English and read the newspaper before she lost her sight, rarely spoke it, using Paiute almost entirely. Her extensive experience with the non-Indian world had not diminished her Paiute values. If anything, the experiences had strengthened her belief in the inherent value of traditional Paiute ways.

In the passing of time, she lost all her contemporaries and many of her relatives. She told us, "Now I'm all alone, walking by myself and living with my grandson. Now my house is gone, and my cellar, too. My field is vacant and no one plants for me. I used to plant a lot of potatoes, beans, melons, and squash. The main one I planted was beans, lots of beans. The Mormons used to steal from it. Now I just sit and I am hungry, hungry for melons."

Marie Lehi, younger than Mabel Drye, was still physically active. She had her own flock of sheep and goats, which she tended herself. She wove blankets, a skill she learned from the Navajos, with wool from her sheep. She made beautiful baskets, which she sold to Navajos and tourists, and she walked occasionally the seven or eight miles from her home on the plateau to Willow Springs. Like Mabel, Marie most missed old kinds of food and the activities associated with them: "Sometimes I miss cornmeal and getting up and grinding the corn. It was a lot of work, but I liked the food. I don't like to eat potatoes all the time. When I can, I still gather and eat the old foods like *paas* [a grass seed similar to wheat].

"I feel good almost all the time," she said. "Once in a while, however, I feel 'old age.' And then I think it's time to kick the black bucket."

NOTES

1. Isabel T. Kelly, "Southern Paiute Bands," *American Anthropologist* 36 (1934): 548–60.

2. Richard Stoffle and Michael Evans, "Resource Competition and Population Change: A Kaibab Paiute Ethnohistorical Case," *Ethnohistory* 26:2 (spring 1976).

3. Pamela Bunte and Richard Stoffle, "The 1918 Flu Epidemic and Southern Paiute Territorial Re-arrangement," unpublished paper presented at the Ethnohistory meetings, Colorado Springs, Colorado, 1981.

4. This was a common practice. Grandparents, because they usually had more time, often were the primary caretakers of children. Besides the obvious economic benefit in allowing adults in their prime to hunt and gather, this practice had the further benefit of exposing the children very early to the knowledge of the elders.

5. All the material quoted directly from Mabel Drye and Marie Lehi has been translated from Southern Paiute. The orthography of the Paiute words in this paper was developed by Pamela Bunte and Lucille Jake. The vowels *a, i, o, u* are pronounced like those vowels in Spanish and Italian, except for the Paiute *ʉ*, which is a *u* pronounced with the lips spread and unrounded. The consonants are similar to the corresponding English consonants with the exception of Paiute *x*, which is similar to German *ch*.

6. Owls are dangerous creatures associated with evil and witchcraft.

7. Historical evidence suggests that a closely related group, the Havasupai, rather than the Walapai, had ties to the land and the people in the Tuba City area. See David M. Brugge and J. Lee Correll in *Partition of the Surface Rights of Navajo-Hopi Indian Land* (S 441–26), Government Document 8/13:N22/9.

8. Agave.

9. *Atatsiv* (Sands), was a traditional dance place, at least as far back as the mid-nineteenth century.

10. Stoffle and Evans, "Resource Competition and Population Change."

11. This refers to the 1918 influenza epidemic.

12. Captain Frank is the Chuarumpi-ak mentioned in Powell's accounts: Don D. Fowler and Catherine S. Fowler, *Anthropology of the Numa: John Wesley Powell's Manuscripts on the Numic Peoples of Western North America, 1868–1880* (Washington DC: Smithsonian Institution Press, 1971).

Frontiers 7:1 (1983): 44–49.

From the Yazoo Mississippi Delta to the Urban Communities of the Midwest

Conversations with Rural African American Women

VALERIE GRIM

African Americans had a particularly difficult existence in the rural South during the early twentieth century. For those who wanted to own land, houses, and other property, who desired participation in the political process, and who hoped to improve themselves socially, culturally, and economically, the rural South was deadly. Racism and intimidation killed blacks in body and in spirit, diminishing their emotional and mental strength and limiting the ability of their communities to survive. Among those who suffered the effects of racism, none endured worse hardships than rural African American women who labored diligently on farms in order to contribute economically to their family's survival and well-being.

The pains rural African American women suffered were most evident in the Yazoo Mississippi Delta, where their life was orchestrated around the beat of the cotton planter, the scrape of the hoe, and the rasp of cotton sacks moving swiftly over the fields. Cotton became "white gold," taken from the hands of black sharecroppers and day laborers to support the agricultural enterprises of white landlords. "Life was hard," said Eva Glenn, one of thirty-seven women I interviewed who moved from the South to northern Midwest cities, "and us black women had no choice but to grow hard along with it."[1] "You could let it beat you," explained Mae Liza Williams, "or you could take control over it by not lettin' what white folk did to you or said 'bout yo' people bother you."[2] Or, according to Estella Thomas, "You could leave and go up North and try to find a better life for yo'self."[3]

Leaving was exactly what many African American rural women did. They left the fields and farms by the hundreds of thousands and moved to urban communities across the United States. Many, like Mary Alice Williams of

St. Louis, packed their bags for the same reason as did her husband, Isom: They wanted to make more money and to find better social, cultural, and educational opportunities for their children.[4] According to Willie McWilliams, some women wanted to see "just how different the city was, especially if black people voted and held some kind of office to help they people."[5] Other women made the journey from the field to the city to reunite with family members, especially aunts, uncles, and siblings who had gone ahead of them. These pull factors were particularly strong on those living in rural communities following World War II, but African American female cotton pickers also left because life in the rural South was too hard on women and devastating to their sense of womanhood. Many rural black women left the cotton fields, as Annie West did, because "there was no way to be protected from physical, sexual, and spousal abuse." She proclaimed: "The law was not interested in keepin' black field women safe from any kind of attack, so the fields, because they were so far from town and the lack of enforcement of the law, worked together and actually became a form of imprisonment for many women."[6] "Surrounded by cotton and cotton fields," Jessie Easter explained, "you felt, at times, that you could not get out and no one could get to you because you was livin' in a closed off community where you did not see many things or folks from the outside. . . . So the only way to escape the madness caused by greed and the power white folks got from raisin' King Cotton was to run, run, and run away as fast and far as you could."[7] Migration became an attractive alternative to the Delta's cotton fields because it offered many women the opportunity to search for a new identity and a different sense of community.

However, once settled in the North, the women worked hard to maintain some of their rural heritage and culture. "We still like to eat the same foods because it reminded us of home and our traditions," Rosie Fountain explained.[8] "It is so important for my children and the people in this community to understand that black farm women, like me, came from a rich tradition and that all of us did not come off of white people's farms, but actually lived on land owned by our parents and other blacks, went to schools and churches our grandparents helped to build, and shopped in little stores black country people sat up so we could see some positive role models in our little rural community," explained Clementine Coleman of St. Louis.[9]

Upon arriving in the city, many African Americans faced harsh realities. The industrial landscape also presented problems similar to the rural South. Poverty was rampant, and every form of social, cultural, and economic limitation existed. They could only expect difficulties in securing employment, and in finding decent housing, health care, and nutritious food. Transportation and telephones, when they could be afforded, enhanced their lives by helping connect their urban communities to their home communities in the South.[10]

Housing was never plentiful, and that made available to blacks was substandard and wholly inadequate for the large families migrating from farms. Rent was exorbitant, draining families of the majority of their income. Because migrants had been told by promoters of industry needing a cheap workforce that the city offered better housing than in the South, many had looked forward to efficient plumbing and bathroom facilities and bedrooms large enough to house their families. Such accommodations were scarce and costly. Indeed, respectable housing seemed available only to those who brought money with them for a down payment and only in certain neighborhoods. Women with this kind of money were few, and for the majority, housing "projects" were the only alternative to overcrowded, substandard urban housing.[11]

African American women migrants and their families also needed health care. Down South, doctors willing to treat blacks were few and expensive, and, as a result, many did not seek medical care regularly until the 1970s post–Civil Rights period. In contrast, health care was more readily available in the North, and public assistance was in place to help the poor without the kind of discrimination practiced by white landlords who determined who would receive public aid. "Up here, I always had a doctor when I needed one, and my children could go, and we did not have to worry 'bout settlin' accounts at the end of the year like we did when we was a woman sharecroppin' to make a livin'," said Gayle Davis of Chicago.[12]

Between 1964 and 1980, poor and working-class women migrants off the farm found their greatest support in government-funded social services in the city, which helped them pay medical expenses for themselves and their children. "There was so many doctors, black and white, who was available to treat you," explained Dollie Williams of Columbus, Ohio. "All you had to do was to work out some form of payment if you did not have all of the money."[13] Having better health care was important because "women had to be concerned about child bearin', treatin' heart disease, common colds and other kind of illnesses."[14] So important was having access to better quality health care that each of the women sought it out with the understanding, as Bernice Ware said, "that it was goin' to take time to find everything we needed and the right doctors to treat us and our children."[15]

Tied to the issue of health care was a concern about quality food for the women's families. Rural migrants in general had used fresh dairy produce, meat, fruits, and vegetables they had raised themselves, and farm women were accustomed to performing this role. However, because the majority of the migrants did not own houses with large back yards, raising and acquiring fresh food in the city was difficult. With limited resources, many migrants were forced to eat canned goods and government commodity staples of cheese, peanut butter, powdered milk and eggs, dry beans, and canned beef. Each of the women stated that their family diet suffered because the city did not offer an opportunity for them to control the production of their food supply. "As long as we had a place, we could eat well and keep the children fed with a minimum of three meals a day," explained Jessie Mae White.[16] Lack of land combined with low incomes made it difficult for poor and wage-working women to afford quality food. This condition contributed to these women's concerns about health conditions such as heart disease and diabetes.

When they arrived in the city, rural migrants could see that technology had greatly improved urban women's lives. "We was surprised at how good some of them had it in their housework, with electric irons and washing machines as well as gas stoves and refrigeration, since the women down South lagged behind in buyin' household devices that saved them time," Mary Alice Williams recalled.[17] Ann Gordon remembered, "Women in the city had the luxury of bein' entertained as they did their housework because they could listen to the radio, or watch television, or even talk on the phone to take some of the boringness away and to make their work load seem lighter and less of a burden."[18] Mary Tucker said, "These things—the radio, and television—was way, way different than what we knowed or had seen because they connected us to the world. . . . Many of us remained isolated until we left the farm."[19] By the 1960s, television was much more common in these migrants' homes than those they left in the South. As soon as families could afford it, they added telephones to their homes to improve their contact with family members they had left behind.

According to the women, the car was the most valued piece of property one could own in the city. "You need a way to get around because the bus didn't go everywhere back then," remembered Canary Coleman.[20] As a significant investment, owning a car "meant no mo' mules and wagons, ridin' on a horse's back on broken down back roads, no mo' getting' dirty as you travel, and you sure enough didn't have to be a hobo no longer."[21] The acquisition of a car was similar to a farmer's purchase of a new tractor, both were symbolic of economic profitability on the farm. "When a woman was able to get herself a car, she had arrived, movin' immediately into a new social circle where few blacks traveled in the 1950s and early 1960s," Canary Coleman remembered.[22] Nevertheless, because cars were expensive, most African Americans used public transportation to go back and forth to work. Many rural migrants did not have the economic power or the political connections to acquire such expensive possessions until the late 1970s and early 1980s, when wages and the economy improved.

Discrimination based on race, gender, and class were experiences remembered vividly by all participants in the study. Throughout the rural communities of the southern United States, racism established a social stratification that placed African American women at the bottom of the socioeconomic and cultural ladders. Black women were valued as important laborers in rural manufacturing, domestic servitude, and fieldwork, but as a group were considered loud, unattractive, and lacking the social skills of white women. These African American females in the rural South had no chance of achieving white society's standard of womanhood because of these kinds of attitudes combined with discrimination. As a result, many black women fieldworkers left the farms of the Yazoo Mississippi Delta to find places where they hoped more positive views of black people existed. Many never found their utopia. Rosie Fountain elaborated: "When I came up here to St. Louis, I thought my race wouldn't matter as long as I was willin' to work, but I found out white society is basically the same everywhere, especially if they detect you are a southern black person who should expect no more than to be treated with no respect and who didn't mind bein' on the bottom."[23] According to Rose Jackson, "We could get jobs and we worked hard, but that did not stop our factory boss from treatin' us like a second-class citizen."[24]

Some of the women were satisfied with the way whites and blacks interacted. "I moved up here to find work, not to become the best friend of white people," said Ann Hearon.[25] She explained: "When I found work, my mission had been accomplished, and I did not need to interact with them to know I was a good worker, and neither did I need to seek out their blessin' to understand who I was because I was proud to be a southern-born, rural black woman who understood what it took to make it. And for me, my survival did not depend on race mixin' because I was quite comfortable spendin' my time away from them, as I enjoyed my life in my community with so many other black folk who had walked out of them Mississippi Delta cotton fields."[26]

While Ann's attitude seems positive and uplifting and represents the perception of six other women participants, other women were distressed about race relations in the city. Betty Williams of Indianapolis explained: "I didn't like it because we left the Delta for this reason, too much racism and prejudice existed, and now to have come up here and find that racism was just as bad, and that white folk in the North had a place for black folk just like they did down South, was disappointin', but I wasn't willin' to be on another plantation, a field hand in the factory workin' like a Mississippi slave."[27]

Primary and secondary sources support the experiences discussed by these women. The research indicates that racism did not prevent rural African American women migrants from securing employment, but it forced them to take the lowest paying jobs, thereby causing the majority to live in abject poverty in their adopted urban communities.

While the racial attitudes of the dominant white society were frustrating for rural black women, they were not the most painful. Self-imposed prejudices favoring lighter skin among African Americans was the most hurtful. As Patricia Adams explained, black women "never forgot what society thought 'bout 'em."[28] However, what mattered was "what the black people in the city thought about who you were and your reason for comin' North, knowin' that jobs were not as plentiful as they had been during the forties and early fifties," said Linda McWilliams.[29] Doris Lindsey elaborated: "Due to competition for jobs, people's practice of racism spreaded over into the black community where blacks began to practice a form of color prejudice among themselves, believin' that skin color was important and that the lighter your skin, the easier it would be to get a job from white people and to separate from those who white folk despised 'cause they skin was dark."[30]

The majority of the African American rural women participating in this study suggested that their sense of self was affected by how their skin color was perceived. "The North was supposed to represent a kinder place for black women," explained Bernice Black, "and it was suppose to be the place where the black woman was treated well, 'cause people had said women could have a better life in places like St. Louis, Chicago, Indianapolis, and Detroit."[31] That better life was difficult to achieve, especially because black women were also victims of northern-based sexism.

Sexism in the North was difficult for black women off the farm to understand. Although they experienced male patriarchy in agrarian societies, they had nevertheless held a respectable place in the economy that rivaled black men's because their labor was essential and they were successful in performing their duties and roles. In rural communities, sexism for these rural African American women migrants was largely a theoretical position because male and female responsibilities overlapped in the home, church, and community, preventing, to a degree, the inhibition of the activities of black women. However, in the North, African American women migrants found gender discrimination to be more real. Men's labor was more highly valued, and they were chosen more often for the skilled and semi-skilled jobs available in the factories.

"We thought makin' mo' money would eventually remove the northern stigma of what a black woman from the farm could do," Ann Gordon explained. "We didn't understand their notion of a woman's place, and we did not like the hard separation of the sexes because to us there was no such place as a woman's or man's place; it was just a role to be played, and whoever could do the job, did it and kept movin'."[32]

Segregation was a major issue in urban communities. It existed in the factories, some of the schools, and in neighborhoods. While manufacturers encouraged blacks to migrate to the city to work, whites and other communities of color did not look favorably upon blacks moving into their neighborhoods. "One of the most disappointin' things was to realize that segregation was as much a problem up here in the city as it had been for us down South," said Ann Gordon.[33]

Every woman interviewed disliked segregation as a system because it reminded them of the second-class citizenship from which they had migrated. Canary Coleman explained: "Up here, you did not see the signs, but you understood where you could go and what you could do, and folk didn't necessarily want you eatin' in they restaurants, swimmin' in the pool with they children, workin' the same good job they had, or goin' to school with they children."[34] Despite their dislike of institutional segregation in their urban communities, these women were not sure that integration would solve the problems between the races. In their former community, each had interacted with whites in a number of interracial and cross-cultural contexts but had gained very little from the exchange.

The women primarily encountered whites in the work place. Working as agricultural laborers, domestic servants, or low-wage factory employees, the black world was controlled by the white world, was predictable, and offered little in the way of empowerment to blacks. For the majority of women, integration offered more struggle than opportunity. "When you are always with them," explained Annie Harris, "you have to be conscious of who you are and what you are doin' and sayin' because they was always actin' like they had done us a favor by allowin' blacks to be in their presence."[35]

According to Linda Rice, because of the stress associated with racial, social, and economic integration, "blacks in the city had to think through how to make integration work in order to minimize its impact on their lives."[36] Consequently, the women migrants attempted to control the level of stress school integration caused their families. "When our children went into those white schools, them white people wanted to know every thing about them, their mamas and daddies and what was goin' on in they home, even if nothin' appeared to be wrong," explained Linsey Billups.[37] Sherri Hooper explained, "Such an intrusion into our private affairs did not take place when black teachers and parents was controllin' the education of black children in segregated communities. Even if black teachers had to ask such questions of the children, the objective was not to shame the child or embarrass his family, but to point out that help was available."[38] To avoid such unwelcome intrusions, each woman instructed their children to keep silent about family and community affairs when they attended school.

Positive aspects of school integration were experienced by those who migrated between 1980 and 2000, as was the case with ten of the women. They received a better education and as a result were able to secure much better jobs and improved housing, which was not commonly opened to earlier generations of rural black women off the farm. According to the women, migration was most effective for those rural blacks who already had acquired an education and had the type of credentials that would allow them to compete for social, political, and economic opportunities. Indeed, according to Ann Gordon, "This is one of the ways younger generations of rural black women off the farm can regenerate themselves."[39]

Maintaining family ties has remained the most significant way that the women who were interviewed have renewed or revived themselves. Family celebrations also provided the opportunity for old-timers and newcomers to share their experience of migration. Linda Robinson points out, "We needed to keep that connection because it reminded us of our value as persons and our importance within the kinship circle."[40] "Down South, family connection meant everything," explained Deborah Walters, "from the time you spent with parents, grandparents, siblings and other kinfolk to what you all actually did together, and everyone knew that crashin' parties and takin' part in any other community celebration was acceptable because everybody was family."[41]

The women seemed especially revived when community celebrations occurred. "This was a time that you could let yo' hair down and have fun the old way, laughin' and talkin' as loud as you wanted and enjoyin' each other because you had so much in common," explained Delores Brown.[42] Easter, Mother and Father's Day festivities, Fourth of July, Memorial Day, and Labor Day cookouts, and especially the joy they experienced during Thanksgiving and Christmas celebrations regenerated the women interviewed.

Because some of these women and many other rural black women migrants have been forced to reside in the inner city, they have created other celebratory activities in keeping with their rural heritage, such as Blues, sewing, quilting, and garden parties. Annie Williams recalled, "These help us remember our heritage and tradition of takin' care of yo' family with yo' hands, similar to the way we celebrated rice, cotton, and corn harvests and the completion of the cannin', quiltin', and huntin' seasons."[43] By doing so, explained Joyce Fountain, "We remained committed to treatin' each other with love and functioning as a civilized community among ourselves."[44]

African American culture in the northern cities was a diverse mixture of rural and urban traditions. In the South rural black women had a limited choice of entertainment and recreational activities, and they dressed in a way that reflected the cotton culture. Rural southern towns also had a relatively low crime rate because there was not much to do beyond going to church, work, and juke joints. The migrant women marveled at the recreational and fashion opportunities that existed in urban communities in the North. They were also amazed at the high crime rate, "since nobody told you 'bout all the killin', stealin', prostitutin', drinkin', and gamblin' befo' yo' move up here, because they didn't want you to change yo' mind 'bout leavin' the farm."[45]

Along with the desire for better jobs and improved race relations, the desire to have access to better entertainment, recreation, and community involvement was reported by each of the women interviewed as a reason they migrated. Because letters from family members and editorials in newspapers described the culture in the city as blossoming and exciting, migration emerged in some households as the answer to the oppression families suffered "down South." The North not only promised work but also places to relax and to establish community, which could lead to organizing for social change.

In the city, as it was in the rural black South, recreation was vitally important to a family's sense of community and kinship. Large parks and movie theaters provided the opportunity for families to spend time together, an activity greatly needed because family members were now working outside of the home. Maxine Johnson explained: "Every Saturday the children and

I went to the stores, lookin' for things for the house, and sometimes, after the shoppin' was finished, I would take them to a movie or to eat a burger, the kinds of things I could not do as a young girl livin' in a rural town."[46] Because of these kinds of opportunities, the women expressed general satisfaction with the recreational alternatives that were available, even though some missed the simpler types of activities available to children in rural environments. Dollie Rogers remembered: "A lot of us was not all that excited because it cost money to go to movies and museums and to enjoy yo'self outside the home, especially when you did not make much money on yo' job, and when what you had, had to be used to first feed and clothe your children, it was enough to make you want to move back home where yo' children could run around, fish, and hunt free of charge."[47]

Indeed, recreational participation depended on having money available to buy new clothes and go to movies, concerts, museums, community meetings, and parties. Yet it was fashion that consumed much of the women's discretionary money and time. Style, to some degree, indicated a level of economic success. The majority of the women participating in this study liked the fashion that existed in the city, but each generally disapproved of the emphasis placed on clothing and "looking good." "Down South, we could wear anything because folk didn't care," explained Louise Dillard, "and we only paid attention to how we looked at church, and that did not require much, just a decent suit and a couple of nice dresses, but no pressure, like up here, when folk think you ought to be dressed up just to go to the store."[48] Like the purchase of a home or car, improvement in one's personal appearance was an indication that migration had been a good decision.

In cities throughout America, many blacks believed they had acquired new status when they secured employment. This new social standing suggested that families now had the resources to purchase fashionable clothes, modern appliances, and household items. Ironically, these new acquisitions brought the constant fear of being burglarized. "Folk just believe that you had money not only to pay yo' bills, but to spend on fun, and to loan to other people, and to keep buyin' things if someone broke into yo' house and stole yo' stuff."[49] The perception that employment equaled wealth was so powerful that many working women feared for the safety of their home and children.

According to those interviewed, working outside of the home often meant that their children faced potential danger due to the growing crime rate in the inner city. All of the women felt that the city was somewhat unsafe, but one woman stated that "in the neighborhood, there was police on constant duty, so that if somethin' happen, they could get to you or yo' house much quicker than they could down South."[50] In fact, the majority of the women said they had confidence in the ability of the police to investigate crime and protect citizens. Many cited examples of the police arriving quickly when a crime had been committed, but they were not convinced that quick response time was the long-term answer to crime-infested cities.

Despite the opportunities northern cities offered for work and recreation, they were not enough to offset women's fear concerning the criminal element that preyed upon urban black communities. The women expressed constant fear for their children's lives, of their children becoming involved in gang activity, of their daughters being raped, and of the visibility and availability of drugs. Some of the women were concerned about police brutality, gambling, prostitution, and other social problems that some children viewed as exciting urban entertainment. An overwhelming majority of the women interviewed are mothers, and their concerns were not unrealistic or exaggerated. While they were aware that crime existed in rural towns throughout the United States, to them, southern rural crime was not as life-threatening since, as Fannie Williams explains, "No black person on a farm, back then, could earn a good livin' like some blacks in the city from drugs, gang activity, gamblin', or prostitution."[51] Only within the last two decades of the twentieth century has rural America fostered the kinds of criminal activity long established in urban areas.

Family relationships ultimately determined whether or not migrants appreciated African American urban culture and whether they would adjust to living in the inner city. Each of the women believed some form of family association was necessary just to survive. The question was whether they would rely solely on family living in their urban communities or maintain relationships with family members they left behind in the South. The majority of the women believed it was very important to maintain family ties generally, and they adopted a number of strategies to do so. "We visit back and forth," said Eva Glenn, "and we write and send messages and gifts by travelers livin' in the city where our folk lived."[52] Because their income was limited, traveling and keeping in touch by telephone were difficult. When limited funds inhibited close contact with family far away, migration became a liability, a process that gradually separated them from their extended network of kin.

For some women, maintaining family ties was not an option. A few women in this study chose to sever their relationship with family members they left behind because they still struggled with the physical and sexual abuse they experienced growing up. Two women had witnessed ongoing physical abuse of their mothers and other female family members and, as a result, decided that it was best for them to let the past go, including contact with all family members, until they could heal from the emotional suffering they were forced to live through.

But, for most, the vibrancy they felt from the energy in the city was enough to keep them hopeful and believing that their families had an opportunity for a better life in their adopted urban communities. The African American culture in which they became involved nourished them and retained enough of their rural traditions to make them feel somewhat comfortable living among "city folk."

For some women, the need to migrate had less to do with their desire to be in the industrial workplace than with the pains they suffered as young girls. In the American South, where there was no respect for African American women and little concern for their right to have their bodies protected, black women were often violated. The migrants interviewed discussed the sexual exploitation of black women in order to provide an understanding as to how migration influenced family and gender relations. Their stories included not only descriptions of sexual exploitation but also how wives and children were abused. Women who participated in this study stated that they migrated because they were concerned about their daughters and other girls becoming emotionally and physically abused. Joyce Fountain put it in very plain words: "The country was a place where people lived so close together in their physical and housing space, and it was the perfect place where little girls, because they were always working around grown men, were at a risk of being sexually abused in the fields. . . . So I left because I wanted my children to be safe, and since I was a professional, no longer working all day in the field with them, and because I needed to know they would be under watchful eyes in the city, I decided to migrate and move to a community that offered after-school, all-day, and year-round child care for working and professional women."[53]

While no woman or child was totally free of the potential threat of abuse, the general consensus among these women was expressed by Shirley Bullock: "The law, up here, seemed more likely to protect you because the police wasn't concerned about causin' the white landlord a loss of labor in the event they had to arrest the person."[54] However, protection was far from guaranteed, as Faye Williams explained: "These urban communities up here was not foolproof, but you did have better protection under the law, just in case a mother might detect her child was being physically or sexually abused, and in case she, herself, was being battered."[55]

Each of the women who participated in this study recalled conversations with her mother concerning safety as young girls. Not only were their parents concerned about protecting them from the white male gaze, but also from any man making sexual advances toward young girls. African American women who left the rural South to find safer communities for their daughters were, however, often disappointed at the amount of sexual exploitation that existed within black communities outside the South. Each woman in this study indicated that sexual abuse continues to be a concern, even though a few safety nets are built in, such as leaving their children, especially the girls, with trusted family members and friends when responsibilities require them to be away from home. Fifteen of the thirty-seven women interviewed felt satisfied or very satisfied that their daughters were safe and did not face the kind of pressure that existed in the rural South. However, an overwhelming majority of twenty-two disliked the urban environment. Irene Scott said: "The city often proved to be more dangerous because we had to leave our children alone."[56] Canary Coleman elaborated, "Down South we kept up with them, especially durin' the day, 'cause they was in the field workin' with us eight to ten hours a day, and when they wasn't workin', they was with us in church or workin' in the garden, quiltin', and when all other work was done, they was asleep."[57] Being able to keep a watchful eye over their children was a privilege that farm life offered, but this privilege was diminished considerably when women went to work in northern factories.

Since the late nineteenth century, tens of thousands of African American men, women, and children left the cotton fields in search of improved social, economic, political, and cultural opportunities. By the end of the 1940s, as many as five million African Americans were gone from the fields and were working in various factories, packing houses, and domestic industries. As these migrants labored in their new industrial fields, they also expended energy transplanting their rural cultures and values to their adopted cities.

Among the large groups of migrants searching for freedom, justice, and opportunity were great numbers of African American women with ambitions of becoming financially able to provide for their children and in the process hoping to purchase a little respect for themselves. They had hope, and they believed God was leading them to a "better land." What this process involved in its entirety is not yet fully known, but a significant amount of information exists concerning how these women attempted to reestablish themselves through their family, work, church, and social activities. The question for these women became not whether they could find jobs, but what quality of life they and their children would have far from their close-knit communities in the rural South, where families and friends shared resources to survive. The research that comprises this article presents these women's experiences primarily in their own words and reveals the kinds of struggles rural African American women migrants endured as well as their attitudes and perceptions concerning their hardships. Far more research of this type needs to be done in order to fully comprehend the significance of gender in the multiple migrations experienced by African Americans.

As researchers and historians are increasingly attempting to put faces and voices to historical developments to help us better understand the human-istic and emotional aspects of change, studies such as this one can serve that need. The conversations I had with these thirty-seven women revealed much about their feelings, perceptions, and expectations concerning migra-tion and the kind of life it was supposed to lead to for hardworking families who moved to northern cities. More research is needed in order to incorpo-rate women's ideas, actions, reactions, and behavior into recent scholarship that focuses on how migrants survived or assimilated into urban life.

NOTES

This article is based on preliminary findings from a survey and data obtained from oral history interviews conducted with thirty-seven rural African American women for a book manuscript entitled, "African American Rural Women in the City." The women who participated in this study resided in six different Midwestern commu-nities and represent diverse social, cultural, educational, and economic positions. This research addresses issues pertinent to how these women have experienced ur-ban life. The women interviewed migrated north to Midwestern cities over a period of fifty years following World War II, the period known as the Great Black Migra-tion. A larger percentage of African American women left the rural South in the last half of the twentieth century than they did during the previous exodus of African Americans from the South between 1915 and 1950. Once they arrived, educated and uneducated rural African American women alike competed for jobs more fiercely than ever before during the first half of the twentieth century, and they coped with severe housing problems and alarming crime rates to do so.

1. Eva Glenn, interview with the author, April 28, 1988, Drew, Mississippi. For a discussion, see also Douglas Massey and Nancy A. Denton, *American Apartheid: Segregation and the Making of the Underclass* (Cambridge, Mass.: Harvard University Press, 1993); and Darlene Clark Hine and Kathleen Thompson, *A Shining Thread of Hope: The History of Black Women in America* (New York: Broadway Books, 1998).

2. Mae Liza Williams, interview with the author, April 30, 1989, Minter City, Mississippi. For a discussion of life in general for African Americans and of black women in particular, see Virginia Yans-McLaughlin, *Family and Community: Italian Immigrants in Buffalo, 1880–1930* (Ithaca, N.Y.: Cornell University Press, 1977); Oscar Handlin, *The Uprooted* (Boston: Little, Brown, and Company, 1973); David M. Katzman, *Before the Ghetto: Black Detroit in the Nineteenth Century* (Urbana: University of Illinois Press, 1973); and Richard W. Thomas, *Life for Us Is What We Make It: Building Black Community in Detroit, 1915–1945* (Bloomington: Indiana University Press, 1992).

3. Estella Thomas, interview with the author, April 30, 1989, Drew, Mississippi; and Estella Thomas, interview with author, May 25, 1991, St. Louis, Missouri. For a discussion of how African American women have responded to crises and stresses they have experienced due to segregation, exploitation, and domination, see Robin Kelley, " 'We Are Not What We Seem': Rethinking Black Working-Class Opposition in the Jim Crow South," *Journal of American History* 80:1 (1993): 75–112; Joe William Trotter, "African Americans in the City: The Industrial Era, 1900–1950," *Journal of Urban History* 21:4 (1995): 438–69; and Kenneth Kusmer, "African Americans in the City since World War II: From the Industrial to the Post-Industrial Era," *Journal of Urban History* 21:4 (1995): 470–504.

4. Mary Alice Williams, interview with the author, December 21, 1990, St. Louis, Missouri. For a discussion of the many issues that influenced black women's migration from the rural South, see Peter Gottlieb, *Making Their Own Way: Southern Blacks' Migration to Pittsburgh, 1916–1930* (Urbana: University of Illinois, 1987); James R. Grossman, *Land of Hope: Chicago, Black Southerners, and the Great Migration* (Chicago: University of Chicago Press, 1989); and Earl Lewis, *In Their Own Interest: Race, Class, and Power in Twentieth-Century Norfolk, Virginia* (Berkeley: University of California Press, 1991).

5. Willie E. McWilliams, interview with the author, May 1, 1990, Drew, Mississippi; and Willie E. McWilliams, interview with author, June 30, 1997, Detroit, Michigan. For a discussion, see James Borchert, *Alley Life in Washington: Family, Community, Religion, and Folklife in the City, 1850–1970* (Urbana: University of Illinois Press, 1991); Allen B. Ballard, *One More Day's Journey: The Story of a Family and a People* (New York: McGraw Hill, 1984); and Joe William Trotter, *Black Milwaukee:*

The Making of an Industrial Proletariat, 1915–1945 (Urbana: University of Illinois Press, 1985).

6. Annie West, interview with the author, June 25, 1994, St. Louis, Missouri. For a discussion of how important the issues of safety and protection were to African American women in rural and urban communities, see Arna W. Bontemps and Jack Conroy, *Any Place But Here* (New York: Hill and Wang, 1966); and Elizabeth Clark-Lewis, *Living In, Living Out: African American Domestics in Washington DC, 1910–1940* (Washington DC: Smithsonian Press, 1994).

7. Jessie Easter, interview with the author, Chicago, Illinois, June 15, 1991. For a discussion of the feeling of enclosure and the problems associated with living in a closed society, see Anne Moody, *Coming of Age in Mississippi* (New York: Dial Press, 1968); and Reynolds Farley, "The Urbanization of Negroes in the United States," *Journal of Social History* 1:1 (1968): 241–58. See also Kathryn Grover, *Make a Way Somehow: African-American Life in a Northern Community, 1790–1965* (Syracuse, N.Y.: Syracuse University Press, 1994).

8. Rosie Fountain, interview with the author, St. Louis, Missouri, December 22, 1993. For a comparative discussion of how rural black women attempted to maintain their cultural heritage and rural values in northern, eastern, and western communities, see Albert S. Broussard, *Black San Francisco: The Struggle For Racial Equality in the West, 1900–1945* (Lawrence: University Press of Kansas, 1993); and Quintard Taylor, *The Forging of a Black Community: Seattle Central District, 1870 through the Civil Rights Era* (Seattle: University of Washington, 1994).

9. Clementine Coleman, interview with the author, May 25, 1997, St. Louis, Missouri. See Florette Henri, *Black Migration: Movement North, 1900–1920* (Garden City, N.Y.: Anchor Press, 1975); and Carole Marks, *Farewell— We're Good and Gone: The Great Black Migration* (Bloomington: Indiana University Press, 1989). See also Joe William Trotter, ed., *The Great Migration in Historical Perspective: New Dimensions of Race, Class, and Gender* (Bloomington: Indiana University Press, 1991).

10. For a discussion, see Jacqueline Jones, *Labor of Love, Labor of Sorrow: Black Women, Work, and the Family from Slavery to the Present* (New York: Basic Books, 1985); Dolores Janiewski, *Sisterhood Denied: Race, Gender, and Class in a New South Community* (Philadelphia: Temple University Press, 1985); Darlene Clark Hine, "Black Migration to the Urban Midwest: The Gender Dimension, 1915–1945," in Trotter, *The Great Migration in Historical Perspective*, 126–46; and Elsa Barkley Brown, "Womanist Consciousness: Maggie Lena Walker and the Independent Order of St. Luke," *Signs: Journal of Women in Culture and Society* 14:3 (1989): 610–33.

11. Nell Irvin Painter, *Exodusters: Black Migration to Kansas after Reconstruction* (1976, reprint, Lawrence: University Press of Kansas, 1986), 45–52. See also Kenneth L. Kusmer, "The Black Urban Experience in American History," in *The State*

of Afro American History: Past, Present, and Future, ed. Darlene Clark Hine (Baton Rouge: Louisiana State University, 1986), 91–122; Joe William Trotter Jr., "African Americans in the City: The Industrial Era, 1900–1950," *Journal of Urban History* 21:4 (1995): 438–57; Thomas, *Life for Us Is What We Make It*; and Kimberley L. Phillips, *Alabama North: African-American Migrants, Community, and Working-Class Activism, 1915–1945* (Urbana: University of Illinois Press, 1999).

12. Gayle Davis, interview with the author, Chicago, Illinois, July 11, 1994. For a discussion of health and other living conditions faced by African American rural women migrants when they arrived in Midwestern cities, see Nicholas Lemann, *The Promised Land: The Great Black Migration and How It Changed America* (New York: Knopf, 1991); Jones, *Labor of Love, Labor of Sorrow*; Vincent P. Franklin, *Living Our Stories, Telling Our Truths: Autobiography and the Making of the African-American Intellectual Tradition* (New York: Scribner, 1995); Darrel E. Bigham, *We Ask Only a Fair Trial: A History of the Black Community of Evansville, Indiana* (Bloomington: Indiana University Press, 1987); and James O. Horton, *Free People of Color: Inside the African American Community* (Washington DC: Smithsonian Institution, 1993).

13. Dollie Williams, interview with the author, Columbus, Ohio, June 1, 1997. For additional discussion, see Phillips, *Alabama North*; and Lillian Serece Williams, *Strangers in the Land of Paradise: The Creation of an African American Community, 1900–1940* (Bloomington: Indiana University Press, 1999).

14. Mary Tucker, interview with the author, St. Louis, Missouri, December 11, 1992. For a discussion, see Ulf Hannerz, *Soulside: Inquiries into Ghetto Culture and Community* (New York: Columbia University Press, 1969); Tamara Hareven, *Family and Kin in Urban Communities, 1700–1930* (New York: New Viewpoints, 1977); and Robert B. Hill, *The Strengths of Black Families* (New York: Emerson Hall, 1972).

15. Bernice Ware, interview with the author, Chicago, Illinois, June 6, 1994. See also Andrew Billingsley, *Black Families in White America* (Englewood Cliffs, N.J.: Prentice-Hall, 1968).

16. Jessie Mae White, interview with the author, St. Louis, Missouri, October 12, 1996. For a discussion of rural black women migrants' concerns about food, diet, nutrition, and health, see Lehmann, *The Promised Land*; Thomas, *Life Is What We Make It*; and Lewis, *In Their Own Interest.*

17. Mary Alice Williams, interview with the author, St. Louis, Missiouri, December 10, 1992.

18. Ann Gordon, interview with the author, Detroit, Michigan, November 15, 1993.

19. Mary Tucker, interview with the author, St. Louis, Missouri, December 11, 1992.

20. Canary Coleman, interview with the author, St. Louis, Missouri, December 12, 1992.

21. Mary Tucker, interview with the author.

22. Canary Coleman, interview with the author. See also Lehmann, *Promised Land*; Jones, *Labor of Love, Labor of Sorrow*; and Kenneth W. Goings and Raymond A. Mohl, eds., *The New African American Urban History* (Thousands Oaks, Calif.: Sage Publications, 1996).

23. Rosie Fountain, interview with the author, St. Louis, Missouri, September 15, 1994. For a discussion, see Trotter, *The Great Migration in Historical Perspective*.

24. Rose Jackson, interview with author, Detroit, Michigan, August 5, 1991. For a discussion of the kinds of jobs that were available to rural African American women migrants, see Gilbert Osofsky, *Harlem: The Making of a Ghetto* (New York: Harper and Row, 1968); St. Clair Drake and Horace R. Cayton, *Black Metropolis: A Study of Negro Life in a Northern City*, 2 vols. (New York: Harper and Row, 1945); and Carol Stack, *All Our Kin: Strategies for Survival in a Black Community* (New York: Harper and Row, 1975).

25. Ann Hearon, interview with the author, Detroit, Michigan, May 28, 1995. For a discussion of racial interactions between blacks and whites as well as other ethnic groups, see John Bodnar, Roger Simon, and Michael P. Weber, *Lives of Their Own: Blacks, Italians, and Poles in Pittsburgh, 1900–1960* (Urbana: University of Illinois Press, 1982); James Weldon Johnson, *Black Manhattan* (New York: Arno, 1968); and Bigham, *We Ask Only a Fair Trial*.

26. Ann Hearon, interview with the author. See also Mary White Ovington, *Half a Man: The Status of the Negro in New York* (1911, reprint, New York: Hill and Wang, 1969); and Goings and Mohl, *The New African American Urban History*.

27. Betty Williams, interview with the author, Indianapolis, Indiana, June 21, 1995. For a comparison between southern and northern racism and its impact on rural migrants and immigrants to American urban cities, see Josef J. Barton, *Peasants and Strangers: Italians, Rumanians, and Slovaks in an American City, 1890–1950* (Cambridge: Harvard University Press, 1975); and Andrew Hacker, *Two Nations: Black and White, Separate, Hostile, and Unequal* (New York: Scribner's, 1992).

28. Patricia Adams, interview with the author, Chicago, Illinois, June 13, 1991. For a discussion of the treatment of African American women in the public and private spheres, see Jones, *Labor of Love, Labor of Sorrow*; Billingsley, *Black Families in White America*; and Andrew Billingsley, *Climbing Jacob's Ladder: The Enduring Legacy of African-American Families* (New York: Simon and Schuster, 1992).

29. Linda McWilliams, interview with the author, Detroit, Michigan, October 15, 1995, and Chicago, Illinois, November 15, 1999. For a discussion of issues pertaining to African Americans' self-imposed color prejudices and discriminations,

see Franklin, *Living Our Stories, Telling Our Truths*; and Allan H. Spear, *Black Chicago: The Making of a Negro Ghetto, 1890–1920* (Chicago: University of Chicago Press, 1967).

30. Doris Lindsey, interview with the author, Minneapolis, Minnesota, May 29, 1997. For a discussion of available economic opportunities in the cities and how rural black women entered the work place, see Bigham, *We Ask Only a Fair Trial*; Spear, *Black Chicago*; Drake and Cayton, *Black Metropolis*; and Trotter, *Black Milwaukee*.

31. Bernice Black, interview with the author, Columbus, Ohio, May 30, 1997. For a discussion, see Goings and Mohl, *The New African American Urban History*; Kathryn Grover, *Make a Way Somehow*; and Hacker, *Two Nations*.

32. Ann Gordon, interview with the author, Detroit, Michigan, November 15, 1993. For a discussion of how African American women confronted issues of sexism in the home, workplace, church, and larger African American community, see Jones, *Labor of Love, Labor of Sorrow*; William Julius Wilson, *The Declining Significance of Race: Blacks and Changing American Institutions* (Chicago: University of Chicago, 1978); and Hacker, *Two Nations*.

33. Ann Gordon, interview with the author, Detroit, Michigan, November 15, 1993.

34. Canary Coleman, interview with the author, St. Louis, Missouri, December 12, 1992. For a discussion, see Philip S. Foner and Ronald L. Lewis, *Black Workers: A Documentary History from Colonial Times to the Present* (Philadelphia: Temple University, 1989).

35. Annie Harris, interview with the author, Columbus, Ohio, July 25, 1996.

36. Linda Rice, interview with the author, Indianapolis, Indiana, August 10, 1995.

37. Linsey Billups, interview with the author, Indianapolis, Indiana, August 12, 1995. For a discussion, see Vincent P. Franklin, "Education for Life: Adult Education Programs for African Americans in Northern Cities, 1900–1942," in Harvey Newfeldt and Leo McGee, *Education of the African American Adult: An Historical Overview* (Westport, Conn.: Greenwood, 1990).

38. Sherri Hooper, interview with the author, Detroit, Michigan, September 7, 1995. For a discussion of African American parents' involvement in their children's education, see Rayford Logan, *The Betrayal of the Negro* (New York: Collier, 1965); and Bigham, *We Ask Only a Fair Trial*.

39. Ann Gordon, interview with the author, Detroit, Michigan, November 15, 1993.

40. Linda Robinson, interview with the author, Chicago, Illinois, September 23, 1994.

41. Deborah Walters, interview with the author, Chicago, Illinois, September 26, 1994. See Goings and Mohl, *The New African American Urban History*.

42. Delores Brown, interview with the author, Columbus, Ohio, June 5, 1997.

43. Annie Williams, interview with the author. See also Franklin, *Living Our Stories, Telling Our Truths.*

44. Joyce Fountain, interview with the author, Minneapolis, Minnesota, July 10, 1998.

45. Mary A. Williams, interview with the author, St. Louis, Missouri, December 10, 1992.

46. Maxine Johnson, interview with the author, St. Louis, Missouri, August 10, 1995. For a discussion, see Lehmann, *Promised Land.*

47. Dollie Rogers, interview with the author, St. Louis, Missouri, October 29, 1994.

48. Louise Dillard, interview with the author, Minneapolis, Minnesota, December 20, 1997. For a discussion of this issue, see Phillips, *Alabama North.*

49. Mary Tucker, interview with the author.

50. Rebecca Fitzpatrick, interview with the author, Indianapolis, Indiana, August 16, 1990.

51. Fannie Williams, interview with the author, Chicago, Illinois, June 10, 1991.

52. Eva Glenn, interview with the author, Drew, Mississippi, April 28, 1988. For a discussion, see Borchert, *Alley Life in Washington*; Ballard, *One More Day's Journey*; Grover, *Make a Way Somehow*; Franklin, *Living Our Stories, Telling Our Truths*; and Marks, *Farewell—We're Good and Gone.*

53. Joyce Fountain, interview with the author, Minneapolis, Minnesota, November 19, 1997. For a discussion of rural women migrants' concerns for their children, especially their daughters, see Elliot Liebow, *Tally's Corner: A Study of Negro Streetcorner Men* (Boston: Little, Brown, 1967); Lehmann, *Promised Land*; and Kenneth W. Goings, "Blacks in the Rural North: Paulding County, Ohio, 1860–1900," (Ph.D. diss., Princeton University, 1977). See also Drake and Cayton, *Black Metropolis.*

54. Shirley Bullock, interview with the author, Minneapolis, Minnesota, April 15, 1998. See also Nicholas Lehmann, *Promised Land*; and Trotter, *The Great Migration in Historical Perspective.*

55. Faye Williams, interview with the author, St. Louis, Missouri, September 15, 1997. See Liebow, *Tally's Corner*; and Lehmann, *Promised Land.*

56. Irene Scott, interview with the author, Drew, Mississippi, May 1, 1990.

57. Canary Coleman, interview with the author, St. Louis, Missouri, December 12, 1992. For a discussion of occupational opportunities and changes among migrants in Midwestern cities between 1945 and 1980, see Goings and Mohl, *The New African American Urban History*; Beverly A. Bunch-Lyons, "And They Came: The Migration of African American Women From the South to Cincinnati, Ohio, 1900–

1950," (Ph.D. diss., Miami University, Ohio, 1955); Jack S. Blocker, "Black Migration to Muncie, 1860–1930," *Indiana Magazine of History*, December 1996, 297–320; Kusmer, "The Black Urban Experience in American History," in Hine, *The State of Afro American History*; and James E. DeVries, *Race, Kinship, and Community in a Midwestern Town: The Black Experience in Monroe, Michigan, 1900–1915* (Urbana: University of Illinois Press, 1986).

Frontiers 22:1 (2001): 126–44.

Domestic Violence and Poverty

The Narratives of Homeless Women

JEAN CALTERONE WILLIAMS

Among the many reasons for homelessness, domestic violence and low-cost housing shortages experienced within a context of poverty are fundamental for low-income women living in shelters. Women interviewed in homeless and battered women's shelters in Phoenix, Arizona, describe a process of becoming homeless that usually involves a combination of interlocking events and factors, such that it is impossible to isolate one explanation for a woman's homelessness. Nonetheless, women's stories indicate a pattern in their persistent poverty and battering relationships prior to becoming homeless.

Most research distinguishes between the women who live in homeless shelters and those in domestic violence shelters. Likewise, the environments and programs offered by the two types of shelters vary significantly, and shelter staff usually argue that a homeless woman has different issues and needs than a battered woman. This study concurrently analyzes both kinds of shelters and points to the striking similarities in women's reasons for seeking emergency housing whether they reside in domestic violence or homeless shelters. Specifically, women discuss similarly impoverished circumstances and often indicate that their past histories include abusive partners. Partly, the similarity in women's stories can be traced to the overlap in populations at the two types of shelters. A woman who has left an abusive relationship may enter a homeless shelter after spending thirty days at a domestic violence shelter. Shifting to a homeless shelter is in part the effect of battered women's shelter policies, which encourage women to look for other accommodations after thirty days have expired. Other women may go directly from their relationships to homeless shelters because domestic violence shelters are full. Others prefer the attention paid to economic issues or even the generally later curfews found at homeless shelters. The overlap in client populations in the two kinds of shelters and the similarities among women's stories—in particular, the centrality of battering—suggest a complex connection between battering and homelessness. Such a connection is rarely captured by the easy distinctions generally drawn between women who are identified by shelter staff either as battered or homeless.

The distinctions drawn between battered women and homeless women by shelters are reflected in academic and popular literature. Though some homelessness studies address domestic violence as a central concern, such violence is more often mentioned only in passing as a reason for women's homelessness, and most studies neither explore its significance for homeless women nor examine the process of becoming homeless as it results from domestic violence.[1] For their part, analyses of domestic violence take more seriously the link between women's financial status and their ability to resist violence,[2] but only a few seriously explore homelessness.[3]

Though much attention has been paid to the "feminization of poverty," there has been less emphasis on the significance of poverty for increasing the likelihood that women will become homeless.[4] Female single-parent families rose from 23.7 percent of all families in poverty in 1960 to 52.6 percent of all families in poverty in the mid-1990s.[5] According to the 1995 U.S. Conference of Mayors's report on homelessness, the poverty of female-headed families is reflected in the composition of the homeless population. Of the twenty-nine cities surveyed for the report, twenty-three reported that at least 70 percent of homeless families in their cities were single-parent families, with nineteen citing from 80 percent to 98 percent single-parent families, the majority of them female headed.[6] As a proportion of the homeless population, families grew from 27 percent in 1985 to 43 percent in 1993 and dropped slightly to 38 percent in 1996.[7] Moreover, seventeen of the twenty-four cities that responded to a set of questions from the U.S. Conference of Mayors regarding requests for shelter by families indicated an increase in requests. Some cities reflected as much as a 100 percent increase from 1994 to 1995. As a result of historical growth in women's poverty and female-headed family homelessness, it has become increasingly important for research to focus on the unique sets of issues and problems that women's homelessness presents.

Women interviewed for this study emphasize the impact of divorce, battering, and other family disruptions in combination with economic insecurity and primary responsibility for their children on their paths to homelessness. Notwithstanding the complex story each woman tells when asked what events led her to seek temporary shelter, the combination of persistent poverty, domestic violence, and low-rent housing shortages were most often cited as causing crises. Just as social ethnographers have discovered in interviews with people receiving government assistance, most women and their families managed to survive for some time with little income and precarious housing, in other words, in an uncertain financial situation.[8] However, when financial difficulties occurred—problems like a car breakdown that would not cripple a middle-income family—there was no surplus money to finance the unexpected. Many of the women's parents and circle of friends were low-income as well, but had not themselves experienced homelessness. Nevertheless they lacked the resources needed to assist their homeless relatives with substantial amounts of money or long-term housing.

Recent changes in the availability of welfare benefits through Aid to Families with Dependent Children (AFDC) will also have an impact on women currently living in shelters or those who are borderline homeless. Low-paid or seasonally employed workers' loss of welfare benefits, however meager, may create more homelessness as people are unable to meet rent, utility, and food expenses during bouts of unemployment. The current services and shelters designed to assist homeless people will likely be overwhelmed by an increase in the numbers of the homeless. In fact, surveys of homeless shelters have found significant numbers of homeless families and individuals already are unable to find shelter due to a lack of space. Families often comprise a disproportionate number of those unable to find a shelter with an opening, as they are in Maryland, where families and children comprised 57 percent of all people turned away in 1990 and about 50 percent in 1991, despite making up closer to 30 or 40 percent of the homeless population nationwide.[9]

METHODOLOGY

This study is based on research that was conducted in homeless and domestic violence shelters in Phoenix, Arizona, from 1994 to 1996. The research included in-depth, semistructured interviews with thirty-three homeless women and participant-observation in several homeless and battered women's shelters with approximately one hundred shelter residents and the caseworkers, usually professional social workers, hired to work with them.[10] A review of fifty randomly chosen 1995 case files at one family homeless shelter supplements the interviews and participant-observation. In addition, I worked for a year as a part-time caseworker at Rose's House, a domestic violence shelter.

Interview questions were open-ended and as general as possible, encouraging women to formulate their own narratives of homelessness. In this sense, interview participants could include the information that to their minds explains homelessness and delete parts of their life histories that they believe do not count as an explanation of why someone loses housing. Their stories are, of course, mediated by the author to the extent that I asked certain questions and not others, and have the power to frame their stories in a specific context. Though some women probably left out embarrassing or incriminating information about themselves, most who discussed violence, drug use, and sex work offered this information without direct questioning, usually in response to an initial, general question regarding how they became homeless.

In addition to relaying homeless women's lived experiences, this project offers a story about the meanings attached to homelessness and domestic violence, a story that has been shaped through interviews and informal talks with homeless women. These interviews are rich in paradox and contradiction, indicating a great diversity in personal experience. With such diversity, I do not claim to offer the "homeless point of view"; rather, these voices are multiple and conflicting.[11] Yet they ultimately yield a story that gives significance both to homelessness and domestic violence that helps to make sense of their cultural and social meanings in the United States.

Most of the women interviewed came from two fairly small family homeless shelters, The Family Shelter and Lighthouse, and two domestic violence shelters for women and children, Rose's House and Casa Para Las Mujeres (La Casa). These shelters vary in size, housing from five to thirty families. All have cumbersome sets of rules and a significant amount of client and staff contact. In contrast to larger or armory-style homeless shelters, which tend to have fewer caseworkers per client and fewer expectations of residents, the smaller, more tightly controlled shelters offer more privacy and amenities, and fewer clients per caseworker. Although the more comfortable living environment is accompanied by more stringent regulations, these shelters are almost always full and consistently have to turn away people because of a lack of space. Staff at the smaller family homeless shelters tend to accept those who appear most "motivated" or most likely to secure housing within the three months that they are allowed to live at most shelters.[12] This practice usually excludes those who are severely mentally ill and heavy substance users because they are probably least likely to have the ability or desire to obey stricter shelter rules.[13]

SHELTER ORGANIZATION

As argued above, the interviews completed for this study point to the difficulties in citing the *one* reason women turn to domestic violence and homeless shelters. But analyses of homelessness often divide shelter residents and other homeless people into groups of those who have lost housing as a result of drug use, mental illness, or the vagaries of the economy. Although categorization is usually offered as the first step in calculating how many people are homeless and why, and how government and private agencies can best respond to them, Peter Marcuse criticizes the practice.[14] He argues that it is symptomatic of a reliance on "specialism, or calling a general problem the sum of a number of different special problems."[15] Rather than focusing on the systemic structural roots of homelessness, specialism both reflects and encourages a cultural understanding of homelessness as merely a "mental health, substance abuse, or criminal justice problem."[16] The tendency of such research to categorize people based on the one reason they lost housing precludes a focus on the *process* of becoming homeless, on how, for example, domestic violence, drug use, and poverty actually intertwine to lead to homelessness.

Much like analyses of homelessness, each emergency shelter tends to direct its services toward a certain subpopulation of the homeless. Abused and neglected teens, drug addicts, homeless families, and battered women are each assisted in a different program, to the exclusion of others who are similarly without housing. Most shelters do not offer services to women unless they conform to the criteria that ostensibly make them part of the particular group the shelter program targets. These classifications are delimited by a range of "experiences and characteristics" that do not necessarily match the women's lives who wish to gain entrance into a program.[17] As a result of their reliance on such categories, programs geared toward battered and homeless women vary considerably in the importance given to housing and employment considerations, lifestyle and behavioral issues, and emotional state.

Women who do not clearly fit into either the battered woman or homeless woman identity have great difficulty locating a program to assist them, or may redefine their experiences in order to correspond more closely to an identity looked for by a shelter. For example, a woman who is defined by staff at a battered women's shelter as "streetwise" (often a euphemism for "homeless" or "drug user") will have difficulty gaining entrance into that shelter, whether or not she has left an abusive partner. Likewise, some homeless shelters refuse to accept women who become homeless when they leave abusive relationships, even if battered women's shelters are full, because they do not define these women as "homeless." As the women's stories that follow make clear, however, many women have multiple issues for which they seek assistance but learn to emphasize one problem and to conceal another in order to gain acceptance into a particular shelter. Women's stories in this study indicate that the distinctions between "battered woman" and "homeless woman" are not as straightforward nor absolute as they often appear in cultural narratives drawn upon in the academic literature, by shelter employees, and sometimes by shelter residents themselves.

Although they know all too well the financial constraints that have colored their own decisions, battered women nevertheless often support and further construct a differentiation between homeless and battered women apparent in the emphases at different shelters. Unlike those who are in homeless shelters, "battered women" can rely on an identity that names them "victims" or perhaps "survivors," identities that do not hold them responsible for living in a shelter and assumes a supportive community of women in similar circumstances. Analyses of battering have noted that "women who have lived through such violence, who know the immense daily expenditure of strength and attention and self-discipline it takes to survive, rarely identify themselves as 'victims.' They think of themselves as strong women who can somehow 'cope.'"[18] Though it could be as easily argued that the women in homeless shelters develop personal fortitude through their struggles to survive, they tend not to be constructed as "survivors." Culturally, "battered women" are congratulated for turning to a shelter, as leaving their relationships is constructed as the defining act of "helping themselves," while those in homeless shelters generally are constructed as lazy and having turned to shelters as a way to "live off the system."

Phyllis, a fifty-five-year-old Euro-American resident of Rose's House, provides an example of the ways in which domestic violence shelter residents distinguish themselves from "homeless women." She contends that homeless people seek shelter after they have allowed their financial and personal lives to completely deteriorate, while battered women are in shelters because they want to change their lives, which have been ruined by someone else: "I think I just ended up in this place through no fault of my own. . . . I've found so much caring here, we really support each other, we have that sister-love." Kim, a Euro-American woman in her mid-forties and also a resident of Rose's House, responds similarly to a question about whether she considers herself homeless: "No, not really. I've always been very resourceful. . . . I've got friends who are battered women and come to shelters like this, but I don't know anyone who's been homeless. We're survivors, most of us. We've learned to be very strong and resourceful because of everything we've been through. Financially, it's a big hurdle. If you don't have a job or skills, then you've got a problem." Despite cultural narratives of domestic violence that historically have constructed battered women as "masochists,"[19] and a more current concentration on the psychologically debilitating effects of battering,[20] Kim represents women who view leaving as courageous. Indeed, she argues that battered women are stronger than most specifically *because* they have experienced such violence. Tammy, also a Euro-American resident of Rose's House in her early forties, echoes Kim's construction of battered women as survivors. In response to the same question asked of Kim regarding whether she thinks of herself as homeless, Tammy asserts: "No, and it's bizarre because I guess I have been [homeless], but when someone says homeless you just go 'yuck' — I think of a bag lady. I guess since I've always been able to provide for myself, I just think of myself as in transition instead of homeless."

Those women who become homeless for reasons other than domestic violence display a similar desire to separate themselves from the label "homeless." "Homeless" suggests a woman mentally ill or drug addicted, unwashed, helpless, and hopeless, a person mired in a permanent "lifestyle" rather than "in transition." Though the inclination remains as strong for homeless women who are not battered, battered women make the move to claim an alternative status to "homeless" more successfully, in large part because they have recourse to the "battered woman" identity. Such an identity relies partially on a feminist narrative that constructs the "battered woman" as a person "in transition," a "survivor," stronger than other women for having experienced and left a violent situation, or a participant in a "sisterhood" that includes many other women assumed to have similar histories and needs.

Like other residents of Rose's House, Latanya, a twenty-eight-year-old African American woman with two children, also does not consider herself homeless, asserting that homeless people have different problems than she does, particularly that they have "given up." Claiming that "there is always a way out of homelessness," Latanya can never picture herself "on the street," and states that people become homeless because, unlike her, some are lazy, others "like to live like that," and still others "have been hurt badly in life." She argues that she would do anything to keep from becoming homeless, such as collecting cans for money or relying on public welfare payments until she could find work.

Despite her wish to distinguish herself from homeless women, Latanya's own story supports the contention that many women seek shelter for a multiplicity of reasons. Latanya grew up in a family with eight children, with a father who was an alcoholic and abusive to her mother and to the children. Like Latanya, most of her sisters have also had violent relationships, and she remains close to only one sister who also lives in Phoenix. Latanya had her first child at age seventeen, dropped out of high school, and lived with her son's father for five years. When she left him, Latanya moved with her son to an apartment subsidized by the Department of Housing and Urban Development (HUD). With subsidized housing, work in a fast food restaurant and cleaning houses, and some help from her sister, she managed to support herself and her child.

Two years later, Latanya met her current boyfriend, Emil. After two years together the couple had a son, and she gave up her subsidized housing a year later to move into his home. Over the course of the past year, Latanya left Emil several times and stayed with her sister when he became violent toward her. Finally, she decided to leave him for good and called the shelter: "My sister wanted me to stay with her, but I wanted counseling, so I went to Rose's House." Although she claims that she is not "really" homeless because she has the option of living with her sister, Latanya's sister's husband already works three jobs to support the family, and two or three more people would certainly strain their resources. Moreover, Latanya has applied for subsidized housing again, but she faces a significant delay in obtaining such housing because of a two-year waiting list.

Like Latanya, Betsy describes multiple, interlocking factors that led to her residence first in a domestic violence shelter and then in a homeless shelter. And like Latanya, Betsy does not clearly fall into either the "battered woman" or "homeless woman" categories. A thirty-one-year-old Euro-American woman with three children, Betsy begins the story of how she became homeless when she ran away from home at age fifteen, saying, "I guess I've been homeless from fifteen to twenty-one, but I didn't think of myself that way then." For those six years, Betsy supported herself through sex work and as a relief driver for truckers, riding back and forth across the country with truckers who paid her one cent a mile to drive while they slept. She had to sleep on the streets only twice during those years, but supporting herself through sex work was difficult for her emotionally. Her voice lowers to a whisper and she cries when she talks about it.

For a few years in her early twenties, Betsy worked alternately as a live-in housekeeper and as a cashier in a retail store. She then met her husband and had her first child, who is now four years old. Because the couple had difficulties getting by on the money her husband made at his appliance repair business, they were repeatedly evicted when they were short on rent. In the four years prior to Betsy's arrival at the shelter, they had moved twenty-two times. During the past year, cocaine had played an increasing role in their marriage, and Betsy's husband had become increasingly violent. As the couple became more involved in using drugs, his violence escalated and he grew less interested in and committed to working. Betsy blames him for their homelessness, arguing, "The main reason I'm homeless is that Ron didn't want to work." Because Ron did not want Betsy to work, and three births in the past four years kept her at home for some months with each baby, the family's financial problems intensified. The last time they were evicted, the landlord would not return what was left of their security deposit for fourteen days, and they had no money to pay for a motel or another apartment.

Betsy had tried to leave her husband some months earlier, after she felt his drug use and the violence had gotten "out of control." However, she asserts, "the only place I had to go was my father's house. I was trying to quit using drugs, but he's an addict too, and they would knock on my bedroom door at night saying, 'Betsy, do you want to get high with us?' I knew if I didn't get out of there I wouldn't be able to quit using." With three children in tow, her friends were not willing to take her in or able to spare the room or the funds to feed and house four more people for any period of time, so Betsy returned to her husband. She tried for the next two weeks to get into Rose's House, but either the shelter was full or the staff did not think Betsy's "problem was domestic violence, because I wasn't defining it that way. I didn't understand that was the issue." Eventually, Betsy went to another organization that assists homeless people, sometimes directing them to area shelters. They helped Betsy get into Rose's House the following day by emphasizing her battering relationship. She stayed there for the next six weeks, then went to The Family Shelter.

It is difficult to point to the one reason Betsy became homeless. Even before she and Ron began using cocaine, neither had education nor skills that translated to jobs that paid enough to adequately support their children and themselves. The couple faced great difficulty finding low-income housing. Their repeated evictions meant yet another obstacle to stable employment, as they were constantly in the process of moving from one apartment to another, sometimes a fair distance from their former residence and jobs. Nor did they own a car to facilitate travel to work. Moreover, Ron tried to start his own repair business, working out of his apartment, but continual moves made it difficult for customers to locate him. Both had cultural expectations that a husband would take care of "his" family, expectations that made Betsy reluctant to work full-time and Ron less likely to encourage her to do so. Thus, they had to forego a badly needed second income. On the other hand, with three children, the cost of childcare during work hours would have demanded a large portion of their second income. Ron's violence created even less stability in their household, and Betsy's inability to rely on a family she had fled at age fifteen created few options for her when she attempted to leave him.

DOMESTIC VIOLENCE

Rather than approaching domestic violence as a direct (or the single) "cause" of women's homelessness, this study considers how such violence can help to create the circumstances that might particularly make a low-income woman more susceptible to homelessness.[21] Domestic violence and poverty may intersect with other issues to produce the circumstances that often lead to homelessness, creating conditions that leave women no other choice but to seek temporary shelter for the short-term, and thereafter to remain precariously housed. Because of the extensive resources a woman who leaves a violent relationship needs in order to support herself and her children, the shelter presents one of the few choices available to low-income women. It demands a significant amount of money to avail oneself of other options, such as staying in a hotel, renting an apartment alone, or moving to another city.

Ella's story provides an expression of the ways that domestic violence and poverty may intersect to create the very elements that often lead to homelessness. A forty-three-year-old Euro-American woman with three children, Ella left her husband five years ago and entered Rose's House domestic violence shelter. By the time she left, the violence in their eighteen-year marriage had escalated to the point that her husband, Jim, often threatened her with knives and guns. She believes that if she had stayed longer, he eventually would have killed her, and as a result Jim still does not know where she lives. During their marriage, the couple was homeless off and on, at one time sleeping for four months in the woods and for two years in their camper, getting most of their food from dumpsters. Ella worked sporadically as a waitress and her husband in construction, but primarily they lived isolated lives in rural areas. Ella notes that the poverty and violence escalated simultaneously over time, to the point that in the last year and a half of their marriage they rarely bought groceries: "One time, we lived off canisters of candy thrown away by the supermarket for one month. We lived off chicken thrown away from the supermarket deli. I would have to pick off the dirt and mop strings before serving it." After she left Jim, Ella stayed at Rose's House for two months.

The violence in Ella's marriage made a fragile economic situation worse and contributed to her need for social services or a shelter when she left. She needed a supportive shelter or program in order to ensure her and her children's safety and allow her time to finish school and find employment. Women like Ella who leave violent partners are much like other homeless women who do not have family on whom to depend or whose families are too impoverished to offer them many resources. Because an abuser often isolates his partner from friends and family, and a woman's shame for the beatings encourages her to remain isolated, women fleeing violence may lack a network of friends and family upon whom to rely for housing, money, food, or clothing. Moreover, low-income women who wish to leave such a relationship often do not have any money saved that they can use to support themselves until they find employment. Others cannot find a job that pays a living wage. Even a woman leaving a middle-class home may have earned a salary well below her husband's and may find it difficult to live on her income alone. Although Ella possessed a high school diploma, during her marriage she "felt like there was no way out . . . that it was possible only to get waitressing and fast food jobs" that she did not think would support herself and her children. At the same time, however, she began to realize that she could obtain assistance from the social service organizations (from which she and her husband had occasionally obtained food boxes) without her husband, and she saw that as providing an escape from the marriage.

Ella currently juggles a full-time university schedule (she has a 4.0 grade point average), part-time employment as a case manager working with elderly men and women as a counselor and advocate, and raising her three children, ages nine, ten, and thirteen. In addition to subsidized housing, she receives a Pell Grant and some support from AFDC as her work at the hospital is an unpaid internship, a requirement for her graduation. She also participates in a transitional program for homeless families called Endowment for Phoenix Families (EPF). The program's goal is to help people become financially secure enough to permanently leave behind government-subsidized housing. In the three-year program, families find their own housing and pay a portion of their incomes to the landlord for rent, while HUD pays the balance with a voucher. Despite all her accomplishments,

Ella and her children continue to live in constrained economic conditions. Their old, sparsely furnished house has torn window screens, and the carpet is worn through to the concrete floor in several places. Ella explains, "we still run out of almost all food except beans and rice by the end of the month."

In pointing out the influence of poverty on the lives and choices of women currently living in domestic violence shelters, my interest is not to argue that low-income men are necessarily more abusive than their well-off counterparts. Rather, I am exploring the reasons that primarily low-income women go to the shelters. This study is done in a context, however, of an association of domestic violence with low-income people, which includes a sociological approach to the analysis of battering that concentrates on various "subcultures."[22] This is driven by the perspective that social variables, such as class, race, ethnicity, gender, and age, influence the tendency toward violence. As a result, it is argued that African Americans, Latinos, and members of the working class have a greater tendency toward violence in their relationships because of the "social stress" of higher unemployment rates and impoverishment.

This view, however, is not universally accepted. For example, Linda Gordon's work suggests that both historical and current correlations between differing rates of violence and specific groups of people may warrant further attention. Gordon criticizes the historical view that "family violence is a problem of poor people," an understanding of violence in the 1930s that led organizations to address poverty as a key to eradicating violence.[23] Gordon cautions that measuring "the contribution of economic stress to family violence" historically has produced ambiguous findings.[24] She comments on the inconsistency of 1930s and 1940s statistics that correlate poverty with family violence, concluding that in some cases "what is being measured is as much the sensibility of caseworkers as the conditions of clients."[25] As this paper argues, the association of battering with racial "others" and impoverished people continues to define popular cultural understandings of battering in the present. This study supports Richard Gelles's suggestion that a critical perspective like Gordon's might be brought to bear on discussions of battering today. Gelles proposes that the higher incidence of violence found in present-day Latino and African American families may be in part attributable to overreporting relative to reporting on violence in white families.[26]

Although Gelles also maintains that current studies indicate the risk of violence is higher for people under stress from unemployment and poverty, his and Gordon's arguments should caution researchers of battering to consider the complexities involved in creating measures and interpreting statistics in this area. First, in terms of this study, a predominately low-income population at La Casa and Rose's House may be traceable to the limited options available to low-income battered women relative to higher-income women wishing to leave their relationships. It does not necessarily suggest a higher incidence of battering among poor people. Moreover, just as is the case with many researchers and academics, caseworkers at domestic violence shelters are overwhelmingly middle class and Euro-American. Their participation in constructing meanings for domestic violence is influenced by their own social locations and biases, in particular, their assumptions that abusive relationships are most likely to occur in the families of racial "others" and low-income people. This paper argues, then, that surveys measuring the incidence of violence within certain groups of people are wrapped up in cultural understandings of battering that depend to some extent upon racialized and class-based assumptions about what "kind" of men beat their wives or partners.

The existence of such assumptions invites further examination of the cultural meanings of "abuser" and "battered woman." In addition to enumerating the everyday experiences of the women interviewed for this study, it is important to understand the ways in which reality is socially and culturally constructed through narratives of domestic violence. Culturally available narratives provide a way for people to understand battered women's experiences, a shorthand that explains a woman's behavior and delineates her status as "domestic violence victim" or "survivor," as "battered woman" or "not battered woman." The subject positions available to a woman experiencing violence are bounded by a limited number of narratives that tell us what domestic violence entails and who is a "battered woman."

Much of the writing and public discourse on domestic violence suggests that a woman who escapes a violent relationship is almost always in serious physical danger and therefore needs a battered women's shelter in which to hide from a mate who probably will stalk her and possibly eventually kill her if she leaves him without going into hiding.[27] In this narrative, a woman remains in a battering relationship for fear of incurring increased violence should she leave, and sometimes more importantly because, despite her fear of her partner, she still loves him. Because he has decreased her self-esteem to the point that the battered woman on some level believes she does not deserve better treatment, she needs counseling.[28] Without counseling and attention to her emotional condition, in particular that of "learned helplessness" (in which a battered woman becomes increasingly depressed, anxious, in denial about the seriousness of the violence, and less likely to fight back), she is more likely to return to the relationship.[29]

This narrative does not provide a space for a "battered woman" to be anything other than "agent" or "victim," identities that are set up as binary opposites with little middle ground or possibility that a woman may be both active in her own defense and in pursuing strategies to end the violence *and* abused mentally, emotionally, or physically.[30] An either/or dichotomy between helpless victimization and powerful agency equates agency with leaving the relationship and psychological victimization and impaired self-esteem with staying. Women involved in violent relationships may, however, be active agents freeing themselves from abuse, many remaining in a relationship while incorporating a "vast array of personalized strategies and sources . . . to end the violence in their lives."[31] Such strategies may entail remaining in the relationship for a period of time while trying to negotiate an end to the abuse, or to save money, or to finish school or job training in order to leave with more resources. Requesting family networks to pressure the abuser to end his violence or turning to social service agencies for assistance are other strategies.[32]

A competing feminist narrative argues that violence against women is part of a cultural milieu that accepts and rewards male violence.[33] According to Kersti Yllö, a feminist perspective on domestic violence situates male violence within a discussion of gender and power, thereby rejecting the "gender neutral" sociological explanation of "family violence."[34] Yllö points out that the sociological perspective makes little of the fact that relationship violence is primarily a "*male* phenomenon," that in cases where women have reported violence toward their partners it generally has been in self-defense, and that domestic violence is a "tactic of entitlement and power that is deeply gendered" rather than about a "conflict of interest."[35] Women protesting against male violence or trying to leave their relationships may face indifference or disapprobation from the police, the courts, the church, and their families. As such, leaving a violent partner is complicated by women's lack of community support and the possibility of increasingly violent repercussions from abusers. Feminists and formerly battered women argue that shelters were founded in response to women's need for protection from their partners and for counseling and support from other women. A feminist perspective argues that all women who have abusive husbands or lovers are victimized, yet even women who return to their relationships may be "agents," as such women may be actively involved in trying to end their partner's violence.

Women of color have argued that such alternative narratives on issues of rape and battering offered by white feminists often ignore the specific experiences of women of color, or worse, utilize the racist stereotyping relied upon in the dominant narrative.[36] In her study of battered women's shelters in Los Angeles, Kimberlé Crenshaw reveals the dynamics of "structural intersectionality" as they play out in the lives of low-income African American, Latina, and Asian American battered women, arguing that women of color suffer multilayered subordination based on race, gender, and class. Crenshaw suggests that persistent poverty and its attendant issues of housing shortages and underemployment are particularly important in considering the experiences of battered women of color:

Economic considerations—access to employment, housing, and wealth—confirm that class structures play an important part in defining the experience of women of color vis-à-vis battering. . . . [S]helter policies are often shaped by an image that locates women's subordination primarily in the psychological effects of male domination, and thus overlooks the socioeconomic factors that often disempower women of color. Because the disempowerment of many battered women of color is arguably less a function of what is in their minds and more a reflection of the obstacles that exist in their lives, these interventions are likely to reproduce rather than effectively challenge their domination.[37]

Much like those women Crenshaw describes, the women who entered the domestic violence shelters in Phoenix have few personal resources such as savings, significant education and job training, or family or friends who can take them in for any period of time. Most women have housing and job needs that often are not addressed at the shelter. Rather, the shelter is designed principally to shield women from danger and offer counseling and emotional healing in hopes that a woman will not return to her relationship. African American, Latina, and American Indian women interviewed in the Phoenix shelters contend with racial discrimination in the past and present that make their journeys to stable housing more difficult. Despite, then, the construction of "battered woman" that intimates that all women leaving a violent relationship need psychological counseling or are in serious physical danger, many low-income women look to shelters to provide housing. As Crenshaw argues, women of color are disproportionately low income and face significant financial obstacles in leaving abusive relationships.

Staff members of Phoenix battered women's shelters present yet another competing narrative of domestic violence, which shares some commonalities with both the feminist and dominant narratives.[38] In this interpretation, like the feminist one, women are victims of controlling male violence and need the shelter in order to hide from their husbands or lovers who are likely to be more violent should they locate their escaped partners. Alternatively, others need the shelter in order to work on their diminished self-esteem while finding housing and a job. Shelter staff identify emotional, verbal, and sexual abuse as domestic violence as well as physical abuse, and in this sense recognize that all women seeking shelter do not necessarily need protection from their abusers. Despite their claim that many women do not need physical protection, however, some staff operate as if they assume that most women do need the shelter for physical safety. For example, some staff members argue that a woman who visits her abuser while she resides in the shelter, thereby proving that she is not hiding from him and not in severe physical danger, does not "really" need shelter. In other words, she is not a "real" battered woman.

Although Rose's House and La Casa are not among them, two of the seven domestic violence shelters in Phoenix have instituted "closed" programs, based on the argument that both battered women and their partners are sometimes "addicted" to their relationships. These shelters dictate that women entering their programs remain literally on the shelter premises, eschewing any contact with friends, employers, and especially their partners for a period of several days to up to two weeks. Women must get a leave of absence from work, reschedule any appointments or meetings during that time, and generally upset their daily schedules. One woman called Rose's House wanting to transfer there from a shelter with a closed program, complaining that she had already missed one housing appointment. She had scheduled the appointment in anticipation of leaving her husband and was in danger of missing more if she stayed at the shelter. Thus, those women who have been working on separating from their abusers even before calling a shelter, in particular by arranging for housing, find themselves forced to put most practical considerations aside in such closed programs.

Supporters of closed programs argue that a woman in a violent relationship, much like a drug addict or alcoholic, is on some level addicted to the relationship and needs a period of intense "in-patient" counseling in order to ensure her "recovery." By mandating resident confinement for a period of time, closed programs strive to "break the addiction" to an abusive partner, suggesting that at the end of a period of intensive counseling, a woman will be less likely to return to her partner. The rationale for canceling appointments for low-income housing or demanding that a woman miss work lies in the argument that a battered woman's most pressing need is for counseling, supported by the notion that women remain in abusive relationships primarily because of low self-esteem, codependence, or fear of being alone. While these psychological factors may affect a woman's decision about whether to leave her relationship, closed programs basically ignore the economic insecurity that many Phoenix women factor into their decisions about their relationships. Likewise, even in programs that are not closed, women are sometimes not allowed to accept a job if it interferes with regularly scheduled weekly or nightly group counseling meetings.

In addition, like the dominant narrative, shelter workers tend toward a dichotomization of agency and victimization. Caseworkers at Rose's House, for example, may suspect that those women who do not appear "helpless" or have "low self-esteem" might simply need housing from the shelter, or might be lying or not telling the whole story about their experiences with abuse. In fact, I discovered that many women were primarily seeking housing from the shelter. Although they, as well as other women interviewed, said that the counseling and group support at the domestic violence shelter helped them, they had entered the shelter because they had few options regarding a place to live and financial support for themselves and their children.

Marta's story, like Ella's, indicates the centrality of both domestic violence and poverty to women's homelessness. Moreover, Marta describes the extent to which economic dependence played a role in the dynamics of her battering relationship. A forty-year-old Latina, Marta was staying with her five children at The Family Shelter when I met her. She had tried leaving her twenty-year marriage several times in the past, but, because she did not know that shelters existed, Marta lived in her car with her youngest child for five months while attempting to become financially independent of her husband. Unable to make the transition from the car to housing, she returned and lived with her husband for a few months. During a fight between Marta and her husband that resulted in a fire in the house, the police were called, and they provided Marta with a list of battered women's shelters. She applied to Rose's House and was accepted within a week, staying for a month before moving to The Family Shelter.

The day I met Marta, she had only two weeks left in the shelter before her ninety days expired. When she spoke about her search for housing or another program for her family, her face clouded with worry: "I have too many children to get into the Endowment for Phoenix Families. Other people have found me eligible, but no one has a place open." Nor could Marta find an apartment building that would accept her, even though she had enough money saved to pay her deposits. As soon as the managers learned that she had five children, lived on an income of $561 per month from AFDC, and had a problematic credit history, they refused to rent to her. The caseworker at The Family Shelter was pressuring Marta to ask her husband for money to help support their children. Indeed, her stay at the shelter for the next two weeks was contingent on her demanding money from her husband. Marta did not want to involve him in her financial difficulties, believing that a request for his assistance would be the first step in returning to her husband. In thinking about her options, Marta remarked, "I'm in a position now where I will remain homeless or go back with my husband." She did not want to live with him again, saying that she had spent a weekend with him and saw his "old behaviors coming up" and felt that it was "dark and tense" at his apartment.

In the ensuing weeks, shelter staff allowed Marta to stay beyond their usual ninety-day limit, but she still could not find housing. She spoke with increasing anxiety about her inability to find a place to live and spent hours sitting by the phone in the community area near the office, making calls and checking messages repeatedly to see if an apartment manager or program director had returned her calls. When Marta's extensions at the shelter had run out, she refused to return to her husband. A month after the first interview she was sleeping in her car and her children were sleeping in a tent trailer behind an acquaintance's home.

As Marta's story illustrates, the scarcity of low-cost housing plays a significant role in narrowing the choices available to battered homeless women trying to live on their own. Veronica's and Lisa's experiences have some parallels to Marta's in that their inability to pay for housing and other living costs without a male partner's assistance critically affected the choices available to them. Indeed, a number of Phoenix women were forced to enter shelters when they found that their low-wage jobs or AFDC benefits were not enough to pay for rent, utilities, food, and clothing. Veronica is a twenty-five-year-old Latina with two children, ages two and four, living at La Casa: "I came to the shelter yesterday. I was living with my boyfriend on and off for six years. . . . I left him before and stayed with my mom. I went back because I didn't get along with my mom, and I didn't have anywhere else to go. The last time he beat me up, I called the cops for the first time—he's in jail now. I was tired of the abuse, and I felt like if he didn't care about me, if he could do that to me, I shouldn't care about him."

Veronica receives $347 per month from AFDC for her two children, with which she is supposed to pay for rent, utilities, and other necessities.[39] With an eighth-grade education, she possesses few marketable skills. She says she lied to the welfare department, telling them that she did not live with her boyfriend in order to receive benefits. Even with benefits, however, she and her boyfriend survived only because his father took them in and accepts $150 per month for rent and utilities, which, according to Veronica, "was nothing compared to getting your own place." She had attempted to rent her own apartment in the past: "I tried to get a place on my own, but I couldn't keep up with the electricity payments, so I went back to my boyfriend." Another time, she had tried to leave her boyfriend and live with her father, but his new wife did not want her and her children to live with them. Veronica hopes that the shelter staff can help her find housing and pursue her GED and computer training. She remarked sadly, "My boyfriend used to threaten me that if I left him, he'd come find me. . . . Now he says he beats me because he *wants* me to leave."

Though she has more resources than Veronica, Lisa, a Euro-American woman in her late thirties, experienced similar housing problems when she came to Phoenix with her two children, ages eight and four, to hide from a fiancé she describes as "paranoid and abusive." When she realized that her fiancé would try to track her down if she left him, Lisa decided to move to a city where she had no family or friends, so he would be less likely to find her. She and her children arrived with no car, no employment lined up, and little money, since in the last months of their relationship Lisa had depended on her boyfriend financially while she tried to start her own business. After two weeks in Phoenix during which Lisa stated she had not had a full meal, she resigned herself to the need for assistance and applied for AFDC: "People always say that getting on AFDC is a cop-out. The easy way would have been to stay with [my fiancé], but it took more integrity to leave and get on assistance."

Unable to afford an apartment on her AFDC allowance, Lisa rented a room for herself and her children in a house owned by a woman who lived with her emotionally disturbed young son. However, the mother and son's constant physical fighting caused Lisa and her children considerable stress. Moreover, the woman began locking the phone and answering machine in her room, both of which were crucial in Lisa's efforts to develop a career as a freelance writer. The family then moved in with an older woman, who seemed to be relatively stable but who Lisa soon learned was a "closet alcoholic." Complaining that the family was home too much, after a month the woman was no longer willing to rent to them.

By this time, Lisa had made a friend who owned his own business in Phoenix and arranged for her and her children to sleep in his office until they were able to find better housing. They slept on the floor in the unheated office for the months of December and January, piling on blankets to try to stay warm. Lisa finally decided to look into shelters, though she feared a drug-infested and unsafe environment. She met with a case manager from The Family Shelter, who, she asserts, had to convince her to come to the shelter: "I thought a shelter would be so unsafe that I'd rather be on the street than there. I agreed to go because of rules like no drugs or alcohol [allowed on or off the shelter premises], people have to sign in and out, and no one's allowed in the rooms." Surprised by the structure and support offered at The Family Shelter, Lisa moved her children there in early March. From there, a longer-term, transitional program for homeless families accepted her. Analyzing her struggles over the past year, Lisa asserts that women's ability to leave abusive partners "all comes down to economics": "So many women stay in abusive situations for economic reasons. . . . I tried for a year to get on my feet, but you can't do it without a stable living environment. . . . It was a blow to my pride and self-esteem to end up in a program like this."

Describing her life before moving to Phoenix as a combination of generally stable periods alternating with tumultuous intimate relationships, Lisa has been married twice, both times to abusive men. After her children were born and Lisa had divorced her first husband, she completed a college degree while holding down a job. Though she had some difficulty supporting her family during those years, since completing her degree five years ago Lisa has managed to live a relatively comfortable lower-middle-class life. With her college degree, she worked as a freelance desktop publisher, which did not afford her a consistent or wholly reliable income. Still afraid that her fiancé will find her, since moving to Phoenix Lisa has contacted only one family member, her sister, though even she does not know where Lisa lives.

Like Lisa, Veronica, and Marta, many Phoenix women describe significant obstacles to finding housing that is both affordable and safe. With more than three low-income renters for every low-cost apartment available in Phoenix, compounded by lengthy waiting lists for subsidized housing, the housing shortage contributes enormously to women's vulnerability to homelessness. A low-income woman's problems with securing an income that pays a living wage, and thereby an apartment, may be complicated by her wish to avoid her ex-husband or partner and in most cases by her primary or sole responsibility for financial support of her children.

Women in domestic violence and homeless shelters tell notably similar stories about their paths to emergency shelters, regardless of whether those shelters are for battered women or homeless women. Listening to their stories suggests that the distinctions drawn between the identities of "homeless woman" and "battered woman" are often arbitrary. The organization of homeless and domestic violence shelters, however, demands that women define themselves in one way or another in order to receive services. Women who cannot find an opening in a battered women's shelter may have to conceal their histories with abusive partners in order to gain entrance into a homeless shelter. Other women may repackage themselves in order to receive assistance from a battered women's shelter.

Shelters reinforce the distinction between homeless and battered identities through the services they offer. Notwithstanding the pattern of persistent poverty and battering, homeless shelters are likely to focus on women's housing and employment needs, while battered women's shelters concentrate on the psychological ramifications of violence, often to the exclusion of providing staff time to help with housing and job searches. In addition, both kinds of shelters have three-month time limits that preclude serious attention to women's skill levels and training, making receipt of subsidized housing—with waiting lists of up to two years—an undependable option. Although women usually receive federal or state preferences once they enter a shelter and so will be placed at the top of most housing lists, three months may easily pass before housing becomes available. Because battered women's shelters define their services as "crisis" housing, most initially accept women for no more than thirty days so women cannot always depend upon even ninety days of shelter.

Women counter the story of homelessness suggested by such a shelter system by emphasizing their persistent poverty and precarious housing arrangements in concert with battering relationships. Women in both kinds of shelters express their desires to receive respectful, individualized treatment from a staff who will respond to their experiences with battering and their housing and employment needs. However, when their ability to gain entrance into a shelter depends upon their conformity to certain identities—"battered woman" or "homeless woman"—women in Phoenix shelters will self-consciously manipulate their histories in order to fit into these socially constructed categories of need.

NOTES

1. See Jan L. Hagen, "Gender and Homelessness," *Social Work* 32 (July/August 1987): 312–16; Joan Zorza, "Woman Battering: A Major Cause of Homelessness,"

Clearinghouse Review 25:4 (1991): 421–29; David Wagner, *Checkerboard Square: Culture and Resistance in a Homeless Community* (Boulder, Colo.: Westview Press, 1993); and Doug A. Timmer, D. Stanley Eitzen, and Kathryn D. Talley, *Paths to Homelessness: Extreme Poverty and the Urban Housing Crisis* (Boulder, Colo.: Westview Press, 1994).

2. Linda Gordon, *Heroes of Their Own Lives: The Politics and History of Family Violence* (New York: Viking, 1988); Kimberlé Williams Crenshaw, "Mapping the Margins: Intersectionality, Identity Politics, and Violence against Women of Color," in *The Public Nature of Private Violence: The Discovery of Domestic Abuse*, ed. Martha Albertson Fineman and Roxanne Mykitiuk (New York: Routledge, 1994), 93–118; and Ann Jones, *Next Time, She'll Be Dead: Battering and How to Stop It* (Boston: Beacon Press, 1994).

3. Lee Ann Hoff, *Battered Women As Survivors* (New York: Routledge, 1990).

4. Hagen, "Gender and Homelessness."

5. U.S. Department of Commerce, Bureau of the Census, *Income and Poverty: 1994* (Washington DC: U.S. Government Printing Office, CD-ROM).

6. Laura DeKoven Waxman, Kimberly Peterson, and Matthew McClure, *A Status Report on Hunger and Homelessness in America's Cities: 1995* (Washington DC: The United States Conference of Mayors, 1995), 70.

7. Laura DeKoven Waxman and Shannon Hinderliter, *A Status Report on Hunger and Homelessness in America's Cities: 1996* (Washington DC: The United States Conference of Mayors, 1996), appendix.

8. For example, Mark Robert Rank, *Living On the Edge: The Realities of Welfare in America* (New York: Columbia University Press, 1994).

9. National Coalition for the Homeless, *A Place Called Hopelessness: Shelter Demand in the 90s* (Washington DC: National Coalition for the Homeless, n.d.), 21.

10. The names and identifying background information of interview participants (both shelter staff and residents) and that of homeless and domestic violence shelters have been changed in order to protect the anonymity of participants.

11. Aihwa Ong, *Spirits of Resistance and Capitalist Discipline: Factory Women in Malaysia* (Albany: State University of New York Press, 1987).

12. Shelters that receive funding from the Department of Economic Security may provide ninety days of shelter per person during each fiscal year.

13. For a more detailed description of the environments and rules of the shelters, see Jean Calterone Williams, "Geography of the Homeless Shelter: Staff Surveillance and Resident Resistance," *Urban Anthropology* 25:1 (1996).

14. For example, Peter H. Rossi, *Down and Out in America: The Origins of Homelessness* (Chicago: University of Chicago Press, 1989); Robert C. Coates, *A Street Is Not a Home: Solving America's Homeless Dilemma* (Buffalo, N.Y.: Prometheus

Books, 1990); and Christopher Jencks, *The Homeless* (Cambridge: Harvard University Press, 1994).

15. Peter Marcuse, "Neutralizing Homelessness," *Socialist Review* 18 (1988): 88.

16. Wagner, *Checkerboard Square*, 5.

17. For a discussion of the "experiences and characteristics" associated with battered women, see Donileen R. Loseke, *The Battered Woman and Shelters: The Social Construction of Wife Abuse* (Albany: State University of New York Press, 1992).

18. Jones, *Next Time, She'll Be Dead*, 83.

19. Florence Hollis, *Women in Marital Conflict: A Casework Study* (New York: Family Service Association of America, 1949).

20. Lenore Walker, *The Battered Woman* (New York: Harper and Row, 1979), and "The Battered Woman Syndrome Is a Psychological Consequence of Abuse," in *Current Controversies on Family Violence*, ed. Richard J. Gelles and Donileen Loseke (Newbury Park, Calif.: Sage Publications, 1993), 133–53.

21. Timmer, Eitzen, and Talley, *Paths to Homelessness*.

22. Richard J. Gelles, "Through a Sociological Lens: Social Structure and Family Violence," in Gelles and Loseke, *Current Controversies on Family Violence*, 31–46.

23. Gordon, *Heroes of Their Own Lives*, 151.

24. Gordon, *Heroes of Their Own Lives*, 149.

25. Gordon, *Heroes of Their Own Lives*, 149.

26. Gelles, "Through a Sociological Lens."

27. Loseke, *The Battered Woman and Shelters.*

28. Walker, *The Battered Woman*; and Del Martin, *Battered Wives* (New York: Simon and Schuster, 1983).

29. Walker, "The Battered Woman Syndrome."

30. Martha R. Mahoney, "Victimization or Oppression? Women's Lives, Violence, and Agency," in Fineman and Mykitiuk, *The Public Nature of Private Violence*, 60–63.

31. Lee Bowker, "A Battered Woman's Problems Are Social, Not Psychological," in Gelles and Loseke, *Current Controversies on Family Violence*, 155. Also see Gordon, *Heroes of Their Own Lives*; and Mahoney, "Victimization or Oppression?" 62.

32. Susan Schechter, *Women and Male Violence: The Visions and Struggles of the Battered Women's Movement* (Boston: South End Press, 1982), 232–33.

33. Kersti Yllö, "Through a Feminist Lens: Gender, Power, and Violence," in Gelles and Loseke, *Current Controversies on Family Violence*, 47–62; Gordon, *Heroes of Their Own Lives*; and Schechter, *Women and Male Violence.*

34. Yllö, "Through a Feminist Lens."

35. Yllö, "Through a Feminist Lens," 57. See also Gordon, *Heroes of Their Own Lives.*

36. Kimberlé Crenshaw, "Whose Story Is It Anyway? Feminist and Antiracist Ap-

propriations of Anita Hill," in *Race-ing Justice, En-gendering Power: Essays on Anita Hill, Clarence Thomas, and the Construction of Social Reality*, ed. Toni Morrison (New York: Pantheon Books, 1992), 402–40.

37. Crenshaw, "Mapping the Margins," 95–96.

38. Schechter has written of the tensions involved in defining the components of battering, tensions that increased as shelters and shelter staff professionalized in the late 1970s and early 1980s. In Phoenix shelters today, these tensions sometimes play out as a battle between feminist understandings of battering and understandings based on the model used by professional social workers. Social workers became the primary staff at shelters as public and private grants to run shelters became more available. See Schechter, *Women and Male Violence*, 101–3.

39. The poverty level, as calculated by the Department of Health and Human Services in 1994, was $12,320 per year for a three-person family (see *Federal Register*, vol. 59, February 10, 1994, 6277–8). However, the maximum median state AFDC grant for the same size family was $4,392, excluding food stamps and other in-kind benefits such as Medicaid.

Frontiers 19:2 (1998): 143–65.

Gender, Sexuality, and Class in National Narrations

Palestinian Camp Women Tell Their Lives

ROSEMARY SAYIGH

Western feminism emerged in a historical context of established nation-states, whereas most Third World women's movements have been inextricably entwined with anticolonialist national struggles. These struggles have inspired, mobilized, and constrained women's movements in culturally and historically specific ways.[1] R. Radhakrishnan links anticolonialist, nationalist discourses with feminist ethnographers' interest in personal narratives in an essay that questions what gives nationalism its ideological power to dominate and speak for women's issues.[2] Building on Partha Chatterjee's theory of rupture between the political programs of anticolonial nationalisms and their systems of knowledge and ethics,[3] Radhakrishnan translates this rupture into a crisis of individual agency and collective representation:

The nationalist subject straddles two regions or spaces, internalizing Western epistemological modes at the . . . purely pragmatic level, and at the inner level maintaining a traditional identity that will not be influenced by the merely pragmatic nature of the outward changes. In other words, the place where the *true* nationalist subject *really* is and the place from which it produces historical-materialist knowledge about itself are mutually heterogeneous. The locus of the true self, the inner/traditional/spiritual sense of place, is exiled from processes of history while the locus of historical knowledge fails to speak for the true identity of the nationalist subject.[4]

The tendency of anticolonialist nationalism to construct an "inner level" or "inner domain" as sanctuary against alien domination has implications for women, identifying them with home and cultural authenticity. As part of the same process, gender ideology is exempted from historic change, becoming part of a reconstructed "traditional identity" preserved fossil-like within a modernizing nationalist program. For example, the Palestinian Declaration of Independence (1988), while pledging gender equality in the future Palestinian state, speaks of "the brave Palestinian woman, guardian of sustenance and life, keeper of our people's perennial flame."[5]

Although Radhakrishnan criticizes nationalism for its suppression of alternative narratives of gender and class, he curiously fails to specify the gender of his "nationalist subject." Yet his description of the subject as "straddled" between two unconnected epistemologies implies masculinity. Women's positioning vis-à-vis nationalism's "problematic" and "thematic" (Chatterjee's terms for the dual levels of nationalism) is clearly very different from that of the male nationalist subject. Women are mobilized by nationalist movements to take part in the struggle alongside men, but they are also simultaneously compelled to symbolize an ahistorical inner domain. Woman is thus situated centrally *within* the contradiction between Chatterjee's problematic and thematic. This is what gives women's narratives their great theoretical interest. We need to conceptualize a female nationalist subject, whose narrative subverts the dominant one through revealing what the national narrative has effaced, historicizing the home, gender, and sexuality, and registering actions and experiences that would otherwise be forgotten. Here lie crucial tasks for a feminist ethnography.

THE PALESTINIAN NATIONAL MOVEMENT AND WOMEN/GENDER

Some currents and phases of Palestinian Arab nationalism have demonstrated an alignment of dichotomies similar to those that stamped nineteenth-century Indian nationalism: inner/outer, politics/home, men/women. Yet from its beginning, the Palestinian Arab national movement has encompassed varied and contradictory discourses on women and gender, attempting to steer a middle course between active and symbolic forms of mobilizing woman. For women, national mobilization began almost with the beginning of British occupation, was relatively self-initiated, and has always contained elements of indigenous feminism, however suppressed by nationalism's priority.[6]

The history of the Palestinian community in Lebanon has been one of historical fluctuation and insecurity, reflecting regional political upheavals and Lebanon's own sectarian instability. From the exodus from Palestine during the war of 1948 until the founding of the Palestine Liberation Organization (PLO) in 1964, Palestinians had no recognized national institutions or identity. Arising in exile, post-1948 Palestinian nationalism's manifesto was one of unity, international recognition, and armed struggle for return. In 1969, the formerly clandestine Resistance movement took over the leadership of the PLO. After the defeat of the Resistance in Jordan in 1970–71, its headquarters and forces moved to Lebanon where, allied with the Lebanese National Movement, it controlled a large part of the country until the Israeli invasion of 1982.[7] Though the call to mass armed struggle encouraged women's full participation in the Resistance movement, even the leftist parties and activist women deferred class and gender issues until after national liberation. In Lebanon, activist women were divided organizationally by their work in an expanding complex of offices, institutions, and unions, and ideologically by Resistance group affiliations. Nationalist discourse stressed "organic unity" between the women's movements and the national movements, and stood against any move to formulate women's issues or to single out women as a category. In contrast to women living in Palestinian diasporic society in Lebanon, women in the Occupied Territories were less constrained by nationalist ideology and Resistance group loyalties.

As framework to examining camp women's oral histories, the camps themselves need to be set in relation to their Lebanese setting, to Palestinian diaspora society, and to the PLO/Resistance organizations that exercised control over the nationalist movement from 1969 until 1982. Classified as refugees and without civil rights, Palestinians of rural and poor urban origin formed a marginal stratum within Lebanon's society and polity. Camp residence separated this poorest refugee stratum from the educated, urban Palestinians who assimilated without much difficulty into Arab host societies. Thus camp communities constituted a defensive space against refugee destitution, against Lebanese society, and against oppression by Lebanese authorities. Gender norms formed a strategic cluster within this defensive position. Though camp discourse until recently represented gender norms as unchanging, oral evidence suggests that exile intensified some aspects of gender ideology, for example, the surveillance of young women and violence against those who deviated from assigned gender roles. Gender rules changed, becoming more explicit, more central to identity, and more strictly enforced. Young girls were taught from an early age to censor their own bodies, movements, facial expressions, and interactions. The subject of sexuality was made terrifying through suppression, as well as by stories of what happened to "bad girls."[8]

Despite intensified enforcement of gendered comportment, camp women took part in clandestine activity against the Lebanese Army in 1969. This radical change weakened the Lebanese state, alarmed many Lebanese, and accelerated the slide toward sectarian civil war. When the PLO took over control of the camps in 1970, its call for mass mobilization had complex, contradictory effects, on the one hand engaging an already existent, though minority, women's activism, and on the other confronting family and community norms directed at "protecting" women from change. The movement's solution to this problem was to combine pragmatic mobilization of women in a wide variety of work, with a gender discourse that emphasized Arab and Palestinian "traditions." In relation to the national leadership, the people of the camps constituted a subordinate yet essential stratum, one that the Resistance depended on for recruits and support. Secular, progressive ideas about gender were tempered by concern not to alienate *al-ahali al-mukhayem* (the families of the camp). During the PLO period, gender norms became an arena of conflict as women struggled with their families to join the Resistance or marry men of their own choice. Through such processes, gender became a topic of ideological contest, with women voicing their rights to education, employment, and a role in marriage decisions. At the same time, however, gender norms became nationalized, as this quotation forcefully suggests:

As to honor, I say that if our Palestinian society has managed to preserve its unity, it was on this basis. Migration and refugee status usually lead to unemployment, and to girls going out to seek work, whatever it may be. As for us—and I consider this something to be proud of—the Palestinian family has preserved its traditions in spite of social liberation. When there's promiscuity and moral breakdown, moral values are lost. Then every family thinks of itself, and every family member thinks of himself. When there's distancing within the family, they will be distanced from society, and when there's distancing from society, a man won't think about Palestine. When he doesn't care about his sister, his mother or his family, he won't care about his country. It's all connected together.[9]

This brief review of camps as context for women's life stories points to the many reasons, both structural and ideological, that explain why nationalism should still dominate women in 1991–92, when the life stories that form the basis of this paper were recorded, a decade after the departure of the PLO leadership to Tunis.[10] The twelve years, from 1970 to 1982, when the camps had been the main sites of Resistance rallies and recruitment, had left a deep imprint on popular discourse there, while developments after 1982—the Shi'ite-based Amal militia attacks (1985–87) and the outbreak of the Intifada in 1987—intensified nationalist feelings. Yet the absence of an "official" national history and schooling system left space for particular histories—those of village, city, family, class, gender—to live on. This helps explain why, though nationalist themes dominate camp women's life stories, they never do so completely or uniformly. Careful listening enables us to hear narrations that reflect both dominant discourses on women (nationalist and communal) and women's own appropriations of their female and nationalist identities.

Insecurity and poverty need to be underscored as context during the period when the life stories were recorded, 1990 to 1992. After the battles of 1985–88, most homes in Shateela camp were shattered, and most survivors were living in places of temporary refuge. Most of the stories were recorded in places of temporary refuge outside the camp. The Syrian army intervention in 1988 to stop militia fighting began a large-scale campaign to arrest Palestinians accused of Arafatism. International and regional events, especially the Gulf War (1990–91), exacerbated economic hardship and Resistance decline. These events had mixed effects for this feminist research project. Women were burdened with daily life problems, most had lost close family members in recent fighting, and none knew how they would rebuild their homes. These conditions formed a discouraging context in which to be asked to recall their lives. Yet harsh conditions also stirred traditions of testifying, so that several subjects explicitly spoke through me in order to convey their appeal for justice to "the world." In spite of fear generated by the Syrian arrests, I met few refusals. This particular historic moment appeared to allow the narration of personal and gendered experience that, before the PLO leadership departed in 1982, the Resistance would probably have tried to obstruct, or women themselves would not have voiced.

TESTIMONIES AND TEXTS

The empirical basis of this paper is formed by life stories recorded with eighteen women from Shateela camp. Life stories have been criticized on many grounds, most radically by those who challenge the concept of a singular, bounded, coherent "self."[11] Yet, as Luisa Passerini convincingly argues, life stories are not only about selves but are multilayered, containing fragments of larger collective narratives.[12] Further, the global adoption of the autobiography as a genre points to connections between narrations of the self and collective crises, and, in a global matrix of competing identifications, gender clearly occupies a central and strategic place.[13] Essential to the physical and cultural reproduction of collectivities, women members reflect and contest ideologies binding them to gender-specific tasks and roles. Women's personal narratives, whether written or oral, mono- or polyphonic, structured story or fragmentary testimony, have value in illuminating this contested subjective domain that national and social movements repress.[14]

Yet difficult issues arise when the testimonies of women of marginal groups are recorded by researchers from another class and/or cultural background, among them narrator autonomy, the interpretation and textualization of spoken words, and control over publication.[15] The politics of choice of speakers, involving the representation of the collectivity, is always problematic, and more so in the case of marginal groups. Are research ethics breached if the researcher/writer selects speakers that the collectivity might repudiate as "untypical," or highlights passages that might cause offense to some members? These are questions that need to be faced in a paper that focuses on the problematization of sexuality in three of eighteen women's life stories. In most of the life stories sexual references were suppressed to the extent that even marriage and husbands were mentioned briefly, if at all. Suppression of sexual reference is also the rule of most everyday speech in camps. But there is also another tradition of bawdy talk and sexual explicitness, za'rani, rooted in rural life, its existence a reason why camp families generally do not allow their daughters to sit in on married women's gatherings. I have written about these three speakers here because they raised problems of sexuality spontaneously, not in response to questions from me. This warrants the presumption that they wanted to be heard. In their view at least, these are serious social issues that need to be aired and discussed rather than repressed. On a more theoretical level, I argue that their explicitness points to the historicity of everyday speech about gender.

The three interviews analyzed here were among the eighteen life stories I chose to record, a relatively large number of women because—though this choice sacrificed the possibility of a "real" relationship—a larger sample gave me the opportunity to include women of a variety of ages, enriching generational comparisons and historicization of the domestic domain. Speakers ranged in age from twenty-six to ninety-one, dividing fairly evenly among the three historic generations marked in camp speech as the "generation of Palestine" (those who were born and reached maturity before 1948), the "generation of the Disaster" (those born in Palestine who reached maturity in exile), and the "generation of the Revolution" (those born in Lebanon who grew up under the Resistance). I formed the sample from my own visiting network and by consulting with friends. Aside from age, the speakers differed in marital status, employment experience, relationship to the national movement, and in socioeconomic background.[16] All but five speakers had lost children, parents, husband, or siblings; one speaker had lost three sons, another all six brothers; two had children in prison, and two had missing sons, presumed dead.

The life stories were mostly recorded at home, in front of family and neighbors or in Resistance offices with speakers' colleagues present. My intention was to "naturalize" the life stories so that they might resemble stories the speakers might have told in real life. The presence of family and friends helped older women overcome shyness. Audiences not only provided encouragement, they also offered prompts and often acted as second, more interventionist interviewers. Though such audience interventions reduced the autonomy of some of the life stories, I determined that this was an advantage because the resulting texts could be regarded as the product not only of my request but also of the milieu. Such interventions also produced insights into themes and concerns of Palestinian refugee collective memory. For example, when a female speaker was describing her wedding in the 1930s, she was interrupted by a male visitor who commanded her, "Tell her about the lands you owned." The same speaker was criticized when describing an old rural healing practice called *tirqa* for "not telling history." To make accounts as autonomous as possible, I repressed questions that particularly interested me, or kept them for follow-up sessions.

All eighteen of the life stories contain rich reflections of the way that gender ideology and practice have been played out over time in camp women's lives. They show the degree to which the primary institution of control of women is marriage, which was practically obligatory in camps and always subject to parental agreement. Marriage controls women beforehand through the importance attached to virginity and afterwards through the responsibilities of childbearing, housework, and the many kinds of social labor attached to the housewife role. The life stories also illustrate the heavy demands of household labor: Many of the speakers had brought up families of seven or more children (often undergoing yearly pregnancies), and all but three had also worked for wages outside the home, undertaken voluntary political work, and/or helped husbands in shops. Gendered and class experience was also manifested in the anxieties of raising children in camps in Lebanon in a period of mobilization and violence; in the hardship of being left to bring up children alone; and in separation from adult children when offspring migrated to work, or were imprisoned or killed. The gendering of the life stories was expressed not only through their content, but also through references, language, and style.

I assumed that recording in public would suppress all references to sexuality, since camp norms are even stricter on this point than those of diaspora society in general.[17] That this was not so in the three cases that form the grounds for this paper calls for examination. What were the situational, interactive, or temporal factors that helped produce such unsolicited evidence? What do these revelations suggest about issues that lower-class Arab women consider most important? Does nationalism suppress gender issues, and, if so, in whose interests and with what kind of cooperation from women? How does class influence women's experience and narration of sexuality? Do perceptions of researcher identity influence what speakers say? In the case of the Shateela life storytellers, speaking frankly about problematic aspects of sexuality could have been related to personal crisis and perhaps also to my identity, neither outsider nor insider, and aged.[18] But I should emphasize that no special circumstances surrounded the recording of the stories of these three speakers. One was someone I knew well, but another I had met only twice before recording, while the third I met for the first time when inviting her to record. In all three cases there were others present.

COMPLAINTS, REBELLIONS, CRITIQUES

Umm Ghassan was the oldest of the three speakers and gave a strong, autonomous narrative in which the national story predominated but in the course of which she also castigated her husband's excessive sexuality, his neglect of the children, and the inadequacy of his contribution to the family's survival.[19] With the other two speakers, the sexual problematic constituted the core of their narratives. Umm Marwan formed her story as a critique of the coercive marriage that had frustrated her own sexuality, while the youngest speaker, Dalal, gave a complex, introspective narrative focused on inner conflict between a nationalist and a feminine "self."

Umm Ghassan, from a small village in Galilee, was born in 1930, remained unschooled, and married in 1945. Umm Ghassan had thirteen children who survived infancy out of a total of twenty pregnancies. One of her sons had been killed; another was missing and presumed dead. When I recorded with her, she was busy preparing a mountain of stuffed zucchini for a household that included four orphaned grandchildren. Also present were her husband and two older daughters. Umm Ghassan's remarkably sustained life story was marked by the rhythms and repetitions of the 'ataaba (plaint or dirge), which Arab rural women use to express grief or reproach.

More than any other of the life storytellers, Umm Ghassan described the materiality of refugee poverty, dwelling on its daily detail: cold and heat, the hunger and sicknesses of young children, leaking roofs, police oppression, and insecurity. She elaborated on the insufficiency of her husband's earnings as an itinerant coffee-seller: "He was the only one working. And what was his work? What could he bring? What could he give? . . . What he earned today, we spent today. Barely enough to buy milk for the children." At this point Umm Ghassan addressed me directly, "Do you think you can take a child to the doctor, and buy food, when you only have one person earning in the house?" Later in her story she listed and described military attacks against Shateela camp: army shelling in 1973; Lebanese forces shelling in 1975–76; the Israeli invasion and massacre of 1982; the Amal sieges of 1985–87. She had lost two sons and was raising their children. Her home in Shateela had been destroyed in the sieges. Such experiences are specific to camp Palestinians, and the detail of her narration of them to me set in relief the relative immunity of middle-class Palestinians to whom, by marriage, I belong.

Umm Ghassan's husband figured centrally in her life story as a low earner, as foolishly getting himself imprisoned for three years during which there was no one but herself to provide for the family, as being sexually excessive, and as leaving all the burden of child raising to her. Here is the passage in which she complains of the burden of repeated childbearing, placing the responsibility squarely on her husband: "By the end he got thirteen children. . . . After forty days [from delivery] I'd get pregnant again, and after nine months I'd give birth.[20] And so it went on. I suckled them and I got pregnant, that's how it was. Thirteen children! . . . I'd just be sitting, and *yallah* — I went on having babies." Notice the phrase, "I'd just be sitting, and *yallah* . . ." Generally *yallah* means "let's move," but here Umm Ghassan uses it to indicate a sexual approach. Later, in a discussion of contraceptive methods, I asked whether Abu Ghassan knew of her attempt to use abortifacients. She said, "No, he wasn't concerned. Many things happened and he didn't care." When I asked if he had helped with the children, she answered, "Him? No, no, no, *no*! In his whole life he never touched a child."

It needs to be noted that Umm Ghassan's complaints against her husband formed a small part of a strongly nationalist- and class-based narrative and cannot be read as rebellion against gender norms. In a later discussion about bringing up daughters, Umm Ghassan affirmed a central element of gender norms when she said, "A mother is responsible for teaching her daughters what is shameful, but [a girl] should know what is *haram* [forbidden, wrong] and what is *halal* [permitted, licit] without anyone telling her." Complaints against husbands are, I would argue, an indigenous form of women's consciousness that operate not to criticize or challenge the sex-gender system but to remind men of their responsibilities within it. Blame of particular persons rather than the sex-gender system as a whole reflects both national and communal gender ideology.

Umm Ghassan's story also points to ways the domestic domain—specifically conjugal relations, childbearing, and housework—was affected by refugee displacement. Histories like hers of yearly pregnancies and more than ten surviving children are not rare in camp women who became mature just before or after 1948, possibly due to a reduction in infant mortality. Desire for sons as way of escape from refugee poverty was a factor increasing family size, while changes in household composition and in male and female labor must also have affected conjugality and fertility. The transformation of male refugees into a disenfranchised, unskilled labor force separated them from home and community. Housewives became more isolated than they had been in rural Palestine, leading, among other things, to a loss of rural methods of contraception and abortion. When I asked Umm Ghassan whether she had sought contraceptive advice, she said she had been too ashamed to do this even from other women. Two decades later, though Resistance discourse encouraged large families, schooling and a changed cultural climate that made contraceptive advice more generally available allowed younger camp women to voice their own wishes about family size.

Umm Marwan was born in 1938 in a village in Galilee. Unschooled, married in 1956, and widowed after bearing five children, Umm Marwan had worked to maintain an independent household. During the Amal sieges she had lost her home, and one of her children had been kidnapped and was presumed killed. The recording session was carried out during her first visit to her mother after years of estrangement, an unusual lapse that her story sets out to explain and justify. Its leitmotif is marriage to a man she did not want, forced on her by her mother. Though she had come to seek reconciliation, anger was still foremost in her recollections. A second circumstance encouraging Umm Marwan's frankness may have been the approaching marriage of one of her daughters after graduation, a moment of triumph in a saga of poverty and marital unhappiness. After a brief résumé of early life, she launched into her real subject: "As for our daily life I was married to a sick man. From the beginning. Because *she* wanted this. I married him and he was sick, he had a heart problem. She wanted him because he was a relative. I wanted someone else."

Such explicitness of sexual reference characterized Umm Marwan's presentation throughout. She emphasized the long wait before she became pregnant and the dreariness of her life without love. She contrasted her own fertility with her husband's impotence: "We had children with difficulty. But I am fertile, when you have good land anything you plant will grow. I'd get pregnant, and he'd go to hospital." Her husband's impotence was made ridiculous by quoting the joke of the hospital staff: "What, Muhammad, you did it?! Straight to Emergency!" Such explicitness harks back to older rural women's speech style, declining today as educational levels rise. Umm Marwan contrasted her frustration in marriage with her fulfillment as a mother: "When I gave birth I began to have a life. This child came to me—he was beautiful! I started to work for him. Afterwards the girls came. . . . I wanted children. . . . they would compensate for other things, money, a man, everything." In a striking metaphor, Umm Marwan told me, "My children carry my flag, my self-respect." The flag image points to the profoundly social nature of the maternal role in Arab culture. It also underscores how, for a woman, feelings based in motherhood build a lifelong structure of reciprocity, compensating for the conjugal disharmony that often results from coercive marriage.

Widowed when her children were still young, Umm Marwan found work as a cook in a large institution. Her attachment to her children and how this determined the way she raised them—in conscious opposition to her own upbringing and forced, early marriage—forms the other main theme of her story. It was on their account that she broke with her family, and it is in this story of struggle for independence that Umm Marwan reveals the strength of her rebellion against gender norms. Among Palestinians of rural origin, the family of a man who has died usually appropriates the children, while the widow's family presses her to remarry.[21] But Umm Marwan insisted on working and keeping her children, explicitly linking rejection of her family's interference to coercion in marriage: "According to our traditions, the family of the father dominates, but in our case they didn't want the children. My family were near me. . . . they came, they tried to dominate, I didn't want it. . . . I wanted to raise my children myself. . . . I separated myself from people for fifteen years, I was outside my family. They had forced me to get married, that was it! I didn't let them impose anything on me, nor on my children. I stood against them." Elsewhere Umm Marwan asserted, "I wouldn't put my children as slaves to anyone." Asked to explain, she said that orphaned children are often expected to provide domestic labor in the households of their grandparents. Usually they are less well fed and clothed than cohabiting cousins.[22]

A third major theme of Umm Marwan's narrative was women's need for education, professional training, and economic independence, ideas still not fully accepted by more conservative Palestinians. Herself unschooled, she had learned to read and write in order to be able to help her children with schoolwork. All her daughters had been educated to the limits of her means, and she had refused to allow them to marry before they had acquired a *shehadeh* (diploma). Here she explains why women need to be able to work: "Work is not shameful. I encourage women to work and to struggle. . . . A woman shouldn't depend completely on a man. . . . Maybe her husband will come and tell her, "You are divorced. Goodbye!" He will give her the *mu'akhar*, and throw her out.[23] The money won't feed her two days."

However strong and challenging its tone, it would be a mistake to read Umm Marwan's life story as a critique of gender norms. Although Umm Marwan trenchantly criticized practices that hurt women, such as coercive marriage, she also reaffirmed central elements of the sex-gender system: Sexuality outside marriage is forbidden; women must exercise self-control in the workplace; marriage should only be postponed until a girl has completed her education. This is clear in the way she emphasizes her avoidance of promiscuity: "I did any job except one that would hurt my dignity, for the sake of my children." A woman who works must have the strength to resist sexual pressures. Even a woman unhappily married, like herself, must not yield to temptation—"this is totally refused." Elsewhere she remarks, "All eyes are on women," but she does not comment critically on this state of affairs. At the time I recorded her, Umm Marwan was eagerly looking forward to dressing her youngest daughter in the *bedli baidha* (white wedding dress), symbolic not only of her daughter's virginity but also—perhaps more importantly—of her own successful fulfillment of a mother's duties. The importance she attached to this forthcoming event underlines the way the responsibility of mothers for their daughters' proper upbringing helps maintain gender norms.

Like Umm Ghassan's, Umm Marwan's life story illuminates the impact of history on the domestic domain. Extreme poverty in early exile undoubtedly increased the incidence of early, coercive marriage. Rebellion against her family was made economically possible by the availability in urban areas of employment for "unskilled" women, while refugee rights to shelter, services, and rations offered further means of independence from family. Land loss and dispersion weakened the capacity of extended kin groups to control and protect female members. Such conditions were specific to a particular period, the first two decades of exile. It is interesting to note that coercive marriage of daughters at early ages reappeared in the camps after 1982, when unemployment and extreme poverty became prevalent. Before 1982, during a period when the PLO guaranteed employment and minimum living levels, age at first marriage rose and parents consulted daughters before betrothing them. These trends point to a connection between coercive marriage and poverty and underscore the susceptibility of gender norms to historic change.

Dalal is the youngest of the narrators, born in 1965 and hence a member of the generation of the Revolution, educated to university level, and unmarried. Dalal came from a poor urban background. Both her parents were dead, and the family home had been destroyed. Although I had often visited Dalal, I first recorded her after the second of the Amal sieges of Shateela camp in 1986. Shortly before the life story recording, the Resistance group to which she had been affiliated since childhood had been dissolved, leaving her unemployed and deeply shaken by the loss of a path to which she had earlier dedicated her life.[24] What to do? Economic and social pressures pointed to marriage, but Dalal found she could not conform to the configuration of "Arab woman/wife" after years of exercising power in a Resistance cadre. These difficult personal circumstances obviously shaped the content and form of her narrative. A younger sister and nephew were present during recording.

Alternating between recollections and self-analysis, Dalal's narrative revolved around a "self" experienced as always having been problematic. Alone among the life storytellers, she gave a detailed description of her childhood, emphasizing the way poverty had given birth to her sense of class and gender oppression: "We were deprived—no toys, no clothes. I used to feel the difference between me and my friends. . . . My mother favored the boys. She loved us [girls] but she gave them better food and clothing. What I liked best was to get sick so as to feel loved." She describes their family life as "closed," the result of poverty reinforced by the conservatism of her father, who was much older than her mother and had been a sheikh in Palestine: "My father was very strict with us. Everything was forbidden—dancing, singing, visiting friends. We were very isolated. When I started working [part-time, at age thirteen], the thing I most wanted to buy was a transistor. All my friends had cassettes. But my father didn't allow me to. This incident is still stamped on my mind." Relations with friends were marked by consciousness of "something lacking" and of "difference": "My friends wore pretty clothes, they listened to music and talked about the latest hits. I couldn't join in their conversation. Sometimes I pretended I'd heard these songs when in fact I hadn't." This memory launched Dalal on her first bout of self-analysis: "I feel that deprivation and inferiority are deep inside me. Perhaps this is what made me try to be superior. I like to succeed in everything I do."

Coming from a "miserable environment," Dalal "grabbed with passion" the public role opened up for her at age sixteen by full-time salaried work with a Resistance group. Nationalist politics satisfied her deep desire to "be somebody," assuaging her sense of class and gender deprivation. Yet at the time of recording, she regretted her total absorption in politics, feeling that it had imposed on her another kind of deprivation, preventing her from becoming a woman like other women: "I paid a price, I didn't live the stage I ought to have lived. If someone said to me, 'You're pretty,' I'd think, 'Who does he think he is! I'm above that sort of thing.' I acted as if he was committing a crime against me."

In the 1986 interview, Dalal described how her struggle with her parents to persuade them to allow her to become a Resistance member involved accepting their principles regarding her behavior outside the home:

My mother completely refused that I should work with young men. She wanted me to marry so that she could relax. Every day she kept telling me, "You've got to marry. As soon as someone comes along, that's it!" As for my father, he was very fanatical; he kept after me to wear a headscarf. I was forbidden to wear jeans, I was forbidden to cut my hair.

Though I was still at school at the time, I confronted my parents. I told them, "I don't want to marry, I want to do national work. But if ever anyone tells you that I'm not behaving correctly, you have the right to do what you want." So I worked, and stayed far from anything that could cause gossip.

A story of a broken engagement, framed by regret for a lost opportunity, offers both social commentary and rich cultural and psychological insights: "He [the fiancé] gave me money to buy the 'alameh.[25] The same day he said, 'I don't want you to sleep in Shateela, and I don't want you to work in the [Resistance].' This was the cause of our disagreement." Dalal added to the story of her failed engagement a long self-critique: how she had imposed her opinions on her fiancé, forcing him to join the Resistance movement, refusing to allow him even to hold her hand. Her strongest motive in rejecting him, however, was fear that he would jeopardize her role in the Resistance.[26] Now, in retrospect, she regretted having lost a man who "really loved me and gave me everything I asked for."

Regret precipitated in Dalal a complex critique of "self" and society. First, she felt that the "strong personality" her Resistance role prematurely gave her complicated gender relations: "A man won't accept to be led by a woman. Socially this can't happen." But on a deeper level, Dalal perceived this strong personality as a fiction, an appearance that masked inner contradictions and weaknesses. The fragmentation of her narrative reflects a painful search for self-understanding, a digging into the self and the past that suggests, through the metaphor of a "missing stage," irreparable damage. The contradictions she discovers inside herself proliferate: between a strong outer self and inner weakness; between an outer self that appears "liberated" and inner self that is "closed"; between a desire to "be somebody" and a desire to be "feminine"; between her need for others' respect as a "good girl" and her need for self-expression.[27] Her self-analysis seems to focus, in the end, on emotional and sexual blockage: "If someone holds my hand, I feel it's a sin. I feel as if something inside is locked, there's an obstacle between me and a man. I hold society responsible for this basic failure. It oppressed something deep inside me. I suffer; it hurts. I want to live my life and I can't."

Yet rebellion against society is contradicted by other passages, particularly those related to her mother: "Of course my mother taught us the values that have to be taught. . . . She taught us that if a girl is unclean, her family will kill her. When we were small she told us stories, that so-and-so's daughter loved somebody, and her parents killed her. She used such stories to teach us."

Other Resistance women would probably have criticized my selection of Dalal as speaker by claiming that she is not representative. Yet, I would argue that her life story is only unusual in its frankness and degree of introspection, that it reveals widespread gender-based problems that most activist women do not admit.[28] One of my translator-colleagues, herself an ex-cadre member, commented while we worked on Dalal's testimony, "The Resistance movement did something to girls." From her I learned more of the movement's sexual politics, how leaders often manipulated in-group relationships or tried (as in Dalal's case) to prevent members from marrying "out." Dalal's testimony corroborates Julie M. Peteet's observation that women could only achieve full integration in the Resistance if they defeminized and desexualized themselves.[29] Yet society demanded of them an eventual return to gender norms through marriage, a constraint that the Resistance had not attempted to challenge, only to defer. Dalal herself expressed this dilemma when she said in 1986 that if she were to marry it must be to a man "in the movement, preferably in [her Resistance group]," and that he must "understand the role of woman" (that is, not insist that she give up politics). But defining such a man instantly provoked her skepticism: "Where is this person? When you come down to reality, [Resistance] men usually marry women who are completely outside the Revolution."

Few Resistance women have not faced this dilemma, a result of the nationalist movement's failure to create change in social attitudes to gender and women. Through mobilization, the Resistance had changed them as women but had not tried to form "a new Palestinian man" to be their partners. Or, put another way, it had spoiled their social identity as women without offering them a viable identity as "female national subject" or "citizen." Dalal's story illuminates a specific rupture between nationalist politics and culture, the Palestinian problematic and thematic. It also suggests how, in Arab society, class interacts with gender subordination to motivate women like Dalal to enter politics, and how they combine again to depoliticize them.

For Third World women, national struggle has been simultaneously an entry point into public life and a source of transformed constraints, altering gender values by making them explicit, "fixing" them newly at the core of national culture. Chatterjee's theory of problematic/thematic rupture helps explain why women's situations never follow a unilinear or "progressive" trajectory but shift with historic change and the rise of new national elites. By linking the theory of rupture to narratives of identity, Radhakrishnan helps us to formulate the concept of female "nationalist subject" whose position vis-à-vis the problematic/thematic rupture is different from a man's—pivotal rather than "straddled." The three cases presented in this paper demonstrate the way narratives illuminate the interaction between the political and the domestic that nationalist ideology suppresses. Their life stories reflect national history, but in a transverse manner that reveals gender-specific modes of incorporation into national politics that change over time. Moments of historic rupture—1948, 1969, and 1982—are revealed in camp women's stories as having effects on domestic labor, conjugal relations, child rearing, work, and women's representations of self.

Each of the three cases represented here show in their different ways how history enters the most private part of the domestic domain—sexuality—and alters it. Umm Marwan's narrative points to a particular moment of collective history, early exile, when destitution reinforced coercive marriage, a practice that may have been in decline prior to 1948, and to economic conditions in the 1960s that made an independent female-headed household possible. Umm Ghassan's story also throws light back on the early exile period, suggesting how altered patterns of labor, household composition, and residence affected conjugal relations and levels of fertility. Set in a later epoch, Dalal's life story illuminates the complex ways in which female subjectivity was affected by contradictions within the national movement as well as by the historic break between the period of PLO autonomy and that of post-1982 Resistance decline. Inner conflict between her nationalist and her feminine self reflects a specific case of problematic/thematic rupture. The sharpness of her dilemma underlines the way representations of the self reflect collective as well as personal crisis.

History enters the life stories in another way, through the moment of their narration. I doubt whether these three narratives would have taken the form they did if they had been recorded before 1982, when Resistance discourse on gender predominated, and when selection of speakers would have been mediated by organized women who would have chosen strong nationalist speakers. Given that no research-related factors encouraged these three speakers to raise problems of sexuality, the inference is justified that it was the historic conjuncture, and more specifically, the decline in national mobilization that made some women speak more frankly and personally than would have been the case under the PLO. History surely affects narration of the female self, repressing or liberating the expression of gender-specificity and sexuality, as well as influencing the way women reflect and appropriate gender norms, rebelling against some while speaking for others. All three speakers formulated critiques of the sex-gender system, but they did so selectively, in line with community values that condemn sexual promiscuity. Such affirmations point to the renewed importance of non-national frameworks, such as family and local community, in a period when the national movement was in decline and the refugee community lacked security.

Class enters our reading of camp women's life stories at several levels. At one level, Palestinians in camps formed a special marginal sector within both host and diaspora Palestinian societies, which remained stratified despite a common status as refugees. Later, from 1969 to 1982, camps in Lebanon constituted the movement's main population and territorial base, becoming in consequence a prime target of Israeli and Lebanese attack. This class specificity is particularly evident in the degree of hardship, displacement, and loss that the life stories tell. Class is present in all three narratives, as is the interaction between national, class, and gender oppression. Umm Ghassan's story tells how, in the most marginal stratum of refugees, housewifely and child-rearing burdens were exacerbated by refugee destitution. The narrative of Umm Marwan links coercive marriage to poverty and suggests other conditions in early exile—employment openings for "unskilled" women, the weakening of kin relations—that gave her scope to assert economic and social independence. Dalal's story shows many of the objective and subjective consequences of low-income status in Palestinian exile society, including strong parental pressures on daughters to marry, dependence of women on the national movement to legitimize their entry into the public domain, and a desire to "be someone" rooted in class- and gender-based deprivation. Beyond this, her narrative speaks of the contradiction between pragmatic Resistance mobilization of camp women and the absence of campaigns to change gender norms.

Selection of the passages I have quoted as well as my interpretation of them is, of course, open to question. The selection of passages focusing on problematic sexuality creates a much stronger impression than when the passages are read or listened to as part of entire interviews. Yet critics should not ignore the possibility that these speakers, who chose to use life story recordings as vehicles for complaints or critiques, were doing so intentionally, to be heard. In raising the question of intentionality here, I stress the open, informal, and ambivalent nature of the life story as genre, able to be private and/or public, mono- or duo- or polyphonic, a structured story or a series of conversations conducted over time. The unregulated generic boundaries of the life story have a value in allowing speakers a more uncensored, more contextualized expression of topics that are usually repressed, in contrast to interview questions that predetermine contents, form, and language of responses. As for the researcher, the processes involved in producing life stories open up multiple angles of vision that nuance interpretation.

NOTES

1. Kumari Jayawardena, *Feminism and Nationalism in the Third World* (London: Zed Books, 1986); Nira Yuval-Davis and Floya Anthias, eds., *Woman-Nation-State* (Basingstoke: Macmillan, 1989); Kumkum Sangari and Sudesh Vaid, eds., *Recasting Women: Essays in Indian Colonial History* (New Brunswick: Rutgers University Press, 1990); and Partha Chatterjee, "The Nationalist Resolution of the Women's Question," in Sangari and Vaid, *Recasting Women*, 233–53.

2. R. Radhakrishnan, "Nationalism, Gender, and the Narrative of Identity," in *Nationalisms and Sexualities*, ed. Andrew Parker et al. (New York: Routledge, 1992), 77–95.

3. Partha Chatterjee, *Nationalist Thought and the Colonial World: A Derivative*

Discourse (London: Zed Books, 1986), 36–53. Chatterjee borrows from existentialism the terms "problematic" and "thematic" to designate two fundamental elements of anticolonialist nationalisms. The "problematic" is that part of nationalist ideology that asserts the possibility of autonomy, while the "thematic" is its moral/epistemological framework.

4. Radhakrishnan, "Nationalism, Gender, and the Narrative of Identity," 85.

5. Quoted by Mary Layoun in "Telling Spaces: Palestinian Women and the Engendering of National Narratives," in Parker et al., *Nationalisms and Sexualities*, 406–23.

6. Sources on the Palestinian women's movement include Matiel Mogannam, *The Arab Woman and the Palestine Problem* (London: Herbert Joseph, 1937); Khadija Abu Ali, *Introduction to Women's Reality and Her Experience in the Palestinian Revolution* (Arabic) (Beirut: General Union of Palestinian Women, 1975); Julie M. Peteet, *Gender in Crisis: Women and the Palestinian Resistance Movement* (New York: Columbia University Press, 1991); Orayb Aref Najjar, *Portraits of Palestinian Women* (Salt Lake City: University of Utah Press, 1992); and Ellen Fleischmann, "The Nation and its 'New Women': Feminism, Nationalism, Colonialism, and the Palestinian Women's Movement, 1920–1948" (Ph.D. diss., Georgetown University, 1996).

7. For Palestinian history in Lebanon, see Helena Cobban, *The Palestine Liberation Organisation: People, Power, and Politics* (Cambridge: Cambridge University Press, 1984); Rex Brynen, *Sanctuary and Survival: The PLO in Lebanon* (Boulder, Colo.: Westview Press, 1990); and Rosemary Sayigh, *Too Many Enemies: The Palestinian Experience in Lebanon* (London: Zed Books, 1994).

8. Proverbs in use among camp people, such as, "She should not show as much as the tip of her tooth" (that is, not laugh or talk too much), illustrate the disciplining of girls' bodies. Note also later in this paper the remark of Umm Ghassan that a girl should know what is forbidden (*haram*) without anyone telling her and Dalal's remark that her mother told them warning stories of girls whose families killed them because they were "bad."

9. Samira Salah, a leading cadre in the Resistance and Palestinian Women's Union, interview, March 1992, Beirut.

10. The life stories were recorded as part of a doctoral dissertation: "Palestinian Camp Women's Narratives of Exile: Self, Gender, National Crisis" (Ph.D. diss., The University of Hull, 1994).

11. For a political critique of life stories, see Daphne Patai, "Ethical Problems of Personal Narratives, or, Who Should Eat the Last Piece of Cake?" *International Journal of Oral History* 8:1 (1987): 5–27; Dorinne K. Kondo critiques the "I" concept as Eurocentric in *Crafting Selves: Power, Gender, and Discourses of Identity in a Japanese Workplace* (Chicago: The University of Chicago Press, 1990), 3–33; see also Lila Abu-Lughod, *Writing Women's Worlds: Bedouin Stories* (Berkeley: University of Califor-

nia Press, 1993), 31. Lourdes Torres takes a different view in "The Construction of the Self in U.S. Latina Autobiographies," in *Third World Women and the Politics of Feminism,* ed. Chandra T. Mohanty, Ann Russo, and Lourdes Torres (Bloomington: Indiana University Press, 1991), 271–87.

12. See Luisa Passerini, *Fascism in Popular Memory: The Cultural Experience of the Turin Working Class,* trans. Robert Lumley and Jude Bloomfield (Cambridge: Cambridge University Press, 1987), 17–63.

13. V. Spike Peterson makes the connection in "Reframing the Politics of Identity: Democracy, Globalization, and Gender," *Political Expressions* 1:1 (1995): 1–16.

14. Jo Stanley, "Including the Feelings: Personal Political Testimony and Self-Disclosure," *Oral History* 24:1 (1996): 60–67.

15. See Daphne Patai, "U.S. Academics and Third World Women: Is Ethical Research Possible?" in *Women's Words: The Feminist Practice of Oral History,* ed. Sherna B. Gluck and Daphne Patai (New York: Routledge, 1991). Also see Rosemary Sayigh, "Researching Gender in a Palestinian Camp: Political, Theoretical, and Methodological Problems," in *Gendering the Middle East,* ed. Deniz Kandiyoti (London: J. B. Tauris, 1996).

16. Eight were married, six were widows (of whom two were in the youngest age group), three were single, and one was divorced. Ten of the speakers were or had been employed fulltime (four with the PLO or Resistance), five had done casual waged labor or worked in a family shop, and three had apparently never worked for money. Fourteen were of village origin, four from cities. Eight lived in family-owned or rented homes outside the camp, six had rights to shelter in Shateela, and four were currently homeless.

17. Most of the life storytellers suppressed all sexual references and this was particularly marked in the case of older women. But two younger women, both cadre members, also omitted personal details such as marriage and divorce.

18. Most of the life storytellers had faced crisis in the period leading up to recording, and the crisis may have been particularly severe in two of the three cases presented here. My status as an in-marrying foreign woman possibly encouraged confessions and critiques that would not have been made to a community member, a complete outsider, or a male researcher. My age definitely helped since women past menopause in Palestinian communities are liberated from many suspicions and constraints.

19. In non-Westernized Arab communities women are usually called "Mother-of-(name of eldest son)." All the names used in this paper are fictional. To protect the speakers, I have been sparing with details that might identify them.

20. It is unusual for Arab women to use the masculine pronoun in relation to

"getting children." Umm Ghassan clearly does so to underline her husband's irresponsibility in producing more children than he could provide for.

21. On widows' struggles to avoid this fate, see Hilma Granqvist, *Marriage Conditions in a Palestinian Village* (Helsinki: Societas Scientiarum Fennica, 1935).

22. When I asked others about such discrimination in grandparental households some interlocutors denied it, but one young Palestinian woman said that this had indeed been her own experience.

23. The *mu'akhar* is the part of the marriage settlement held back in case of divorce.

24. In the 1986 interview Dalal had said, "I've been in the [Resistance] nearly twelve years, a long experience. I feel now that I can't leave, I have tied my future to this march."

25. The *'alameh* here refers to the gold "set" composed of necklace and earrings that marks a formal engagement. Etymologically related to *'alam* (news), it is also used as a marriage announcement.

26. The Resistance groups are said to have discouraged marriage outside the group. Such objections were more forcefully expressed in regard to women than to men members.

27. The full text is: "Everyone who sees me coming and going, wearing normal clothes, would think I'm liberated and coquettish, whereas deep inside I'm more closed than I appear." Dalal uses the same word *munqhalaq* (closed, locked) to describe her home in childhood, and her inner personality.

28. This is a difficult political and moral issue, but I take Shula Marks's position that it is the lives of victims of gender systems that tell us most about them. See "The Context of Personal Narrative: Reflections on 'Not Either an Experimental Doll,'" in *Interpreting Women's Lives: Feminist Theory and Personal Narratives*, ed. Personal Narratives Group (Bloomington: Indiana University Press, 1989), 39–58.

29. See Peteet, *Gender in Crisis*, 152–56.

Frontiers 19:2 (1998): 166–85.

Women of the British Coalfields on Strike in 1926 and 1984

Documenting Lives Using Oral History and Photography

JACLYN J. GIER-VISKOVATOFF AND ABIGAIL PORTER

Mrs. Evans fach, you want butter again
How will you pay for it now, little woman
With your husband out on strike, and full
Of the fiery language?
  Idris Davies, "The Angry Summer. A Poem of 1926"

Most Rhondda women are ambidextrous. They can throw just as well with their left hands as with their right.
  Glamorgan Free Press, *July 10, 1926*

What is this feminism anyway? I don't think I am a feminist, but if what we're doing [in the women's support group] is helping the women, then I guess we're feminists, too.
  Margaret Donovan, South Wales Women's Support Group, March 12, 1985

Throughout the first half of the nineteenth century, women played an active role in various forms of community-based social protest in Great Britain. But as industrialization progressed, the emergence of a distinct sexual division of labor and a gradual separation of work and home redefined gender roles and relations. With the rise of a largely male labor movement in Britain that derived its structures of support from the male-dominated coal industry, avenues for political protest became increasingly formalized in mining communities. Moreover, the nineteenth century witnessed the development of a domestic ideology associated with industrialization that further circumscribed the role of women, limiting the scope and acceptability of female forms of protest. While changes in both the nature and base of social and political activism curtailed the use of some popular forms of protest by women, certain elements have remained part of the repertoire of vernacular culture in coalfield society even to the present day.

A comparison between the tactics used by women protestors during the Great Lockout of 1926 and the protest activities of women during the Great Miners' Strike of 1984–85 suggests a number of common themes.[1] These forms of popular protest reveal an underlying continuity in the construction of gender relations and the reinforcement of community values associated with them during periods of communal crisis. They are also difficult to ascertain because women's protests have generally occurred outside the institutional organs of labor, such as trade unions and the Labour Party. The use of oral history and photography provide another avenue, alongside conventional research methods, for reconstructing the history of mining community women in the twentieth century.

THE TRADITION OF WOMEN'S PROTESTS IN MINING COMMUNITIES

The history of female popular protest in British mining regions points to an older tradition of protests by women that suggests a continuity of form, if not content, in women's activism. The historical evidence is highly evocative when viewed in relation to the protests of women in twentieth-century mining communities. It is critical to understanding more contemporary forms of female popular agitation and the role they play in the formation of a collective political identity. Incidents of female protest against community "blacklegs" (men who continued to work in the mines during periods of strike) have been documented for the nineteenth and early twentieth centuries. During the 1873 lockout, Dowlais women and girls publicly denounced the blackleg miners with cries of "turncoat."[2] Men who refused to join the union, like strikebreakers, were similarly abused, as in a 1906 episode in Maesteg in which the miners' wives splashed the unlucky victim with pig slop, removed his shirt, and painted him with blacklead (a type of graphite commonly used on fireplace grates).[3]

The blackleg miners were sometimes taunted with poles hung with women's clothing—a symbolic questioning of their manhood. By the 1920s and 1930s, this practice, known as "white shirting," was a common and largely female tactic for intimidating blackleg miners. Oral testimony relating to strikes in the 1920s confirms the effectiveness of this method: "There was a man that was lodging in the village here and he went to work. And so we women got together, we decided to go to the pit to meet him coming out. And we had sticks and brooms, you know, like you had and one of our members pinned a white nightdress on a broom and we marched right to the pit and waited for him to come out. And when he came out we marched behind him bleating and whatyoucall until he came up to a house up here in the avenue where he was lodging and we chanted outside and then went away to our homes, like. And we heard the next morning that he had gone away in the night."[4] Menna Gallie, a Welsh novelist from the anthracite mining area of South Wales, recalled in an interview the following incident from her childhood: "I was still a child, you see, at the time of the 1926 strike, and I remember hearing a lot of noise outside one evening and, peeking through the curtains, I was terrified to see this man being paraded down the street. He looked as though he'd been tarred and feathered, anyway he was covered in black and white and the crowd was carrying him on their shoulders and quite a lot of shouting and screaming going on. He must have been a blackleg."[5] The incident left such an indelible impression on the young Menna's mind that during the 1984–85 strike she attended a conference of mining community women held in South Wales to recount her remembrances of the 1926 strike, some of which had been incorporated into her novels about mining community life (see figure 1).

During the 1926 strike, women figured prominently in twelve major prosecutions. The common thread in all of these forms of female social protest was first and foremost a communal ethos—a sense that what was done was done not only for one's own benefit but also for the benefit of others. Their purpose became aligned with a higher law or moral authority, neither determined by the courts nor enforced by police but imposed by the community itself. Thus, the protests of miners' wives were the public manifestation of communal consensus. Cartoon representations of women that appeared during the 1926 strike in *The Miner*, the official publication of the Miners' Federation of Great Britain (MFGB), portray two sides of the experience of mining community women on strike. The first depicts the miner's wife as a powerful figure, tossing the aristocratic politician out of her yard; the second shows the beleaguered miner's wife, exhausted, head on the table, still rocking the cradle of her baby with her other foot (see figures 2 and 3). Indeed, neither cartoon was far from the truth. Mining community women had the largest number of children of any occupational group in early twentieth-century Britain, and photos from the collection of the Welsh Folk Museum show miners' wives as they appeared in the earlier part of this century. Figure 4 is a typical mining community street scene in Wales, circa 1913, where the

1. Welsh author Menna Gallie speaking at the Miners' Welfare Hall, Onllwyn, South Wales, at the Coalfield History Conference, May 25, 1985 (Photo: Abigail Porter).

women standing outside their doorways, babes wrapped in their arms, await news concerning an accident in the mines. For comparison with more recent conditions, figure 5 shows typical miners' homes in 1985, often called "council" homes because they were built with local and state subsidies and were offered for rent or purchase at rates affordable to working-class tenants.

The tradition of women's protests in British mining communities has always been largely community based, deriving its authority as well as its form from commonly understood values. However, it would be misleading to argue that none of the women's protests of the interwar years took their cue from formal political institutions. Many women, especially in the Rhondda Valley, were active members of the Communist Party. Others, such as Elizabeth Andrews, a South Wales miner's wife who testified before the Coal Industry Commission in 1919, launched political careers through the Labour Party. The strategies for change employed by these women relied less on spontaneous protest than on carefully planned and organized initiatives that paralleled those of the men. In the 1926 Lockout, for example, miners' wives and their supporters used both types of strategies—informal community protest and involvement with political organizations—to cope with the seven-month crisis. In order to get a clearer picture of how these strategies overlapped and reinforced each other during a long-term dispute, we will look more closely at the activities of miners' wives during the 1926 Lockout and then consider the historical significance of female activism in that strike in comparison with the more recent history of women in the 1984–85 Miners' Strike.

1926: HOUSEHOLD AND COMMUNITY ON STRIKE

The story of the General Strike of 1926 has been well documented in the annals of labor history.[6] However, historians have paid little attention to the role of South Wales miners' wives during the 1926 Lockout and to the long-term elements of continuity in their activism during mining strikes in general. From the turn of the century onward, strikes were endemic throughout the British Isles, with an estimated two thousand strikes involving 2.5 million workers taking place between 1919 and 1920. In coalfield regions such as South Wales, major strikes in 1898, short-term work stoppages in 1900 and 1901, and major disputes in 1910 and 1921 lead up to the General Strike of 1926. This pattern of mining disputes continued across the British coalfields during the 1930s with little intermission until the Second World War.[7]

The years preceding the 1926 strike were a period of intense activity among the working class of South Wales. The Labour Party had numerous triumphs throughout the coalfield valleys, and the Communist Party developed an especially strong presence in the Rhondda area. The success of both political parties was facilitated by the unions, particularly the South Wales Miners' Federation (SWMF). By May 3, 1926, when the general strike began, it was already obvious that the South Wales miners would be solidly behind the strike that had, in any case, begun with the national lockout in their own industry.

Although there were specific differences between the 1926 strike and the more recent 1984 strike, the fundamental issue of the industry's unprofitability and the government's refusal to continue to subsidize it were in fact key issues in both disputes. Similarly, mass mobilization took place in all of the coalfield areas. Local strike committees, councils of action organized to deal with the crisis, and an assortment of ad hoc organizations maintained the soup kitchens, brought in food supplies, and collected and distributed boots and shoes during 1926. In the 1984–85 miners' strike, community support groups, local miners' wives support groups, and the nationally

The Adventures of "The Duke" (No. 11). By FLAMBO

2. Cartoon from *The Miner*, May 1926, depicting a miner's wife chasing Prime Minister Baldwin out of her yard.

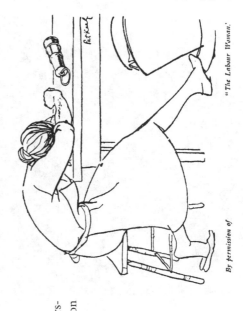

3. Cartoon from *The Miner*, June 1928, depicting a miner's wife in the worsening depression that followed the 1926 Lockout (Note the miner's lamp on the table and the cradle below).

4. Miners' wives outside their homes, Rhondda Valley, South Wales, circa 1913 (Photo courtesy of the Welsh Folk Museum Archive).

5. Members of a miners' support group waiting for a bus in front of council homes, 1985 (Photo: Abigail Porter).

6. South Wales Women's Support Group Members organizing food parcels, November 1984 (Photo: Abigail Porter).

organized Women Against Pit Closure, among others, performed similar functions. Figure 6 shows a typical scene from 1984 of several miners' wives from the South Wales Women's Support Group organizing food parcels for distribution in the community.

What stands out about the 1926 strike, apart from the high level of community militancy, was the level of deprivation and in some instances outright starvation that eventually forced the miners back to work. Oral testimony confirms that many families took years to pay off the debt accumulated during the seven-month strike.[8] No amount of careful budgeting on the part of miners' wives could overcome the absence of some form of regular income. But the onus of feeding their families fell squarely on the women's shoulders. Evidence suggests that most women fed their husbands and children first, often going without food for themselves. Although work in the mines had stopped for the men, the household chores of cleaning and preparing meals did not cease for the miners' wives. Mrs. Davies recalled her mother's role as a miner's wife during 1926, "My brother ended up the strike very, very sunburnt, whilst my mother was worn out."[9]

One miner's wife, Mrs. S. J. of Maerdy, explained how she budgeted and, with the help of her mother and the local soup kitchens, was able to get through the long periods of strike during the 1920s:

We got married in 1920. And then they were three days in and three days out, not much luck. And then the strikes were coming and everything was hard to get. A month after we got married, his mother died. Well, then I had a family to look after, two sisters, his brother, and his father. Well, things were more difficult again, of course, there was another little one; she was born in the '21 strike. Well, we weren't having a penny from anywhere. There were soup kitchens then; well I couldn't go down because I was going to have my baby. But the girls were going down [husband's sisters] and Will [husband] was going down to help Dad, Will's father. He used to go down to carve all the meat, he was great at carving. And because I couldn't go down he used to bring home on soup days, "Give me the biggest jug you've got now Sal," and then he said, "I'll bring my share up see and both of us can have a share." Well then the money, the money side now as you can imagine. Mind, my mother was very good, as good as she could afford to be, but I mean they weren't well off themselves.[10]

Mrs. S. J. goes on to explain in great detail how she fed the family during the extended period of strikes:

Well, we used to manage, we used to go, send the girls down, "Three pennyworth of your hearts," stuff them with sage and onion stuffing, mind you, beautiful because it was all Welsh meat then. And we used to have them for Sunday, and three for Monday, cut them up and all have a share. Six for threepence, and sometimes if they were a little bit small they might throw another one in and you might have seven. Well then we used to, in the week then you would have to have, I used to go down to Liptons in Ferndale and you know the long back bacon, don't you, there's a nice piece and then it comes streaky toward the end, well you could have a piece about that big of the streaky part. Yes, about six inches. Well, then we used to have the short back, the streaky, and we were able to have that for tu'pence ha'penny a pound. I used to go down on a Friday and I used to have four pounds of that, so that would make ten pence. Well the two leanest pieces I would keep for frying to make a dinner, with boiled potatoes and cabbage, make a nice dinner out of it. And then the other two I used to boil and we used to make pea soup out of it. Well, then the meat was coming for you to make some chips for dinner another day. And then I would send down for threepennyworth of cuttings [bits of meat and fat the butcher trimmed off to square a larger piece of meat]. Then I would make broth. We had the allotments so it meant that we had plenty of vegetables to go into it, so plenty for everybody, no meat. The next day then I used to boil fresh vegetables and I would cut up the meat into smaller pieces again now and I used to make a big pie so that we would have enough, because there were seven of us to help. Well, out of the threepennyworth of meat you were having fourteen meals, and out of ten pennyworth of bacon you were having more than fourteen meals, because we used to have soup one day and the meat the next day.[11]

The detail Mrs. S. J. provided in describing her meal preparations more than fifty years later indicates the extent to which she carefully planned the use of food for her family's survival. She explains how it was next to impossible to predict how much money would be coming into the household in a given week. Sometimes her husband would have three days' pay when he was working, or, if he was out of work, three days' dole. Even when the men were not on strike there might not be work in the mines for weeks, and "You would have to go down to the Reliefing Officer, and have a lot of cheek, and have a ten shilling food note."[12] As Mrs. S. J.'s testimony illustrates, the household budget and the ability of the miner's wife to cope with the unpredictability of her husband's income was important to the mining family as a whole.

Although direct support of their husbands through protest and activism was certainly crucial for the maintenance of community morale, the indirect forms of support carried out by the miners' wives, such as shrewd household management during periods of strike, could be just as significant. The notion of accommodating their husbands' needs, particularly in matters relating to the miners' work and union activities, is one that remains prevalent among miners' wives to the present day. And while it may be argued that in certain respects this attitude was merely an extension of the domestic ideology, it was one that both Labour and the unions continuously promulgated in their publications during the interwar period.[13]

The labor movement encouraged women to enter the political arena during the interwar years. The aforementioned career of Elizabeth Andrews, a miner's daughter and a miner's wife, who was a justice of the peace and recipient of the Order of the British Empire and a Labour Party Woman Organizer for Wales from 1919 to 1948, or Jennie Lee, the North Lanark miner's daughter who became a Labour MP for her area during the 1920s and subsequently married Welsh Labour leader Aneurin Bevan, are both good examples of Labour's successful female working-class politicians. Their involvement in the institutionalized labor movement provided one avenue of access to social and political change for miners' wives, and, indeed, both women were active in promoting pit-head baths and other measures to improve conditions for the miner's wife and family.

During the 1926 Lockout the activism of miners' wives in formal political channels played a central role in mitigating suffering across the coalfields of South Wales. In her memoirs, Andrews described the structure of the relief organizations: "The Miners' Lockout following the General Strike will ever be remembered in the mining valleys of Wales. Our Advisory Councils worked with the Relief Committee of the Standing Joint Committee of Industrial Women's Organizations, of which Dr. Marion Phillips was secretary, Mrs. Ayrton Gould, chairman, and Lady Slesser, Treasurer. Under the guidance of these three great women, we set up in Wales in a very short time a wonderful network of organizations to look after expectant and nursing mothers, children, and sick people."[14]

The organizations set up in Wales were only part of an extensive national network to provide relief to miners' wives and children during the 1926 Lockout. Marion Phillips, chief woman officer for the Labour Party, headed this national effort through her leadership of the Women's Committee for the Relief of Miners' Wives and Children. Her account of this period, *Women and the Miners' Lockout,* which she described as the "only noncontroversial history of the 1926 Lockout," documents how the organization was able to relieve "the miseries of want and starvation."[15] The Women's Committee for the Relief of Miners' Wives and Children was in fact the only body officially sanctioned by the MFGB to collect funds on their behalf. By the end of the strike the committee had collected and distributed more than three hundred thousand pounds.[16]

In South Wales, the work of Labour Advisory Councils was geared toward assisting those in greatest need. In addition to parcels of food, medical supplies, and clothing, the councils established boot repair centers fueled by voluntary help—primarily the miners themselves. Among those who were most active in fund-raising activities during the 1926 Lockout were miners' wives from South Wales, who made public speeches in London on behalf of the miners' cause. Andrews recalled: "Mrs. Beatrice Green of Abertillery, well known for her ability as speaker, addressed meetings in London to raise funds for the Committee. . . . Mrs. Johnna James, Tonypandy, and Mrs. Herman, Pentre, also addressed meetings in London. The three were miners' wives and good speakers."[17]

It is noteworthy that a number of miners' wives from South Wales delivered fund-raising speeches in London during the 1984–85 miners' strike, following in the tradition of institutionalized protest established by their predecessors in 1926. Among them were Sian James and Margaret Donovan, who regularly traveled to London to do fund-raising for the miners (see figures 7 and 8). These women crossed over the line between the private world of home and the public world of men and union politics. In 1984, as in 1926, the crisis precipitated by the strike seemed to justify, and even to necessitate, the involvement of women in public activities where they became the voice of their communities.[18]

The miners' wives who engaged in speech-making, fund-raising, and other types of institutionalized forms of protest and political activism were the exception, however. The vast majority of women participated in an indirect way, facilitating their husbands' political activities by their work in the home. But the most direct form of political activism available to women was popular protest, and this usually meant harassing strikebreakers. Although women were officially barred from work in the mines after 1842, many continued to collect coal for their own use or for sale off the slag heaps, in some areas working as "pit brow lasses." They were the sort of community women who might be involved in harassing the hated blacklegs, for, whether or not these women's labor was paid, they had a vested interest in keeping the mines open on their own terms — to collect coal themselves or to protect the interests of the working males in their families. Figure 9 shows a typical scene of miners' wives and daughters collecting coal in early twentieth-century Wales.

Although this form of protest received no official sanction from the union or the Labour Party, it did not go unrecognized by other women of the coalfields. During the Eighth National Conference of Labour Women, held in May of 1927, Mrs. Rose Davies of Aberdare, South Wales, asked the conference to remember how women in the mining areas had struggled nobly and well, helping in all relief work, such as communal kitchens. She reminded her audience that the miners' wives had also taken up the fight against "the dirty blacklegs," and as a result many of the women had been sentenced to prison. Davies maintained that it was now the work of Labour women to get those victims of class "justice" out of jail.[19]

Who were these victims of class "justice"? In the standard Labour history accounts of union politics and the 1926 Lockout in South Wales, their identities are virtually unknown and their protests mentioned only in passing.[20] Most of the women who were adults at the time of the 1926 Lockout have already passed away, making the task of collecting oral testimony impossible. Apart from some legal records and community documents, such as records from the Maerdy Distress Committee, there is little information

7. Sian James giving a speech as head of the South Wales Women's Support Group, March 1985 (Photo: Abigail Porter).

available on the miners' wives who engaged in protest and collective action. The legal records and accounts of court proceedings refer only to those who were arrested and prosecuted, and in many cases women successfully avoided both.[21]

A limited number of interviews were conducted with miners' wives during the 1970s, and some of the women interviewed refer to women's involvement in protest. However, the majority of these refer specifically to the Communist Party of Great Britain (CPGB) or to women's relationship with the union vis-à-vis their husbands.[22] Although the Communist Party was behind some women's protests, particularly in parts of the Rhondda Valley, there is no conclusive evidence linking the majority of women's protests during mining disputes to the CPGB, the SWMF, or the Labour Party. While each of these organizations was important to interwar coalfield society, the coalfield society's aversion to scab labor was essentially a moral stance, not expressly political—which is to say that a blackleg was a blackleg to communists as well as to Labour Party members.

Women were particularly well suited to the traditional role of confronting strikebreakers. Questioning the offender's manhood underscored his failure

8. Margaret Donovan and her son Owain, March 1985 (Photo: Abigail Porter).

9. Mining community women picking coal at the tip, circa 1910 (Photo courtesy of the Welsh Folk Museum Archive).

to live up to the masculine ideal of the miner, an especially potent form of censure. Gender difference, or in some instances *sexual* difference, as illustrated by the account below from the 1926 Lockout, could be used to shame the blacklegs into retreat: "We used to go up in the night and watch them coming out, and the women, and what do we now, because we got hold of them, and we used to give them a rough time, and I said, 'Take their bloody trousers off, they won't go to work without any trousers.' So that's what we did, we used to take their trousers off, take their food off of them and throw it away, and they were cunning, they used to overtime, and different shift work, but the place was like a beehive up there, with the police. We used to be up there every night, and all day long we'd be out there."[23]

The 1984–85 miners' strike provided ample opportunity to observe miners' wives continuing this tradition of protest. An incident in the village of Pontyberem, for example, reveals the extent to which such protests have remained similar in form. When about twenty women from surrounding communities assembled outside of a blackleg's house in November of 1984, they created their own rough music with a drum that one of their members proudly beat to the accompaniment of various imprecations against the working miner. The group refused to depart until several vans of about twenty police officers arrived on the scene.[24]

The historical significance of this type of event in relation to the activities of miners' wives during the 1926 strike is twofold. First, it underlines the continuity of this kind of protest by women in coalfield society. Second, it suggests that the reasons for female protest were not necessarily narrowly political. The women involved in the Pontyberem incident, for example, were not affiliated with one particular political party, nor were any of them acting under the directive of a single organization. The bond that united these women was that their husbands worked in the same local colliery, and all of them were on strike.

For the most part, the protests that involved women during the 1984–85 miners' strike remained relatively peaceful. However, there was plenty of evidence of police violence against male pickets captured by television cameras and photographers throughout the strike and at least one death. During the 1926 Lockout, on the other hand, the level of desperation in the coalfield valleys meant that the women's persistent protests against blacklegs occasionally took on a violent form. Stone throwing and other forms of intimidation were fairly common, and the courts were swift in their condemnation of women who participated in these protests. One judge was reported as saying, "You threw the first stone at the police constable and you set a very bad example to the women of the district. I find that the women have been taking too prominent a part in these disturbances and I must impose a penalty that will be a deterrent to others."[25] The majority of women involved in the protests were married and many had young children, yet despite that fact the courts were reluctant to show leniency. Appeals made to the Home Secretary requesting that married women with children be released from prison were generally unsuccessful.

The determination and vigilance of the miners' wives in both strikes is especially remarkable when we consider the depth of deprivation they and their families regularly endured in the order to bring about a successful conclusion to the dispute. Women like Mrs. L. P. understood the meaning of poverty. She was married at the age of eighteen during the 1926 Lockout, and for months had only a ten-shilling-a-week public assistance voucher to live on. The experience of poverty and her husband's political involvement led to her membership in the Communist Party and her participation in several riots in the Bedwas community against the colliery company's attempts to eliminate the seniority rule during the early 1930s. In 1933 she was arrested along with her husband and four other miners' wives. She and her husband served a four-month prison sentence for their participation in the riot.[26]

For Mrs. L. P., as for many women of her generation, the turning point in their political awareness was the 1926 Lockout. Kenneth Morgan writes, "This almost spontaneous expression of class and community solidarity made an immense impact on the young men and women who took part in it."[27] Indeed, Mrs. L. P. had indicated that before her marriage in 1926 she had virtually no interest in political matters at all.[28] Like the 1984–85 miners' strike, the 1926 Lockout drew larger numbers of working-class women into the political arena than ever before. Union records from the Rhondda Valley include a "list of persons in receipt of summonses arising from civil disturbances at Ferndale" during November 1926. The list of women includes a description of those convicted who had especially difficult family circumstances:

Mrs. Blodwen Pearce, 6 Gwernllwyn — Sentenced to three months. Husband unemployed. Six children, youngest a few months old. Oldest eight years. A young girl has been engaged to look after the home. Paid by voluntary contributions from the neighbors.

Mrs. Millard, 35 Gwernllwyn — Sentenced to four months. Her husband just started to work. There are five or six children, dependants. Youngest two years old. The eldest girl at home (fifteen) takes charge; she looks a total wreck through sheer starvation during the Lockout.

Mrs. Rose Owen, 45 Gwernllwyn — Sentenced to four months. Husband unemployed. Three children dependent. Her son, D. J. Owen, sentenced on the same day to three years Borstal. Rees Owen, son-in-law, of the same house sentenced to two months.

Mrs. Marion Jones, 46 Gwernllwyn — Sentenced to three months. Husband unemployed. One child, very young.

Mrs. Esther Laurence, 12 Dolycoed — Sentenced to three months. One child (adopted). Husband very ill in Cardiff Hospital.[29]

The disturbances referred to by the records took place between the first and fourth of November 1926. The complete list of defendants arrested numbered 201; of those charged, 115 were sent to prison, 30 were bound over, 35 were acquitted, and one was sent to Borstal. Although some of the charges against women were dropped, or they were found not guilty, those who were not acquitted went to prison regardless of their family circumstances.[30]

The mining communities expressed a moral ethos of their own in a full range of extralegal and extraparliamentary activities. Women's protests borrowed heavily from accepted and traditional forms of collective action, yet they were confronted with external forces, such as the police and courts, which challenged the expression of the community's moral authority. As a consequence of protests during the 1926 Lockout there were 395 intimidation charges that were heard in Swansea Court alone, not to mention the numerous prosecutions that took place in other parts of the coalfields.[31]

The 1926 Lockout was catastrophic for coalfield society in Britain in general and in South Wales in particular. Miners who had participated in the strike were victimized for years to come, and families were burdened with excessive debts they could not repay. The union was all but destroyed, and, with little or nothing left of its negotiating power, the men were forced to return to work for lower wages and longer hours. Miners' wives who had starved themselves to feed their families and support the strike found themselves facing long-term and continuing deprivation, which deepened as coalfield society slid into the Depression. At the annual Labour Party Conference in 1926, Arthur Horner, head of the miners' union, called upon the participants to express their gratitude to the women for "having saved the British Labour Movement from disgrace."[32]

The suffering endured by the women in coalfield society strengthened the sense of a common purpose and for some inspired a greater political awareness. In the case of Mrs. L. P., that awareness found expression in her involvement with the Communist Party. But not all women directed their newfound political identities toward the traditional institutions of labor politics. There were those who believed that the needs of miners' wives were best served not by the Labour Party, or the Communist Party, or even the Miners' Federation. The failure of the 1926 strike had left many women uneasy with regard to the political agenda of other groups. These women proposed an alternative solution that would work with the existing organizations but give them a voice of their own—a "union" of miners' wives.

THE AFTERMATH OF 1926 AND THE "UNION" OF MINERS' WIVES

The 1926 strike raised questions in the minds of many miners' wives about their relationship to their husbands' union. They questioned the way in which the MFGB and, in the case of South Wales, the SWMF had handled the dispute. Letters to *The Miner* revealed some of their concerns. Here a miner's wife expressed her opinion in regard to a newly established MFGB "Distress Fund": "Permit me, through the columns of *The Miner*, to express my appreciation of the eloquent appeal for cash, clothing and boots made on behalf of the suffering miners and their families. It is cheering to note that the officials are mindful of the terrible poverty and privation rampant throughout the British Coalfields. But on the other hand, surely the appeal in itself is an indictment of the inability of the MFGB to protect its members? The time is surely ripe for a thorough overhauling of the Miners' Federation."[33] The most striking feature of the letter is the writer's direct questioning of the MFGB and her proposal that the organization be overhauled. Indeed, in the two years following the 1926 Lockout, letters from miners' wives regularly appeared on the pages of *The Miner* from all areas of the British coalfields, and many expressed similar discontent or raised serious questions about their political identity as the wives of miners. The following anonymous letter to the editors is a case in point: "A militant women's movement determined to alter things, determined that they will understand why they and their children have to suffer, that is what is wanted. . . . I am looking forward to the day when the Boss will have to meet a deputation of women. He would be glad to kneel and pray for nationalization! May we women march forward is the earnest wish of—'The Wife of a Hy Hon. Miner.' "[34] The anonymous miner's wife who penned the letter challenged traditional institutions of the Labour Party while at the same time proposing a method whereby she, and others like her, might have a voice—a militant women's movement and the election of a miner's wife to Parliament.

Perhaps the most extraordinary development in the aftermath of the 1926 Lockout was the development of an organization of miners' wives in various parts of the British coalfields. In February 1927 *The Miner* published a photograph of Mrs. Maude Cannon, who was announced as the president of the first women's section of the MFGB in Basford, Nottingham.[35] Following a request in a letter to the editors from a Rose Lillie of Sunderland,[36] *The Miner* published a description written by Cannon (in the section entitled "The Home Page") of the formation of the first women's section of the MFGB: "The idea of a Women's Section was first suggested by a comrade who was victimized, and I addressed the women in September during the dispute [the 1926 Lockout]. The same month I was asked to be president and we are still going strong!"[37]

The notion of a "union" of miners' wives suggested the same type of institutional organization as that of the miners, but apart from that it implied that the women might also have a voice in mining community matters that was distinct from the MFGB—whether they became a section of the MFGB or a separate union of their own. In a second article for *The Miner*, Tess Nally, another miner's wife, made an even stronger plea for enlisting miners' wives and challenged the miners to face the consequences of 1926 and take action: "I am not a feminist, but say that the majority of miners' wives and mothers are more class conscious than their men. Some weeks ago I made an appeal in *The Miner* asking you men to seriously consider the organizing of your women-folk. Asked you to send resolutions from your lodges re the importance of miners' wives sections. Have you done anything?"[38] Nally concludes this piece by calling upon the men of the coalfields to accept the help of the women and recognize their strength and power. She queries, "Why do you not treat us with the respect and dignity our sufferings and sacrifices (entirely due to conditions imposed on you) deserve?"[39] In March 1927, a large gathering of Labour Party members from the Nottingham area was held at Kirby. The speakers included Marion Phillips, Maude Cannon, and Tess Nally. They debated whether women's sections of the MFGB were essential. The majority concurred that such sections were necessary and should be initiated throughout the coalfields immediately.[40]

Throughout 1927 and 1928, announcements of the activities of miners' wives sections appeared in *The Miner*, but there was no evidence that these women's groups were ever granted any sort of access to union meetings or, for that matter, official affiliation. In the case of South Wales, there is no historical evidence that an organization of miners' wives had any success in the region, where the male-dominated union was closely allied with the Communist Party in the late 1920s and early 1930s. Without the support of the union, the women's groups could have little more than a cosmetic function. Moreover, with the onset of the Great Depression, large numbers of miners and their families unable to find work in the region left their communities, immigrating to Australia and elsewhere. The expulsion of Communist Party members from the Labour Party during the interwar years marginalized the more radical aspects of mining community politics and the female activists allied with it.

The advent of the Second World War served to further disrupt labor organizers, as men and women redirected their energies into participating in the war effort. The postwar period of consensus politics in Britain led to some gains for mining communities and, with the long-sought nationalization of the industry in 1947, the impetus for radical political agitation ended for a time. As in the United States, the 1950s reaffirmed more traditional roles for women as wives and mothers; mining community women, whose lives had always been circumscribed by limited employment opportunities and exclusion from union politics, were no exception.

The 1960s and 1970s, which gave rise to feminism and the women's liberation movement elsewhere in Britain, all but bypassed the women of coalfield regions who were isolated by the tradition and practice of a domestic ideology that had served the needs of the male labor union and the industry for more than a century. As the power of the union (renamed and reorganized as the National Union of Mineworkers or NUM since the 1940s) grew inexorably throughout the 1960s and 1970s, the need for a women's organization had disappeared, and the historical tradition of activism among mining community women during periods of industrial crisis was lost, only to be rediscovered once more during the protracted Miners' Strike of 1984–85.

A TRADITION OF FEMALE ACTIVISM RECONSIDERED: WOMEN AGAINST PIT CLOSURE AND THE 1984–85 MINERS' STRIKE

The Miners' Strike of 1984–85, one of the longest industrial disputes in British history, pitted the Marxist revolutionary Arthur Scargill, head of the NUM, against the prophet of free-market capitalism, Prime Minister Margaret Thatcher. The process of deindustrialization and the closing of unprofitable mines had begun in the 1950s but was delayed for several decades by the political power of the miners' union. It was the goal of Thatcher to bring the NUM to heel and permanently subdue the power of the unions to the government. Scargill believed the coal industry should be run for the benefit of the workers; Thatcher believed it should succumb to the power of the market. Thus, the strike was not about wages or hours, as so many of the previous conflicts had been, but a protest against colliery closure. In a much larger sense, it was also a tug of war between the Left and the Right, an ideological confrontation that would have profound consequences for the British working class in the decade that followed. The government decided to apply a new law requiring the union to hold a one-man, one-vote referendum before calling a strike; this led to the strike (initiated by the NUM) being declared illegal. The consequences of that decision galvanized the mining communities, particularly the women, for in practice it meant that the miners and their families would not be permitted to collect strike pay, nor to collect the standard welfare benefit they might otherwise have been entitled to. Union funds that might have been used to assist members were impounded by the government. The Thatcher government and the National Coal Board struck at the very heart of mining community life by its actions, forcing deprivation on these communities in an attempt to short-circuit the strike.

In short order what had begun as a simple protest against colliery closure developed another dimension. For as months passed and entire communities mobilized in support of the miners, the dispute took the form of a moral protest, a crusade to protect not only the right to work, but also a whole way of life. At the forefront of that moral crusade to save the collieries, their communities, and the right to work were the miners' wives. Almost spontaneously what were loosely described as women's support groups sprung up across the coalfields—small groups of local women who were involved in all aspects of the fight to sustain their households and communities during the strike: from fund-raising, to distributing food parcels, to standing on the picket line with the men. Figure 10 shows several women from a miners' support group standing on the picket line in the early days of the strike; some of the police in the background of the photo are clearly amused by the presence of the women. Less than five months into the strike, these local groups came together and founded what was hailed by the British Left as the first national movement organized by working-class women, Women Against Pit Closure.[41] This group, and the miners in general, received extensive support, from left-wing and student groups, from the Greater London Council (before it was disbanded by Margaret Thatcher), and from gay and lesbian organizations that were active in organizing support and exchange visits for miners and their families.

Certain parallels between the Great 1926 Lockout and the 1984–85 Miners' Strike are unavoidable. Yet, despite the similarities in the size and scale of the effort to organize relief, it would be naive to give weight to any such observation without considering, albeit briefly, the tremendous changes that have occurred in mining communities in little more than half a century. As late as 1927, for example, the families that comprised coalfield society reared one out of every ten British children.[42] In South Wales the proportion was even higher. In 1921 it was estimated that one man in every four in Wales worked in the mining industry, and along with their families miners constituted roughly 40 percent of the entire population in that country. A population of approximately 270,000 miners in 1921 in South Wales had dropped to less than 20,000 by 1984–85, or less than 2.3 percent of the Welsh working population.[43] These changes have occurred gradually over the past sixty years, but they are nonetheless representative of the declining coal industry in Britain. To the social historian, such changes mark the demise of coalfield society, its material as well as political culture and that complex structure of beliefs, values, and traditions that shaped and were shaped by the lives of the men and women who comprised it.

As we have seen in the case of the 1926 strike and the 1984–85 strike, oral history and photography can provide a means for exploring the history of mining community women. As women identified by their connection to their spouses' occupation, miners' wives have never been in the vanguard of feminism. Nevertheless, as evidenced by their participation in both the 1926 Lockout and in the 1984–85 Miners' Strike, the lives of these women are an integral part of the history of British coalfield society and an important chapter in the history of women and working-class feminism.

CONSTRUCTING A HISTORY OF MINERS' WIVES USING ORAL HISTORY AND PHOTOGRAPHY

Given the absence of any large archival collections on the social history of mining communities in Britain, oral history seemed the most promising method for exploring the historical experience of mining community women, a topic I had selected for my Ph.D. research in the mid-1980s, despite the fact that I was told by the members of my thesis committee (and most of the British Labour historians I had consulted) that such a project was doomed to failure for lack of available sources. The reason: The lives of mining community women had left few traces, especially after 1842 when they were legally barred from working as miners by act of Parliament. The unions kept no record of women's activities, and their entrance into the public domain could be found only in the registry of marriages, births, and deaths, and in the occasional newspaper reports of scandal. Their work as housewives and mothers was hidden by a domestic ideology, defined as nonwork in census reports, and depoliticized by the very workers' movements that had sought to liberate their husbands from their capitalist oppressors. The history of their households, of their struggles during strikes, of their sufferings in childbirth, of their skill as household managers, of their networks of friendship, family, and community, all defined by the largely male labor movement of coalfield society as nonhistory, was glaringly absent or at best tentatively presented in the existing scholarship pertaining to twentieth-century coalfield society.

10. South Wales Women's Support Group member on the picket line as police look on (Photo: Abigail Porter).

The possibility of using photographs in the research did not occur to me until, quite coincidentally, I met up with another researcher, Abigail Porter, whose own project involved using photography to document the process of sociological change in the mining valleys of South Wales. Although our research projects used different approaches and had different aims, events would conspire to throw us together on the picket line, in the miners' pubs, and at the support group meetings, one wielding a camera, the other a tape recorder. As the 1984–85 strike wore on, we found ourselves sharing the same concerns and friends, each of us wanting to understand and as much as possible be a part of the communities we had come to study.

The magnitude and duration of the strike was something neither of us had anticipated. Nor could we have begun to imagine the extent to which our personal histories would be bound up with the events of 1984–85. The idea of combining our efforts to use oral history as well as photography to interpret the lives of mining community women was born partly out of necessity and partly as a consequence of historical circumstances. Although we maintained our separate projects, it was clear from the outset that each of our projects would benefit from exposure to the talents and expertise of the other.

Our collaborative work did not begin with a clearly defined methodological strategy. In conducting the oral history interviews, I was less concerned with acquiring specific information, especially at the outset of my research, than I was concerned with allowing my interviewees to tell their stories. I very quickly realized in my interviews with miners' wives that many of the women did not believe they had anything of historical interest to offer. Women who had never worked outside the home generally believed that their lives, some reaching back as far as the First World War, had nothing to do with history. Many of the women who had agreed to talk with us would refer us to their husbands shortly after their interview began, believing that their experience in the union was what history was about. But when we had follow-up interviews with the husbands we began to discover that much of the information presented was in some way homogenized, so that the experiences of ten different miners who belonged to a particular branch of the union would sound very much the same. It was clear that this type of data was a kind of oral history in the public domain; these were the stories miners told amongst themselves, so that it seemed at times as if there was a kind of group consensus about past events and their meaning.

In the case of mining community women, our experience was quite the opposite. While there were common experiences that the women shared—such as marriages, childbirth, financial struggles—these events were recalled with a particular accuracy. Some women, well into their eighties, such as Mrs. S. J. who was interviewed about her household budget during the 1926 strike, could remember with remarkable clarity the details of weekly meals, while others recalled with almost military precision the strategy they employed to keep their houses free from coal dust. In several instances when the women I interviewed deferred to their husbands, I redirected the conversation and asked them what their surname had been before marriage, something that usually led them to talk about themselves, their childhoods, the days of their youth, courtship with their husbands, and other experiences they associated with growing up. These women revealed a modest pleasure in our interest, all the while maintaining that, "this isn't history." As outsiders to the community and to the British working class, we were viewed with warm curiosity and rarely with suspicion. Whether our long-term presence in one area led our subjects to accept and trust us more than they might have otherwise, we may never know, but we were gratified at the end of the 1984–85 strike to be invited to a closed meeting of the regional women's support group. Relegated to the kitchen to help with tea and sandwiches before the conference opened, I was told, "Roll up your sleeves; you're one of us now."

The presence of a photographer during the interviews tended to confirm the idea that we were making a kind of history and that it was serious business. To anyone born in the twentieth century, photographs tend to signify the idea of remembering and recording in ways that a mere tape recorder cannot. On more than one occasion, the presence of a photographer kept intrusive relatives at bay, adding a certain solemnity to the event. It created a different dynamic in the interviewing process, making the interviewee more aware, in some instances more self-conscious, of her own physical presence. In general, photos taken during the interview tended to be formal. Most interviewees wanted to look their best or wished to be surrounded by things that were important to them, whether that consisted of a child sitting on their knee (as in the photo taken of Margaret Donovan) or a strike poster hanging in the background.

Of course, many photos that were taken outside of the formal interview process document and interpret the ongoing events of the 1984–85 Miners' Strike as those events unfolded. Just as the interviews elicited memories of bygone days, past strikes, and other experiences in the lives of mining community women, the photographs—whether taken with the awareness of the subject or without it—presented an opportunity for exploring the present and its relationship to the past. Yet they are also the interpretive statement of the photographer; just as the historian selects, reviews, and sometimes edits oral history interviews for the purpose of reconstructing historical events, the photographer selects the moment to record and, after many rolls of film, determines which moments best tell the story.

The excerpt from the oral history interview that follows is only part of the story that we wished to tell about the women of the South Wales mining valleys. It is a story that goes beyond the mythologized view of the Welsh Mam presented in the popular novel by Richard Llewellyn, *How Green Was My Valley*, beyond the endless tabloid headlines that described the role of women in the 1984–85 Miners' Strike as "the petticoat pickets on parade" or "the strike that turned wives into warriors," and beyond the working-class adaptation of a domestic ideology to the demands of life in a mining community, with the implicit separation of spheres for male and female activity. For just as we shared in the lives of these mining community women, they became part of our lives, of our lived and shared experience, and of our historical understanding, not only of them, but of ourselves as well.

In the interview below, Margaret Donovan, at the time a thirty-eight-year-old mother of two and one of the leaders of the women's support group movement in Wales, describes how the group came about. She recounts her first experience on the picket line, which involved protesting the electrical plant at Port Talbot, Wales, for its delivery of imported coal. She describes the strategy employed by women of lying down to block the entrance of coal-bearing lorries to the plant and her feelings concerning her first encounter with the police:

JGV: How did you become leader of the local support group?

MD: Well, really, I'm not the boss, everybody in the group works together, I wasn't elected or anything, I started organizing the food parcels for twenty-five families and just kept doing it.

JGV: How did the South Wales Women's Support Group get started?

MD: From each village doing their own thing the nine villages got together, and Kath in Cardiff [leader of the women's support groups for the whole of South Wales] decided we needed to coordinate what we were doing, so we met like, and we saw that it was the same for all of us, nobody knew what we were doing, nobody knew what money was coming in or going out [in support of the strike] and the South Wales Women's Support Group was formed then, that's how we got started. We got coordinated with other groups, and at the meeting it was decided that we'd do a mass picket of Port Talbot. And we just came back and reported to our group and then we just showed up.

JGV: Can you describe what happened during the picket?

MD: Oh, it was frightening.

JGV: Was that the first time you decided to go on the picket line?

MD: The first time I went on any kind of demonstration—we had lots of valleys represented there, everyone in the valley. And I didn't sleep the night before and I had my rosary beads, because you know there had been trouble in Port Talbot with the men in the week prior to that. So we knew there would be trouble with police. We arrived, oh, five, half-past five in the morning, and the men were standing around laughing. It was suggested we sit down in protest, but we were all very wary of it. We weren't actually sure we were going to do it until the very last minute. In the end we had about twenty-five women come along. There were many more men, the word had gotten around the lodges and they were organized, so it was a big demonstration. So we were hanging around, all of us women, but the police didn't know how to handle the women. There had never been women on the picket lines in South Wales ever before. Then some of the women went to sit down in the middle of the road and someone shouted, "Come on, all women together," and it was just instinctive. We all just ran out into the road and sat down and we just blocked it. And then the men followed suit. Then the police came over to them and they tried to get them up. And they started on us then.

JGV: Did they arrest any women?

MD: All told there were six women arrested and there were six women from the peace movement [Campaign for Nuclear Disarmament] and we were all doing the same thing. But whether they knew it or not, they were dressed differently from us, 'cause we were all dressed quite all respectable going there, in high heels and hose. I was quite frightened when the policeman lifted me up, but then I just got carried along, and the same policeman picked me up and said if I came back again he'd arrest me. Looking back, he probably wouldn't have arrested me, but he frightened me then so I didn't go back. I was frightened then, but I wouldn't be frightened now. But there were more than forty of us then, and there was no way the lorries were coming. So eventually they arrested a few of the women. When they arrested the men, one of the girls there was with her husband and two of the girls were actually trying to pull the policeman off of him, and we would have never imagined these people would have done that; they actually attacked the policeman!

JGV: So you were surprised by the police reaction?

MD: Yes, I think so. You know we seen it all on television, but until we actually saw it, it didn't actually sink in, what was happening, the way they were actually treating the men. And the way they were treating the women as well, they picked one up and they just sort of bundled her, sort of just literally threw her over the barrier! There was absolutely no need for that at all. We did complain to an inspector who was there, but he said we had to go through the proper channels and it wasn't his place to take complaints by the roadside. We knew the convoy went in, so it had to come out, so we tried to think of doing something different then. So we decided, we'd walk down the road and all the women went to sit on the roundabout and the policeman followed us and when they got there we walked back to where we were and the policeman just stood there. So we thought we'd walk down the highway to distract the police, so the men could take some action, and it was great. We were singing peace songs; it was a lovely atmosphere. But when we turned round all the men were following us, they thought we were having such a good time.

JGV: Did that experience give you confidence?

MD: Oh yes, and we went back there many times, but we couldn't stop the lorries unloading there.[44]

Margaret Donovan's account of her gradual politicization during the 1984–85 Miners' Strike was not unlike the experience of Mrs. L. P., who claimed that her interest in politics and her later decision to protest was fueled by her experience of the 1926 Lockout. But the miners' wives who banded together to form support groups during 1984–85 had no knowledge of the long tradition of mining women's activism in South Wales or elsewhere in the British coalfields. Indeed, the strike itself presented a unique opportunity for the older generation of women, scholars of coalfield history and others such as Menna Gallie, to share their knowledge and experience with the younger generation of miners' wives.

It also provided an unusual opportunity for these otherwise isolated industrial communities to share their experience of the strike with other groups in British society who were prepared to offer their support, in particular university students and academics, gays, lesbians, feminists, and the members of Campaign for Nuclear Disarmament. In this respect the strikers and their supporters forged connections that crossed the lines of race, class, and gender, providing new opportunities for creating broadly based coalitions, such as the "London Wales Congress" formed in the aftermath of the strike to strengthen ties between the mining communities and the nation's political capital and to address the broad concerns of these communities above and beyond the specific agenda promoted by Arthur Scargill and the NUM.

The 1984–85 Miners' Strike may well be considered as much of a debacle as the Great 1926 Lockout. From the point of view of the rank-and-file miner and the NUM, it certainly was. In the immediate wake of the 1984–85 strike, the NUM was in disarray, in much the same way that the MFGB had been in 1926. Just as the miners' wives who sought to gain official affiliation to the MFGB with their "union" of miners' wives were ultimately left standing outside the union door, Women Against Pit Closure and the South Wales Women's Support Group were denied the right to have official representation at NUM meetings in the poststrike period, even though the NUM, like the MFGB in 1926, acknowledged with gratitude the splendid support of the miners' wives.

After months of taking on the work of fund-raising, picketing, and organizing food parcels on behalf of a union they were not allowed to join, many women were told by their husbands to "get back to the kitchen." Indeed, the strike took its toll on many marriages, and the mining community witnessed its share of divorces in the poststrike period. But for some women the story did not end with the photo that was taken of them standing on a picket line, nor with the fund-raising speech they had given in London. For a few women in the Women Against Pit Closure movement, the strike was the beginning of their political awakening. Several women decided to return to full- or part-time study at university; several others became active in Campaign for Nuclear Disarmament and the Labour Party, in one case winning a local political election.

When British Coal announced on October 13, 1992, its plan to close thirty-two of its remaining fifty mines, it was patently obvious to even the most optimistic observer of mining community life in Britain that any hope the miners and their wives had had of "saving" the industry for the next generation was lost.[45] Nevertheless, the women of coalfield society had gained something in return for their struggle in 1984–85: a sense of political identity and a place in history. Perhaps the official song adopted by Women Against Pit Closure (written and performed by Mal Finch of Flamin' Nerve in November 1984) tells their story best:

Here We Go (for the women of the working class)
You are women, you are strong, you are fighting for your lives
Side by side with the men who work the nation's mines
United by the struggle, united by the past
And it's here we go, here we go, for the women of the working class.

You don't need Government approval for anything you do,
You don't need their permission to have a point of view,
Don't need anyone to tell you what to think or say,
You've strength enough and wisdom of your own to go your own way.

They talk about statistics, about the price of coal,
The cost is your community is dying on the dole.
In fighting for your future you've found ways to organize
Where women's liberation failed to move, this strike has mobilized.

Yours is a unity that threats can never breach,
Yours an education that books or schools could never teach;
You face the taunts and the violence of Thatcher's thugs in blue.
When you're fighting for survival you've got nothing, nothing left to lose.[46]

NOTES

1. In the Great Lockout of 1926, the owners of the coal pits literally locked the miners out of the mines until they agreed to work for lower wages. The lockout, which began on April 30, 1926, precipitated the General Strike of 1926, a nine-day strike of approximately two million workers in other industries who went on strike to show support for the miners. This strike, led by the Trade Union Congress of Great Britain, was the largest strike in British history at the time. After the general strike failed to persuade the government to force coal owners to keep wages at the same level or reduce the length of the workday, the miners remained on strike for another six months. Eventually they were forced to return on the owners' terms after losing more than sixty million pounds in wages.

The 1984–85 Miners' Strike was precipitated by the National Coal Board announcements in early March 1984 that more than twenty mines would be closed in the coming year with a projected loss of 84,000 jobs. By the end of March some 165,000 miners were out on strike, with approximately 30,000 remaining in the mines. The strike, which lasted until the first week in March 1985, was the longest mass strike in British, European, or American history. It led to one murder, thirteen deaths, thousands of injuries, and almost ten thousand arrests, and cost more than seven billion pounds of British taxpayers' money. But the strike also led to the first large-scale organization of working-class women, Women Against Pit Closure, and to a host of regional women's support groups that changed the public face of British coalfield society.

2. Angela John, "A Miner Struggle? Women's Protests in Welsh Mining History," *Llafur* 4:1 (1984): 78.

3. Rosemary A. N. Jones, "Women, the Community, and Collective Action: The 'Ceffyl Pren' Tradition," in *Our Mothers' Land: Chapters in Welsh Women's History, 1830–1939*, ed. Angela V. John (Cardiff: University of Wales Press, 1991), 27.

4. John, "A Miner Struggle?" 78.

5. Menna Gallie, personal interview, February 13, 1985.

6. See, for example, Margaret Morris, *The General Strike* (London: Journeyman Press, 1980).

7. Kenneth Morgan, *Rebirth of a Nation: Wales, 1880–1980* (Oxford: Oxford University Press, 1982), 146–47. For general information about industrial disputes in Britain, see Clayton Roberts and David Roberts, *A History of England*, vol. 2 (Englewood Cliffs, N.J.: Prentice-Hall, 1985), 748–49.

8. Hywel Francis and David Smith, *The Fed: A History of the South Wales Miners' Federation in the Twentieth Century* (London: Wishart, 1980), 62–65.

9. John, "A Miner Struggle?" 82.

10. Mrs. S. J., Maerdy Community Study Interview, July 4, 1973, University of Wales, Swansea, Oral History Archive, South Wales Miners' Library, tape 86.

11. Mrs. S. J., interview.

12. Mrs. S. J., interview.

13. Many examples of this type of "propaganda" may be found in *The Miner*. Every issue examined for the period from 1926 to 1931 contained some reference to miners' wives, and many articles specifically mentioned their role in supporting the cause of Labour and their husbands.

14. Elizabeth Andrews, *A Woman's Work Is Never Done* (Ystrad Rhondda: The Cymric Press, 1956), 24.

15. Marion Phillips, *Women and the Miners' Lockout* (London: Labour Party, 1927), 1–5.

16. Marion Phillips, "A Message for 1927," *The Miner*, January 8, 1927, 9.

17. Andrews, *A Woman's Work Is Never Done*, 25.

18. The transition from miner's wife to public speaker was not always made easily. Oral testimony from miners' wives who were asked to represent their communities in London for the purpose of fund-raising described being terrified by their first public appearance (Margaret Donovan, personal interview, Swansea Neath and Dulais Valley Women's Support Group, April 12, 1985).

19. *Report of the Eighth National Conference of Labour Women* (1927), 30.

20. Francis and Smith mention the presence of women in a number of protests during 1926 and in the 1930s, but the details they present are limited and viewed primarily in relation to the swMF and the Communist Party rather than in relation to the longstanding tradition of protest and collective action by Welsh women (*The Fed*, 60–67).

21. Francis and Smith, *The Fed*, 65.

22. University of Wales, Swansea, Oral History Collection, South Wales Miners' Library.

23. Mrs. L. P., interview recorded October 25, 1974, University of Wales, Swansea, Oral History Archive, South Wales Miners' Library.

24. The author was privileged to have been invited along as an observer of this particular event, November 3, 1984, at Pontyberem, South Wales. None of the women were arrested as all agreed to cease their intimidating activities after a stiff warning from the police. However, the police did record the names and telephone numbers of all of those present.

25. *South Wales News*, November 3, 1926, quoted in Francis and Smith, *The Fed*, 65.

26. Mrs. L. P., recorded interview.

27. Morgan, *Rebirth of a Nation*, 285.

28. Mrs. L. P., recorded interview.

29. "Material Relating to the 1926 Disturbances," Ferndale Lodge, file E, numbers 1–3, South Wales Coalfield Archive, University of Wales, Swansea.

30. Ferndale Lodge, file E, number 3.

31. Ferndale Lodge, file E, number 3.

32. *Report of the 26th Annual Conference of the Labour Party* (Margate, 1926), 177.

33. Tess Nally, letter, *The Miner*, September 29, 1928, 12.

34. Anonymous letter, *The Miner*, February 5, 1927, 5.

35. *The Miner*, February 19, 1927, 8.

36. Rose Lillie, letter, *The Miner*, February 26, 1927, 12.

37. Maud Cannon, letter, *The Miner*, March 19, 1927, 9.

38. Tess Nally, "Women and the War: A Plea for Enlisting Miners' Wives," *The Miner*, April 7, 1928, 8.

39. Nally, "Women and the War," 8.

40. By a Woman Rebel, "Notts Notes," *The Miner*, April 9, 1927.

41. Sheila Rowbotham and Jean McCrindle, "Women in the Miners' Strike," *Feminist Review* (1986): 74–76.

42. *Report of the Ministry of Health on the Investigation of South Wales Coalfield, 1928–1929*, VIII, Cmd. 3272.689.

43. Gwyn Williams, "Women Workers in Wales, 1968–1982," *Welsh History Review* 2:4 (1983): 530–48.

44. Margaret Donovan, personal interview, March 12, 1985.

45. William E. Schmidt, "Britain to Shut Most of Its Coal Mines," *New York Times*, October 14, 1992, C1.

46. Chrys Salt and Jim Layzell, *Here We Go: Women's Memories of the 1984/85 Miners' Strike* (London: London Political Committee, Retail Services Ltd., 1985), 86.

Frontiers 19:2 (1998): 199–230.

Contributors

SUSAN H. ARMITAGE, editor of *Frontiers,* is a professor of history at Washington State University. She is best known as the coeditor (with Betsy Jameson) of two important anthologies on western women's history, *The Women's West* (1987) and *Writing the Range* (1997). She first found her way into the history of women in the U.S. West through oral histories that she conducted and directed in the 1970s.

DOLORES DELGADO BERNAL earned her Ph.D. from the University of California–Los Angeles and was a University of California President's Postdoctoral Fellow in Chicana/o studies at the University of California–Davis. Her research includes an examination of the sociohistorical politics of Chicana/o schooling and an oral history study of Chicanas/os in the Midwest, both grounded in a Chicana epistemological and methodological perspective.

CONNIE BROUGHTON is part owner, with her husband, Irv Broughton, of Mill Mountain Productions, a company that has produced a literary magazine, poetry chapbooks, short films, and film documentaries but not a lot of revenue. Located in Spokane, Washington, Broughton worked fifteen years as an audiovisual writer-producer and has also taught composition and American literature at local colleges. She has an M.F.A. in creative writing from Eastern Washington University and is pursuing a Ph.D. in American Studies from Washington State University. She presently works for the Washington State Board for Community and Technical Colleges as the managing director of WashingtonOnline, an online consortium of thirty-four community and technical colleges.

PAMELA BUNTE is a professor of anthropology and linguistics at California State University in Long Beach specializing in Southern Paiute language and culture and applied anthropology with Native American communities. She worked with Evelyn James and other San Juan Paiutes on their successful federal recognition case and has continued to work with the San Juan Paiute Tribe on land claims and other applied projects. She is presently working with tribal members on a language socialization study as well as a language revitalization/maintenance program. Bunte has also continued to do ethnohistorical research and is presently working with the Little Shell Chippewa tribe of Montana on their federal recognition project.

ANNE M. BUTLER is editor of the *Western Historical Quarterly* and a Trustee Professor at Utah State University, where she teaches western and women's history. The author or coauthor of six books and numerous articles and essays, she has published extensively on the social history of the American West. She is currently working on a study about Roman Catholic nuns who established missions, schools, and hospitals in western environments.

JACQUELINE CHURILLA, now Jacqueline Russiano Miles, was an educational therapist and doctoral student in social-clinical psychology at the Wright Institute at the time she wrote the article that appears in this collection. Her Ph.D. work explores the value of reminiscing for the elderly, which she pursued while working with a population from Andrus Gerontology Center at the University of Southern California.

JACLYN J. GIER-VISKOVATOFF is an associate professor of history and the director of European studies in the Pennsylvania State System of Higher Education at Slippery Rock, where she teaches graduate and undergraduate courses in European and women's history and women's studies. She is the author of *The Last Days of Remembering: Gender, Culture, and Society in the British Coalfields, 1890–1990* and, with Laurie Mercier, coeditor of *Mining Women: Gender, Race, and Global Capitalism, 1800–2000*. She earned a Ph.D. from Northwestern University and has been a British Council Fellow to the Center for Research on Women, University of Adelaide, S. Australia, and a recipient of a Woodrow Wilson Foundation Doctoral Fellowship in

Women's Studies, among other awards. She resides near Pittsburgh with her partner and a family of cats.

SHERNA BERGER GLUCK began doing women's oral history in 1972, when she founded the Feminist History Research Project. In 1977 she joined the women's studies program at California State University and continues to direct the oral history program there. Her books include *From Parlor to Prison, Rosie the Riveter Revisited: Women the War and Social Change, Women's Words* (coedited with Daphne Patai), and *An American Feminist in Palestine: The Intifada Years.* Gluck is semi-retired and is directing the CSULB Virtual Oral/Aural History Archive project, which is mounting the original audio recording of many of her own interviews on the Web, including those with suffragists, women garment workers, and radicals and reformers (*www.csulb.edu/voaha*).

VALERIE GRIM is an associate professor of Afro-American studies at Indiana University in Bloomington. She is a historian and teaches courses on African American experiences in America. Her area of research is African American rural and agricultural history. She has published in numerous journals as well as edited collections. She is currently completing a manuscript entitled, "African American Rural Life and Culture in the Yazoo-Mississippi Delta: Stories of Families in the Brooks Farm Community, 1920–2000."

LUCILLE JAKE was a Southern Paiute elder of the Kaibab-Paiute tribe in northern Arizona. Besides her involvement in her tribe's affairs, she was an accomplished craftswoman in traditional Paiute leatherwork and basketry, as well as an expert in native wild foods and medicines. Jake died in 1997.

EVELYN JAMES is a Southern Paiute. Her work includes acting as spokesperson for the San Juan Southern Paiute tribe and contributing to her tribe's Federal Acknowledgment Project and other tribal endeavors.

AMY KESSELMAN is a professor of women's studies at SUNY–New Paltz. She is the author of *Fleeting Opportunities: Women Shipyard Workers in Portland and Vancouver during World War II and Reconversion* and *Women: Images and Realities, a Multicultural Anthology,* as well as several articles on the history of United States feminism. She is currently working on a book on women's liberation in New Haven, Connecticut.

ALISON MARCHANT is an artist based in London, England. She is also head of photo-visual at the Fine Art Department at Cardiff School of Art, University of Wales. Since the early 1980s she has constructed and shown a number of research installations both nationally and internationally, representing working-class women's history and culture. In 1998 she wrote and produced *Living Room*, a book of research on the redevelopment of an East London housing estate. In 1999 she produced *Relicta*, a full-color catalog and installation based on the self-representations of servant Hannah Cullwick (1833–1909). During 2000 she produced *East Londoners*, a major artwork of over two hundred billboards from collected family photographs, loaned after working with over three hundred members of the East London public over the duration of one year. The billboards were placed in ad shells and on panoramic billboards along major East London through-roads. Alison is currently touring and developing the *Relicta* project into a larger body of research toward a Ph.D. and compiling her East Londoners documentation into a book and CD sound work.

MARY MURPHY is an associate professor of history at Montana State University–Bozeman. She is author of *Mining Cultures: Men, Women, and Leisure in Butte, 1914–41* and coauthor of *Like a Family: The Making of a Southern Cotton Mill World*. Oral history has been and continues to be central to her historical analysis and writing.

ABIGAIL PORTER is a historian, writer, and photographer. She holds degrees from Harvard University and George Washington University, and she also studied photography at the Museum School in Boston. Over the last fifteen years she has pursued her interests in history and the visual arts by planning or working on a number of major museums or exhibitions in the United States and abroad, including The Sixth Floor Museum in Dallas, the Women of the West Museum, the South African Breweries Centenary Centre in Johannesburg, and the Museum of African American History and Culture in Baltimore. She lives in Washington DC, with her husband, David Kay, and their daughter, Emma Claire.

DIANE SANDS has been a feminist activist and educator for thirty years. She is the former director of the Montana Women's History Project and the

Montana Women's Lobby. A former president of the Montana Oral History Association and a former Montana legislator, she is currently codirector of the Montana Feminist History Project.

ROSEMARY SAYIGH is working to record displacement stories from (mainly) Palestinian women onto a website, Al-Mashrek, created by a Norwegian colleague. The recordings were carried out between 1998 and 2000 in Gaza, the West Bank, Jerusalem, and Israel. The multimedia project, which will have the original voices as well as photos and editorial text, will include English translation. The study was supported by the Diana Tamari Sabbagh Foundation.

GERRI W. SORENSON completed a master's degree in history from Utah State University in June 2001. Her thesis explored the world of a Mormon polygamist woman of the late nineteenth century in Utah and is entitled "The Bishop's Second Wife: The Life and Diary of Ellen Ricks Nibley." Currently residing in Heidelberg, Germany, with her two youngest sons, she is traveling and learning German while completing a post–master's degree in education at National-Louis University in Heidelberg.

MARGARET STROBEL is interim director of the Jane Addams Hull-House Museum at the University of Illinois at Chicago, where she has a faculty appointment as professor of gender and women's studies and history. She is writing a book about the Chicago Women's Liberation Union. She is a member of the editorial board for *Women Building Chicago 1790–1990: A Biographical Dictionary*, edited by Rima Lunin Schultz and Adele Hast. She has published works on African women, including *Three Swahili Women: Life Histories from Mombasa, Kenya*, and articles and book chapters on African religious and secular ideology, on gender, race, and empire, on the development of the fields of women's history and women's studies from a personal perspective, and on oral history and public history. She is series coeditor of Restoring Women to History, with volumes on Africa, Asia, Latin America, the Caribbean, the Middle East, and North Africa. Her book *Muslim Women in Mombasa, 1890–1975* won the Herskovits Award from the African Studies Association.

TINA TAU has recently published her third poetry chapbook. She is clerk of the local Quaker meeting. She lives in Portland, Oregon, and is currently a full-time parent of two young daughters, who were adopted from China.

SHERRY THOMAS was a cofounder and editor of *Country Women* magazine. She is the author of two books of nonfiction, *Country Women* and *We Didn't Have Much, but We Sure Had Plenty.* After four years at Old Wives' Tales women's bookstore in San Francisco, she became publisher of Spinsters Ink Books.

SALLY ROESCH WAGNER is one of the first women to receive a doctorate in this country for work in women's studies, at the University of California–Santa Cruz. She was a founder of one of the first college women's studies programs, at California State University–Sacramento. Having taught women's studies for twenty years, she now tours the country as a writer, lecturer, and historical performer, "bringing to life" Matilda Joslyn Gage and her better-known woman's rights ally, Elizabeth Cady Stanton. A scholar in residence for the Women's Rights National Historical Park in Seneca Falls, New York, during Celebrate 98, Wagner was curator of two exhibits, developed a curriculum, and performed as both Elizabeth Cady Stanton and Matilda Joslyn Gage. She is currently the executive director of the Matilda Joslyn Gage Foundation in Fayetteville, New York. Recent books include *She Who Holds the Sky: Matilda Joslyn Gage*; a Modern Reader's Edition of Matilda Joslyn Gage's 1893 classic, *Woman, Church and State; Daughters of Dakota* (six volume series); *The Untold Story of the Iroquois Influence on Early Feminists; A Time of Protest—Suffragists Challenge the Republic: 1870–1887*; and *Celebrating Your Cultural Heritage by Telling the Untold Stories.*

KAREN WICKRE wears many hats, including those of oral historian and communication strategist. In the early 1980s, she shepherded the Northwest Women's History Project through its most exciting project: capturing the stories of World War II–era women shipyard workers in the Northwest. She resides in San Francisco, where she herds corporate cats (internet variety) through web development and communication strategies.

JEAN CALTERONE WILLIAMS did her graduate work at Johns Hopkins University and taught in the gender studies program and government program at St. Lawrence University. She has been active in the battered women's movement and other feminist movements, and she writes and teaches on homelessness, poverty, and domestic violence.

HARRIET WRYE attended Vassar College, and in 1961 received her undergraduate degree in English literature and painting from the University of

California–Berkeley. She earned a master's degree with honors in English and teaching from Harvard University in 1963 and her Ph.D. in social-clinical psychology from the Wright Institution in Los Angeles, with a dissertation entitled "The Belief Systems of Women with Breast Cancer." Following an internship in adult and child psychiatry at Cedars-Sinai Medical Center, she was an NIMH Post-Doctoral Fellow at the Reiss-Davis Child Study Center. She completed psychoanalytic training in 1983. She is past president and a training and supervising psychoanalyst at the Los Angeles Institute and Society for Psychoanalytic Studies (LAISPS). Wrye is in private practice as a psychoanalyst in Pacific Palisades.

JUDY YUNG is a second-generation Chinese American born and raised in San Francisco Chinatown. She has worked as a public librarian, community journalist, and director of two Asian American women book projects. She is currently chair and professor in the American Studies Department at the University of California–Santa Cruz. She is the coauthor of *Island: Poetry and History of Chinese Immigrants on Angel Island, 1910–1940* and the author of *Chinese Women of America: A Pictorial History*; the award-winning book *Unbound Feet: A Social History of Chinese Women in San Francisco*; and, most recently, *Unbound Voices: A Documentary History of Chinese Women in San Francisco*.

Index